DISTURBING PRACTICES

Disturbing Practices

History, Sexuality,
and Women's Experience
of Modern War

Laura Doan

The University of Chicago Press / Chicago and London

Laura Doan is professor of cultural history and sexuality studies, codirector at the Centre for the Study of Sexuality and Culture, and subject leader for English and American studies at the University of Manchester. She is the author of *Fashioning Sapphism: The Origins of a Modern English Lesbian Culture*.

The University of Chicago Press, Chicago 60637
The University of Chicago Press, Ltd., London
© 2013 by The University of Chicago
All rights reserved. Published 2013.
Printed in the United States of America

22 21 20 19 18 17 16 15 14 13   1 2 3 4 5

ISBN-13: 978-0-226-00158-6 (cloth)
ISBN-13: 978-0-226-00161-6 (paper)
ISBN-13: 978-0-226-00175-3 (e-book)

Library of Congress Cataloging-in-publication data
Doan, Laura L., 1951–
    Disturbing practices : history, sexuality, and women's experience of modern war / Laura Doan.
        pages.   cm.
    Includes bibliographical references and index.
    ISBN 978-0-226-00158-6 (hardcover : alk. paper) — ISBN 978-0-226-00161-6 (pbk. : alk. paper) — ISBN 978-0-226-00175-3 (e-book)   1. Women—Sexual behavior.   2. Lesbians—Sexual behavior.   3. Women and war.   4. Queer theory.   I. Title.
HQ29.D57   2013
306.7082—dc23
                                                                        2012018795

♾ This paper meets the requirements of ANSI/NISO Z39.48–1992 (Permanence of Paper).

CONTENTS

PREFACE

In the final months of the First World War the Hon. Violet Douglas-Pennant suffered intense public humiliation when ordered to stand down from her post as head of the Women's Royal Air Force (WRAF), accused of lacking the necessary skills, competence, and experience to do her job properly.[1] Warmly praised for her work performance just weeks earlier, this highborn lady was convinced that a few disgruntled women she had turned down for promotion had engineered her downfall by circulating malicious and unfounded rumors alleging sexual misconduct. Although she had the means and social connections to demand that the British government give a reasonable explanation for her discharge, Douglas-Pennant would wait thirteen years before her suspicions became public knowledge: that she had been the victim of a whispering campaign intimating that young women under her command were deemed unsafe with an alleged sapphist. Here is a good example of how the new homosocial arrangements engendered by modern war — military or paramilitary units, voluntary organizations, nursing and ambulance corps — entailed risk in rendering women of all class backgrounds vulnerable to similar accusations. At the same time, the vicissitudes of war allowed "hundreds" of "sexually inverted women" an opportunity, as novelist Radclyffe Hall put it, to perform "noble and selfless" service to the nation — their greater freedom of movement, it is sometimes asserted, accelerating the development of a nascent lesbian subculture in modern Britain.[2]

In my project's earliest stage I sought historical evidence to better substantiate claims that women serving in military organizations were thought "abnormal" or "peculiar" or that the war "heightened visibility of lesbianism" and led to "greater self-awareness among British homosexuals," a view popularized in Hall's classic "lesbian" novel *The Well of Loneliness* (1928), which idealizes the activities of an all-female ambulance unit working near the front lines and fantasizes about erotic possibilities.[3] Of the myriad forms of war service, ambulance driving attracted a number of well-known adventure-seeking women we now identify as lesbian, such as Gertrude Stein, who was joined by her partner Alice B. Toklas; the flamboyant Dolly Wilde, niece of Oscar; the eccentric speedboat racer Joe Carstairs; the former suffragettes Vera "Jack" Holme and the Hon. Evelina Haverfield (rumored to have been lovers); and Barbara "Toupie" Lowther, the model for Hall's protagonist, Stephen Gordon.[4] Soon my research interests expanded to include women like Douglas-Pennant, who had been accused or suspected of same-sex relations. But then something unexpected happened that completely transformed the project: I began to take seriously theorist Lee Edelman's proposition that "queerness can never define an identity; it can only ever disturb one," which struck me as profoundly unsettling in its suggestion that the efficacy of queerness for the historian of modern sexuality was methodological rather than ontological.[5]

This seemed a far cry from current practices in lesbian, gay, or queer history making, intent on recovering, remembering, imagining, or reconstructing lesbian, gay, or queer beings in the past. Edelman's provocative statement about the queer refusal to name left me wondering whether queer history's destabilization of sexual identities such as lesbian or gay had really gone far enough, since blurring the boundaries between, say, hetero/homo, straight/gay, or normal/abnormal, or calling for more fluid and capacious categories (all vital strategies in response to the imperative "to queer") still constituted a conversation with identity and thus represented a preoccupation with queerness-as-being. My interest in figuring out how and why this intriguing predicament mattered or, conversely, might not matter (depending on the purpose of the historicizing) meant that *Disturbing Practices* was becoming less a history of lesbianism (or a queer history of lesbianism) than a historiography of sexuality, especially of the discourses of sexuality, with (at least) two objectives: first, to examine the specific political interests, purposes, and investments of the project of recuperating and/or tracing a lesbian, gay, or queer past as continuous or discontinuous in relation to present conceptualizations and, second, to envisage alternative histories of sexuality to think differently about the sexual past, practices *uninterested* in recuperating or tracing queerness-as-being but nevertheless eager to exploit queerness-as-method. Current practices in the historicizing of queerness-as-being have deployed queerness-as-method to good effect, producing powerful narratives shaped by the paradox of not-knowing as a way of knowing.[6] Still, I have concerns that history making framed by "identity knowledge" constrains even as it illuminates, because it is mobilized by the epistemological and social structures of modern sexuality.[7] This dilemma, I argue throughout, is best explained through historical example, which is the rationale that informs this book's two-part structure in its movement from historiographical and theoretical problems to a set of case studies.

To ascertain precisely what the air minister had been told about the WRAF commandant's character, I traveled to the University of Glasgow Archives to inspect the papers of the person who fired her, the Scottish industrialist and politician William Douglas Weir.[8] Over several days I sifted through a vast archive of materials relating to the long career of a man based first in the Ministry of Munitions before moving to the Air Ministry, a man known for his expertise in the field of civil aviation, who later advised lawmakers on rationalizing the electrical power industry — hardly the usual terrain of a cultural historian interested in a queer investigation of sexuality. Since Weir was a government official who saved each shred of paper, I skimmed hundreds of daybooks detailing his every meeting, every hour of the day during the war. I knew that Weir dismissed Douglas-Pennant based on information he had received from Lady Rhondda (then director of the Women's Department of the Ministry of National Service)[9] about the WRAF leader's alleged immorality — intelligence Rhondda, in turn, had received from someone else. If only I could uncover notes from this meeting between Weir and Rhondda I might learn, through these material traces, how people in 1918 were able to talk about sex between women.[10]

Locating the hard evidence of this exchange proved difficult in light of the voluminous evidentiary base — the catalog description alone ran to over 150 pages. At one point I came across a small brown envelope (postmarked August 24, 1931)[11] addressed to the Right Hon The Lord Weir in Scotland. Expecting a letter, I was taken aback to discover that it was stuffed with several white feathers, a symbol of cowardice, presumably sent by Douglas-Pennant's ardent supporters to goad Weir into coming clean about his shabby treatment of the commandant, a topic on which he remained obdurately silent throughout his lifetime.[12] Eventually my perseverance paid off, and I found the elusive daybook with dates corresponding to Rhondda's visit to Weir that would show presumptively "beyond a scintilla of doubt" that lesbianism was no longer a subject off-limits for respectable people in mixed company.[13] Here in my hands, I believed, might be sufficient proof that the accusation of improper sexual relations between women had attained such a level of coherence and legibility as to destroy one woman's career, endanger the smooth running of a vital women's service organization, and generate unease across the highest levels of government. Political intrigue within the fledgling WRAF would prove a rich site for tracing how one woman's enemies effectively floated accusations of sexual malpractice to oust an unpopular leader, their utterances of same-sex acts or identities an indication of a shared cultural understanding of the lesbian. Unfortunately, the thrill of unearthing this document quickly dissipated when I saw that the three relevant pages had been razored out. Whether excised by Weir himself or by an aide, whether in the aftermath of the government's review of the case or later in preparation for deposit in the archive, whether part of a sinister cover-up or the routine clearing out of old business, the only fact I could establish was that, inexplicably, the material was deemed "unkeepable."[14]

For the historian of lesbianism accustomed to scant tangible evidence, razored pages represent irredeemable loss in that this apparent act of censorship disrupts and frustrates the genealogical urge to know with certainty. Historicizing a being once oppressed and now liberated describes the workings of a progressivist project that believes in the existence of an "official history" from which it has been excluded, and it is this gravitational pull toward writing narratives of collective belonging that animates the making of both lesbian and gay stories in dialogue with current understandings of sexual identity.[15] A queer slant, on the other hand, might regard loss or disappointment as an opportunity to speculate differently about the meaning of fragments or absence. Queer work often presents itself as different from lesbian and gay history making, but this book will argue that, for all their differences, gay and lesbian historiography and queer historiography emanate from the similar genealogical impulses.

Lesbian, gay, or queer history—whether invested in identity or in the project of identity's undoing—is as pleasurable as it is purposeful in sustaining political identities and communities; yet, while I am no stranger to those zingy sensations of the archival hunting expedition, I have found myself increasingly troubled that identity history itself excludes and disallows in its bid for inclusion. Gathering up those white feathers gently wafting across the table and drifting onto the reading room floor strikes me as an apt metaphor for this historiographical approach, which can be seen in my first book, *Fash-*

ioning Sapphism: The Origins of a Modern English Lesbian Culture (2001), its very title emphasizing a search for the family roots of modern lesbianism.[16] The feathers were clearly visible, and while each nearly escaped my grasp, with persistence and concentration I slowly and carefully nabbed each one and put them back into a tidy package; nonetheless, it would be misleading to pretend that identifying likeness is really this simple. Over time some feathers had deteriorated — disfigurements suggesting a need for another historiographical practice with interests in what is dissimilar or deviant, one closely aligned to the first in seeking a thing (and relations between things) but open to more expansive notions of featherness and fascinated by objects that are not quite feathers. What vexes me now about my earlier account of a nascent lesbian subculture in modern Britain is that — from the very start — I believed I knew more about female sexuality in the 1920s than the individuals I was researching; equally troubling was my inattentiveness to the purpose of my history writing.

In *Disturbing Practices* I want to address these and other historiographical problems, not to assert that the time of identity history has passed. Operationalized by lesbian, gay, or queer inhabitants of the present, the political, ethical, cultural, and affective value of identity history (inside and outside the academy) cannot be denied — indeed, my respect and admiration for its accomplishments have only increased in writing this book. Neither do I propose here how to do lesbian and gay *or* queer history better, though I hope practitioners will find my critique of current practices suggestive of new directions in navigating the conceptual difficulties of a mode of historicizing sometimes "blind to all but the group it binds": blind, that is to say, to alternative historical frameworks beyond its borders.[17] I have come to believe that identity history's struggle to recognize other frameworks is not unrelated to its persistent invisibility and marginality in academic history. This is why I seek to know more about the workings of each historical practice, noting also where practices converge and diverge, assessing their respective advantages and disadvantages as well as different points of embarkation in crafting narratives about the past.

Understanding the limitations and possibilities of lesbian, gay, and queer history is the main concern of this book — a task that calls for analyzing the historiographical consequences of an identity history that tends to regard the past as something already constructed and therefore available to be touched, traced, remembered, encountered, and documented, either to affirm a lesbian and gay historical existence that has been denied or to examine multiple and fluid ontologies within the rubric of knowing and unknowing the queer being. Above all, I posit the usefulness of "critical history" as a mode of historicizing (empirical and theoretical) that acknowledges the historian as the producer of a "representation of the past."[18] In the wake of the queer historian David Halperin's pathbreaking work on the history of homosexuality, many queer scholars already understand their practice as a form of "critical history," but I will argue that touching or tracing an already constituted past (which is the maneuver of any historicizing that begins with a notion of the modern homosexual or queer subject), or detecting repetition across time, constitutes a profoundly different stance than a critical historical practice that believes the past does not exist until conjured into existence in the making of history.[19] To be sure, there are significant alliances between queer history as currently practiced and critical history: both, for instance, are fully committed to making "creative futures," and both grasp the importance of subjecting identity to radical questioning and the need to rethink categories as well as the relations between categories.[20] Where these practices part company is the subject of this book, which considers their aims and purposes and determines how and why each elects to historicize differently. Hence also my call for a new practice — "queer critical history" — not to displace ongoing trajectories in the historicizing of lesbian, gay, and queer lives but to disentangle queerness-as-method from queerness-as-being and, in doing so, subject "every regime of truth or knowledge" to critique, including the regime of modern sexuality.[21]

What these ruminations about feathers and razored pages highlight, in the end, is the crucial importance of paying serious attention to the purpose of historicizing as well as to the range of tools and methods at our disposal. This anatomy of the practice of sexual history marks an attempt to persuade queer scholars to take another look at academic history and to invite academic historians who have hitherto shown little interest either in sexuality or in the history of sexuality to consider (or reconsider) the usefulness of the concept in historical analysis. I am still very curious about the history of sexuality in Britain in the early decades of the twentieth century, but even more curious about how historical practices might be disturbed.

ACKNOWLEDGMENTS

This book was written in a remote corner of the western Lake District, in a cottage that looks out on a field of sheep, with views to the Irish Sea and the Isle of Man in the distance. Over the past couple of years I've often thought about beginning the acknowledgments with an expression of my appreciation for the Cumbrian weather, since I've rarely felt deprived sitting at my desk. Even more helpful were the numerous intense conversations with a small group of good friends who share my passion for probing the conundrums of historicizing sexuality, friends utterly generous with their time in reading drafts and offering their thoughts and ideas. In particular I want to thank David Alderson, whose rants kept me energized and focused on the big questions; Matt Houlbrook, whose perceptive and witty commentary on drafts of every chapter enabled me to sharpen my arguments — his encouragement and support were unflagging; Valerie Traub, who pushed me to rethink the larger conceptual organization of the project and always listened with exceptional care; and Chris Waters, who helped me to figure out how historians think. I now associate each of these individuals with particular epiphanies, whether sitting on a bench in the garden, communicating via e-mail several times an hour, or sitting chastely on a double bed in a Bloomsbury hotel, creeping out late at night past the concierge, who likely ascribed flushed faces to reasons other than the intensity of historiographical debate.

As with any book project that has evolved over a number of years, there are many other individuals I want to thank (in alphabetical order): Ana Carden-Coyne (who taught me to nugget); Anne Carter (for research assistance beyond the call of duty); Anna Clark (whose valuable feedback was always worth the wait); Hal Gladfelder (a.k.a. Zen Master Oliver, whose mantra on the five hundred words a day and wise advice on how to destroy and rebuild sustained me); Liz Harvey (for her reminder that the women who stayed home to knit socks are sometimes as interesting as those who went off to the Western Front); Hilary Hinds (whose well-timed intervention got me through the first impasse and clarified the need to break the book into two parts); Annamarie Jagose (whose theoretical insights kept me up well after midnight); Carol Mavor (who ordered me to stop rewriting and upload the manuscript); Jackie Stacey (a.k.a. the Seer, whose queries on the workings of history clarified the queer perspective); Martha Vicinus (who gave a thumbs-down on an earlier title for the book and told me to try harder); and Janet Wolff (who knows full well why her name appears here). Others I wish to thank include Adrian Bingham, Lucy Bland, Patricia Briggs, Terry Brown, Gavin Butt, Bridget Byrne, Mary Cappello, Jerome de Groot, Graham Drake, Jane Garrity, Jeff Geiger, Laura Gowing, Sue Grayzel, Lesley Hall, Helen Hills, Kali Israel, Amelia Jones, Deborah Lambert, Alison Oram, Monica Pearl, Sharrona Pearl, Krisztina Roberts, Sheila Rowbotham, Bev Skeggs, Penny Summerfield, Bertrand Taithe, Ursula Tidd, and Jean Walton. I owe a special debt to Doug Mitchell, executive editor extraordinaire at the University of Chicago Press, whose significant and now legendary contribution in the history of sexuality is the stuff of history books.

A British Academy Small Research Grant (2006–7) allowed me to visit several key archives to research the Douglas-Pennant case. I am also grateful to the Arts and Humanities Research Council (Research Leave Scheme 2010) for support that allowed me to complete the book.

A shorter version of chapter 1 appeared as "Topsy-Turvydom: Gender Inversion, Sapphism, and the Great War," in *GLQ: A Journal of Lesbian and Gay Studies* 12, no. 4 (2006): 517–42. A section of chapter 1 is an earlier draft of "Forgetting Sedgwick," published in *PMLA* 125, no. 2 (March 2010): 370–73.

Finally, thanks to Mar—for everything.

History and Sexuality/
Sexuality and History

Rethinking history . . . means rethinking what is new and "unheard of."
HAYDEN WHITE (2007)

The queer must insist on disturbing.
LEE EDELMAN (2004)

Disturbing Practices explores the friendships, communities, and work of a few British women who served in various capacities during the First World War. It looks at women such as Elsie Knocker and Mairi Chisholm, who lived together near the Belgian front lines for most of the war and captured national headlines for their personal courage in caring for the wounded; the Hon. Violet Douglas-Pennant, the onetime head of the Women's Royal Air Force until her career was ruined by rumors alleging sexual immorality; and Florence Eva Harley, a former nurse in the British Red Cross, who initiated legal action against a man she believed had besmirched her honor. Their letters, diaries, and memoirs, as well as their words as reported in the press, attest to the many "extraordinary" changes wrought by the unusual circumstances of war, for life in Britain between 1914 and 1918 "was not a normal time."[1] New forms of meaningful employment tested these women's physical, mental, and moral strength, expanded the configurations and expressions of gender, and allowed greater independence and mobility, even adventurous travel. Above all, for the historian with interests in sexuality, war work threw these women together with others of their sex. Yet while parliamentary papers and newspaper stories confirm that sex talk was rampant, little is known about how the sexual was understood or talked about by the women themselves or by others. My purpose in closely examining the material traces of these women's lives is not to find acts or identities that warrant inclusion or exclusion in a modern British lesbian history or queer history. Instead, I turn to these historical examples to disturb current practices in historicizing sexuality, in particular practices that position the homosexual or queer subject near the center of investigative curiosity. Let me say at the outset that I do not regard the project of historicizing homosexuality as somehow intrinsically flawed, naive, useless, outmoded, epistemologically compromised, or in any other way irredeemably problematic. On the contrary, unlike those who call for its undoing, in this book I seek to clarify its ethical value and political purpose, indeed its very capacity to give rise to new practices born of sustained dialogic exchange between two fields at present so distant that their intellectual affinities have gone unrecognized: queer studies and critical history, the latter committed to producing historical knowledge grounded in the empirical and framed by critical theory.[2]

I did not start out with the aim of anatomizing the diverse practices of lesbian, gay, and queer history, a subfield of academic history but also carried out by multiple practitioners who configure their work in accordance with the rules of their respective disciplines. This undertaking came about by accident when I realized that many of my discoveries about the structure and organization of female sexuality in the modern sexual past made little sense in the context of a historiographical practice in conversation with "lesbian and gay" identity or even a practice alert to a "queer" identity as fluid, mutable, or unstable. As I explain at length, the predominant historiographical mode of lesbian, gay, and queer history is genealogical, which is the reason I refer throughout to the "genealogical project." A slippery and ill-defined concept, genealogy denotes—confusingly—both the act of tracing one's lineage, as in family history, and the name of a "critical history" practice most often associated with Michel Foucault, who called for denaturalizing and defamiliarizing categories taken for granted in the present in order to understand the subject as constructed within history.[3] Writing this book would have been far simpler if lesbian and gay history (what I term "ancestral genealogy") could be seen as pursuing narratives of origins, displaced by a queer history (a practice I call "queer genealogy") informed by a Foucauldian genealogy renowned for problematizing narratives of origins. Unfortunately, the history of the historicizing of lesbian, gay, and queer lives is much messier, with elements of earlier forms of politically infused lesbian and gay practices embedded in queer practices. And to add to the confusion, once mobilized these distinctive trajectories are ongoing and address different readers for a range of purposes.

No example captures as succinctly the shared concerns, but also fraught relations, between ancestral and queer genealogical practices as the debates concerning the cultural meanings of the notorious Allan/Billing case of 1918. This case involved the Canadian dancer Maud Allan, who sued the radical right-wing member of parliament Noel Pemberton Billing for claiming she belonged to the "cult of the clitoris"—a designation ancestral practitioners equate categorically with modern female homosexuality, though queer observers prefer to hedge their bets.[4] In the context of a narrative of subcultural emergence, women's studies specialist Deborah Cohler positions the lesbian at the center of the proceedings and points to the influence of sexology (in tandem with the rhetoric of a related trial in 1918 concerning the government ban of Rose Allatini's novel *Despised and Rejected*) as crucial in securing "female homosexuality" as knowable.[5] Reading this case queerly, literary critic Jodie Medd reorients the interpretive frame to unpack the spectacular phrase "cult of the clitoris," which she explains as a "hermeneutical enigma" to invoke "the suggestion of lesbianism."[6] Albeit for different purposes, both assert the case's huge significance in raising public awareness of female sexual deviancy and reach conclusions so similar it is difficult to tell them apart. Either the trial exposes "wartime nationalistic homophobia," "highlights the increasingly direct relationship of lesbian erotics to the law," and "cements the bond between an expanding rhetorical power of female homosexuality and British nationalism during World War 1," or it foments "national wartime paranoia," "conflate[s] spy fever with homophobia," and offers "a sensationally effective and exquisitely elusive means of figuring Britain's political and epistemological crises of modern history."[7] To a greater or lesser extent, both accept the lesbian's "value" for Billing as a tactic in fueling the highly charged atmosphere of the courtroom, thereby maximizing publicity for his criticism of the government's conduct of the war.

Still, this case merits little more than a footnote in social and cultural historical accounts of the war's impact on British society—a lack of interest I find exceptionally interesting in suggesting that the persistent marginalizing of the history of sexuality is not unrelated to the objectives of ancestral *and* queer genealogical practices.[8] The focal point of the ancestral may be the sticking point for the queer, but either way the discussion pivots around the relative salience of a modern category, lesbianism. Whether coherent or incoherent, knowable or unknowable, speakable or unspeakable, secure or suggestible, these scholars understand the objective of historical explanation as measuring the past against current understandings—and in so doing, they "discover" danger and deviance because it is the lesbian (or lesbianism) that matters. This is not a "wrong" conclusion, as if there were a "correct" historical interpretation that eludes them. My point is that these practitioners trace back from the present moment, so each detects "homophobia" in wartime nationalist discourses (a term first available in 1969) or collusion and "conspiracy" between a magistrate and counsel.[9] I have different questions about this case. As a historical example of insalubrious name calling, this trial provides a good opportunity to see how sexuality was structured and organized in 1918. This is why *Disturbing Practices* calls for analytical frameworks alert to meanings outside the context of identity. To account for contradictions and illogicalities of a "lesbian" both central and irrelevant entails a mode of historicizing that does not construct "a past reality" of the "covered over, hidden or repressed" or dismantle an "ornate cover story which blocks access to the past" as seen in the trope of "suggestibility."[10] I do not see alternative practices shedding new light on the darkness of identity history; rather, I envisage the potential of practices that acknowledge the "vast domain of historical unknowability."[11]

In this book I want to critique and assess what identity history can and cannot deliver — not to dismiss it as inadequate for its singular and abiding interest in the force of modern identity categories, which would seriously underestimate and undervalue the power of its insistence on recognition (as connected or disconnected), its cogent reminder of sexuality's importance. I am curious what a "queer" critical history of sexuality might look like were it to embark with an unknowingness about the past to discover what is now "unheard of." I see scope for a different practice that draws on the methodologies of queer genealogy *not* to trace queer beings at any given moment, but to understand how sexual difference "is established, how it operates, [and] how and in what ways it constitutes subjects who see and act in the world."[12] I am fully aware that some queer scholars believe their work *already* seeks to understand sexuality in precisely this way — how difference is established, its operations, and how it constitutes the subject. Why ask for a queer critical history practice when this is already being done? In a sense, *Disturbing Practices* offers a long-winded answer by drawing attention to the impulses of identity politics that linger in queer genealogical practices. Queer genealogy *has* a history itself, and if those residual elements drive its interest in the pursuit of sexual pasts, we need to grasp how this complicates its ambitions to be genealogical in the Foucauldian sense.

To reiterate, I did not begin this project feeling an urgent need to rethink the purposes of historicizing vis-à-vis the epistemological apparatus of sexuality on which identity history is based. This book changed as a result of the peculiarities and conceptual roadblocks I encountered in the archive. How, for instance, could a landlady's testimony in 1920 that her husband gave her permission to sleep with the female plaintiff be accepted as proof of virtue beyond all doubt? Stranger still, why did no one in my case studies, either during the war or through the 1920s, appear to understand sexuality as an orientation or a category of being, knowable as deviant or normal? Some things just didn't add up.

What I understood as "sexuality"—a modern analytical concept that structured erotic desires and sexual acts through taxonomies and identities—did not map onto the women I was investigating. Queer methodologies acutely alert to the significance of the unsaid are adept at clarifying the cultural meanings of "talk" that circulates "from mouth to mouth" and is "never formulated on paper"—yet in my materials the individual as a sexual being did not appear to lurk in people's "nasty thoughts." "Dirty things" proved "extraordinarily difficult" to nail down.[13] Rumors and accusations of a sexual nature put some of the women in my case studies in the national spotlight, but I found no private papers disclosing their innermost thoughts about their romantic entanglements or their sexual desires, preferences, or inclinations; and during the war and into the interwar period, none ever spoke of themselves or others in reference to modern categories of sexual identity. Particularly fascinating, however, were the reformulations of wartime events and experiences recounted later in interviews conducted in the 1960s, in which interviewees readily latched on to the labels and habits of thought familiar to us now.

Captivated by the conundrums of sexual knowledge itself and the problems of historicizing that knowledge, I began to worry about the limitations of any historiographical practice mediated by the knowledge structure of a "science" that was invented and developed in the late nineteenth century and flourished into the early decades of the twentieth: sexology (or sexual science), a project especially influential in modern Britain.[14] To what extent, I wondered, were my questions about the sexual past informed by a scientific way of knowing "sexuality" as an edifice comprising categories and identities built out of a "host of different biological and mental possibilities, and cultural forms—gender identity, bodily differences, reproductive capacities, needs, desires, fantasies, erotic practices, institutions, and values"?[15] Equally disturbing, were the historiographical objectives that motivated my visits to the archive already determined by the residual forces of sexology's operational habits of thought in constructing sexuality as categorizable and identifiable? Unraveling the cultural meanings and discursive formations of female sexuality in the early decades of the previous century demanded I step outside the logic of identity history because its knowledge apparatus seemed to bring sexuality into the light at the expense of casting other knowledge regimes into the dark. Lesbian, gay, and queer historians and historically minded (or historicist) critics have thought long and hard about questions concerning the discursive inadequacies of the infrastructure of sexological knowledge, its modern system of sexual classification, and the vexing problem of using identity labels to describe sexual subjects in the past. This project's concerns lie elsewhere in highlighting the effects of the relative absence of self-reflexivity in the making of identity-based sexual history — the terrain, in other words, of historiography.

This book aims to anatomize the history of sexuality as a project divided by disciplinarity *and* the historiography of sexuality as a project divided by purpose; hence its two-part structure: "The Practice of Sexual History" and "Practicing Sexual History." Part 1 lays the groundwork for part 2 in examining the complex historical conditions that shaped the historiography of sexuality as a field practiced across multiple disciplines, to serve competing agendas. Although the topic is largely unfamiliar in queer studies and often judged uninteresting by social and cultural historians, I regard historiography as a crucial starting point in encouraging intellectual exchange between queer studies and academic history and, more specifically, between queer studies and critical history, the latter an approach to, or method of, historical writing interested in a critical interrogation of "how that-which-is has not always been."[16] The two parts of the book — the historiographical overview in the context of disciplinarity and the case studies — engage a similar set of questions from two directions, to speculate on a praxis forged out of dialogical exchange between queer studies and academic history.

For some time now, relations between these two fields have been strained, if not estranged — a predicament not only puzzling and frustrating, but also profoundly disappointing because, in several respects, queer studies and critical history are the products of the same post-Enlightenment critique; both, for instance, are skeptical of universalist metanarratives, transcendent categories, sequential linearity, narratives of progression, and "empty sameness."[17] If, this book asks, the queer genealogist and the critical historian reach into the same tool kit to create "possibilities of resistance" and "emancipatory futures," what are the epistemic repercussions — for practitioners and their practices — in splitting apart at the level of historiographical purpose?[18] This is perhaps the toughest question of all — and it cannot be explained solely by surveying lesbian, gay, and queer historiography. What is required, I argue, is actually showing the roadblocks through the writing of critical history, which is the reason the book's second part grounds the abstract, theoretical discussions about the historiography of sexuality in the materiality of the sexual past through case studies. Illustrating some of the conceptual obstacles through specific examples foregrounds the importance of a self-reflexive practice in addressing questions relating to how historical knowledge of modern sexuality is organized and produced.

The Historical Past and the Practical Past

Harnessing disciplinary frictions and incompatibilities to the mutual advantage of multiple disciplines to broaden the historical understanding of sexuality, as this book attempts, is a risky venture. Nowhere is the strain more visible than in the frustration historians, even those well versed in theory, feel in seeking a secure hold on the word queer. Sociological historian Jeffrey Weeks wisely begins his account of the term with an apt reminder that queer originally denoted a figure linked with what was odd, twisted, or bent — a meaning lesbian and gay activists would later appropriate to describe a militant collective sexual politics.[19] With the advent of queer theory in the early 1990s, queer signaled a privileging of dissidence, subversion, transgression, and above all a radical critique of sexual identity. For nearly two decades the "queer" of queer theory and queer studies has proved extraordinarily useful for literary and cultural critics in unsettling the power of the hetero/homo binary, but its highly abstract and esoteric language has made it a difficult theoretical perspective for outsiders to navigate. No other concept in sexuality studies has so vexed and confused as "queer," which, whether deployed as verb, noun, or adjective, revels in open-endedness, its playful resistance to definition rarely deterring ongoing speculation about its capabilities and limitations. Highly contested and lacking scholarly consensus, queer is valued by some for its inclusivity, as seen in its use as an umbrella term for LGBT (lesbian, gay, bisexual, and trans) communities and identity politics, and treated by others as a rejection of identity — *non*identity as identity.

Yet another stumbling block for historians is that the queer characterization of historical practices, protocols, or methods maps only unevenly onto the ways historians understand their work. This is partly because the "history" queer studies encountered at its inception was a mode of social history content to leave theorizing to others. With the cultural turn (that is, the impact of the poststructuralist critique of language on historical practice), academic history has changed in ways that have largely gone unnoticed by queer practitioners, who sometimes mistake the distinctive concerns of lesbian and gay social history as representative of all historical practice. Queer *mis*understanding of the discipline of history allows queer studies to depict it as enthralled by empirical evidence and truth claims. Now cut off from the dominant practices of history, queer scholars variously ignore it, reject it, misconstrue it, reinvent it, or uncritically conflate the discipline with "pastness." This disconnect needs to be examined closely to appreciate why even historical arguments play out differently between these two scholarly fields. Queer scholars, for instance, have been deeply influenced by historian Dipesh Chakrabarty's emphasis on the "elements of empathy, sincerity, intuition, generosity of spirit, and a sense of the possible."[20] Historians, on the other hand, are divided in their judgment of work that appears to privilege affect over "forensic skills," to the point of suggesting that Chakrabarty's project more closely resembles "a literary work than a conventional history."[21] This prospect, of course, is more threatening to historians than to historically aware queer scholars accustomed to negotiating the problem of evidence by cultivating a special relationship with literary expression. For philosopher of history Hayden White, Chakrabarty's "poetic history" produces "not so much history" as "the 'history effect'" and is therefore only tenuously related to history "proper."

Crafting arguments that speak to scholars with shared interests in history and sexuality across these disciplinary divides is further complicated by differences in style and expression, but more fundamental incompatibilities relate to the conventions and habits of praxis. However exaggerated these differences between disciplinary cultures, it is not uncommon to hear practitioners of one field caricature the other; thus, historians reputedly prize accessibility and lucidity above all else, while queer theorists are famous for enunciating their findings with impenetrable density and sometimes playful abstraction. Instances too of queer appropriation of concepts such as the "archive" or "historiography" strike some professionally trained historians as unsettling and pointless. The more urgent concerns are far-reaching, deeply entrenched, and intransigent at the level of modes of analysis, basic foundational assumptions, and stances toward material evidence and the status of truth claims. To some extent that gap will never be narrowed because there are "indispensable" elements in the practice of history that some queer practitioners will not countenance, such as the importance of "factual knowledge" not merely "about events but, however problematically, on more structural and comprehensive levels, such as narration, interpretation, and analysis."[22] Needless to say, locating points of connection is hardly straight-forward. Initiating cross-disciplinary discussion starts with an awareness that historical practices (or the practices of historically minded literary and cul-tural critics) informed by "the cultural politics of recognition"—in this case, sexual identity—must discern what different practices have to offer, which is another objective of this book in its attentiveness to use value.[23]

A helpful preliminary schema in determining the diverse uses of history can be found in the work of political philosopher Michael Oakeshott, who, in accounting for the professionalizing of history in terms of its service to the nation-state, identified two modes that "have nothing whatever in common": the "practical past" (what "most of us carry around with us in our minds and draw on in the performing of our daily tasks") and the "historical past" ("which could be studied scientifically, disinterestedly, as an end in itself and 'for its own sake'" and "possesses little or no value for understanding or explaining the present, and provides no guidelines for acting in the present or foreseeing the future").[24] The explanatory force of this differentiation lies *neither* in its characterization of the current state of an academic history that largely welcomes and encourages the incorporation of the experiences of groups previously excluded *nor* in its anticipatory vision of the possibilities of a critical history practice alive to the future. Oakeshott's conceptualization of two kinds of pasts instead elucidates why an old discipline places a high value on professional training (and remains tacitly invested in what consti-tutes proper and improper history) and therefore tends to regard politically motivated outsiders with suspicion.

Queer historicist work such as Elizabeth Freeman's *Time Binds: Queer Temporalities, Queer Histories* (2010) perfectly exemplifies the tensions be-tween these two pasts in her invocation of "traditional historical inquiry," "history 'proper,'" "historiography," or "official history," which attempts to establish distance between the "historical" and "practical" pasts to mobi-lize bold reconceptualizations of queerness and to disrupt temporalities and generate "a discontinuous history of its own."[25] In an eloquent preface to the volume, Freeman interweaves a close reading of a poem titled "It's a Queer Time," written by the British poet Robert Graves *during* the First

World War. Positioning her critical and political intervention as satisfying the intense queer longings for "becoming-collective-across-time," Freeman interprets the poet-officer's inciting his men to go over the top ("You're charging madly at" the enemy "yelling 'Fag!'") as indicating the "homophobia necessary to fuel masculine violence."[26] Forging a queer practical past entails confronting how queer lives have "been forgotten, abandoned, discredited, or otherwise effaced," but this is often at the expense of subverting the purposes of the historical past, which can be observed in Freeman's claim that Graves used a 1920s American slang word for the male homosexual rather than, more plausibly, an ancient Gaelic battle cry, adapted by his regiment in the Royal Welsh Fusiliers (*Fág a' Bealach*, meaning "clear the way").[27] What appears as an egregious error within the context of the historical past registers as exhilarating inventiveness in a practical past off-limits to the scholar trained in a disciplinary culture that bears the residual traces of scientific investigation. "Proper history" elevates the status of the fact, advocates the development of techniques, methods, and values to cultivate detachment, and subscribes to the promise that history should teach "no lessons"; its interests are "strictly impersonal, neutral, and in the best cases, objective."[28] In contrast to the purposes of professional historians who alone—as producers of a "historical past"—are qualified to circulate work in approved publications, the practical past is available to anyone because it is "made up of all those memories, illusions, bits of vagrant information, attitudes, and values which the individual or the group summons up as best they can to justify, dignify, excuse, alibi, or make a case for actions to be taken in the prosecution of a life project."[29]

To the delight of some and the annoyance of others, the history of sexuality is a site where these two pasts—the historical and the practical—collide, crisscross, and blur. The difficulty, from the perspective of producers of the historical past, is that queer movements in "that warehouse of archived memories, ideas, dreams, [and] values" are determined by specific political investments, informed by the modern organization of sexuality that predetermines and overdetermines what can be said, asked, thought, or written about the sexual past.[30] The queer practical past creates "possibilities of resistance," but its purposes can also impede investigation of sexualities that have vanished without trace. For example, returning to the circulation of sex talk during the war, dangerous talk behind closed doors may have intimated that "something" was going on without differentiating the sexual subject as a "thing." Critical historians seek to know how it was possible to know *in the* past: "Not just to tell the past, but to incorporate in that telling the reasons why the past can talk meaningfully to us today" — an interest shared by some queer scholars but realized in ways critical historians might view as limiting in reinscribing the way we know now.[31]

Disturbing the History of Sexuality

From the vantage point of the twenty-first century it is easy to forget that the inclination for thinking of ourselves either as "sexual" *or* as sexual beings is relatively recent. The very word sexuality does not appear until the late nineteenth century, when it was decreed to be "the most powerful factor in individual and social existence" and psychiatry came to regard sexuality as "the way in which the mind is best represented."[32] Before the classificatory systems and values of late nineteenth- and early twentieth-century sexology slowly began to trickle down into public culture through the interwar period (a process we still know little about), a plethora of referents were available to denote same-sex and different-sex acts and desires. Attaching identity labels based on choice of sexual object would not become widespread in North America and Western Europe, outside scientific and medical circles and the educated elite, until about the mid-twentieth century, as a result of the work of early sexologists such as Richard von Krafft-Ebing, Havelock Ellis, and Magnus Hirschfeld, who developed a knowledge practice for understanding sexuality based on taxonomies of desiring subjects compiled through case histories.[33] This great classificatory project has been subjected to intense scrutiny by scholars who debate its relative usefulness and internal contradictions and track, for instance, how older formulations — such as contrary sexual instinct, sexual inversion, or reproductive physiology — gradually evolved into the clinical discourse that allowed sexuality to be historicized.[34]

Claiming a history for sexuality is no longer controversial. Queer scholars declare the subfield so "respectable" that we "no longer feel much pressure to defend the enterprise — to rescue it from suspicions of being a palpable absurdity."[35] Practitioners exude confidence about the future direction and possibilities of this burgeoning and vibrant field, as seen in the introduction to *The Modern History of Sexuality* (2006), in which the editors Harry Cocks and Matt Houlbrook take it as axiomatic that the field has a proper subject. Building on the foundational work of Weeks, these historians describe a "protean discipline that allows us to enter a world of meaning [and] to understand the most fundamental assumptions about everyday life that shape the social, cultural, and political life of modern Western societies."[36] Historians of sexuality, they further claim, aspire to nothing less than writing "a total history of modern Western culture." Cultural historian Geoff Eley's inclusion of the history of sexuality—alongside labor history, the history of women and gender, and histories of empire, colonialism, and race—in his thoughtful discussion of scholarship that has challenged and energized social and cultural history through the 1970s and 1980s seems to acknowledge its growing importance. Yet while these other areas are fully documented by lengthy footnotes identifying representative work, for the historiography of sexuality Eley points to a couple of special issues of *Radical History Review*, one collection of essays originally published in the *Journal of the History of Sexuality* (*JHS*), and Kathy Peiss and Christina Simmons's anthology *Passion and Power: Sexuality in History*—each a worthy and important project in its own right but hardly an adequate representation of the field's range or intellectual ambitions.[37] The brevity of Eley's sample notwithstanding, it stands in stark contrast to similar overviews of historical practices (and there are many) that typically note only the influence of Foucault in relation to history and sexuality.[38] In some respects the position of the history of sexuality within academic history is oddly reminiscent of women's history before the conceptual shift to gender—at once thriving intellectually in terms of academic publishing and conferences and languishing on the sidelines of so-called mainstream history or, to borrow Eley's phrase, "left safely to its own devices."[39] While I would certainly not want to dash hopes for a practice with the potential to transform and reconfigure current historiographical practices, a more sober assessment of the subdiscipline's current influence in academic history presents a gloomier picture. Historians with lively interests either in writing about the sexual past or in using the concept of sexuality as a tool (to illuminate, for instance, gender, the law, politics, class, race, nation, empire, divisions of public and private, or the body) frequently express frustration that many of their colleagues dismiss the subject as narrow, trivial, or marginal.[40]

From the perspective of disciplines such as literary studies or sociology, which have long accepted sexuality's importance in studying human societies and behavior, the defensive and exasperated tone of an introductory volume called *Sexuality in World History* (2009) seems of another era: "A study of sexuality in history can understandably evoke several skeptical responses: (1) This is a frivolous topic, not worthy of historical attention. . . . (2) This is an inconceivable topic . . . for sex is a basic behavior, biologically determined, so it has no real history. . . . (3) This is a disgusting topic, certainly not fit for student audiences. . . . (4) . . . Sex is such a private behavior that its real history is impossible."[41] Or to take another example, historian Joanne Meyerowitz notes that in the past the history of sexuality "had to (and maybe still has to) justify itself in ways that other new subfields did not, to dissociate itself from the seemingly trivial and embarrassing, from the lingering sense that sex is private and therefore distasteful when aired in public."[42] And this kind of response is not atypical. As early as 1995 cultural critic (and trained historian) Lisa Duggan famously complained that academic history regarded sexuality as "more about gossip than politics, more about psychology than history."[43] Nearly twenty years on, little seems to have changed. In fact, a recent *American Historical Review* forum on the contribution of the history of sexuality in the context of transnational history reaffirms historians' sense of the field as "fairly new and somewhat marginal" (a curious chronology in that Weeks's pioneering history of homosexual politics appeared in 1977 and *JHS* was founded in 1990).[44] Is it any wonder that sexuality's usefulness as a category of historical analysis persistently slips off the radar?

It doesn't help that outsiders frequently conflate the history of homosexuality with the history of sexuality, a predicament that must be particularly irksome for investigators of other facets of human sexuality in relation to the sexed body, feminism, gender and gender variance, age, race, ethnicity, nation, empire, class, culture, and religion. The history of sexuality encompasses all periods and geographical contexts and a huge range of topics (including sexology, erotica and pornography, masturbation, fetishism, bestiality, transvestism, pedophilia, prostitution, abortion, birth control, venereal disease, marriage, adultery, divorce, sex education, sexual abuse, illegitimacy, morality, and naturism). Recent new studies on bisexuality, transsexuality, transgenderism, and intersexuality have enriched our understanding of underinvestigated areas of research, with the added benefit of unsettling homosexuality's dominance, thereby revealing how identity drives a wedge between those who organize their historicizing around it and those who insist on disavowing it (though always keeping it in the frame).[45] However, as a perusal of any issue of *JHS* makes abundantly clear, the history of homosexuality is the field's gravitational center.[46] Queer historical work, despite its emphasis on discontinuities, habitually locates what is "queer" in and around same-sex behaviors, desires, and identities, which is one reason some historiographers view lesbian, gay, and queer history as a collective project with a progressivist agenda, its political inflections posing an obstacle to those seeking to convince professional historians of sexuality's analytical value outside the identity framework.

Ancestral and Queer Genealogies

One way to move forward is to invite lesbian, gay, and queer chroniclers to become as interested in *writing* their histories as in *reflecting* on the foundational premises and assumptions that govern and shape their work.[47] Let me be clear that I recognize the extraordinary degree of critical reflection on questions about the nature of historical evidence in positioning sexualities as either essentialist or socially constructed. Neither is there any doubt that a significant body of scholarly work on the shifting cultural meanings and dissonances of, say, the sexed body, gender, desire, erotic pleasure, love, friendship, or sexual behavior represents one of the field's greatest intellectual achievements. Disentangling the theoretical investments across the genealogical project entails examining the procedures of a historiographical project that remains tethered to the logic of lineage and roots. Genealogy in the sense of bloodline emphasizes the tracing of lines unbroken, as seen in the "genealogically patterned" chronicles of medieval European cultures that were structured "by the principle of hereditary succession" so that "historical figures and events in the past" were presented "as part of one continuous *interrelated* stream of history."[48] In a historical practice expressly designed to serve the political interests of ruling families and dynasties, it was not uncommon for chroniclers to invent "mythical ancestors."[49] Beginning in the 1970s historians of homosexuality similarly shaped their chronicles in linear fashion to advance their political agendas, some tracing back an essentialized, transcendent, or universal lesbian or gay being and others understanding sexual categories as culturally contingent and historically situated, the project I call ancestral genealogy.[50]

Ancestral inquiry has often centered on whether the homosexual is defined by acts or identities or whether homosexuality is essential or socially constructed.[51] With roots in political activism and animated by identity politics, ancestral genealogists ask who "hid" their history and characterize their project as a struggle for visibility, a breaking of the silence, an emergence from the shadows, or the desire for community. All are causes to be fiercely defended to preserve its political purpose, as seen in the sometimes acrimonious debates over terminology or the intensive interest in further refining the taxonomies of sexual beings.[52] In seeking to affirm lesbian and gay existence, some investigators work comfortably with certainty and, in the face of indecipherability, gloss over the features that make little or no sense, highlighting what appears salient. For the ancestral genealogist, the case of Nurse Harley (an example I discuss in chapter 5) — depicted in one newspaper as "an amazing story of a girl's love for another girl" — would be seen as pertaining to modern lesbianism.[53] Preoccupied with similitude while keeping the queer messiness of identity at bay, ancestral genealogy has tended to avoid an investigation of the emotional or psychic motivations that have mobilized its fascination with origins, as queer commentators point out.[54] Ancestral genealogy is particularly valuable in rectifying exclusion; locating women such as Knocker, Chisholm, Douglas-Pennant, or Harley within teleological narratives of emergence allows for the further consolidation of individual or collective identities, recovery work that in turn gives voice and presence to sexual minorities otherwise denied entry to the historical record.

Later iterations of the genealogical project deeply influenced by Foucault's *History of Sexuality* largely shifted attention away from the search for origins (essential or socially constructed) toward an equally politicized project: the attempt to *queer* Foucauldian genealogy, which, as I explain in detail in chapter 2, is a tricky maneuver within the framework of a critical history practice suspicious of "transhistorical continuities."[55] The preeminent theorist of "queer genealogy" is David Halperin, who, in a theoretically bold move, set in motion a new way to historicize sexuality:

> A genealogical analysis of homosexuality begins with our contemporary notion of homosexuality, incoherent though it may be. . . . [I]t is this incoherence at the core of the modern notion of homosexuality that furnishes the most eloquent indication of the historical accumulation of discontinuous notions that shelter within its specious unity. The genealogist attempts to disaggregate those notions by tracing their separate histories as well as the process of their interrelations, their crossings, and eventually, their unstable convergence in the present day.[56]

Without question, Halperin's *method* is as fully committed to "an inquiry into the alterity of the past" as that of any other *critical* historian. Moreover, this attempt to harness the power of a Foucauldian genealogical practice for tracing back a queer subject has been highly effective and deeply influential in activating and animating historicizing markedly different from lesbian and gay practices. Arguably, however, any practice that begins "with our contemporary notion of homosexuality" sutures two definitions of "genealogy" into a single project. Don't get me wrong — I do think it is possible to write a critical history of the homosexual and homosexuality, but it is a historical narrative that, in the popular realm in modern Britain, starts about the middle of the twentieth century and runs into the early decades of the twenty-first. Hence my interest in positing the efficacy of a *queer* critical history of *modern sexuality* that does not seek to "look for" or "trace back" an idea or being we know about now; as Foucault explains, the critical historian must "produce something that doesn't yet exist and of which we can have no idea of what it will be."[57]

This turn toward queering the sexual past has successfully problematized the search for similarity or continuity (a chief objective of lesbian and gay history) through illustrating the "limited use" of categories of identity "that have often been taken for granted since the 1970s."[58] Open to plurality and strangeness, practitioners emphasize the need for a dialogue with difference, discontinuity, alterity, and rupture and argue that the discovery of fixed and stable identities cannot be an investigatory end point. In sharp contrast to ancestral genealogy, queer genealogists might read the cultural meaning of the "amazing story of a girl's love for another girl" as more equivocal and indeterminate.[59] At the same time, queer genealogy's call for "undoing . . . the straitjacketing of the homo/heterosexual binary" to discern "a more universal as well as diverse effulgence of nonnormative identifications" betrays a lingering conceptual investment in the discursive logic it claims to repudiate and problematize.[60] In effect, embedded in queer genealogy there remain at least some of the impulses and structuring habits of the ancestral, which — provocatively — exposes the potential of one of the most unlikely of alliances in that *both* queer deconstructionists (the scholars most outspoken in their criticism of academic history practices) *and* critical historians are profoundly skeptical of the "resemblances" the queer historian or historicist perceives shimmering "unsteadily and unevenly" on the sexual landscape.[61] For the critical historian — who proceeds with a different set of questions to meet other objectives — those "retrospective identifications . . . are imagined repetitions and repetitions of imagined resemblances."[62] Despite periodic calls for rapprochement, the critique of queer deconstructionists who regard the historical enterprise as overempirical and undertheorized has only intensified, with queer history dismissed as teleological in its attempts to account for a deviant sexual past thought coextensive with a lesbian and gay past, as evinced by a continued interest in sexual identity, stable or not.[63] These tensions and misunderstandings inhibit exchange and point to a need for heightened awareness of how the protocols of disciplinarity challenge an interdisciplinary field practiced both by professional historians who must adhere to strict disciplinary expectations regarding "accuracy, lucidity, and specific detail" and by queer critics who have more freedom in imagining what "history" is and how it works.[64]

What the Book Does and Does Not Do

Part 1 broadly outlines the position of the history of sexuality inside and outside the academy, then moves to consider how the genealogical project constrains and obscures historical explanations of the sexual past even as it facilitates, animates, and illustrates — opposing tensions best understood as a legacy of sexuality's epistemic construction forged in the nineteenth century by sexology and psychiatry. The subtitle of my first chapter ("The Discipline Problem Reconsidered") is a tribute to Lisa Duggan's pioneering essay "The Discipline Problem: Queer Theory Meets Lesbian and Gay History" (1995), a perspicacious diagnosis of the effects of academic history's difficulties with politicized identities as well as lesbian and gay history's reluctance to engage with queer theory.[65] As happens with other oppressed groups — women, workers, colonized peoples — lesbian, gay, and queer history hovers at history's edge, suggesting that the discipline problem has not gone away. More positively, intense queer interest in temporality and historicity is a good indication of the timeliness in reassessing Duggan's earlier call for lesbian and gay historians to meet queer theory. This meeting has now taken place, but queer genealogy remains indebted to identity practices grounded in resistance and in oppositionality as an act of protest, complicating efforts to mobilize queerness to disturb identity. Meanwhile, we also need to reassess the discipline problem in light of the "cultural turn," because academic history's greater familiarity with critical theory has rarely extended to a sustained engagement with queer theory, perhaps accounting for the relative neglect (in comparison with gender) of sexuality's usefulness as an analytical concept in historical work.

To what extent homosexual historiography is unwittingly complicit in creating some of the epistemological problems in which it now finds itself is the subject of chapter 2, which anatomizes the diverse strands of the genealogical project. While I interrogate the distinctive investments and protocols of historicizing homosexuality, I believe it is also useful and illuminating to view lesbian, gay, and queer history as a collective project rooted in identity politics as well as the postmodern critique of identity — a field born out of the 1970s struggle for homosexual rights *as well as* 1990s queer activist politics and queer theory. Above all, it is a field shot through with paradox and contradiction in its embrace of two different meanings of genealogy, its predominant historiographical mode. This book carefully traces the evolution of these two intermeshed genealogical practices to argue for the advantages of a different starting point — a queer critical history that seeks to destabilize not simply the hetero/homo binary but the logic of oppositionality itself. As I stated above, the objective is not to abandon identity history, for it is important to continue recognizing its political value; instead, the aim is to grasp genealogy's various meanings and, after seeing how it works, determine whether it is necessary to devise new historical frameworks. The organization of this book is informed by my belief that there is no better way to test the shortcomings and blind spots of the genealogical project than through the materiality of past lives as seen in newspapers and magazines, photography, legal documents, parliamentary papers, war writing, memoirs, and private correspondence, to prise apart conceptual apparatuses — old and new — by which sexuality is known.

There is, of course, a more substantial historiography beyond the purview of this book. In setting specific geographical and chronological boundaries (modern Britain during the First World War), coverage of the extensive work by historians and literary critics on modern America or Victorian England, for example, is glaringly absent. Although a subfield of academic history, lesbian, gay, and queer historiography is simply too large to cover comprehensively even if this were my ambition — and it most emphatically is not. Charting modes of historical analysis that have evolved over the past several decades has been hugely challenging, since praxis is never static but works like an escalator "in perpetual motion."[66] These risks — and many others — come with the territory, because I am less interested in presenting a comprehensive survey of lesbian, gay, and queer historiography, or in pigeonholing scholarship within ever more nuanced subcategories, than in sketching the broader contours of historiographical trajectories animated by an engagement with identity or informed and determined by the ways modern sexuality is known now. To readers discomfited by my use of the phrase genealogical project, I acknowledge it overstates conceptual affinities — separating intellectual work into phases inevitably appears to schematize an ever-shifting body of scholarship. Again, this is a necessary hazard in attempting to outline larger arguments about the historicizing of sexuality inside and outside the intellectual project that is identity history.

Focusing particularly, though not exclusively, on lesbian historiography over a period of nearly forty years means I have overlooked other significant examples of identity history. The immediate relevance of this most marginalized of the histories of marginalization to larger debates and problems — a field widely seen as lacking in "intellectual respect, existential weight, and moral and aesthetic gravitas"—may not be readily apparent.[67] In my view, this field's internal debates over the past several decades (in addressing problems in naming and understanding same-sex acts, desires, and identities in relation to the performance of gender) elucidate in concise ways the wider concerns of historical work on gender, male homosexuality, and other sexual minorities as well as constructions of heteronormativity. As a subject "undervalued . . . and neglected," with only "an insubstantial foothold" in the academy and "complacently" overlooked by many historians, there are certainly aspects of lesbian historiography that do not extend to other fields.[68] Documenting the sexualities of women calls for particular tools and methods because, in the context of modern Britain, the question of female subordination to men is highly contested. The so-called fact of male dominance must be seen as less an inescapable feature of female sexuality than a force to be reckoned with, since some women (particularly New Women, suffragists, and feminists) found it possible to escape, subvert, or challenge such cultural imperatives. Equally, lesbian history has been constructed from an evidentiary base significantly different from that of men's same-sex relations, which were subject to social and legal regulation.

Neither do I undertake an exhaustive survey of the intricate connections between gender and sexuality in relation to wider social and cultural formations during the First World War and its aftermath. Rather, in part 2 I seek to illustrate through historical example events and cases resistant to the explanatory frameworks of ancestral and queer genealogy. The Great War is exceptionally useful for this purpose because it is a cultural moment widely perceived — by social historians and historians of lesbianism — as crucial for emergent homosexual subcultures. The tumult of war, it is often claimed, gave rise to "the first widespread public linkages between representations of female masculinity and female homosexuality in British culture."[69] Commentators such as Havelock Ellis, writing in 1916, believed the conflict had "changed so many things," especially "in the sphere of women's activities."[70]

Newspapers too helped enforce the popular view of the war as a "crucible" in which the "dross was purged away" to allow new configurations of womanhood to emerge.[71] I am less confident, however, that such configurations signaled either a heightened visibility or a growing awareness of female homosexuality between 1914 and 1918. Claims that lesbianism was "almost invisible" before the outbreak of hostilities or that the war was especially transformative for masculine women "who were beginning to think of themselves as lesbians" tell us more about ourselves than about public understanding of the modern sexual subject (or sexuality in general) in the early decades of the twentieth century.[72]

The three chapters that make up the book's second part scrutinize the concepts that underpin genealogical work — categorization, identity, normativity, and deviance — always in relation to specific aspects of the gendered experience of modern war. We have long suspected the inadequacy of our terminologies and categories but have not confronted how they persistently distort even as they illuminate. Following Foucault's influential observation that the evolution of nineteenth-century sexology established a great divide between a sexual act and a species (the sodomite and the homosexual), historians of homosexuality have mapped social relations in terms of power and regulatory regimes, but somehow classifying as a system survives unscathed. This is why part 2 critiques the sexological underpinnings of lesbian, gay, and queer history by situating in the context of the war and its aftermath, first, the exceptional fluidity and interconnectedness of sexuality and gender; second, the limits of categories of sexual identity in talking about sexuality; and third, the cultural habit of assigning to sexuality the value of "normal" as pitted against its opposite, a binary configuration that remains dominant even as it is troubled in queer studies.

Chapter 3 examines how gender historians and historians of sexuality each discuss the First World War's disruptive effects in "bringing together large numbers of like-minded women in war work and the military" but reach separate conclusions about the nature and significance of homosociality as a source of cultural anxiety.[73] The former show little interest in how the war contributed to the development of a more "coherent narrative of female homosexual identity" or "distinct models of female homosexuality"; their larger concerns focus on the perceived changes in the moral and social regulation of sexual relations between women and men.[74] Noting the "gendering effects of World War 1" as "class differentiated," historians of women and gender typically address sexuality in the context of marriage, motherhood, abortion, birth control, illegitimacy, prostitution, and venereal disease, as it pertains to family, work, or the home front rather than as evidence of shifts in the public perceptions of agency, identity, power relations, sexual knowledge, or self-understanding, the theoretical terrain of queer studies.[75] Historians of lesbianism, on the other hand, regard the First World War as a "turning point in the way in which homosexuality was represented."[76] This origins myth summons us "to more *affective* narratives of human belonging" but is founded less on painstaking archival research than on the writings of Radclyffe Hall, who imagined the female sexual invert as an ambulance driver with tremendous physical strength, stamina, personal courage, and a willingness to perform the manly skills of motoring and maintenance.[77] This chapter examines how the systems of categorization we rely on now may not be the best guide in explaining how ordinary Britons made sense of gender variance.

Chapter 4 turns to the problem of sexual identity, which — as a historical concept and historicized process — has facilitated the retrieval of a lesbian and gay past even as it elides the variations, deviations, and complications of actual lives of individuals who resist that fixity or who were unaccustomed to sexual self-reflexivity. Situating the "great scandal" surrounding the dismissal of the Hon. Violet Douglas-Pennant as commandant of the Women's Royal Air Force in a recuperative mode of lesbian history satisfies the need for a knowable sexual subject, yet yielding to the explanatory force of a queer identity also makes it difficult to decipher how a woman like Douglas-Pennant saw herself or how others saw her in 1918.[78] Resisting the very modern urge to define sexuality as fundamental and knowable through categories of identity — naming, name calling, and self-naming — invites alternative understandings of modern formations of selfhood, including the inability or refusal of women such as Knocker, Chisholm, and Douglas-Pennant to "identify." Finally, chapter 5 assesses the epistemic ramifications of a queer history dependent on conceptual tools inherited from early sexology, notably the impulse to categorize based on binaries ("normative" or "deviant," for instance). Turning to the slander case of Florence Eva Harley, I examine the queer elision of "normal" and "norm" that haunts queer historical work. Despite Halperin's famous articulation of queer as "*whatever* is at odds with the normal, the legitimate, the dominant" (and note here the several potential registers),[79] historians of modern sexuality are sometimes inattentive to sexuality's governance across multiple and contradictory regulatory norms, which in turn reduces the strategic openness of the "whatever" to a universalist formulation of the normative as normal. The story of the rise of the normal/deviant binary as a descriptor of sexuality begins only about the early 1930s, and although it is a discursive success story, the normal does not supersede or displace prior regimes. This chapter offers a new perspective on how it is possible to test the limits of a conceptual framework operating outside the oppositional tensions of normative/queer, to gauge the legibility of sexuality outside the precarious nature of normativity, and to locate new pathways in comprehending the fluidity of female sexualities.

Enacting New Futures

The aim of this exploration of how and why the history of homosexuality is produced, and who it is produced for, is not to spell out how to do it better — there is already excellent work on that topic.[80] Rather, I examine the material lives of a very few and move across a wide historiographical and theoretical terrain to see what lesbian, gay, and queer history has already achieved, staying mindful of the difficulties inherent in practices that reproduce the conditions of the epistemological structure that made sexuality modern. I am troubled by historical investigative work that embarks with a notion of the modern lesbian or homosexual, because I have different questions about the sexual past. What interests me is figuring out how one epistemological structure jostles against another, since my own case studies suggest that the modern organization of sexuality was still evolving in British public culture during the First World War and into the interwar era. The transcripts of courtroom hearings and parliamentary meetings show that while one or two speakers may have been familiar with a modern knowledge of sexuality, others found such talk baffling, as seen in the Allan/Billing case or parliamentary exchanges about the Douglas-Pennant case. If we turn to the past with a primary interest in the nameability or intelligibility of the lesbian or even queer being, it is as if we are sitting in a crowded courtroom amid hundreds of murmuring observers but can hear only one conversation, our attention drifting away when things seem incomprehensible or irrelevant — or perhaps words are so softly spoken that we hear nothing at all. My experiences in the archive forced me to confront a paradox: How was it that the same epistemological structure of sexuality that impelled me to historicize sexuality in the first place also hindered and obscured other ways the "sexual" might have been configured, talked about, and known?

In what follows I want to suggest that making sense of the *modern* sexual past (or discovering the usefulness of the concept of sexuality) may demand at least two historical practices: one structured within the logic of sexological knowledge, with its taxonomies and labels organized in relation to a "normal," and another organized differently. Before mapping future directions, it is essential to examine current practices inside and out. This is why part 1 splits the genealogical project apart, especially queer genealogy, a hybrid practice that begins (like the ancestral) "with our contemporary notion of homosexuality" to produce "a genealogical understanding of the emergence of (homo)sexuality itself."[81] Hybridity is by no means a flaw — after all, the evidentiary base for my case studies was organized around a set of questions more closely related to queer genealogy than to queer critical history. To produce a queer critical history of sexuality entails an attentiveness to purpose in order to make visible how practice itself shapes and reshapes the way we think about the sexual past.

If this book encourages dialogue between scholars with shared interests in the power of queerness-as-method in historicizing the sexual past as well as greater self-reflexivity in terms of practice and purpose, I will be satisfied. Like the queer genealogist, the queer critical historian too is alive to the usefulness of queer methodologies in determining how any historiographical pathway expands or curtails the investigatory range. My speculations — tentative, provisional — relate to the possibilities of new ancillary practices in the history of sexuality forged out of a productive conversation between scholars whose intellectual interests diverge in purpose yet converge in their recognition of history's power to enact new futures.

PART 1

The Practice of Sexual History

1 / An Uncommon Project

The Discipline Problem Reconsidered

The emergence of queer theory in the early 1990s posed difficult challenges to the practice of lesbian and gay social history, still largely in a recuperative mode of discovering a hidden past. Already under considerable pressure to rethink its foundational assumptions in light of what is commonly known as the "cultural turn" (the turn toward cultural analysis in historical investigation in response to poststructuralist and postmodern theory), lesbian and gay social history faced a particularly determined and highly specific queer critique of its research methods and paradigms.[1] To queer observers, social history's ways of understanding the world, its faith in the progress narrative of liberation politics, its investment in making hidden things visible, its confidence in the knowability of the sexual self, and its methodological relation to historical evidence (often characterized as an empiricist window onto the past) were no longer sustainable.[2] Any attempt to summarize succinctly either the transformative effects of the cultural turn in academic history or the queer negotiation of history inevitably oversimplifies. Nonetheless, there is little doubt that lesbian and gay social history — intellectually enthused and politically motivated by its core belief in a coherent and identifiable sexual subject — was profoundly at odds with a queer theory that, despite its own internal disputes about the cultural significance of sexualities, blasted to smithereens the possibility of fixed identities, stable meanings, and knowable truths.[3] To satisfy its intellectual, affective, and imaginative needs for history (its "overwhelming desire to *feel historical*"),[4] queer studies soon turned away from a social history it judged unpersuasive and grew increasingly disenchanted with an academic history insistent on the enduring importance of the empirical. Gravitating not to the new cultural history but to cultural theorists such as Frederic Jameson (whose configurations of "history" as the name given "to the impossibility of reconciling personal life with the

27

movements of a total system" were deemed more compelling), queer studies would take little notice of the changes wrought by the move from the *social* to the *cultural* in historical practice.[5]

I am by no means the first to notice this. As early as the mid-1990s queer historian and cultural critic Lisa Duggan published an influential essay ("The Discipline Problem: Queer Theory Meets Lesbian and Gay History")[6] in which she outlined, first, the wobbly status of lesbian and gay history within academic history. Departments of history, she warned, were so unconvinced about sexuality's importance in historical investigation that younger scholars risked professional suicide in investigating the lesbian and gay past. It is still true — as evinced in numerous recent historiographies — that academic history remains largely unreceptive or indifferent to the proposition that sexuality is as crucial a category of historical analysis as gender, though, as I discuss in chapter 2, there is evidence that this too is now changing.[7] Duggan's second point was her prediction that queer studies would be unforgiving in its treatment of social historians who failed to come to terms with queer theory. If the prospect of long-term unemployment wasn't scary enough, those who persisted in writing "underdog history" without engaging with the queer critique of sexuality would go "unacknowledged" or be "dismissed with an implied sneer."[8] According to Duggan, lesbian and gay social history as practiced in the 1980s and 1990s was thus doubly stigmatized by a mainstream history that deemed its project worthy but marginal and by a queer theory that ignored its findings or dismissed its methods as naive (though in the latter case the feelings of disdain were reciprocal in that some lesbian and gay social historians regarded queer theory as jargon-ridden, trendy, star-obsessed, and elitist).[9]

In the years following Duggan's one-two punch, historians of homosexuality have responded differently to the unhappy predicament that Martha Vicinus described — in her judgment of the state of lesbian history in 1994 — as "all theory and no facts or all facts and no theory."[10] A random perusal of the leading journals in sexuality studies (*Journal of the History of Sexuality* or *GLQ: A Journal of Lesbian and Gay Studies*, for instance) suggests that most scholars fall somewhere in between, with very few social historians wholly resistant to theory and with theoretically sophisticated specialists in fields such as LGBT studies (lesbian, gay, bisexual, and trans) attentive to, and respectful of, historical work, even if refraining from entering the archives themselves. With lesbian, gay, and queer historical work entering a new phase in the early decades of the twenty-first century, the polarizing effects of mutual distrust seem to be receding, as historians interested in homo-sexuality have, to a greater or lesser extent, heeded Duggan's caution that ignoring queer theory would be "a devastating mistake."[11] Far less evident is a thoroughgoing assessment of the losses and gains of the turn, for some prac-titioners, toward queer or an assessment of the epistemological consequences of a queer critique that sometimes invents what it thinks history means and how it operates. In other words, it is important to reconsider the discipline problem, because sexual history is produced within academic history but also across disciplines where, on the one hand, the impact of new theoretical perspectives such as queer theory is felt unevenly over time (embraced early on in literary and cultural studies, for example, and negotiated much later in academic history) and, on the other, the gap between history as practice and "history" as an idea conveying "pastness" obscures the object and objective of historical inquiry.[12]

In 1993 queer theorist Michael Warner pointed to the historical as a ma-jor force in producing theories of sexualities, alongside — though not equal to — psychoanalysis (thus placing history at something of a disadvantage). Warner credits psychoanalysis with providing the more "rigorous and sophis-ticated" theory of sexuality (clarifying the "psychic structures" of the "pre-oedipal, innate bisexuality, the exchange of women, reverse oedipalization, the instability of identification"), but he argues that psychoanalysis has not been effective in crafting a "subtle" understanding of "historical or cultural differences."[13] Despite Warner's early recognition of history's vital impor-tance in the theorizing of sexuality, queer theorists would be characterized as not interested in "historical questions," and queer studies (despite vibrant interdisciplinary period-based work such as ancient, medieval, early mod-ern, eighteenth-century, and so on) would come to be regarded as a field with primary interests in contemporary cultures and representation.[14] Os-tensibly uninterested in academic history's actual methods and procedures, queer studies became famously and inextricably linked with presentism, even though from its inception queer work was manifestly interested in the power of historical analysis to yield insights about the queer present and inform historicist reading practices of literary and cultural texts.[15] In this chapter my interest in the queer engagement with historicity — the deploy-ment of terms such as "archive," the call for an "erotohistoriography" ("a politics of unpredictable, deeply embodied pleasures that counters the logic of development"), or the proposal that "perverse presentism," "impossible love," or the "fantasmatic" could serve as other models of queer historiography — may exaggerate the presentism of queer studies, but my aim is to clarify how such tendencies and discursive playfulness make little sense to the historian.[16] At the same time, there is no reason the tools and methods of academic history should not be available to, and given another life by, queer scholars based in other disciplines interested in the past and historicity. But equally, history cannot be reduced to a trope, since its practices too require careful and nuanced interrogation. These very appropriations of historical discourse by queer critics suggest the advantages of closely examining what happens when disciplines and subfields rub shoulders.

Queer literary and cultural critics have been fascinated by history's power to bestow political and cultural meaning in the present, and the queer willingness to probe the darker corners of the collective closet and critique a hermeneutic of visibility, decipherability, and recognition is unquestionably provocative and long overdue.[17] With the collapse of a unified political subject and the loss of stable identities, the queer yearning for a lost past is congruent with Jameson's notion of a "nostalgia for the present."[18] Queer critic Heather Love identifies "longing for community across time" as a "crucial feature of queer historical experience," a far cry from Vicinus's characterization over a decade earlier of the queer critique as deeply "ahistorical."[19] Historians have long understood that the past (everything before the present moment) is not the same as history (a constructed account of what came before), but the helpfulness of that distinction eludes some queer critics and theorists who have not been in dialogue with an academic history in flux. No one scholarly community is at fault in failing to initiate critical exchange. The task here is not to assign blame but to open up channels of communication by raising, on the one hand, queer studies practitioners' awareness of history as a discipline interested primarily in change over time and, on the other, professional historians' awareness of the usefulness of sexuality in historical investigation as well as the power of queer analysis. If, as I argue throughout this book, it is not enough simply to incorporate "women, subalterns, primitives, gays, people of color, immigrants" into Western "accounts of 'history'" but a "matter . . . of rethinking history in terms adequate to the present age," it is vital to recognize the common interests shared by queer practitioners and critical historians in exploring the "possibility of the present *as* history."[20] The queer critique of identity similarly points to the advantages of thinking beyond the categories that falsely represent ontology and experience, but the queer entry to the past has often been via literary or cultural studies rather than academic history — and we need to know how and why this different pathway matters. The lateness in considering the epistemological implications of the disciplinarity and interdisciplinarity of the LGBT history project likely accounts, at least in part, for the history of sexuality's status as a still emerging field of academic inquiry, its promise not yet fully realized. Just as the impact of poststructuralist theory on history was "tardy and contested," so too has queer theory been slower in influencing historical practice, ever deferring the famed demise of queer theory.[21]

The usefulness of queer theory to social and cultural historians was first proposed in 1995 by the guest editors of *Radical History Review*'s "Queer Issue," who asked:

> Is queer theory useful for historical work? Can "queer" be a historical, historicized category? What might a queer historical practice look like? Although "queer" is posed as a term that is meant to include men and women alike, might it elide gender in the way the term "gay" tended to in the past? Does queer erase differences between and among those whose variously deviant sexualities correspond to very different histories of marginalization? What is the place of empirical historical research in queer studies? What is the relationship between studies of queer reading strategies and representations and those that seek to explore the meaning and texture of people's lives?[22]

This earliest adumbration of queer historical practice leaves the difficult job of defining "queer" largely to two scholars based outside departments of history, Donna Penn and Martha M. Umphrey (underscoring Duggan's point about institutional resistance).[23] Penn and Umphrey make good use of the work of Foucault, Warner, Eve Kosofsky Sedgwick, Gayle Rubin, and Judith Butler to expose how, in their view, lesbian and gay social history limits "the historical imagination."[24] For Penn and Umphrey, the power of queer theory, by comparison, seems formidable in providing historians with a strategic escape from the hegemony of rigid systems of classification, stable sexual subjectivities, and fixed relational binaries. What, of course, has proved more difficult in queer historical practice — a field still in conversation with identity — is the challenge of working out how to dislodge and destabilize the structure of modern sexual knowledge itself, suggesting a project "divided against itself" in seeking to historicize both queer lives (queerness-as-being) and queerness in the past (queerness-as-method).[25]

Recent queer history has begun to address — often more implicitly than explicitly — many of the *RHR* editors' questions, thus demonstrating that "queer" is very much a historical and historicized category. Thanks to new work on the variations of sexuality, we are beginning to see what a queer historical practice — as an epistemology and a methodology — might look like.[26] The *RHR* cluster of questions anticipates the unsettling effects of the queer troubling of identity for "those that seek to explore the meaning and texture of people's lives"; however, concerns that queer would erase women or collapse "very different histories of marginalization" into an undifferentiated history of deviant sexualities seem unfounded, with the publication of work under the rubric of queer history focusing on both women and men, if seldom in relation to one another.[27] Discrete histories of sexual practices that resist heteronormativity — lesbian, gay, bisexual, or trans — have been deeply informed by aspects of queer theory in ways that preserve the distinctions of recognizable cultures and experiences. Even so, such progress in the development of queer historical practice belies the persistence of an "uncomfortable tension" between "lesbian/gay history and queer studies."[28] Despite insistent calls by Duggan and others for productive intellectual exchange, historians and queer critics have only infrequently engaged in sustained dialogue, and it is this singular failure to communicate that has allowed to go unchallenged the queer depiction of history as a haven of positivist empiricism or historical writing as a "neutral chronicle of events."[29] Only those uninformed about the vibrant and extensive debates in academic history "between those who assert the transparency of facts and those who insist that all reality is construed or constructed" would characterize the field as undertheorized and empirically driven.[30] To reiterate, my aim is not to chastise one side or the other, but to clarify what is at stake in determining how or if the history (or "history") that outsiders produce differs from the professionals' by looking at the results of the border crossings between academic history and queer studies. Some queer critics, often drawing on "the most conservative methodological claims by historians," fashion a historical practice to suit their arguments and show little inclination to deepen their understanding of its range and diversity.[31] Some trained historians, on the other hand, construe queer historical work as cultural criticism and miss opportunities to engage with bold queer theorizing of historicity, transhistoricism, temporality, and change, all topics to be discussed in this chapter and the next. The first task, however, is to unpack a stubborn binary that can sometimes appear to cordon off the practice of history from untrained outsiders.

Proper and Improper History

The reasons for the long-standing marginalization in academic history of the study of homosexuality or queer theory are just as manifold and complex as the reasons some queer critics construct what they think history is and how it works, but one thing is certain: the various constituencies with the most to gain in working across disciplinary boundaries — social and cultural historians interested in lesbian, gay, bisexual, trans, queer, and so-called heteronormative sexualities or in sexuality as an analytical tool; literary and cultural critics interested in writing the history of sexualities or in generating historicist readings of texts; and queer critics and theorists interested in sexuality's historicity — though not estranged, nevertheless too often remain unaware of or uninterested in the epistemological consequences stemming from the very different ways they have gone about their work. Thinking about the vital operations of disciplinarity in producing historical knowledge in relation to sex, the sexual, or sexuality is important because social and cultural historians (with varying degrees of institutional support) have not been alone in their pursuit of a lesbian and gay past. They have always worked alongside popular historians, activists, independent scholars, and scholars based in other fields, especially literary and cultural studies, often sites where queer theory evolved and still flourishes.

A good example of the range of practitioners' backgrounds can be seen in the study of modern British homosexual cultures, though other time periods and geographical locations would serve equally well. In 1977 sociological historian and activist Jeffrey Weeks published *Coming Out: Homosexual Politics in Britain from the Nineteenth Century to the Present*, which has been immensely influential in lesbian and gay studies by providing a captivating narrative of the progression "from sin to crime" and then onward to liberation and community.[32] This major foundational text was followed by a succession of books such as *Making Sexual History*, which played a key role in framing the debates on historiography.[33] Despite Weeks's early example of focusing on both women and men, few others have adopted this approach.[34] Over the decades many scholars have looked at men's friendships and sexual relations in the twentieth century, including popular writers Hugh David, James Gardiner, and Graham Robb, playwright Neil Bartlett, philosopher Morris Kaplan, literary critics Alan Sinfield and Matt Cook, and historians Harry Cocks and Matt Houlbrook.[35] The history of modern lesbian cultures in Britain has often been undertaken by popular writers whom historians

might regard as amateurs of "dubious academic distinction," including biographer Diana Souhami (*The Trials of Radclyffe Hall*) and independent
scholar Emily Hamer (*Britannia's Glory: A History of Twentieth-Century
Lesbians*).[36] Over the past several decades new work has been produced by
scholars with institutional locations in departments of English, cultural studies, and women's and gender studies, including the members of the Lesbian
History Group, Lillian Faderman, Terry Castle, Martha Vicinus, and Nicky
Hallett, as well as by trained social and cultural historians such as Alison
Oram, Rebecca Jennings, and Sally Newman.[37] The presence of significant
numbers of disciplinary outsiders — scholars with no training in or affiliation
with academic history — has undoubtedly enriched the history of homosexuality by introducing new perspectives and expanding the evidentiary base,
but it has also generated disciplinary anxieties and tensions that have wid-
ened rather than bridged the gaps between the disciplines.

Reading intellectual historian Carolyn J. Dean's insightful review of
Scott Bravmann's *Queer Fictions of the Past: History, Culture, and Difference*
superbly illustrates the difficulties that arise when a project appears to be
positioned as a contribution to historiography but fails to observe the disciplinary strictures of academic history. Like many historians, Dean is acutely
attuned to disciplinary training as a group identity, even as she recognizes the
potential of the powerful and "enormously influential" theoretical models
produced by LGBT studies "in English departments and in departments
of literature more generally."[38] While commenting on her disappointment
at the failure of lesbian and gay social historians to engage with the cutting
edge of queer theory through the 1990s, she nonetheless situates historical
work strictly in terms of disciplinarity, noting that there have been only a
handful of "accomplished" social historians of homosexuality (Allan Bérubé,
George Chauncey, and John D'Emilio) in what is otherwise "the province of
fine amateur historians."[39] Taking particular exception to Bravmann's casual
use of the term historian to describe scholars based outside academic history, Dean locates individual scholars in terms of disciplinarity with unusual
specificity: Martha Vicinus is a "literary theorist" (a statement that requires a
footnote, "Martha Vicinus is actually a professor of English"); the historian
of sexuality Vernon Rosario "is not trained as a historian"; and several of the
editors of, and contributors to, *Hidden from History: Reclaiming the Gay and
Lesbian Past* are "not historians by training," a designation bestowed only on
those properly trained and employed in departments of history.[40] From the
perspective of literary and cultural critics inclined to refer to Foucault as a

historian — something historians would never do — this keen interest in aligning individuals within precise disciplinary regimes seems perplexing.[41] However, history is often referred to as an "old discipline," and while there are any number of historians who embrace diverse theoretical perspectives (such as Marxist, feminist, postcolonial, psychoanalytic, postmodern, or sociological), fields of interest (social, cultural, intellectual, family, urban, women, gender, economic, political, military, diplomatic, or public), or areas of specialist expertise defined by national (or transnational) and temporal boundaries, many historians — however irrational — see themselves as members of a club, guild, or "tribe."[42] These terms and relations of professional and amateur, or proper and improper, are familiar to historians and commonly used. That a theoretically sophisticated historian like Dean invokes this binary indicates that this habit of thought (described by White as "always kind of scandalous") is deeply instilled in academic history in ways very unlike literary studies, for example.[43] To those outside the profession of history, such emphatic insistence on positioning scholars as either professional or amateur might seem unnecessarily rigid, even nitpicky, but what Dean endeavors to convey through such specificity is that academic history is professionalized in particular ways, tethered to historical evidence as a means to best understand change over time.

Yet however jarring it might be to outsiders to find themselves slotted inside or outside the discipline, it is important to remember that academic history is not the only discipline to have been invested in "narratives of professionalization."[44] The history of the practice of literary criticism reveals that it too was a field with ambitions of professionalization in the early twentieth century; but with the rise of theory in the mid-1960s, it became more ambivalent about the "theoretical grounds as well as the practical effects of professional expertise and authority": literary theory impelled critics to rethink "authorial intention, historical reference, and textual coherence," therefore "compromising the claim to objectivity in interpretation and with it the sanction of the professional interpreter, . . . [W]hat if anything could now count as our unique critical expertise? And if nothing could, then could criticism still claim to *be* a profession?"[45] The animus of queer theory toward disciplines thought to have remained enmeshed in vulgar positivism can be traced back to this moment when some disciplines responded to theory with enthusiasm while others were less eager or more resistant. To paraphrase philosopher Richard Rorty, history professionalized while literary criticism theorized: "Criticism owes its success to having achieved, through its embrace of theory, a unique *un*professionalism by enjoying from the outset a 'knowledge base,' literature, defined by its refusal to convey knowledge."[46] What for historians is a term of abuse — unprofessional — means something else to the postmodern literary critic; despite such equivocation about the designation of professional, the position of literary studies in the academy as a discipline is secure, and obviously all disciplines demand rigorous training and certain critical skills, tools, theories, and knowledge of methodologies.

Inasmuch as "disciplinarity" literally denotes "control and constraint," all disciplines produce professionals and amateurs by enforcing rules and regulations developed over "several generations," which promotes the formation of "distinct communities of discourse, with distinct methods, vocabularies, and standards of evaluation."[47] The notion of a "professional historian" usefully signals institutional affiliation, specific postgraduate training, and degrees of competency — these attributes, qualities, and qualifications matter to historians, and I will respect this by reserving the designation for scholars whose training or institutional home is in academic history or who, as the historian Geoff Eley puts it, "practice the historian's classic virtues":

> Ground yourself in the most imaginative, meticulous, and exhaustive archival research, in all the most expansive and unexpected ways the last four decades have made available. Embrace the historian's craft and the historian's epistemologies. But never be satisfied with these alone. Be self-conscious about your presuppositions. Do the hard work of abstraction. Converse with neighboring disciplines. Be alive to the meanings of politics.[48]

To outsiders, academic history might seem like a club, but membership is by no means exclusive — otherwise Eley would not have directed these remarks to "my fellow historians, both *within* the profession and *without*."[49] While the protocols of historical professionalism seem to reinforce a dichotomous relational logic that differentiates between insiders and outsiders, thus limiting the conditions of mutual exchange, the discipline's borders are considerably more permeable, and the history of sexuality is an excellent example of this.[50] The "fully credentialed" professional historian has been defined as someone who is "teaching, researching, and writing inside a university history department," but historians of homosexuality, in particular, often frustrate and resist this criterion.[51] Some historians express antagonism toward nonprofessionals out of a mistaken belief that it is possible to preserve the purity of a historical practice that would otherwise be tainted by dialogical exchange with critical-theoretical disciplines; however, Eley observes, the way to keep history "alive and active" is to welcome "cross-border traffic" between the disciplines.[52]

One result of the cultural turn is that historians are now just as likely to examine visual or literary texts as any other kind of document, suggesting that the separation of practices along strict "bipartisan" lines has reached its "sell-by date," but the response by historians is not that simple.[53] For some, the possibilities of an enhanced evidentiary base outweigh concerns that the discipline would somehow be compromised: "Engravings are no longer just illustrations but also evidence for historical arguments. Police reports, memoirs, conduct books, and autopsy reports are not just historical sources but also models, influences, and sources for 'literary' texts."[54] Others urge more caution, partly because of concerns that an undifferentiated cultural studies might supersede traditional disciplinary structures, but also because of a persistent belief that historical questions are "different"—historians and literary critics may use "the same sources," but they do not read these documents "in the same way."[55] As Dean herself recognizes in her approving remarks about the intellectual excitement generated by a field that is the quintessence of interdisciplinarity, queer studies is well positioned to defuse residual skepticism toward more fluid disciplinary boundaries.

Lesbian, gay, and queer history has already proved an ideal site to initiate the kind of animated conversation between history and other disciplines that Hayden White regards as vital in reformulating and reenergizing historical practice, particularly what Joan Scott (following Theodor Adorno) terms "critical history," as evident in the work of literary and cultural critics who disprove the myth of queer presentism and engage — either explicitly or implicitly — with complex historiographical theories, questions, and arguments.[56] In an afterword to a collection of manifestos advocating new and radical directions in the practice of history, White seizes on Foucault's notion of critique:

> Insofar as critique has a meaning beyond the idea of discerning formal structures of expression, meaning, and value in one's own and others' discourses and examining these for logical or artistic consistency, then this meaning is nothing other than the effort to identify the irreducible *historicity* of all things. . . . [C]ritique means historicity, and historicity means attention to the evanescent immanence of everything.[57]

One effect of the meeting between history and queer is recognizing in the realm of sexuality studies what White ascribes to the meaning of critique generally: "The de-transcendentalization of every regime of truth and knowledge, the denial of universals, substances, and essences that are pressed upon us in all times and everywhere, and attention to whatever it is in a thing that makes it a singularity resistant to generalization, abstraction, and reification."[58] For White, as for several other manifesto writers, critical history stimulates self-reflexivity on a field noted for its privileging of the archive and "'primary' sources, its insistence on meticulously accurate chronology, and its mastery of narrative," but this shared sense of what distinguishes historical investigation from cognate fields does not preclude internal debates on every aspect of historical practice.[59]

Critical history too invites scrutiny of history's relations with "other disciplines of the human sciences and arts," a process already well under way in queer history.[60] This is why Dean is troubled, above all, by Bravmann's failure to define what he means by the category of history: "He offers no extensive discussion of historical method, no history of gay and lesbian history, no history of the historical methods used by historians of gay and lesbian identities, nor even a discussion of why this sort of analysis is perhaps unnecessary."[61] In other words, Bravmann's investigation of the lesbian and gay engagement with history is recognizable neither as a work of history nor as the work of a traditionally trained historian, but instead bears the traces of a scholar trained somewhere else — in this case, in a pioneering doctoral program open to alternative reconfigurations of historical practice. While Bravmann's innovative and experimental project (described as a "queer cultural studies of history that focuses on the politics and the poetics of historical discourses")[62] might be considered improper history, its achievement can be more readily gauged by seeing it as a different mode of historical investigation that, in its methodology, fuses the techniques of close reading, often associated with literary analysis, and historical argument. His discussion of methodology is brief but is not wholly dissimilar from methods deployed by professional historians, who also draw on historical evidence to produce theoretically informed accounts of their subjects' "identities, communities, and politics."[63]

The engaging hybridity of this scholarly project — at the nexus of academic history, lesbian and gay studies, and cultural studies — is for some reviewers interesting and troubling, but it is a hybridity fully cognizant of the theoretical implications of the cultural turn and therefore poised to make a valuable contribution to new forms of queer historicizing.[64] Still, Bravmann's project remains vaguely unsatisfying because historians tend to be more attentive to historiographical critiques by scholars who can demonstrate their skill in the basics of historical practice, that is, scholars whose work is grounded in "imaginative, meticulous, and exhaustive archival research," for this is the "craft" of the historian.[65] Thus it is not surprising that John Howard, though appreciative of Bravmann's important theoretical intervention, nevertheless regrets that he has not applied "his considerable talents and his self-reflective theoretical insights to the fashioning of this new history."[66] Eschewing the methods of oral history or archival research, Bravmann's project is somehow incomplete because he has built a solid theoretical foundation not for the purpose of examining material evidence to develop historical arguments, but for examining historical practice itself. What he discovers instead are not what actual informants think about their histories, but the ways the stories (or metanarratives) that lesbians and gay men have invented about a lesbian and gay past — via salient historical events such as Stonewall, the Harvey Milk memorial march, AIDS and other memory projects, and literary representation — are in fact "sites of hermeneutic and political struggle rather than . . . natural, true, or inevitable."[67] Bravmann probes the meaning of the historical past for lesbians and gay men interested in the processes of social, cultural, and political self-definition while insisting that he does not *do* history. Dismissing historiography "as a culturally privileged system of signification," Bravmann's project is nevertheless profoundly historiographical as evidenced by its theoretical interest in the structures of a politicized usable past, specifically how history has shaped the lesbian and gay imagination.[68]

Unfortunately the logic of Bravmann's argument, as is not uncommon in queer criticism, hinges on a metanarrative of academic history before the cultural turn, a history unable to shake off the traces of a "residual empiricist impulse," even though many queer critics are fully aware that theoretically savvy historians have ceased to "search for historical certainty."[69] Understanding the historiography of lesbian and gay sexualities, Dean rightly argues, cannot begin with misunderstanding academic history, which is the reason her trenchant and tough questioning of Bravmann's project needs to be taken seriously: "What is the relationship between gay and lesbian cultural imaginations and historical (and other) scholarship? What is a dominant memory practice and what is *its* relation to so-called official history?"[70] The queer penchant for conflating history with historicism or historicity, as I discuss further in the next chapter, mythologizes a discipline that has not been in stasis. The same queer appropriations of terms and concepts that hold precise meanings in academic history, so helpful in advancing new perspectives on the "queer desire for history," strike some historians as misappropriations in failing to acknowledge the protocols of recognizable fields of historical practice, such as intellectual, social, or cultural history.[71] To a historian, the proposal of historiography as a "culturally privileged system of signification" registers as an attribute, and more often than not, when queer critics refers to "history" they really mean pastness, history as an idea, or the practice of history within lesbian and gay studies. To be sure, there are significant risks in working inside and outside the structure of disciplinarity, which makes it all the more urgent that practitioners flag in more specific ways their appropriations across disciplinary boundaries and avoid uncritical caricatures of the disciplinary "other."

Evidence for Historical Arguments

When I have presented work over the last few years, queer literary and cultural critics have listened respectfully and attentively, but later some have expressed skepticism about what they perceived as my reliance on truth claims. From their perspective, I use "facts" to prove that my interpretation of an event sets the record straight while others were wrong because their arguments were not founded on historical evidence. A good example is how I drew on new archival research to revise myths about the "lesbian" novelist Radclyffe Hall and the obscenity trial that resulted in the banning of *The Well of Loneliness* in 1928.[72] Whereas my careful examination of the daybooks Hall kept for several decades revealed her to be a fashion slave whose hair was elegantly styled at an expensive London department store, Hall's biographers use terms such as "barbered" to reinforce her iconic status as a butch.[73] Also, as I consulted the writer's travel itineraries, it became clear that Hall and her partner rarely left England before the trial and so could not have been, as is often claimed, prominent members of those glamorous sapphic salons in Paris during the early 1920s. According to my colleagues, relying on facts to support one's arguments constitutes an investment in truth claims, and — as anyone with even a passing familiarity of poststructuralist theory knows — since there is no such thing as an objective fact, my work is empiricist. This intractable problem about the nature of evidence cuts to the core of historical practice, with some historians arguing that without some reference to material evidence there can be *no* history, and others surrendering any and all claims to truth. Of course I cannot possibly do justice to this topic here any more than a queer critic might resolve the debates about whether sexuality is defined by acts or identities; however, it should be feasible to sketch briefly some of the discussions that have taken place in academic history concerning the toughest question of them all: "What is the place of empirical historical research in queer studies?"[74]

In the 1990s queer critics charged lesbian and gay social historians with "the most abominable crimes" and treated them with contempt or "condescension" because of their apparent belief in a "transparent 'reality' of 'experience,' and claim to relate, simply and objectively, what happened, when, and why."[75] The myth of historical practice as empiricist is so entrenched it haunts the writings of queer critics, but sustaining this fiction about history is not without cost.[76] The most sophisticated and articulate responses to the problem of objectivity and the status of truth claims by theoretically informed historians would not appear until the first decade of the twenty-first century, so Duggan, writing in 1995 about "the discipline problem," has little choice but to extol the virtues of "empirically grounded work," that is, historical research that is informed by the careful gathering of archival materials.[77] A "stunted archive," Duggan sternly cautions, impoverishes queer criticism.[78] The undertheorized empiricist methods that Duggan ascribes to an earlier mode of social history have not disappeared entirely, but since the cultural turn historians have had to defend their practice from poststructuralists who dismiss their discipline "as a relic of humanist thought."[79] Consequently, historical evidence is treated with far more caution. Since the mid-1990s, when scholars such as Duggan and the RHR editors first pointed to the power of the queer critique for historians, history has become more pliant, more receptive to work outside its boundaries, and more open to theoretical innovations. Fifteen years on, too, the barriers that cut off lesbian and gay social history from either mainstream history or the political agenda and intellectual concerns of LGBT studies have given way to a lively engagement with the new cultural history, cultural studies, and some forms of queer theory. Yet not all historians have embraced indeterminacy as "a general tenet of antifoundational historical methods informed by postmodern theories of the sign," as queer medievalist Carolyn Dinshaw suggests.[80] History is not (and never has been) a unified and coherent discipline. As in other disciplines, there are a few historians who see themselves as truth seekers reliant on objectivity and there are some radical postmodernists, with most positioned between these extremes. Of these, significant numbers just crack on with the time-consuming business of archival research, indifferent to these debates about theory. While one cannot deny that pockets of extreme positivists continue to dismiss theory as elitist jargon, hard-core empiricism is rare, and most historians accept objectivity as unattainable, believing the most anyone might hope for is "plausibility."[81] While Dinshaw presumes the dominance of postmodern history, Duggan sees "a liberal consensus/positivist camp . . . firmly in control of US history departments" that—like a bully—protects its own interests in preserving its authority by pushing to the margins the histories of gender and sexuality informed by feminist and queer theories.[82] We might be tempted to ask which version of academic history is correct, but the best answer is both. There are historians such as Joyce Appleby, Lynn Hunt, and Margaret Jacob—a group Scott dubs "apostles even at the end of the twentieth century of that 'noble dream'" of history's "special objectivity"—who continue to assert the impossibility of postmodern history because "without proof there is no historical writing of any worth," and there are historians who think otherwise.[83] Most egregious, for Scott, are the historians who use theory as a kind of intellectual window dressing, as empty "grand gestures" minus the rigorous, radical questioning that theory demands.[84]

Queer critics need to understand that historians work to a different imperative: "to reconstruct, interpret, and preserve artifacts from the past," a task that involves gathering the "so-called raw material of history (archives, other unpublished sources, and so on) in order to recover the meaning of a text or event."[85] Once gathered (a trawling process that already constitutes a critical intervention), this "raw material" (if the "stuff" collected by any self-reflective act of selection can be so described) becomes "evidence" when historians begin to ask questions and engage in a dialogue with the past. In this way historiography draws on evidence, but proof never speaks for itself.[86] Even the most postmodern of historians express confidence that "with just a little adjustment, the older values of objectivity, empiricism, and emergent causality can still serve to make historical studies worth doing and relevant to the solution of the problems of our modernity."[87] The most prominent historian to voice disagreement is Hayden White, who has spent a lifetime attempting to dissuade his colleagues. Despite his belief that no adjustments—large or small—will ever work, he is reconciled that "historical discourse always involves a truth claim of some kind."[88] The practice of critical history encourages historians to work out their own negotiated settlements with these problems of objectivity and empiricism, and most conclude that truth claims are necessary but should not be misconstrued as an "unproblematic assertion of truth"—historians cannot accept "that the texts with which they work have *no* reference to reality."[89] That the greater number of historians believe the demands of the poststructuralist challenge are not incompatible with their belief in the empirical as a precondition in framing historical arguments might strike queer critics as contradictory. The latter, however, would surely appreciate the willingness of the critical historian to embrace paradox and contradiction, since critical history itself is "neither theory nor practice" but "at once inherently 'theoretical' and irreducibly empirical."[90]

Returning to my reading of Radclyffe Hall's daybooks, I argue that access to certain "facts" allowed me to contextualize aspects of Hall's experiences in new ways and thereby produce an alternative perspective on her gender performance and on her influence on modern subcultural formations in interwar Britain. The daybooks were not my transparent window onto the lesbian past but instead became the raw material to execute an "interpretive intervention" to rethink previous historical arguments about sapphism in the 1920s.[91] Critical history exposes the fissures and controversies of a historical practice that is, in every respect, as "messy" and fractious as fields such as literary studies, to use the qualities Duggan admires about the "literary academy" but finds missing in academic history.[92] Elsewhere Duggan hints that only a literary critic is capable of discovering how "political history might speak to us, not as a disciplining or pedagogical legacy, but as a spiralling, haunting suggestion of resonances and possibilities."[93] But critical history — open-ended, undetermined, self-reflexive — is equally promising in exploring such possibilities. Some have argued that critical history cannot satisfy people's need to "touch, feel, and experience" an ancestral past, and perhaps they are right.[94] A queer critical history may never be as effectual in satisfying affective needs as lesbian and gay social history, but for queer critics who have never been more transfixed by history and temporalities, it may prove a site where debates about evidence and experience, practice and theory, remain (satisfyingly) unresolved and highly contested.[95]

Queer Historicities

There are now several excellent critical introductions to queer theory as well as edited collections showcasing the interdisciplinary field of queer studies, and I certainly have no wish to duplicate that work here.[96] Since the early 1990s the term queer has held contradictory meanings: a shorthand for lesbian and gay; an identity neither hetero nor homo; an anti-identity or repudiation of stable categories of identity. As a theoretical perspective, "queer" also functions as a verb meaning to trouble, subvert, make strange or perverse — its very invocation, queer scholars routinely explain, ruptures, overturns, blurs, and decenters. Queer is about refusal, resistance, indeterminacy, and transgression; paradoxically, it simultaneously thwarts and mobilizes coherent strategies to "bring the hetero/homo opposition to the point of collapse."[97] Queerness-as-method is a critical tool in actively disrupting the "inside/outside" structures of meaning and is a practice attuned to the intersecting, "overlapping and divergent distinctions" between other analytical categories such as gender, race, class, and nation.[98] David Halperin, in an important passage I return to in the final chapter, defines queer more broadly as "*whatever* is at odds with the normal" and therefore "a positionality vis-à-vis the normative."[99] Queer theory is not a cohesive school of thought, and some of its seminal thinkers might object to any attempt to define its core beliefs and positions, but an interest in how queerness-as-method relates specifically to the practice of critical history is a good starting point in addressing the crucial epistemological implications of the final, and perhaps most challenging, question raised by the *RHR* editors: "What is the relationship between studies of queer reading strategies and representations and those that seek to explore the meaning and texture of people's lives?"[100] One objective in examining these border crossings — specifically, the queer attentiveness to historicity, the queer construction of history, and critical history's engagement with (or disregard of) queer methods — is to make it more difficult for either field to mythologize or ignore the other. More positively, cross-fertilization and dialogic exchange across these practices reveal the potential for forging new practices equipped to exploit the productive tensions between fields often positioned as oppositional (such as lesbian and gay in relation to queer, or queer studies in relation to academic history).

Of all the major figures associated with queer theory, Eve Kosofsky Sedgwick, though not a historian of sexuality, was keenly aware of the historicity of sexuality and erotic desire, a fact that has gone largely unnoticed in queer studies and underappreciated in academic history. One example of the historicity of Sedgwick's theories of sexuality can be seen in her now famous critique of Foucault's Great Paradigm Shift — that imaginary moment in the late nineteenth century when the category of the modern homosexual was thought to displace the category of the sodomite. The formulation of axiom 5 in *Epistemology of the Closet* — "*the historical search for a Great Paradigm Shift may obscure the present conditions of sexual identity*" — reveals a deep consciousness of "the irreducible *historicity* of all things . . . discerning the time-and-place specificity of a thing, identifying the ways in which it relates to its context or milieu, and determining the extent to which it is both enabled and hamstrung by this relationship," to cite Hayden White's description of critical history.[101] If Foucauldian genealogy (or a "history of the present") "begins with an analysis of blind spots in our current understanding, or with a problematization of what passes for 'given' in contemporary thought," it is vital to "denaturalize the present, rather than the past."[102] Sedgwick's vantage point on a queer past is based on "homosexuality as we *conceive of it* today," a phrase as resonant now in sexuality studies as was Foucault's reference to the homosexual as a species.[103] So entrenched are the modern categories of identity that Sedgwick repeats the phrase over and over in her cogent analysis of our current conceptions of sexuality. Such insistent differentiation between an alien past and an equally—if not more—alien present, the distinction between "them" and "us," reverberates across the history of homosexuality. Consider, for instance, Matt Houlbrook's discussion of men who refrain from using "'gay' in the way we would use the term today," Jonathan Ned Katz's understanding of the presentness of our present standpoint as "what we today recognize as erotic feelings and acts," or Annamarie Jagose's historical overview of the rise of queer theory, that "there is significant agreement that homosexuality, as it is understood today, is not a transhistorical phenomenon."[104] Sedgwick's understanding of queer temporalities acknowledges Foucault's reminder that history is never simply about what happened in the past but is about "the events that have led us to constitute ourselves and to recognize ourselves as subjects of what we are doing, thinking, saying."[105]

Sedgwick's historical consciousness can also be glimpsed in her scrutiny of Foucault's "act of polemical bravado"—his suggestion that 1870 might serve as the birth date of the term modern homosexual—which informs her discursive analysis of the epistemological consequences of a "unidirectional narrative of supersession," the proposition that any emerging sexual type necessarily effaces earlier models.[106] In an elaborate and stunning account of problems that have arisen as a result of queer theory's colossal misreading of Foucault's phrase "the homosexual was now a species," Halperin clarifies how queer critics invariably "mistake [Foucault's] discursive analysis for a historical assertion."[107] Halperin credits Sedgwick with producing a critique capable of dislodging the category of homosexual, thereby shifting attention away from essentialist-constructivist debates that were going nowhere. In so doing, Sedgwick produces "an original analysis of homo/heterosexual discourse in terms of what she described as a perennial tension among and between four definitional axes, which she identified as minoritizing/universalizing modes of homosexual definition and as gender-transitive versus gender-intransitive or gender-separatist modes of homosexual definition."[108]

Denaturalizing the present allows Sedgwick an opportunity to reformulate historical thinking and ask the kinds of questions White links to the practice of critical history: "What is there about the present that requires revision or reform of the conventional historical 'apparatus'?"[109] But Halperin contends that Sedgwick no sooner initiates this powerful "conceptual move" than she abandons her interest in historical questions and subsequently fails to grasp how her critique falls into the same trap of displacement.[110] In other words, while she believes that residual elements of the sodomite remain in the creature we would come to recognize as the modern homosexual — an insight that animates a major shift in the practice of identity-based sexual history — she neglects to acknowledge how the essentialist/constructivist debates could not be made to disappear. In one of the earliest intellectual exchanges to address the interrelations between queer theory and queer historiography, Halperin praises Sedgwick's critique as "magisterial" but is troubled by what he sees as her reluctance to figure out the "historical reasons" for the "definitional incoherence at the core of the modern notion of homosexuality" — Sedgwick, he concludes, "deliberately set aside historical questions about the emergence of modern sexual categories and described those questions as effectively superseded by her own approach."[111] Halperin then positions his own argument as an "overdue and much-needed historical grounding" that he believes Sedgwick's analysis lacked.[112] His response in an essay equally magisterial is unquestionably significant, but his insistence on Sedgwick's apparent lack of historical grounding obscures how her axioms might also be read as an engaged mode of history as critique.

A helpful primer to Sedgwick's key ideas observes that the primum mobile of queer theory "worried that the urgency, reach, and power of some of her theoretical paradigms may have been limited by the fact that her evidence was drawn from literary texts."[113] Sedgwick also worried about the presentism of queer criticism and called on critics to forge new methods to "access . . . these rich and varied histories."[114] In different ways, critics Ann Cvetkovich, Heather Love, and Scott Herring, all deeply influenced by Sedgwick, have shown a readiness to rethink the politics of identity with a historical consciousness that counters the popular misconception of a queer cultural and literary criticism obsessed only with the present.[115] At the vanguard of queer studies (or what has been termed "late modern queer studies"),[116] Cvetkovich and Love share the political concerns of lesbian and gay social history, as seen in their idealizing of history's power to recover, rescue, or preserve traces of the marginalized, abject, hidden, and invisible. At the same time, their utopian faith in the transformative powers of a Foucauldian-inspired critical history of the present resonates with the imaginings of critical historians such as Joanna Bourke for a practice open to the "possibilities of resistance" and "emancipatory futures."[117] Herring, on the other hand, explores how some writers in early twentieth-century America produced "slumming literature" as a way of subverting "discourses of perversion to present an unknowable underworld removed from a sensationally real gay or lesbian historical body."[118] Believing that unknowability constitutes opting out of the logic of normal and deviant, Herring proclaims that his study marks the "undoing of lesbian and gay history"; his project "has nothing to show . . . about lesbians or gays or their subcultural fashioning. . . . [I]t has nothing to reveal . . . about the debut of homosexual . . . group identity in major urban environments during the late nineteenth and early twentieth centuries."[119] There is no denying that Herring is among the first to sound a wake-up call that deliberately spoils our ability in the present to identify (and identify with) sexual subjects of the past, and while this theoretical maneuver is indebted to historians such as Joan Scott, whose work hovers on the edges of Herring's arguments, his interest in the hermeneutics of the dark, sordid, and sleazy demimonde of slumming reveals a queer impulse to expose as sham what Scott calls the "evidence of experience."[120] Of course, the groundwork for undoing recuperative history begins with Foucault's *History of Sexuality*, but Scott's critique of how the terms of a "'hidden' world of homosexuality" reproduce rather than overturn the "ideological systems" that made repression possible is crucial in rethinking the problem of visibility and evidence in queer history (a topic I return to in chapter 2).[121] For Herring, identification with the past is an albatross around our collective necks, and the loss of a sexual subject and sexual group identities represents the foreclosure of the lesbian and gay history project.

Herring's argument is beautifully illustrated by an account of his experience in the archives of Yale University's Beinecke Rare Book and Manuscript Library when one writer's scrapbooks literally disintegrate in his hands. Whereas Herring reads his encounter with archival scraps as a metaphor for disrupting our ability to claim past sexual lives for lesbian and gay social histories, Cvetkovich invests the queer archive, as opposed to state-funded institutions, with "'magical'" powers in representing "lost histories" and argues that "traditional conceptions of history" can be challenged by collecting the ephemera of sexual intimacy and political movements.[122] For the critical historian it is "memory" rather than "history" that is engaged with the "affective and magical," but all historians might query what Cvetkovich means by "traditional conceptions of history" or "official histories."[123] This is because her own tools and methods seem closely akin to both social history (in emphasizing "material life, class, and society") and the new cultural history (in focusing "on meaning and on the forms of perception and understanding that people make and display").[124] Presumably, unlike the "institutionalized forms of cultural memory" that appear to erase lesbian and gay lives, queer archives serve the purposes of collective memory in becoming a repository of the materiality of their everyday lives by preserving the cultural memory of queer cultures through "oral history, personal photographs and letters, and ephemera."[125] At once political and personal, queer archives (and there are many) "understand the quest for history as a *psychic* need rather than a *science*," although, somewhat ironically, historical investigation of evidence, often located in the archive, is precisely what underpins academic history's claim to be scientific.[126] Leaving aside the fact that meticulous archival research is an empirical methodology in historical practice, it is difficult to see how any archive — whether the "experimental grassroots" work of "volunteer labors of love" or state-supported archives — can ever "represent far more than the literal value of the objects themselves."[127] For Cvetkovich the traces of intimacy in the materiality of the archive are a source of fascination, and the frisson is palpable — the queer archive endeavors to capture and preserve the material evidence of human emotion and sexual desire, "ephemeral, unorthodox, and frequently suppressed."[128] Of course material objects are only material objects, as Cvetkovich points out in her discussion of how the meaning of evidence is never "in any way 'transparent.'"[129]

One result of the cultural turn is that historians are well aware that archival materials hold no intrinsic "literal value": "The Archive is made from selected and consciously chosen documentation from the past and also from the mad fragmentations that no one intended to preserve and that just ended up there. . . . *nothing happens to this stuff, in the Archive.* . . . as stuff, it just sits there until it is read, and used, and narrativized."[130] The historian's task is to situate each archival document — whether a rare book, newspaper article, transcript of an interview, police report, government document, diary, private letter, personal testimony, memoir, home movie, photograph, or other material object — first, within the institutional context of the archive (asking how it landed in the archive in the first place and how it was cataloged and indexed) and, second, in a wider context (social, cultural, political, economic, national, and so on) to clarify how each is culturally mediated.[131] Philosopher and legal expert Morris Kaplan explains with considerable clarity how archival materials come with their own agendas:

> Legal proceedings, from police interrogations to courtroom testimony, impose their own language, categories, and constraints. Newspaper accounts deploy their own sense of what the public requires or can bear to hear. Editors need to sell papers as well as advance their own cultural and political agendas. Private letters capitalize on the shared educational backgrounds and social assumptions of the correspondents. None of these media is free from discursive shaping and constraint. Moreover, each medium bleeds into the others.[132]

Gathering and collecting materials can be fulfilling and meaningful for the activists who create the queer archive, but those materials do not constitute the "material instantiation of Derrida's deconstructed archive," because it is the historian who bestows cultural meaning on the stuff by telling a story about that evidence—as Scott explains, "the facts of history" never "speak for themselves."[133] The political work in creating an archive does not even map onto the same political work in using the archive as a resource to understand the queer past, and therefore the material evidence held in the archive cannot "challenge traditional conceptions of history" or represent a lost history until those materials are mediated and reproduced in alternative ways, such as a public exhibition.

In recognizing Jacques Derrida's lack of interest in the physical archive, Cvetkovich implicitly understands and shares historian Carolyn Steedman's reservations about the usefulness of Derrida's discussion of "archive fever."[134] Psychoanalytic approaches to memory as a way to theorize the physicality of the archive are unhelpful because the archive "is not very much like human memory, and is not at all like the unconscious mind."[135] While this queer "archive of feelings" becomes a tangible site in which to preserve the emotional and cultural textures of actual lives, we can never forget that it is the queer researcher who constructs rather than discovers the past: "What has actually been lost can never be found. This is not to say that *nothing* is found, but that thing is always something else, a creation of the search itself."[136] Steedman points out that the hunt "for what is lost and gone" transmogrifies in sifting through archival traces "so that every search becomes an *impossible* one."[137]

In terms remarkably similar to Steedman's, Heather Love offers "impossible love as a model for queer historiography," a proposition that might not be readily intelligible to historians who understand "historiography" either as a way to view historical practice in terms of analytical perspective or methodology (feminist or Marxist, social or cultural, for instance) or as a field of inquiry in a particular time and place.[138] These queer theoretical negotiations of archival space as a site of resistance or alternative historiographical practices may not seem immediately relevant to historical practice, but there are more significant and valuable insights about historical processes in these queer maneuvers than might first be supposed. The task is to see how queer theorizing of the relations between the present and the past maps onto terms and frameworks more readily grasped by historians.

A particular challenge in recent queer cultural criticism is to determine whether "queer" effectively unravels a lesbian and gay social history that so successfully served the movement's political needs and narrativized desires and longings for a past. Indeed, Cvetkovich's alignment of sexual minorities with "other suppressed and traumatic histories" (such as the Holocaust, civil rights activism, slavery, and genocide) would seem more closely connected to the practice of lesbian and gay social history than a queer history were it not for her impassioned argument for "sexual trauma" as a catalyst in energizing new political communities, signaling an awareness of the power of history making in shaping present concerns.[139] Similarly, Love's juxtaposition of the political struggle for, on the one hand, the institutional recognition of the history of sexuality as a proper subject and, on the other, the history of queer community indicates a desire to link the aims and objectives of an earlier phase of lesbian and gay social history with queer history. From the perspective of a critical history suspicious of links between the present and the past, the search for the "meaning and texture of people's lives" (that is to say, lesbian and gay social history) is intrinsically limiting in reinscribing and naturalizing the terms of difference: "The evidence of experience . . . becomes evidence for the fact of difference, rather than a way of exploring how difference is established, how it operates, how and in what ways it constitutes subjects who see and act in the world."[140] This difficulty suggests the arrival of "queer" as something of a mixed blessing, perhaps marking an end to future possibilities of a discredited recovery project; however, as seen in the next chapter, one mode of history making does not easily dislodge the next, and the historicizing of sexuality is a topic vast enough to accommodate multiple and perhaps contradictory approaches.

Queer critics *and* historians of queer lives (queerness-as-being) have both on occasion succumbed to the melancholy pleasures of nostalgia for "possibilities long lost" with the advent of gay liberation — an event that also seems to have closed down more open-ended sexual expressions and desires, the lingering effects of a "history of marginalization and abjection" no longer available.[141] Citing at length Duggan's assessment of the "discipline problem," Love positions the history of sexuality against those who would deny its validity on the grounds that it "is inevitably a projection of a current state of affairs," though a queer critical history practice reminds practitioners that we are permitted no other means to look backward outside the terms of the present.[142] Ascertaining the cultural meanings of sexuality in the past demands a clear understanding of the purpose of historicizing, whether to serve the political needs of community or to grasp the circuitries of sexual knowledge at any given moment. If Scott is correct in her observation that "emancipation is a teleological story in which desire ultimately overcomes social control and becomes visible," Love's call for a reconciliation of these different modalities of historical practices (lesbian and gay social history and histories of queer lives) merits close inspection.[143] Others such as Christopher Nealon have sometimes misconstrued Duggan's critique of social history as directed to the discipline of history generally.[144] Love also refers to an undifferentiated "practice of history" but nevertheless draws attention to certain inadequacies of the project of recovery that ignore "the dependence of the present on the past."[145] Her observation that "the effort to recapture the past is doomed from the start . . . contact with the dead is impossible . . . we will never the possess the dead," seems indebted to White's call for a critical history that considers "the possibility of the present *as* history."[146] In a compelling essay that advocates the advantages of a critical history over social histories of the marginalized, White explains that "critique means historicity" and thus entails an engagement "with history in terms adequate to the present age. . . . if by history we mean not simply 'the past' but the relation between the 'present' understood as a part of 'history' and the 'past.'"[147] Historians remain perplexed about how to speak of past sexual subjects without lapsing into the language of the present.

It is all very well to call, as Sedgwick did, for dismantling the enforced linkages between gender and sexual object choice, but in the absence of a new lexicon that allows us to speak about any number of possible sexualities, how can new epistemologies evolve? What queer teaches us is that no matter how many new words we invent, none will ever adequately capture the commonalities, contradictions, and confusions of sexual subjects; simply put, according to Sedgwick's first axiom, "people are different from each other."[148] The problem for the historian of sexuality is how to explore the sexual past, even the modern past, without falling back on those seductively simple labels. Sexuality's power — drives, feelings, acts, identities, desires — is poorly harnessed by those arbitrary neologisms first coined in the late nineteenth century. Moreover, the dominance of binary thought — hetero/homo, normative/deviant — has hardly receded, and in historical writing there is no straightforward way of managing Sedgwick's unwieldy notion of sexuality as an "open mesh of possibilities, gaps, overlaps, dissonances and resonances, lapses and excesses of meaning . . . [in which] the constituent elements of anyone's gender, of anyone's sexuality aren't made (or *can't be* made) to signify monolithically."[149]

The historian in Sedgwick understood the historicity of queer theory itself, and as early as 1998 she predicted its demise: "In the short-shelf-life American marketplace of images, maybe the queer moment, if it's here today, will for that very reason be gone tomorrow."[150] Even so, she strenuously advocated an ongoing sense of queerness and envisioned its persistent and enduring usefulness as a theoretical framework across the academy. She would surely have appreciated how a queer theory once chastised for "not customarily [taking] into account the complex historical situatedness and evolution of ideas about the body and sexuality before about 1850" has animated exciting new developments in queer history — a field that has only now (at the start of the second decade of the twenty-first century) begun to flourish, well behind literary and cultural critical practices restless to see if "queer studies has morphed into affect studies, temporality studies, geopolitics, and other things."[151] Sedgwick regarded "queer" as much more than a passing phase — on the contrary, queer might also be "a continuing moment, movement, motive — recurrent, eddying, *troublant*."[152] It seems that any worries about the limitations of her literary examples were only partly justified.

Queering the History of Sexuality

Foucault, Sedgwick, Halperin, and more recently some medieval and early modern literary scholars such as Carolyn Dinshaw, Carla Freccero, and Valerie Traub have radically changed how we theorize sexual history, but the route to understanding their influence on queer history and queer historicizing is anything but straightforward. As I have already suggested, this is partly due to academic history's complicated relationship with poststructuralist theory more generally, and historians based in academic history are no different from their colleagues in other fields where it remains possible to ignore theory. Joan Scott believes that while there will always be diehard resistance in the ranks of the professionals who turn away from critical history, the "less confrontational" are more exasperating because they only give lip service to theoretical concepts in superficial ways.[153] Such work uses the language of theory before retreating into "predictable" accounts that leave unexamined the identity categories themselves, whether sexuality, gender, race, class, age, or nation: "It is as if the requirements of the discipline cancel out the potentially disruptive effects of the theory, blinding the historian to the critical tasks theory enjoins."[154] New and innovative theoretical perspectives rarely emanate from a discipline that prizes above all else the "uniquely authoritative judgments" of the individual historian who has gained "unprecedented access" to unseen or rare archival materials and spent "years of industrious archival labor"—telling phrases that speak volumes about what the profession continues to value and admire.[155] The number of historians known primarily for theoretical work is very small, with Hayden White standing alone as a historian whose reputation "rests almost entirely on theoretical works"; others, such as Scott, Dominick LaCapra, William Reddy, or Dipesh Chakarabarty, established their credentials first through empirical work and often hold joint appointments in a second department, their divided loyalties somehow a license to engage with theory.[156] The contrast with queer studies could not be starker, where high theory is privileged above all else.[157] It would be misleading to conclude that history and theory occupy completely different spheres, but disciplinarity is a powerful structure that continues to exert control on practitioners, and aspects of White's 1978 critique still hold: no discipline "is more hedged about with taboos than professional historiography—so much so that the so-called 'historical method' consists of little more than the injunction to 'get the story straight' . . . and to avoid both conceptual overdetermination and imaginative excess."[158] Even a cursory review of recent historical work on nineteenth- and twentieth-century sexual cultures suggests that, as is typical in so-called history proper, queer theory lies buried "in the interior of the narrative, where it serves as a hidden or implicit shaping device."[159] Queer theory's impact on queer history cannot be charted by skimming footnotes or indexes.

Whereas literary and cultural critics situate their arguments dialogically within a specific theoretical framework, historians are more likely to draw on the seminal ideas of particular theorists to amplify the implications of a historical example, as illustrated by John Howard's reference to Foucault's "repressive hypothesis" ("the idea that sex in Western cultures has been marked by [a progressively eased] repression over time") to shed light on one interviewee's sexual experience.[160] Both Houlbrook and Regina Kunzel refer to Sedgwick's distinction between minoritizing and universalizing discourses not only to suggest the mutual dependence of the hetero/homo binary, but to demonstrate incisively the unease of institutional authorities in dealing with the dangerous threat of homosexuality.[161] Another example of the highly strategic use of theory can be seen in the edited collection *Gay Life and Culture: A World History*, which, its title notwithstanding, evinces the central tenets of a queer critique of identity categories ("no single term encompasses the variety of same-sex attitudes and behaviors . . . that have existed from antiquity to the present"),[162] as if this line of thinking were common knowledge. The obvious influence here is Sedgwick's notion of "*nonce* taxonomy, of the making and unmaking and *re*making and redissolution of hundreds of old and new categorical imaginings concerning all the kinds it may take to make up a world."[163] The scholarship in each of the fourteen essays in this superb overview of "gay life" across time and place exemplifies thorough and up-to-date scholarship, but queer theory per se escapes mention, except as a perspective adopted by the activist group Queer Nation.[164]

Queer theory's critique of how terms such as lesbian, gay, bisexual, trans, queer, and heterosexual are locked into prescribed structures of identity has proved essential for historians interested in excavating the queer and always alien world of the sexual past. Historians have grasped how queer itself can be a "useful rubric" in developing "richer and more accurate histories of deviancy and normalcy" that would "help denaturalize . . . present-day iterations."[165] For the most part, historians do not situate their arguments within specific theoretical frameworks to generate new readings of texts but instead use theory to orient historical thinking in support of arguments built on soundly gathered evidence. Theoretical discussion literally frames the larger project, as seen in Houlbrook's brief though incisive "note on terminology" (tucked discreetly between the acknowledgments and a list of abbreviations), deftly circumventing the conceptual impasse of the "acts versus identities" debates.[166] In the opening of *Nameless Offences* historian Harry Cocks locates in Sedgwick's theorizing of the closet a way to ground arguments about legal discourse in the social regulation of male homosexuality during the Victorian period, but then all mention of her work vanishes.[167]

Kaplan tags on a short conclusion that serves as a metacommentary to explicate his investment in the method of storytelling, deemed especially ideal in queer historiography in that it "offers no theoretical resolution."[168] Kunzel too packs her introduction with an engaging and richly nuanced account of the theoretical discussions that allow her to think of prison sexual cultures outside the hetero/homo binary. The careful arguments in these meticulously researched studies, and others like them, are immersed in queer thought from start to finish, as evidenced in the pervasive skepticism toward modern identity categories in examining sexual lives of the past, but theory has its place. Literary and cultural critics might judge relegating theory to the margins as unacceptably oblique, even evasive, but this strategy should be seen as discipline-specific. From the vantage point of queer studies it might seem imperative to incite history and theory to enter into "continuing dialogue," a prospect historian William Sewell regards as unrealistic, since "historians rarely speak back."[169] Queer thought seeps into queer historical work through an osmosis that is congruent with the disciplinary culture of academic history, as Scott and others observe.[170] Just as queer critics are frustrated that historians never seem to address explicitly the tough historiographical questions that the rigor of their own disciplinary training demands, some literary and cultural critics find it unnecessary to locate textual evidence in specific temporal contexts or to differentiate between fiction and other forms of documentary evidence in ways that frustrate historians.[171] Still, such disciplinary differences are unlikely to fade away. Part of the discipline problem is that the history of homosexuality seems not to be, in all respects, a project we hold in common. Yet I believe it is inadvisable to gloss over our disciplinary differences, because friction energizes our quest to understand the cultural meaning of sexualities of the past. A more viable pathway is to confront more directly how disciplinarity affects our habits of thinking about the history of sexuality by highlighting these differences rather than hiding or ignoring them.

An Uncommon Project

For over fifteen years, scholars have foregrounded the disciplinary differences of an interdisciplinary queer history project undertaken inside and outside academic history, inside and outside queer studies. The history of LGBT history has been about the tensions between lesbian and gay social history and a new queer cultural history, between professionals and amateurs, between proper and improper history, between empiricism and poststructuralism, between academic history and queer studies, and between queer historicity and queer history. Paradoxically, even to those alert to the political implications of praxis, the epistemological consequences of a field open to diverse methodologies have been less visible. Queer historians negotiate queer theory in discipline-specific ways, where some familiarity with its key arguments will suffice. Some queer critics conflate historicity and historicizing and spend too little time familiarizing themselves with the practices of academic history, but many more are scrupulously attentive to historical context. Whether such contextualizing of textuality is similar to the practice of history or different from it has been debated elsewhere, but such disciplinary distinctions need not trouble us unduly as long as we cultivate sufficient self-reflectivity to recognize the differences between queer historicities and queer historical work, set disciplinary expectations accordingly, and move on to capitalize on the advantages of interdisciplinarity in developing our agendas for future work in historicizing sexuality within LGBT history or academic history.[172]

The queer interest in historicity and temporality often seems distant from the concerns of academic history, an investigatory mode that queer critics sometimes need to be outmoded, monolithic, and empiricist rather than dynamic, mutable, and active in ongoing debates concerning theory and practice. Queer criticism has tended to enshrine the transgressive and oppositional. Some critics, as seen especially in the work on contemporary culture, take a perverse pride in cultivating an alternative "historical" practice that deliberately cites "improperly" and misleads with "false testimony"—a practice that "asks little questions, settles for less than grandiose answers, speculates without evidence, and finds insights in eccentric and unrepresentative archives."[173] Queer's brash sassiness is the antithesis of an "old discipline" that seeks to "make statements of a fairly high level of generality" by exercising "evaluation, reasoning, and judgment" and inculcates in its students the importance of honing their skills in undertaking scrupulous and exhaustive archival research.[174] At the same time, the social history of the early 1990s that Duggan and others once fretted might languish forever in a "political and intellectual backwater" has not been in stasis.[175] With the cultural turn, a more theoretically nuanced social and cultural history has been receptive to theories and methods produced elsewhere, including a "queer methodology" defined as "an approach beyond single disciplines and bounded theories that captures the elusive, contradictory movements of queer lives."[176] Yet insouciance toward the workings of disciplinarity—attending to the different ways scholars of different disciplines handle even the same textual evidence — in an interdisciplinary project such as the history of homosexuality constrains by lulling us into imagining discursive equivalences (history as opposed to "history") or methodological affinities that in reality do not exist. Historians such as Lynn Hunt insist they view the world differently than scholars in other disciplines — a point affirmed by new historicists Catherine Gallagher and Stephen Greenblatt, who similarly argue that a literary text and historical evidence "make sharply different claims upon the actual."[177] As we have seen, academic history is not an enclave of narrowly fixed views and methods — historians examine "very concrete and specific records" in order to advance "some form of generalization."[178] Too often simple binary oppositions — fact-finding versus theorizing or professional versus amateur — take the place of a critical interrogation of how historians of homosexuality, working in diverse disciplinary contexts as well as outside the academy, assume multiple ideological positions, operate within numerous conceptual frameworks, and approach questions of evidence or problems in textual readings from an array of angles.

If the field's disciplinary eclecticism is what is most interesting in generating, first, a historiography of academic history's encounter with queer theory and queer cultural criticism and, second, an account of the queer engagement with "history," then it is important to attend to the difference disciplinarity makes in our respective approaches to what has confusingly appeared to be a common project.

2 / Genealogy Inside and Out

Memory is blind to all but the group it binds. . . . History belongs to
everyone and no one.
PIERRE NORA (1989)

There is more than one strategy for entering into a queerer future.
DAVID HALPERIN (2002)

What complicates any account of lesbian, gay, and queer historiography is that the same term — genealogy — describes two different (though interrelated) modes of history writing, one that more closely approximates a family tree, as evinced by an interest in continuities, resemblances, and similarities, *and* another that more closely approximates Foucauldian genealogy, with an interest in rupture and in defamiliarizing and destabilizing categories of identity. Equally troubling, the latter practice frequently expresses antipathy toward the former and situates its methodologies as oppositional (often in disparaging terms), even though both are more co-implicated and interdependent than is generally acknowledged, sharing common interests, for instance, in the nature of same-sex sexuality or the nonheteronormative (whether defined by acts or identities or by what is similar to or different from us now).

To find a pathway through this genealogical labyrinth and highlight what is distinctive about genealogical work (whether undertaken by social and cultural historians or by literary and cultural critics) in comparison with other approaches in constructing historical meaning, I suggest, for clarity's sake, splitting lesbian, gay, and queer historiography into two strands: "ancestral genealogy" (otherwise known as recovery history), which looks for particular kinds of sexual beings in the past, and "queer genealogy," a practice that

58

breaks certain conceptual impasses in its project of "denormativizing" but, its incisive critique of identity notwithstanding, nevertheless remains tethered, albeit precariously, to the logic of lineage.[1] Like all progressivist history, ancestral and queer genealogies proceed with a knowingness about the sexual past and, by definition, search "backwards from the vantage point of the present in order to appraise things in the past and attribute meaning to them" before then tracing "forward" what has already been traced backward to "make a history."[2] To state succinctly the main difference between the two genealogical modes, I see "ancestral" as the history of us and "queer" as the history of "us"—the latter a practice interested both in "transhistorical continuities" and in "the disintegration of our own concepts as we *trace* them backward in time."[3] As David Halperin explains, in a characterization of what I term queer genealogy, "a genealogical analysis of homosexuality begins with our contemporary notion of homosexuality, incoherent though it may be, not only because such a notion inevitably frames all inquiry into same-sex sexual expression in the past but also because its very incoherence registers the *genetic traces* of its own historical evolution."[4] What energizes ancestral genealogy is its confidence in—and political commitment to—the possibility of finding family resemblances to (or dissimilarities from) a largely stable modern homosexual. This is an objective that queer genealogy, while acknowledging ancestral efforts as a necessary early stage in the historiography of homosexuality, ultimately dismisses as theoretically naive, untenable, and even mired in transhistorical "nostalgia."[5]

Sharply critical of ancestral beliefs and methods, some queer genealogists, with equal political zeal, point to new horizons in writing about the queer past. Believing its own project exemplifies Foucauldian genealogy, an ever-increasing body of new queer genealogical work revels in the "capacious analytical capacity of *queer* to deconstruct sexual identity, to illuminate the lack of coherence or fixity in erotic relations, and to champion the radical indeterminacy and transitivity of erotic desire and gender."[6] Yet the powerful queer evocation of history as touching the past or compelling belief in the recurrence of structures and meanings of erotic desire over time reinscribes, to a greater or lesser extent, the logics and circuitries of ancestral genealogy.[7] That the turn toward queer constitutes less a radical and irrevocable break with the ancestral than an offshoot of it might disappoint those wishing to capitalize on queer's power to unsettle and destabilize, but queer genealogists have provided engaging accounts of the sexual past in every way as useful as the ancestral. Neither endeavor is intrinsically flawed, since they reach different audiences and serve different political and intellectual purposes. Indeed, the very struggle of queer genealogy to be critically historical in the production of historical knowledge highlights an opportunity to forge new practices that extend the bold analytical capacities of queer to critical historians interested in working outside the framework of ancestral and queer genealogy to construct different accounts of the sexual past.

To signal some of the conceptual and methodological affinities between ancestral and queer genealogies, I will sometimes refer to the "genealogical project"—a designation that only inadequately represents the complexity of an immense field traversing numerous spatial and temporal contexts. Disentangling these current and ongoing strands of the genealogical project inevitably diminishes the complexity of individual work that fits uneasily into these broad taxonomies, but such risks are necessary in unpacking what currently stands as a vast and often vaguely differentiated project. My schema, and my rationale in placing work under one heading or the other, might strike some readers as arbitrary, self-serving, or imprecise, but to quibble or flatly disagree about whose work is placed where is to miss the more important point that historicizing practices are far messier than any broad characterization of these strands—the ancestral and queer—allows. The genealogical project, as this chapter details, provides usable pasts to diverse constituencies inside and outside the academy, but despite the willingness of some historians to take the queer critique seriously, and the willingness of some queer studies scholars to reflect on historical practice, distance remains.

The first step is to assess the epistemological consequences of those residual elements of the ancestral that pervade later queer work (indeed, seeing both modes as a kind of "conceptual knot held tight by equal but opposite tensions").[8] A salient unifying thread running through both practices is the impulse to relate the lesbian, gay, or queer present to the past—a shared purpose that differentiates ancestral and queer genealogies from, say, a critical history practice that is profoundly skeptical of identities and concepts as touchable, stable, or recurrent, since it regards the past as "*radically unknowable*."[9] Paradoxically, queer genealogy's interest in, and engagement with, the logic of disconnection connects it to the ancestral, because lesbian, gay, and queer historical practices invariably begin (explicitly or implicitly) with the modern category of the "homosexual." At the same time, queer genealogy works methodologically like a critical history practice in that it welcomes "the expansiveness of Foucault's theorizing of history as critique" and fully appreciates "the unlimited nature of its possibility." For the queer genealo-

gist, "prevailing concepts [are] fair game," as is "the idea of their transhistorical meaning."[10] A second step is to carefully examine how queer genealogy's
steadfast interest in sustaining a dialogical relationship between the present
and the past complicates its claims to be a critical history practice that does
not trace back, for its purpose is to interrogate "the very premises upon which
things we take to be foundational are based," such as the modern epistemological structure of sexuality itself.[11] In this latter effort I will occasionally
refer to "queer critical history," a practice I define as making use of queer
analysis to construct the historical meanings of sex and sexuality (in all its
manifold expressions in relation to embodiment and gender variance) not
by tracing back modern sexual·identities with a knowingness of what these
identities mean to us now but by acknowledging at the outset the unknowability and indeterminacy of the sexual past.

As I elaborate in part 2, I see queer critical history working outside the
logic of connections or disconnections that conditions the genealogical
project. Its use value is not to provide a usable past but to explain aspects
of the sexual past that resist explanation in the context of identity history.
I devise this practice, on the one hand, to allow queer practitioners to see
what queer genealogy and queer critical history have in common, but also
to signal their different purposes. On the other hand, I want to clarify to
academic historians certain strategic advantages in rethinking queerness-
as-method outside the identity framework to make available the powerful
methodologies of queer theory in historical investigation. Thus configured,
we can more easily grasp certain of the conceptual congruences between
queer studies and critical history in a bid to position sexuality as an essential concept in historical work. That said, my discussion of queer critical
history in this chapter will be fleeting; its primary value in this critique of
ancestral and queer genealogy is to demonstrate a historicizing practice not
tethered to the habits of tracing back what we think we already know about
the sexual past. This vantage point, I submit, carves out a conceptual space
for anatomizing what the genealogical project allows and disallows—a vital
transaction for a field that has only rarely been inclined toward methodological self-reflexivity.[12] There are, of course, any number of permutations we
might consider, as I conjecture in the epilogue, but one further advantage
in positing a famously dispassionate critical history practice—described as
"all head and no heart"—is that it is the very antithesis of a genealogical
project invested in accounting for "who we are, where we came from, and
to what we belong" or, alternatively, who we are not.[13] Let me state clearly

and emphatically my lack of interest in proposing the undoing of ancestral or queer genealogies, practices that will always better satisfy the yearnings for a lesbian, gay, or queer past than critical history practices narrowly conceived. My concern instead is to figure out the genealogical project's strengths and weaknesses, its potential and limitations, and its distinctive intervention in comparison with a queer critical history practice. Such a thoroughgoing examination will, I hope, demonstrate to the skeptics in academic history that sexuality is less a worthy niche or subfield than a crucial category of historical analysis.

The primary task, then, is to dissect the genealogical project across its several phases, a task made all the more challenging in that its various practices have never themselves been stable or inert but (like identity itself) are mutable and malleable. The point is not to suggest moving beyond a compromised genealogical project, but to envision how a critical history practice might operate at the intersection of queer studies and academic history. In short, there are any number of ways to navigate the sexual past and any number of ways sexuality might be useful in historicizing — possibilities imaginable precisely because of the success of the genealogical project. In this sense my interest in looking at genealogy inside and out signals not its inevitable demise but its strategic importance in giving rise to new mobilizations of the queer critique to discern how sexual relations and desires, and the conditions of sexual knowing and unknowing, are historically contingent.

This chapter scrutinizes the structure, logic, and political uses of this most useful form of historical investigation of sexuality (the genealogical project), first, to clarify — to queer scholars and academic historians — why, in its various permutations, the genealogical project has been ineffective in persuading academic history generally of sexuality's crucial importance as a category of historical analysis. By and large, as I have already discussed in the introduction, the vibrancy of the history of homosexuality is felt more in sexuality studies than in departments of history, though there are important exceptions.[14] Academic history's relative indifference toward the queer critique might seem — to queer scholars — a problem of concern only for historians, but queer studies is poorer for its estrangement from academic history. The time is long overdue to confront both the queer tendency to conflate "history" and the past, which blurs the lines between history as a disciplinary practice and the past as everything that came before the present, and — equally problematic — the queer metonymic reading of the genealogical project as the practice of academic history.[15] A second aim of the chapter is to articulate how the genealogical project differs from what some professional historians continue to regard tacitly as "proper history," that is, a historical practice uninterested in finding the origins of identity or gauging how what is familiar to us now differs. I want to suggest—again, to both queer scholars and academic historians—how the queer critique of sexuality (removed from the logic of lineage and its attendant concerns with similarity and difference, continuity and discontinuity) holds the power to complicate the queer engagement with temporality and transform at least the history of sexuality, if not also the wider discipline of history. In other words, I argue that it is crucial to grapple with the epistemological consequences of, on the one hand, the queer dismissal of academic history as an empiricist and positivist enterprise and, on the other, academic history's relative lack of interest in the value of queer theorizing outside genealogy.

Queer genealogy has not displaced ancestral genealogy; instead, once set in motion, each new trajectory crisscrosses, intermingles with, and diverges from earlier practices, making it harder to see their epistemological incompatibilities and contradictions as well as their congruences and affinities. This means that dissecting the genealogical project cannot be a story of how one mode has moved beyond another or circled back to what came before.[16] Moreover, judging one or the other as right or wrong is less helpful than delineating their respective strengths and limitations, because each practice is responsive to the needs of specific groups and individuals within the academy and beyond. Inasmuch as the historiography of sexuality absorbs rather than overturns or rejects each new development, the historiographer's task is to survey a range of intellectual work that practitioners in sexuality studies and academic history assess differently in accordance with disciplinary cultures and protocols. A significant theoretical intervention regarded as groundbreaking in queer studies, for instance, might not manifest the quality of accessibility admired in academic history. The genealogical project produces work that entices or alienates diverse communities of readers, so it is crucial to examine the uses of history in sexuality studies vis-à-vis the usefulness of sexuality as an analytical concept in the study of history.[17] As I discuss below, in the 1980s gender, ethnicity, race, and sexuality—"powered by the politics of commitment and the ethics of conviction"[18]—all made competing demands on the historian. In recent historiography (that is, historical writing interested in how historical knowledge is produced) genealogical histories of homosexuality are valued for adding new perspectives, challenging old orthodoxies, and problematizing and disturbing naturalized understandings of sexual subjectivities; but in the end historians often deem them to be peripheral or to smack of advocacy, even those historians who regard other analytical categories as critical and durable. This perplexing state of affairs, in part related to problems in defining sexuality, indicates that there is something peculiar about how sexuality has been historicized, something as yet unexplained or unaccounted for. Of course, cultural understandings of sexuality shift gradually, so we cannot overlook that "something very significant happened when sexual object choice became in the course of the twentieth century, at least in some social worlds, an overriding marker of sexual difference. That is an event whose impact and whose scope we are only now learning how to measure."[19] That significant event in the history of modern homosexuality has given rise to an investigatory purpose that differs from that of other fields such as women's history or subaltern studies, whose chronologies have no putative birth moment (however dubiously established).[20] Academic history has a history of sidelining topics it views as "threatening" by casting them as "less intellectually demanding, as overly modish, as not 'proper' history," according to historian Ludmilla Jordanova, who in her overview of "history in practice" mentions "gay" or "queer" only as "oppositional vocabularies."[21] Clearly, another lesson to be learned is that, when it comes to identity politics, not all identities are equal, in the materiality of experience or in structures of oppression.[22]

Assessing genealogical histories of homosexuality (by scholars based in departments of history or scholars and writers based elsewhere) in relation to academic history's dealings with other modes of progressivist history (gender and race, for example) indicates that the status of sexuality is different and, as a category associated more with issues pertaining to identity than power, its usefulness in historical analysis has been only partially realized. What seems to be a constant in the history of homosexuality — from recovery history to the present crisis of recovery history's alleged undoing — is a dominant historiography that perceives a steadfast relation to an identity-based practice with political roots.[23] This stance appears to acknowledge, intuitively at least, a strange affinity between academic history and the queer critique in that both regard a politicized ancestral genealogy warily, though in the case of the latter the feelings are more mixed. Whether (or how) the queer critique might undo the genealogical project is not unrelated to the question whether (or how) there is a future in academic history for a politically inspired queer engagement with sexuality. Any queer scholar genuinely interested in dismantling the genealogical project as a means to escape the logic of lineage will understand and appreciate that, alongside solutions and strategies proposed by queer historicists (that is, literary scholars such as Elizabeth Freeman, Valerie Rohy, or Valerie Traub, among others), it is equally urgent to cultivate any number of historical methodologies.[24] This point, as I argue later in this chapter, is more readily understood in light of history's evolution as a disciplinary practice after the cultural turn. This evolution, as a result of the poststructuralist critique of language, has led to other ways of understanding the "nature of historical reality," the status of evidence and truth claims in historical argument, and the usefulness of interpretive strategies and analytical perspectives from other disciplines, especially literary and cultural studies.[25]

As a sensible way forward, I propose to consider, in relation to the cultural turn, how the genealogical impulse in ancestral and queer work cannot escape an interrogation of the ways — as an approach to writing history — it frames, predetermines, and overdetermines the questions we have been able to pose about the sexual past, bringing some sexual acts, desires, identities, or relations more clearly into focus even as it obscures or excludes others. It is not surprising that the genealogical project imposes epistemological constraints on historical inquiry, for it is a central paradox of all history that it is always engaged in "creating the objects it claims only to discover."[26] In different ways, ancestral and queer genealogies — whether produced by an interested amateur or well-trained professional, a social or cultural historian, a literary or cultural critic, an old-fashioned empiricist or postqueer theorist — are complicit in creating the objects they think they have only discovered. But this does not mean history is a matter of pure invention (though some critical historians believe history is only another kind of fiction). It means instead that historians are the ones who decide what constitutes their "legitimate and coherent objects of knowledge."[27] No degree of critical self-reflexivity mitigates the fact that queer genealogy is "divided against itself" in its links to the logic of lineage *as well as* the "Foucauldian project of producing a history of sexuality" that historicizes "the production of a particular set of discursive apparatuses around sex as the truth of the subject."[28] Historians would be correct, then, in suspecting that queer genealogy has lingering investments in identity politics, but understanding how and why this is so requires a closer examination of the ideological shifts that have taken place across the different genealogical phases in the history of homosexuality — from its inception in the 1970s as a subfield with the express aim of affirming lesbian and gay existence by telling a story about the excluded or hidden, to its social constructivist discovery of the historicity of categories, to its ambitions to create a Foucauldian project interested in speculating on our present desire to understand the sexual past.[29]

Ancestral Genealogy: The History of Us

For over three decades lesbian history — grounded in the "cultural politics of recognition"[30] — has sought correspondences between the present and the past. Unquestionably, its urtext is Lillian Faderman's pioneering 1981 study *Surpassing the Love of Men: Romantic Friendship and Love between Women from the Renaissance to the Present*, informed by lesbian-feminist politics of the 1970s and invested in an understanding of sexual categories that are neither natural nor essential but — as structures of power — culturally mediated.[31] The book's wide-ranging temporal span was, the author admits, something of an accident; she had initially embarked on a more modest study of Emily Dickinson's work and of her intimate relationship with Sue Gilbert. Drawing on her skills as a trained literary critic, Faderman delved into the relevant primary and secondary source materials and, by reading against the grain, believed she had found objective and "irrefutable evidence" of romantic love and emotional attachments between middle- and upper-class women previously undetected or deliberately ignored by earlier biographers.[32] Faderman's interest in women writers who loved others of their sex led from one similar discovery to another until she realized "that it was virtually impossible to study the correspondence of any nineteenth-century woman, not only of America but also of England, France, and Germany, and not *uncover* a passionate commitment to another woman at some time in her life." In 1991 Faderman's *Odd Girls and Twilight Lovers: A History of Lesbian Life in Twentieth Century America* extended her evidentiary base to include oral testimonies, medical and sexological literature, popular journalism, and even song lyrics, hence consolidating her reputation for producing empowering narratives of same-sex relations between women that would inspire others to explore the lives of women who experienced romantic friendships, same-sex desires, passions, acts, and identities as well as women who experimented with or transgressed the boundaries of gender.[33]

A standing ovation of several minutes' duration at the 2006 Lesbian Lives Conference in Dublin suggests the power and pleasure of a shared past and is a testament to Faderman's achievement in giving impetus and direction to modern identity formations, communities, and cultures in the final decades of the twentieth century and into the early twenty-first, though elsewhere

in the academy such work — especially in its earliest phase — has been undervalued, accused by later feminists of essentialism, and relegated to the
margins, regardless of the pleas for its enduring significance. Like an earlier
phase of social history and other histories of marginalization, ancestral genealogy has not fared well in assessments generated either by historians whose
practices were subsequently transformed by the cultural turn or by queer
critics who regarded its ideological framework as outmoded. Reconsidering
ancestral genealogy's objectives and methodologies — as an analytical framework predicated on connections and recognition and thus less interested in
what does not appear to fit or connect us to the past — not only illuminates
its ideological investments in a lesbian-feminist political project of discovery,
but also accounts for its durability outside the academy and its strategic links
to a queer genealogy with shared interests in tracing back from modern formulations.

Underpinning the earliest phase of an ancestral practice noted for its
spatiotemporal "universalizing" of identity was the conviction that lesbians
(and women generally) were subject to the control of the patriarchy and to
a heterosexist ideal so intolerant of difference that it excluded all forms of
nonconformity.[34] The stirring tone of its singular purpose — "simply . . . give
us back our history" — reveals, on the one hand, a confidence in the political
efficacy of tracing the bloodline of modern lesbians and, on the other hand,
its sense of urgency in exposing the impact of homophobia on lived experience in relation to other regimes of power, such as gender, race, ethnicity,
generation, and class.[35] Outing the "fact" of lesbianism (which, as Judith Halberstam and many others note, tended to project a modern lesbian identity
onto historical eras that preceded the Great Paradigm Shift) was thought
crucial in breaking the silence and proclaiming the solidarity of a sapphic
sisterhood across time and place.[36] The discourses of sexology and early psychoanalysis were held particularly accountable for ostensibly pathologizing
lesbianism.[37] The right to a history of origins was enunciated in collective
projects such as the Lesbian History Group's *Not a Passing Phase* (1989), its
very title fixing lesbian identity as permanent.[38] Consciousness raising, the
group endeavored to demonstrate, was vital, first, to the campaign for social
recognition and civil rights and, second, to the education of practitioners
keen to cut through the subterfuge that deliberately obscured lesbian lives,
the "bowdlerization" and "avoidance of the obvious," whether by the sexual
subjects themselves or by any number of oppressors, such as sexologists (always a unified, coherent, and spurious form of knowledge) or biographer-

apologists.[39] Faderman, for instance, actively confronted biographers who thought that silence or denial would protect their subjects from the taint of lesbian perversion or who could not imagine that their subjects' strongest erotic attachments might be to other women, contrary to a wealth of information (letters, diaries, and literary texts) that seemed to suggest otherwise.

Reclaiming a history for lesbians was also regarded as essential to women's history, an argument advanced most persuasively by historian and literary critic Martha Vicinus, who called for a "more open definition of women's sexual subjectivity and of same-sex desire."[40] Highlighting the limitations of a history practice that privileged visibility and depended on women inclined toward sexual self-reflexivity, Vicinus advocated more sophisticated reading strategies attuned to "the possibilities of the 'not said' and the 'not seen' . . . fragmentary evidence, gossip and suspicion"—and a string of historical surveys of modern lesbian lives have largely heeded this sound methodological advice.[41] With their long-standing reliance on imaginative literature as a source of historical knowledge to compensate for the scarcity of hard empirical evidence, these historians of lesbianism have been pioneers in their openness to a wide array of source materials, ranging from published and unpublished literature to authors' letters, diaries, and other personal writings.

Thanks to the efforts of historically conscious literary scholars such as Terry Castle, who has been a lively advocate of the provocative salience of a sapphic figure that appears, disappears, and reappears in the Western imagination, ancestral genealogy's enthusiastic receptivity to literary expression has nurtured lesbian subcultural communities.[42] In her hugely ambitious edited collection *The Literature of Lesbianism: A Historical Anthology from Ariosto to Stonewall* (2003), Castle represents her approach to the "historical genealogy of lesbian writing" as a contribution to the history of ideas and forcefully counters the myth of lesbian invisibility by asserting an "abundance rather than scarcity" of "writing about love between women."[43] Tracing the "serious and abiding human significance" of the lesbian topos from the sixteenth century to the twentieth, Castle eloquently attempts to convince readers that whether lesbians have always existed is "neither here nor there," for what matters is that imaginative literature in all its varied forms has been fully "involved in this historic expansion of awareness" that "women might intimately conjoin for their own sexual pleasure or the sexual pleasure of others."[44] Castle's angle on the problem of "conceptual origins" challenges a familiar discourse of repair and neglect that pervades ancestral genealogy, but her call for a move away from "lesbianism-as-lived-experience" toward "lesbianism-as-theme" is suggestive of how a recuperative project might serve other purposes and might not be intrinsically limited to correcting exclusion.[45] The literary excursions of Faderman, Castle, and others may seem disparate from the material evidence of lesbian and gay social history, with its focus on the lives of individuals not part of the artistic educated elite, particularly in the realms of medicine, education, and law, and its references to other power relations (gender, class, nation, race, and ethnicity). But what binds these strands under the rubric of ancestral genealogy is a shared interest in a type of sexual practice or sexual being that can be located in the past as "a collective act of historical memory, a means of opening lines of transmission of desire and culture," and above all that can allow contemporary women who identify as lesbian to seize "a meaningful space in the present" in the formation of modern lesbian communities.[46]

presentism

The first important social history of the modern lesbian and gay experience in a British context was published a few years before Faderman's first book. Organized as a narrative of "from sin to crime" to the gay liberation movement, Jeffrey Weeks's pathbreaking *Coming Out: Homosexual Politics in Britain from the Nineteenth Century to the Present* pays particular attention to medical and legal discourse in the formation of politically aware communities and cultures, and an updated reissue extends the narrative to the 1980s and 1990s.[47] Early lesbian and gay social history (a far livelier and more productive enterprise in the North American academy) sought to "foreground the disparaged and overlooked," and later practitioners engaged with "questions of ideology, consciousness, and subjectivity."[48] While some practitioners contributed to a project that allowed sexual minorities access to the past by "inventing identities, creating new subjectivities, and imagining communities," others, such as Weeks, stressed "social identities" as "historically shaped."[49] This kind of work has been credited with providing "meaning for sexual minorities today" and encouraging historians "to avoid heteronormativity."[50] Yet these twin objectives, though laudable, have ultimately proved to be at cross-purposes in that those very identity-based narratives crafted for minority communities are often marginalized in contemporary historiography, even in accounts of historical work on gender or women.[51] Some historians, including those sympathetic to the political agendas and polemics of histories of marginalization, admit to feeling queasy about histories organized around identity, notwithstanding their acceptance of a view that all history making is about "finding an identity through the processes of historical identification, [in which] the past is searched for something . . .

that confirms the searcher in his or her sense of self."[52] Unease toward sexuality as an identity category is difficult to locate because resistance is erratic and arbitrary, but it is an unease shared by queer genealogists familiar with the postmodern critique of identity.

Writing in 1989, the Lesbian History Group already understood that "postmodernist ideas" posed a serious threat to its political project, and members fretted that the uniqueness of the lesbian experience would be "reduced" to just another oppressed identity on a "checklist of 'differences.'"[53] The encroachment of postmodern theories, particularly Foucault's call for a critical history of the present, destabilized a lesbian and gay social history forced to confront the theoretical consequences. *The Lesbian History Sourcebook* (2001) is a good example of a scholarly project on the cusp of this disciplinary change from lesbian social history (in searching for past examples of lesbianism and lesbians) to a lesbian cultural history (in acknowledging that "we cannot escape from our own time").[54] The latter is an incipient form of queer genealogy as marked by its scrupulous attention to the unsettling implications of critical history's emphasis on historicizing why we (in the present) want to believe that there are lesbians to be discovered in the past. This volume gathers materials such as literary sources, court records, popular journalism, and advice books to aid researchers "looking for" lesbians of the past, though it repeatedly reminds its readers of the importance of avoiding anachronistic projections of modern categories onto that past. Yet the theoretical challenges of the queer critique and critical history cannot so easily be grafted onto a project that remains invested in the politics of recovery and in fixed and stable categories. In a powerful critique of ancestor hunting, Traub explains that when scholars of lesbianism seek to "discover/recover/reclaim *lesbians* in the past" and "desire to invest those women with identities *like our own*," it is not only "to bridge an epistemological gap in historical knowledge and refute the pretensions of heterosexist history" (the purposes historians most often identify), but also "to fill an existential gap in our own self-knowledge as *lesbians*."[55]

Ancestral genealogy's resilience, and its power to make same-sex love and desire thinkable, writable, and speakable and to celebrate what it perceives as a lost past, has not diminished. On the contrary, no matter how damaging or patronizing the queer critique waged on multiple fronts, the market for popular accounts of lesbian, gay, and queer ancestors endures and flourishes, as is evident both in academic crossover books and in popular histories.[56]

This is in part because ancestral narratives satisfy a hunger for a past that "is not being well fed by professional historians" or queer genealogists—a predicament just as worthy of investigation as the critique that dismisses recovery history as fatally flawed.[57] Arguably, a critical genealogical approach to lesbian history, if such a project were possible, would need to begin by recognizing ancestral genealogy's purpose as foundational and enabling.

Ancestral genealogy is an eclectic body of work, often rich in empirical discoveries and crafted by researchers who provide their readers with political narratives of affirmation.[58] It represents, too, an important archival source for future historical work on consciousness-raising activities such as lesbian and gay history month, observed in countries such as the United States and Britain, or in Pride events that sponsor lectures or exhibits to celebrate ancestral history—cultural work ill served by critical history. As historian Pierre Nora suggests, "Memory and history, far from being synonymous, appear now to be in fundamental opposition."[59] In terms remarkably similar to those of Joan Scott, historian Dipesh Chakrabarty discerns in the discourse of suffering and exclusion another way to understand history as a project of recovery, though his pathway is informed by philosopher Charles Taylor, who contends that a dominant group's "misrecognition" of a marginal group "shows not just a lack of due respect."[60] Misrecognition "can inflict a grievous wound, saddling its victims with a crippling self-hatred" that, in the case of the history of homosexuality, might be evinced by internalized homophobia.[61] Espousing a "politics of recognition" (as opposed to political theorist Wendy Brown's "politics of resentment") Chakrabarty argues:

> *Historical wounds are not the same as historical truths but the latter constitute a condition of possibility for the former.* Historical truths are broad, synthetic generalizations based on researched collections of individual historical facts. They could be wrong but they are always amenable to verification by methods of historical research. Historical wounds, on the other hand, are a mix of history and memory and hence their truth is not verifiable by historians. Historical wounds cannot come into being, however, without the prior existence of historical truths.[62]

This highly significant passage is tremendously evocative for a lesbian history often depicted as the most hidden of the hidden histories of abject people—so (apparently) invisible that historical fiction plays an important part in stories about lesbian lives.[63]

Ancestral Genealogy and Queer Rapprochement

New life has been breathed into ancestral genealogy by queer literary critic Heather Love, whose 2007 *Feeling Backward: Loss and the Politics of Queer History* honors the achievements of ancestral work. In a persuasive effort to elucidate the connections between ancestral and queer, Love offers a rigorous and intellectually generous assessment of the "affirmative bias" of the ancestral's progress narrative, and in doing so recuperates the unsavory or abject dimensions of the homosexual past in the writings of Willa Cather, Radclyffe Hall, and Sylvia Townsend Warner, which emphasized despair, regret, self-hatred, shame, and defeatism.[64] The affective registers of this eclectic and wide-ranging study are palpable, but what I find most interesting about this queer historicist project is its references not to historiography produced *after* the cultural turn, but to the "great work of historical recovery" by the preeminent social historian E. P. Thompson.[65] Here is a good example of how the recent queer "turn to affect" as opposed to reparation (a word that in German [*Wiedergutmachung*] literally means "making things good again") sustains the political momentum of the ancestral impulses of lesbian and gay social history.[66] Love's view that the history of LGBT and queer studies constitutes a "history of the community" is not far afield from the assertive demands of the Lesbian History Group.[67] Positioning her project as a fuller genealogical picture notably resistant to glossing over the negative, in *Feeling Backward* Love attempts rapprochement rather than subversion, producing what might be characterized as late ancestral genealogy, since its urge to "spoil" affirmative ancestral genealogy by turning to trauma, shame, wounds, suffering, or any other feelings of "backwardness" both complicates and reproduces genealogical linearity.[68] In searching the darker corners of the collective closet, late ancestral genealogy might strike other queer genealogists as caught up in the entanglements of analytical structures that pivot around a hermeneutics of decipherability and recognition, thus disallowing what cannot, in the present, be known. Such reparative work — a kind of scholarly trailblazing — is undoubtedly vital and revitalizing, but it is a different project than critical history, emblematic of "not so much history but the 'history effect'" in its privileging of the imagination.[69]

Like subaltern studies, ancestral genealogy has needed to "posit a past reality" of what has been "covered over, hidden or repressed" before undertaking the project of "consciousness-raising in the present."[70] This judgment does not diminish its power — rather, it clarifies how its affective investments ("elements of empathy, sincerity, intuition, generosity of spirit, and a sense of the possible") are fully congruent with the political exigencies of a usable past.[71] In a passionate defense of what he terms the history of "experience," Chakrabarty vigorously asserts his belief that what has been missing in ongoing discussions of the postmodern critique of identity is that it should never have been universalized and needs to be seen as specifically related to concerns about "globalization and late capitalism."[72] Even so, historians such as White regard ancestral genealogy's value more as an "effect" than as critical historicizing.[73] In these exchanges, two points become clear: first, regardless of how debilitating the implications of a critique of identity politics that analyzes the internal logic of identity history, ancestral genealogy—which has contributed in profound ways to securing and consolidating the resilience of the identity of the modern homosexual—will undoubtedly remain central in modern homosexual cultures for the foreseeable future and, indeed, in dominant cultures receptive to its narratives of pain, survival, progress, and affirmation. Second, and here is where things get more problematic, in meeting the needs of emancipatory politics, ancestral genealogy will always be most interested in tracing the ancestries of likeness and resemblance, though willing also to note the mismatches or deviations. I suggest that no matter what one's position in these extensive debates that have preoccupied practitioners (whether similarity should be privileged over difference or vice versa), lineage is lineage: what matters is the possibility of connection with, or disconnection from, that modern construction. In this respect, ancestral genealogy—as lesbian and gay social history or as a literary-historical project practiced by Faderman in the early 1980s, the writer Emma Donoghue in the early 1990s, or Castle in the early 2000s—is similar to other forms of identity history that operationalize a "recuperative" function to allow their stories to become "invisibility's indemnification."[74] At the same time, ancestral genealogy differs from other identity histories in its abiding fixation with a precise chronological reference point that configures the modern conditions of relationality as a narrative of before and after. How or when that reference point is established (whether seen as nailed down with precision to 1870 or as unfolding gradually over time)[75] is less important than the recognition that it is a condition of the genealogical project to trace back.

The reception of identity history by professional historians, though sometimes positive, has often been one of indifference or hostility, as Chakrabarty details in his insightful account of the discipline's "clash" with the "cultural politics of recognition" during the 1980s and 1990s.[76] On one front, many "important historians" regarded such overtly political history making as a threat to the "idea of historical objectivity," since "the presentism built into the rhetoric of 'experience' destroyed objectivity."[77] A second line of attack emanated from historians influenced by the theoretical developments of poststructuralism, postmodernism, and deconstruction, specifically the arguments advanced by Brown and others who charge that identity politics collapses "the past and the present" and is therefore capable of producing "only an irresponsible, if not inflammatory, mix of history and memory."[78] Paradoxically, the discourse of trauma and historical wounding that is so incisive in explicating the psychic investment for a "meaningful space in the present" is also responsible for exposing its political ineffectualness. In a trenchant critique of identity politics, Brown explains the predicament:

> In its emergence as a protest against marginalization or subordination, politicized identity thus becomes attached to its own exclusion. . . . [I]t installs its pain over its unredeemed history in the very foundation of its political claim, in its demand for recognition as identity. . . . Politicized identity . . . enunciates itself, makes claims for itself, only by entrenching, restating, dramatizing, and inscribing its pain in politics; it can hold out no future — for itself or others — that triumphs over this pain. The loss of historical direction, and with it the loss of futurity characteristic of the late modern age, is thus homologically refigured in the structure of desire of the dominant political expression of the age: identity politics.[79]

The explanatory logic of this stunning analysis has been taken up by others for different, though interrelated, purposes. Traub, for instance, dissects the circuitry of a process she describes "as an identificatory relay" in which the "contemporary [*lesbian*] transit[s] certain psychic projects through [early modern *lesbian*] textual traces."[80] Scott, on the other hand, invokes Brown's work not to account for ancestral genealogy's psychic and emotional appeal for researchers and their communities of readers, but to express her profound skepticism about what such reclamation actually achieves for marginalized groups. The political ambitions of the Lesbian History Group, from Scott's perspective, are untenable, null, and void. However earnest and diligent the members' efforts in validating lesbian history as "a step towards our future," theirs seems to be a project doomed before it starts.[81] Put bluntly, ancestral genealogy is a project that has "no future" in historical practice, since it "consolidates the present in terms of the past" and therefore "offers redemption only to the extent that it fixes identity" — which obviously isn't really redemptive at all.[82] Scott and other critical historians have argued tirelessly that critical history is an essential maneuver for academic historical practice in general.

Powerful queer critiques of lesbian historiography also reveal how the "genealogy" of ancestral genealogy has operated in structuring the sexual past to domesticate the category of sexuality and categories of sexual beings, as seen in theorist Annamarie Jagose's unraveling of a vexing conceptual conundrum at the heart of a lesbian historiography "not so much doubled as divided against itself."[83] Reading her analysis of the "current and ongoing genealogy of lesbianism" in relation to academic history practices before and after the cultural turn brings into sharper focus Jagose's discovery that ancestral genealogy's enduring interest in lineage and its embrace of visibility provide no solution at all to the problem of invisibility, "because lesbian invisibility is precisely, if paradoxically, a strategy of representation — even a strategy of visualization — lesbian visibility cannot be imagined as its redress."[84] Thus it must be properly seen as a project "divided against itself." What is remarkable about the analysis of this cultural critic working outside a sustained dialogue with academic history, who therefore does not frame her intellectual project in the context of a historical practice negotiating profound epistemological shifts over time, is her recognition of the unhappy and unsettling epistemological consequences of any form of identity history that attempts to come to terms with the theoretical challenges of Foucauldian genealogy. Jagose argues that history's "apparent promise of recuperation" is overdetermined in that the "historicizing gesture" itself becomes the solution to the problem of lesbian invisibility.[85]

To explain how the problem of visibility/invisibility emerged as a central interest in lesbian history, Jagose briefly traces the influence of Faderman (whose model of romantic friendship obscured sexual relations between women) and Foucault (whose attention to relations between men also rendered women invisible). Illustrating how visibility in lesbian scholarship "cannot be in itself a representational goal," Jagose offers detailed readings of texts drawn from the literary canon (Dickens, James, Woolf, du Maurier) alongside a chapter on lesbian pulp and photographs of the 1950s, to unpack the "logic of sexual sequence" that "disavows the secondary and derived nature of all sexualities, the foundational grammars of which are deferral and displacement."[86] In replacing a concept so "central to the politicized concerns of lesbian representation" with "sequence," it becomes possible to reformulate what has become a "deadlocked and perhaps irresolvable debate in lesbian studies."[87] This line of argument exposes how visibility inevitably "draws on the same logics that it contests," and I would not wish to suggest that Jagose's ambitions are modest in that she hopes to thereby reveal "the derived nature of all sexual subjectivities, the various ways in which sexuality—both in its taxonomic reification and its psychosocial individualization—is culturally produced as a sequential fiction."[88] However, her critique also provides a cogent understanding of why and how a lineage-driven ancestral genealogy finds what it was looking for—which is, of course, the problem Foucault identified. Jagose delineates the two historical concerns of her project as "the articulation of the conditions of possibility that have governed the emergence of 'lesbian' as a meaningful category of identity" and "the reliance on the historicizing gesture as that which might secure for female homoeroticism a *lineage* and hence a value all its own."[89] Observable in the first interest is the methodology of critical history (or Foucauldian genealogy), while in the second Jagose appears to link all history-making practices (through her reference to the "historicizing gesture") to what is specifically the distinctive feature of ancestral genealogy: lineage. In other words, the problem she ascribes to "historicizing" (a term that conflates history as pastness and history as practice) is what ancestral genealogy shares with all histories of marginalization: that it is the very nature of the reparative project to bring the subject into the light, so that the invocation of history becomes the guarantee of that subject's existence. As the next section explains, queer genealogy frequently positions its historical practice as circumventing the conceptual pitfalls of ancestral genealogy, a claim that invites as much scrutiny as the misrecognition of genealogy as a metonym for proper history.

Queer Genealogy: The History of "Us"

Whereas ancestral genealogy situates the object of its analysis within a narrative of continuity about the emergence of creatures who came before or after a particular moment in time, queer genealogy strives to break the stranglehold of identity and disrupt sequential order. Halperin's disquisition on "how to do the history of homosexuality" is the most cogent explanation of queer genealogy's turn away from ancestral confidence in secure taxonomies of identity and toward "partial identity, emergent identity, transient identity, semi-identity, incomplete identity, proto-identity, or subidentity."[90] Traub too has been at the forefront of anatomizing the ontological and epistemological consequences of ancestral genealogy's need for similitude in relation to difference, reading the anachronistic gaze less as "individual misrecognition" than as a "collective melancholic response to the culturally disavowed trauma of historical elision."[91] Drawing on the analytical tools of psychoanalysis to connect narcissism and lesbianism, Traub understands queer genealogy as an investigatory mode that allows scholars to "look simultaneously backward and forward, using our retrospection to imagine and produce a *lesbian*-affirmative future"—an objective, note, that sustains rather than overturns political momentum.[92] Stymied by the residue of ancestral interest in the homosexual as an object to be studied, a being to be located in space and across time from the perspective of the present, queer genealogy operates as a site where it is not only possible but desirable to "stage a dialogue between one queer past and another."[93]

These are precisely the dialogues evident in feminist queer genealogical work by Alison Oram and Martha Vicinus.[94] In a valuable study (*Her Husband Was a Woman! Women's Gender-Crossing in Modern British Popular Culture* [2007]) of the public's perceptions and misunderstandings of working-class women exposed by newspapers to be passing as men, Oram, a social and cultural historian, demonstrates convincingly the inadequacies of reading cross-dressing women simply as butch lesbians. Differentiating between what we think we see now and how such women might have been viewed then, Oram explores the complex relations between gender variance and same-sex desire to reveal the availability of multiple interpretive frameworks that narrowed gradually across a fifty-year period. Oram's conclusion that the gender-crossing woman — "her astonishing transformation, her frisson of mystery, her homoerotic passions, her tricksterish powers, her lighthearted treatment of gender boundaries"—is "as much part of our contemporary sexual identities as the rationalist discourses of science and medicine" signals her project's investment in the dialogical temporalities of queer genealogy.[95] In *Intimate Friends: Women Who Loved Women, 1778–1928* (2004), Vicinus deftly explores a wealth of new source materials (letters, diaries, biographies and autobiographies, literary production, and court transcripts) to expose the historical "'ruptures,' 'discontinuities,' and 'disjunctions'" among a group of economically privileged women, often artistic and well educated (such as the famous Ladies of Llangollen; the minor aristocrat and female rake Anne Lister; Eliza Lynn Linton; Vernon Lee; and Hall and her partner Una Troubridge).[96] Concerned with the discursive formations of sexuality, gender, race, nation, and class, Vicinus situates her sexual subjects in wider historical contexts, considering, for instance, women's access to education and employment and noting change over time. In contrast to ancestral genealogy, however, Vicinus generates new insights about female queerness across specific historical periods. While ancestral interests remain in the frame, the thrust of the argument turns, as Foucault puts it, on the discontinuities of "our very being."[97] Attentive to identity as a construction, the broader aim of queer genealogy is to unravel *"the multiplicity of possible historical connections between sex and identity, a multiplicity whose existence has been obscured by the necessary but narrowly focused, totalizing critique of sexual identity as a unitary concept."*[98] Queer genealogy's investigative curiosity is certainly wide-ranging and multifaceted, but never far from its center is a paramount concern with questions about how the objects we desire in the past relate to current conceptualizations.

In a nuanced theorizing of the problem of alterity/continuism, Traub informs readers that historians would frame the problem slightly differently: "The issue is not whether the past is other or different, but how, when, and if change does occur, which continuities remain or persist."[99] This is precisely the way historian Matt Houlbrook turns to men's queer sexual cultures to rethink the problem of how to search, as Traub puts it, neither for "a mirror image of ourselves" nor a "past . . . so utterly alien that we will find nothing usable in its fragmentary traces."[100] Houlbrook makes subtle use of queer — and feminist — theory to historicize "sexual difference and 'normality'" and the social formations of friendships and sexual desire between men.[101] In the context of regulation and policing, Houlbrook's "queer" signifies "all erotic and affective interactions between men and all men who engaged in such interactions."[102] The book's very organizational strategy (it is divided into four major sections — policing, places, people, and politics) is a first indication of the project's disruption of the familiar ancestral progress narrative that underpins so many earlier accounts of twentieth-century gay history, in which the recent past is seen as a shift from homophobic repression toward homosexual liberation.

Although the advent of a more publicly identifiable homosexual subject in the aftermath of the Second World War paid off in paving the way for the gay liberation movements of the 1960s and after, the rigid sexual binary of hetero/homo would coerce men to pigeonhole themselves rather than pursue pleasurable opportunities in a more fluid realm of sexual desire — a process that Houlbrook, along with other historians such as Harry Cocks and Sean Brady, tracks with particular clarity in the British context.[103] Such insights vividly demonstrate how "normal" is constitutive of "queer," each concept contributing to the consolidation of the other in the public imaginary at this time, though always within the vectors of class, gender, place, race, ethnicity, and age. Houlbrook calls time on earlier accounts of the queer past as hidden, invisible, or "emerging from the shadows," a view shared more recently by Richard Hornsey in a study of the "new experiences of queer self-creation . . . [that were] becoming available to many men."[104] The urban male sexual culture that Houlbrook explores is a queer London and "not a *gay* world as we would currently understand it," and philosopher Morris Kaplan confirms that he is "under no illusion that [he has] simply recovered 'authentic' voices previously 'hidden from history.'"[105] Queer genealogy's interest in identities that do not quite map onto our own marks a turn away from the ancestral, manifesting an awareness of the hazards of transhistorical stable collective identities. But its sustained dialogue with current notions of deviance in relation to assumed norms also distinguishes it from a critical history suspicious of the habits of identification, most often articulated in relation to heteronormativity, a concept frequently understood as standing outside history.

Particularly striking in other recent queer genealogy is the ambition not merely to critique or rethink ancestral genealogy but to initiate its undoing, as seen, for example, in the subtitle of Scott Herring's book (*Slumming, Literature, and the Undoing of Lesbian and Gay History*) or in a chapter heading of Freccero's *Queer/Early/Modern* ("Undoing the Histories of Homosexuality") or in Julian Carter's characterizing a forthcoming project as "unlesbian dishistory."[106] Other historians of sexuality, too, position their "genealogical intellectual history" as a rejection of identity politics, as is evident in the strenuous denial by editors of a special issue of the *Journal of the History of Sexuality* that their engagement with the topic of "feminine sexual pathologies" contributes to "lesbian history."[107] Read against the search by historians for those crucial paradigms and concepts judged as holding continuing value and relevance for the discipline's future, some queer genealogists stake out the importance of their intervention by asserting the urgency of displacing the old — proclaiming rupture and discontinuity as the best way forward. Carter's use of "mother-love" to signal a new relational configuration outside a preexisting identitarian agenda disavows the hetero/homo distinction, even as it reinscribes the relationality of normal and deviant.[108] Herring's response to a politicized lesbian and gay history is to revel in his project's "rotten" politics.[109] He presents his study as an exercise of negation, for it "fails to recuperate or redeem anyone's sexual past. . . . It has little faith in a politics of sexual recognition," and it will not show "lesbians or gays" anything about "their subcultural fashioning. . . . [It] has nothing to reveal . . . about the debut of the homosexual."[110] Queer genealogists underscore the oppositional nature of their work, yet for all their disclaimers of legibility, visibility, intelligibility, or group solidarity, their radical critique of unstable identities represents less an excursion into the terrain of queer "sexual unknowing" (as Herring claims) than a sustained, energetic, rigorous, and sometimes hostile dialogical exchange with ancestral genealogy.[111] In other words, Herring's repudiation of lesbian and gay identity represents a conversation that takes place within — rather than outside — the larger genealogical project, which means it does not escape the logic of lineage. And as long as queer genealogy remains enmeshed in identitarian relationalities and organized around familiar binaries, it does not operate as critical history.

Rather than disparage ancestral genealogy to make room for a project to which it remains inextricably linked, queer genealogy needs to recognize its entanglements with a kindred ancestral practice that produces a "teleological, unifying storyline connecting (by aggressively selecting) historical events over long periods of time into an intelligible arc of progress towards some large telos which itself 'explained' and justified the latent principle of selection."[112] Mistaking genealogical practice as the sole pathway to the sexual past, the brash queer claim to write "bad history" (or, to put it another way, the attempted queer disavowal of the genealogical project) seems an ambition already fulfilled, but queer genealogy cannot rush to critique without also acknowledging how its own preoccupation with categories of identity betrays a kinship with identity politics. If queer genealogy falls short of becoming critically historical, it nevertheless offers incisive articulations on the relations of power, the problems of visibility and intelligibility, and the dangers of reading retrospectively, insights essential in forging queer critical history.

History's Cultural Turn and the Queer Turn to History

All forms of critical history, as discussed earlier in this book, understand the fundamental purpose of history writing as representing the past not — as in the case of queer genealogy — by using a compass to trace back modern conceptualizations from an end point but by abandoning that compass in favor of a more open-ended, undetermined historicizing of the sexual past. This vital distinction is best understood by examining the history of homosexuality in relation to the impact of the cultural turn that has clarified the role of the historian in creating a narrative about "the before now": critical history necessarily and inevitably *makes* rather than *finds* a past that "contains nothing of intrinsic value . . . no truths we *have* to respect, no problems we *have* to solve, no projects we *have* to complete; it is we who decide these things *knowing* . . . that there are no grounds on which we can ever get such decisions right."[113] Whatever new practices emerge as a result of history's encounter with queer theory, only one thing is certain: the limitations of the genealogical project as a history-making venture can be best assessed by inviting queer literary and cultural critics to take an interest in the "massive" and "startling" ways the cultural turn transformed and reshaped traditional historiographical praxis by exposing the conditions under which "subjectivities are produced within and through languages of identification."[114]

Historians debate the impact of the cultural turn, but no one disputes that the discipline has changed irrevocably, and there are no proposals to undo or reverse its effects. Since the mid-1990s, however, historians interested in theory have sensed a sea change, and there is lively speculation about history's future analytical categories and interests "beyond the cultural turn," including ethics, the sacred, cosmopolitanism, trauma, animals, affect, transnationalism, diaspora studies, memory, experience, agency, and religion.[115] Counterbalancing this mood of restive uncertainty about its future, historians — being historians — are contextualizing the recent disciplinary past to account for why the cultural turn came about in the first place and to identify the intellectual work that will have staying power. Of course such judgments are necessarily provisional and preliminary, but the excitement generated by "feminist concepts of gender," for example, has been acknowledged as far-reaching, in asking "how and when . . . and under what conditions" the category of woman was assigned cultural meaning, thus transforming women's history.[116] For historians of sexuality these reflections on the past, present, and future trends of academic history should raise serious concerns in that gender's robust resilience makes sexuality's relative absence, or secondary status, all the more unsettling, whether as a crucial analytical category available across the discipline or as the principal concern of a subfield. Indeed, sexuality does not even appear in these discussions of historiography as ancillary to a gender analysis powerful enough to shake the foundations of historical thinking more generally.[117] At the same time, some readers may wonder if anxieties about sexuality's invisibility in history's future are justified in that sexuality is somehow already embedded in the notion of gender. Gender historians sometimes treat sexuality as merely co-extensive with gender, as is evident even in the work of Joan Scott, the most important theorist of gender in historical analysis, who too often assumes a seamless equivalence between identity categories and thereby relinquishes the usefulness of differentiation.

In a subsection of a 1996 article (titled, ironically, "Processes of Differentiation"), Scott calls on scholars who write on marginal groups to be more attentive to how identity is produced "as a process both of homogenization and differentiation."[118] She cogently argues that we must resist the lure of self-recognition not only because it is inherently ahistorical, but also because the very act of laying claim to identity renders it "static."[119] Scott's explanation of what is at stake in the shift from women to "women," where the latter designation effectively problematizes categorical stability, elucidates the problems in universalizing "difference"—the postmodern sign of "women" allows us to "ask how and in what circumstances the difference of . . . sex came to matter."[120] This argument runs into trouble, however, in her suggestion of the interchangeability of categories of identity, as she demonstrates how this same operation might work in the case of African Americans, homosexuals, and finally, Americanness as a national identity—all these examples, she tells us, can simply be "multiplied."[121] But can they? More recently, Scott again extends to other subjects—in this case, feminists and women workers—Foucault's example of the homosexual, but differentiation again is one casualty of her paramount concern with showing the wider applicability of the Foucauldian imperative to historicize the categories.[122]

The problem of multiple examples is not simply that overlaying one concept onto another is misleading—it is that forms of subjugation are not reducible to each other, as Eve Kosofsky Sedgwick explains: "It was the long, painful realization, *not* that all oppressions are congruent, but that they are *differently* structured and so must intersect in complex embodiments."[123] She continues: "The question of gender and the question of sexuality" are simultaneously "inextricable from one another" *and* distinctive.[124] Obviously this condition of similarity and difference poses difficult theoretical problems for gender historians habituated only to "bringing in" other categories as needed.[125] Early on Sedgwick anticipated objections to her argument that gender and sexuality must be seen as mutually constitutive and separate. Some might argue "that gender is *definitionally* built into determinations of sexuality, in a way that neither of them is definitionally intertwined with, for instance, determinations of class or race."[126] However, "bringing in" a second concept in relation to gender does not adequately account for the inescapable, though fundamental, contradiction that marks the relations between gender and sexuality: that the hetero/homo binary is intelligible only vis-à-vis gender, while sexual object choice may have nothing to do with gender. For Sedgwick the problem of the "narrowing-down" of sexual practices, identities, and desires at the turn of the twentieth century into a single sweeping binary is historical, and it is the move from "lesbian and gay" to "queer" that mobilizes disciplinary practices best equipped to transform "political questions" into "historical ones."[127]

Closer inspection of gender's apparent success reveals a more complex picture in that feminists of all persuasions still worry that gender's political efficacy has been diminished, its critical edge dulled or compromised. That it is no longer necessary "to be a feminist to ask about the effects of World War 1 on gender relations," as historian Lynn Hunt suggests, seems to undermine the political ideals that gave rise to the women's movement.[128] Feminist historian Judith Bennett has been vociferous in her criticisms of an academic history incapable of "owning any political perspectives at all," as if history itself could stand apart from politics.[129] Scott, on the other hand, is troubled because she believes "gender" has been debased, reuniversalized as a "synonym for 'women'" (a similar argument could be made about the concept of "queer," which has functioned as a shorthand for homosexual).[130] These objections to gender's mishandling—its appropriation by those uninterested in its political legacy or its adulteration by those indifferent to its power in historicizing "the very notion of how we came to think of ourselves in the way we did"[131]—put its assumed success in a somewhat different light and call attention to the difficulties in gauging its influence on mainstream history in relation to the persistent sidelining of the history of homosexuality, especially lesbian history.

If, as some gender historians contend, women's history—driven by feminist politics—has occupied a more marginal position than gender in a discipline that once cultivated "impartial, disinterested perspectives," we might expect that most history-making enterprises with overt links to political movements, such as gay and lesbian liberation, would share a similar fate.[132] Yet reading as parallel those shifts that highlight the constructedness of the category (woman to "woman," on the one hand, and lesbian and gay to the queerer formulations of "lesbian and gay," on the other) may be less illuminating than we might think because, while the turn toward gender has transformed academic history, the more recent turn toward queer has not proved equally influential.

The onus in making a persuasive case for sexuality's importance (particularly the queer theorizing of sexuality) to social and cultural historians appears to rest primarily on, for example, a queer critical history that understands how crucial it is to break away from the very practices (ancestral and queer genealogy) that made its existence possible. The queer critique — with its imperative to trouble identity and linearity — has shifted the political ground of lesbian and gay liberation, leading some observers to decry the displacement or loss of those vital links with activist grassroots politics; yet queer distance from the politics of advocacy has not nudged the history of homosexuality closer to the center of mainstream academic history. Caution is necessary in offering a monocausal account of the marginalization of identity-based sexuality studies in academic history, but it is undoubtedly true that the continuing hold of a fascination with identity in the subfield is hugely significant. Tracing an object or concept "backward in time" (as Halperin phrases it in his superb theorization of queer genealogy) — even for the purpose of watching our "modern definitions" disintegrate "to reveal the shape of other, earlier categories, discourses, logics, [and] coherences" — pulls queer genealogy away from critical history.[133] In *How to Do the History of Homosexuality*, Halperin offers an astute and careful explanation of a practice that proceeds differently from critical history: "I begin where all histories of homosexuality must begin (like it or not), namely with the modern notion of homosexuality, which, explicitly or implicitly, defines the horizons of our immediate conceptual universe and inevitably shapes our inquiries into same-sex sexual desire and behavior in the past."[134] This statement represents a new beginning in the history of homosexuality, but critical history begins somewhere else.

No amount of tweaking or revising can enable queer genealogy to become critical history. Jagose, in conceding that on one level her concern with history might seem uncannily familiar (as little more than a "restatement" of the "post-Foucauldian caution against misrecognizing the historical as always in the service of the present"), engages with the fuller and more vexing implications of Foucauldian genealogy.[135] It isn't that practitioners of ancestral and queer genealogy must desist from misrecognizing historical subjects as precursors to modern conceptualizations, but rather that queer genealogy must be seen as a project that has *evolved* from ancestral genealogy, so that the two are intricately interconnected. Too often queer critics take from Foucault only a rule about avoiding anachronism when this mode of historicizing recuperates what it sets out to find in its excursions into the past. The more powerful argument about the nature of history making developed by Adorno, Foucault, Derrida, Michel de Certeau, and many others is not that the desire to see ourselves in the past constitutes a *mis*recognition, because there is no past we do not already construct in the present.[136] For the critical historian interested in what we do not know about the past, there is no past to "encounter," touch, discover, or trace back that we do not invent "to suit ourselves."[137]

History is neither the hide-and-seek of the recuperative project nor the teasing out of discontinuities — we cannot "rely" on it because we are the ones who "cut it up" for our own purposes now.[138] In this sense all pasts are usable, not just those of identity-based genealogy. Implicit in Jagose's densely formulated argument is the recognition of an insurmountable epistemological problem that is the condition of the genealogical project itself either in looking for (and inevitably finding) recognizable beings in the past or in locating what it thinks it already knows about the nonnormative in the past. What is fundamentally troubling for queer genealogy is that it is a condition of its own project that it cannot fully achieve "a critical genealogy in the Foucauldian sense" because, as Carla Freccaro explains, it continues "to work within those very apparatuses to produce truths about people of the past through sex . . . in their distance from and proximity to a modernity defined by sexual identity or orientation" (a familiar line of argument among critical historians).[139] Foucauldian genealogy is not interested in demonstrating historical truth; its objective is to determine "the discursive conditions that contribute to the construction of what comes to be regarded as true."[140] Assiduous in her critique of what she perceives as the genealogical project's abiding investment in teleology, Freccaro (along with early modern queer literary critics Jonathan Goldberg and Madhavi Menon) produces new textual reading strategies, but in so doing she turns her considerable deconstructive powers against history writ large, as if no route exists within academic history to enact a queer practice. Misrepresenting the "pious" operations of history as a "solemn, even dour, marshalling of empirical evidence to prove its point," queer deconstruction can offer little to the scholar interested in drawing on queer thought to historicize the sexual past, and even less to the scholar open to exchange across these fields.[141] Hence the quest for a mode of historical inquiry that is not coextensive with the genealogical project, an alternative that shares the *methodologies* of queer genealogy but generates historical work for a different *purpose.*

Here, I suggest, is where disciplinarity comes into play and seems to drive a wedge through the queer genealogical project, as the imaginative and provocative solutions proposed by queer historicists interested in developing new ways to analyze texts or objects (ahistoricism, homohistory, queer spectrality, feeling historical)[142] prove less tenable for critical historians interested in historicizing the past. Proposals to suspend "determinate sexual and chronological differences while expanding the possibilities of the nonhetero, with all its connotations of sameness, similarity, proximity, and anachronism," might allow the literary critic "to read the past properly," but these "effects" for the critical historian are anything but "liberating"—indeed, in historical practice the shift toward Foucauldian genealogy (critical history) associated with the cultural turn exacerbates rather than resolves the problems posed by practices in conversation with identity or with interests in identity's undoing.[143]

One result of the distance between academic history and queer studies is that, without grasping how disciplinarity and shifts in disciplinary practices have shaped sexual history, we cannot understand the queer indifference to the methods and practices of academic history, the indifference in some corners of academic history toward queer studies, the differences in how ancestral and queer genealogists approach the past, or the differences between the genealogical project and a queer critical history. The relative invisibility of sexuality in mainstream academic history practices—before and after the cultural turn—is integrally related to the current impulse by queer genealogists to undo ancestral genealogy, practices that, in serving the needs of their respective constituencies, should flourish until those readers fade away. The dilemma is that the genealogical project's usable pasts are shaped and animated by the exigencies of particularized political agendas that no sooner are articulated than they are locked down in a locatable time and place. This is why it is misleading to see lesbian, gay, or queer historiography as caught up in a syndrome of supersession that dictates the undoing of the phase that preceded it: lesbian and gay social history is not undone by the queer critique; lesbian social history is not overturned by transgendered history; queer genealogy is not undermined by a postqueer imperative.[144] However dismissive, impatient, fractious, or irascible their relations, these diverse practices represent the multifaceted project of genealogy that engages in "a provocative conversation between the past and the present."[145]

Queer critical history benefits from dialogical exchange with the genealogical project but — as critical history — knows it is not possible to converse with the past. Lineage-driven practices (ancestral or queer) are subject to "the conceptual tyranny of homosexuality" that dictates the terms of engagement as an economy of continuity or discontinuity, which means that current practices in the historicizing of lesbian, gay, or queer beings operate within the modern logic of sexuality as organized through categories, binary structures, and identities.[146] Opting out of the dialogic between the past and the present is queer critical history's greatest epistemological advantage in that it becomes possible to discern how that "referent" we have come to know as the homosexual is not an object to be traced back from the present moment but "something constantly re-created in the recurring movement between past and present, hence ever-changing as that relationship itself is modified *in* the present."[147] Arguably, the queer critique is ideally positioned to make this case to queer critics and historians alike in the form of a theoretically engaged queer critical history, fully committed to enacting emancipatory futures. Traub's acknowledgment that "our desires for these representations constitute them as objects" is reminiscent of the postmodern view that "the so-called past (the before now) doesn't exist 'meaningfully' prior to the efforts of historians to impose upon it a structure or form. . . . [No] historian or anyone else acting as if they were a historian ever returns from his or her trip to 'the past' without precisely the historicization they wanted to get."[148] It is not that we know beforehand what the archive holds — indeed, the pleasure of archival research is encountering the unexpected — rather, it is that critical history (as queer genealogists recognize) understands that our pursuit of desire constructs the past.

Queerness-as-Method and Critical History

Ancestral genealogists trace forebears, prototypes, and antecedents to discover and rediscover a lesbian or gay past, their methodologies judged by the critical historian as resting "on fraud as well as truth," entailing "peril along with pride."[149] To chastise such work for misrepresenting the past is to misunderstand the purposes of collective memory and a politics of affirmation. Queer genealogists, on the other hand, trace "transhistorical continuities" and note "the disintegration of our own concepts as we trace them backward in time" — a purpose equally unavailable to a critical historian who believes no history exists until the historian conjures it into existence by "discerning the time-and-place specificity of a thing" and rejecting universals in favor of singularity.[150] This is not a criticism of the queer desire to write critical history; rather, it is an indication that lesbian, gay, and queer history (like all history) contributes differently to progressive political agendas. Disagreements of practice and theory aside, the strands of ancestral and queer are sedimented into a larger genealogical project because neither can "escape . . . the survival of former structures . . . [and] the weight of an endlessly present past."[151] The value of each strand also varies because the significant theoretical intervention prized by a queer critic might not contribute as effectively to a compelling story of the homosexual past as its close relation. Queer deconstructionists such as Freccaro have soundly thrashed ancestral genealogy as well as mischaracterized the queer genealogies of Halperin and Traub, claiming their work "is not a critical genealogy in the Foucauldian sense."[152] While I agree with this assessment, I see no advantage in dismissing the genealogical project or the practice of history to pursue a "postqueer theoretical critical analysis."[153] Academic history has changed, though some queer theorists prefer their caricature of a discipline enthralled by empiricism, since this serves their own intellectual agenda. Rather than dismiss history, I think queer studies should cultivate an appreciation of the different uses of sexual history and discern the value of *each* practice.

In a different register, queer theorist Lee Edelman reaches a similar conclusion in calling for a queer project that would refuse "every substantialization of identity, which is always oppositionally defined, and, by extension, of history as linear narrative (the poor man's teleology)."[154] Opting out of the "movement toward a viable political future" signals a refusal of "history" as "the continuous staging of our dream of eventual self-realization"—which, in so many words, is the predicament critical historians warned us about all along.[155] In effect, this queer psychoanalytic argument calls queer theory's bluff—no radical critique of identity can sustain a politics of oppositionality, and thus Edelman invests "queer negativity" with the power to challenge the "very value of the social itself."[156] With no telos there is no future—and with no future there is no history. Yet here is where the distinctions between queer genealogy and queer critical history come into play, because the latter eludes the burden of "tracing back" as a project of identity or "denormativizing," and consequently the future looks far less bleak.[157] To demonstrate the potential of a queer historicizing released from the imperative to historicize the queer object, it is necessary to figure out how to write queer critical history.[158]

The earliest adumbrations of the new practice I envisage—that is, historical work uninterested in queerness-as-being, though informed by queerness-as-method — might be glimpsed in the cultural historian James Vernon's excellent article on the extraordinary figure of Colonel Barker (see chapter 3), a life claimed variously for inclusion in histories of marginalized peoples, including lesbian history, transgendered history, women's history, and the history of transvestism. By taking seriously the queer imperative to trouble identity, Vernon insists on reading Barker as "indeterminate, undecidable, and unknowable": "It is the very ambiguity of Barker's story that makes it so interesting, for it enables one to shift attention away from the classification of Barker as an object with a 'real' gender and sexuality to be discovered and revealed to a concern with how Barker was understood and made knowable by his own contemporaries."[159] Literary scholar Sharon Marcus also breaks new ground in troubling "polarized genders and antithetical sexualities"; finding herself "caught up" in the logic of the "heterosexual matrix of gender," Marcus realized she had to "let go of the notion that all bonds between women functioned as the antithesis of heterosexual relations"; in other words, merely abandoning terms such as heterosexual was insufficient — it was necessary instead to reconceptualize through historical contextualization how relations between women and men were understood in Victorian culture.[160] This book seeks to build on work like this to confront not simply the categories of identity we take for granted now but the predetermined and overdetermined structural logic of categorization itself.

Where We Go from Here

Critical history presents the genealogical project with some of the toughest obstacles of all in exposing, first, that nothing in the past is visible until we in the present make it so and, second, that history is always in the service of the present (this is not a problem of history, it is a condition of history). Queer critical history "not only establishes the difference of the past, its remove in time, it also severs its connection — as direct antecedent or precedent — to the present. That which we take most for granted loses its universal or transcendent dimension. It depends only on current time. In this way, the present is historicized."[161] New queer reading practices — such as "queer spectrality" (a deconstructionist "approach to history and historiography") or the queer temporalities of "ahistoricism" — have proved immensely generative in recognizing how "the sign of history has become less the real than the intelligible."[162] Yet these strategies tell us little about how a queer critical historicizing of the sexual past might proceed. In other words, queer historicist work has much to offer historians of sexuality, but pathways drawn from literary and cultural criticism require modification or adjustment, because a shared topical interest is not the same as a shared purpose.

Traub's speculations on why the Renaissance lyric has "had such a compelling hold on *lesbian* engagements with the past" alert us to a genealogical interest in the potential of a textual object to hold cultural meaning over time, and she readily displays the analytical skills to destabilize potential meanings, revealing to her readers competing interpretive contexts.[163] However, queer critical history turns to the past not to "look for" evidence of queerness-as-being in texts and objects, but to deploy queerness-as-method to "look through" the archive to see what is unknown at the present moment. In this way the usefulness of the category of sexuality is its capacity to pose questions rather than provide answers about sexual identities we already know. This is why we need ever more nuanced differentiations in historiographical practice that build on Traub's attempt to explain "continuism versus alterity" in terms more readily understood by the "historian."[164] The positionality of any form of identity history (such as the history of "women" or "homosexuals") is one that measures present conceptualizations against what is discovered in the historical past as continuous or discontinuous, its primary interest in noting resemblance. Critical history also notes change over time, but its positionality does not pivot around what is known in the present moment; hence its privileging of discontinuity.

If Traub's historian-informant had been asked how queer genealogists conceptualize difference and similarity, the response would have been very like the terms used by literary scholars — as difference (alterity) and similarity (continuist) — as seen in women's history, where the meaning of woman is fixed: "The history of women has kept 'women' outside history. And the result is that 'women' as a natural phenomenon is reinscribed, even as we assert that women are discursively constructed."[165] Returning to Jagose's proposition that in lesbian history there is a "reliance on the historicizing gesture as that which might secure for female homoeroticism a lineage and hence a value all its own" reveals not a problem with the "historicizing gesture," but a problem inherent to the genealogical project.[166] If realizing the *purpose* of Foucauldian genealogy is the paramount concern (and it may well not be), we need to worry about how our historicizing gestures secure our sense of ourselves in the present *and* worry as well about how different historicizing practices achieve different purposes. Or, to put it more positively, we need to see that historical work produced inside the logic of lineage and modern sexual knowledge differs from historical work produced outside that logic.

The challenge for the queer critical historian is to see what new historical understandings might be generated in resisting a paramount interest in the categories of identity and identification and rethinking the privileging of the binary relation between normativity and deviance. In other words, queer critical history cannot anticipate in advance what new explanations might emerge. Future work may further test our tolerance for radical discontinuity, and those edgy experiments will likely thwart coherence and perplex. Such work might even be assessed as without purpose, as seen in the historian Chris Waters's question, "What is at stake in reveling in *discontinuity?*" or in Traub's assertion that "a queer genealogy that does not attempt to account for, much less credit, the existence of the category 'modern homosexuality' is . . . a contradiction in terms."[167] These reactions are critical, for they remind us once again of the need for multiple forms of history making, and also of the importance of differentiating when we slip from the discourse of one practice into another.

A good illustration of the consequences of neglecting the purpose of historicizing, the risks in misrecognizing the irreducible otherness of the past, evinced in a discussion of a medicoscientific discourse that flourished at the turn of the twentieth century only to fade away completely, was "reproductive physiology," which asserted the basic hermaphroditic constitution of the human body and coincided with the women's suffrage campaign in Britain.[168] Scholar Lisa Carstens scrutinizes developments in scientific thought that licensed mainstream scientists to seriously entertain the "possibility that patterns of social behavior could trigger physiological sex reversal, particularly in women."[169] Probing the strange beliefs of experts who crafted what seemed like plausible scientific explanations in response to cultural anxieties about female emancipation, Carstens plunges readers into alien terrain, largely steering clear of the topic of homosexuality to account for the ways that "true female identity quite literally depended on protecting a particular developmental relationship between the female body and reproductive-centered behavior."[170] This otherwise savvy and well-researched analysis falters only when the spotlight is on the perceived threat of sex reversal in female militants. Despite the author's recognition that inversion maps only unevenly onto modern configurations of lesbianism, references to the infamous 1918 Billing/Allan libel trial or to 1921 parliamentary debates concerning "acts of gross indecency between female persons" suddenly turn on the modern configuration of the "female homosexual," and consequently all the productive messiness, confusion, misunderstanding, and contradiction so prevalent in the discussion of female sexual inversion evaporates.[171] Curiously, Hall's novel too is seen not as a literary representation of inversion but as centering on "lesbian love."[172] In effect, this author's key discovery that sexual inversion denoted not sexual object choice but an inversion of the reproductive instinct is unraveled and undermined by the straitjacket of taxonomy, which collapses the differences between then and now and relinquishes the ambiguity and radical capaciousness of female sexual inversion. These elisions of sexual inversion and homosexuality are not the result of scholarly ineptitude or unthinking anachronism; the problem is the tremendous power of identity itself that functions like an undertow dragging the researcher back to the familiar. For any historian of lesbianism working within the framework of identity history to generate narratives for readers interested in a lesbian past, the "lesbian" must be conjured into existence — this, however, is not Carstens's purpose; hence, what is jarring about these fleeting appearances of "female homosexuality" or the "lesbian" is not that they are wrong but that two historiographical frameworks (identity history and critical history) collide, the one undermining the other, a predicament best avoided by being mindful of their diverse objectives. From the perspective of queer genealogy, there is absolutely no point in exploring a past where all traces of connection (or disconnection) vanish. The value of critical history "lies in its endorsement of an *undetermined history* . . . [offering] no clear map, no plan for what comes next," though stretching historical analysis to the absolute limits of usability and legibility is not without its costs.[173]

Genealogy — from its early stage of evolving out of the emancipatory politics of the feminist and lesbian and gay liberation movements to its later developments in a queer response to Foucault's call for a history of the present — has been simultaneously the solution (in making such history possible) and the problem (in making nongenealogical sexual history difficult). As yet only a handful of queer historians and literary critics have pushed the boundaries of a lineage framework that, in tracing "our own concepts . . . backward in time," is always more effective in illuminating — as similarity or difference — what we think we already know about the sexual past.[174] That said, of the various practices across the history of sexuality, queer genealogy, with its links to queer negotiations of sexuality, has been essential in paving the way for a productive exchange between critical history and queer studies/queer theory, as seen in Traub's vision of a historiographical approach adept at shifting attention away from similarity and difference toward intelligibility and signification.[175]

Looking at genealogy inside and out reveals how it shapes and conditions the questions we can ask not only about the distant past but about the modern age as well. In part 2 I propose to bring historiographical arguments to life by scrutinizing through historical example the way genealogy sometimes constrains and impedes, paying particular attention to its conceptual underpinnings — categorization, identity, and the tension between normal and deviant — and imagining pathways as yet untried, since these might yield access to sexualities invisible or even inconceivable to the genealogist.

PART 2

Practicing
Sexual History

3 / Topsy-Turvydom
Gender, Sexuality, and the Problem of Categorization

> During the eighteenth and nineteenth centuries . . . taxonomies
> elaborated by scientists ordered human diversity . . . [and] laid
> the foundation upon which the major etiological frameworks of
> homosexuality were based.
>
> JENNIFER TERRY (1999)

> The history of sexuality, as Foucault conceived it . . . [is] an inquiry
> into the historical emergence of sexuality itself . . . rather than with the
> production of sexual categories or classifications.
>
> DAVID HALPERIN (2002)

In 1918 the travel writer Mrs. Ethel Brilliana Alec-Tweedie (1862–
1940) published *Women and Soldiers*—an impassioned extolling of British
women war workers, whose unbridled energies in their service to the nation
were depicted as on a par with the sacrifices men made in the trenches of
the Western Front.[1] Highlighting women's resilience, flexibility, and creativ-
ity in grasping the nettle of any obstacle thrown in their way, Alec-Tweedie's
reconfiguration of the nature and meaning of womanhood in the realm of
work represented—to readers at the time—a radical departure from older
notions of femininity. Recent more nuanced historical accounts of classificatory systems of gender and the First World War suggest the persistence
of gender stratification in the labor market, but Alec-Tweedie's confident
prediction that in the not too distant future Britain would surely see women
fighting alongside men nevertheless constitutes an intriguing historical document in its own right.[2] With hyperbolic flourish she cheerfully welcomed
the new world order, declaring it a state of "topsy-turvydom" wherein "every
man is a soldier, and every woman is a man."[3] Others too saw the war's tem-

porary disturbances in the domain of gender as tantamount to a "revolution" or "complete social upheaval," and the resulting influx of women of diverse class backgrounds into new areas of the workforce meant the British public came in contact with many unfamiliar configurations of modern femininity.[4] Female labor was not simply useful, it was essential. As Lord Derby, under-secretary of state for war, affirmed, "Women are now part and parcel of our great army, without them it would be impossible for progress to be made, but with them I believe victory can be assured."[5] Estimates of the actual numbers involved vary, as I discuss below, but the female war worker was newsworthy, especially the woman in military or quasi-military uniform.[6] In the early days of the war, when uniformed women were still a novelty, photographers sought them out, and journalists reported reactions of shock, laughter, or curiosity; however, as hostilities intensified and the public became accustomed to women clad in uniforms of every color and description on the streets, in the print media, and in newsreels, "distrust" largely gave way to enthusiasm, respect, and admiration for female patriots.[7] Then, in the months following the Armistice, goodwill and support would dissipate, with newspapers and magazines marshaling their considerable energies to persuade or intimidate women "to shed their army manners with the military uniforms."[8]

In reading the militarized and uniformed female body in wartime Britain, scholars sometimes claim that gender deviance (as denoted by clothing, physical appearance, work, or feminist convictions) and what we now understand as "lesbianism" were widely regarded as conjoined. In 1987 Jenny Gould, for example, argues that one "less tangible dimension to the hostility toward militarism in women" was that "people drew links, either consciously or unconsciously, between displays of militarism and masculine women, feminism, and lesbianism," even though "*masculine* as applied to women's behavior was not always a term of abuse."[9] In other words, she contends in this frequently cited essay, people at this time, whether active experts in interpreting culturally appropriate or inappropriate gender performances or only vaguely aware of gender violations as unsettling, were nonetheless apt to connect gender variance with sexual deviance. Gould further explains:

> This association of lesbianism with feminism (and with masculinity and militarism in women) *must have* affected both relationships between women and the public's view of such relationships. . . . Women who displayed "symptoms" of lesbianism (an inclination to dress up in masculine

clothes, to drill, and to shoot) were considered not only distasteful but abnormal and in need of medical help.[10]

Similarly, historian George Robb refers to a "heightened visibility of lesbianism" during the war, a period he sees as "essential to the emergence of a lesbian identity, both through a greater openness in discussing the topic, and by bringing together large numbers of like-minded women in war work and the military."[11] More recently, in a history of the First Aid Nursing Yeomanry (FANY), Janet Lee argues that this "quirky and vivacious" paramilitary group purposely devised "heterosexual exploits" to "avoid the accusations of being 'inverts' or 'mannish lesbians'"; these unsavory labels, she contends, were also imposed on suffragettes and women who served elsewhere in the armed forces.[12] Still others suggest that increased opportunities for female homosociality "awakened in women a dangerous desire for masculine occupations and behavior" that in turn gave rise to "cultural anxieties over women's involvement in the masculine public sphere" and "enabled a new rhetoric of female homosexuality to emerge."[13]

The proposition that manlike uniformed women were thought sexually deviant during the war is troubling for several reasons. First, evidence I have uncovered in the print media and in personal accounts by women themselves indicates that people in general did not understand gender inversion (traits, attitudes, or behaviors culturally associated with "male" manifested in "female" and vice versa) as interrelated with sexuality as either a collective or an individual category of identity. By and large, the educated reading public would not link mannish clothing on the female body or women's masculine behavior with particular sexual proclivities until the late 1920s, as sexological literature became more widely available and popularized in the fiction of writers such as Radclyffe Hall.[14] Indeed, as social historian Alison Oram explains in a highly nuanced analysis of gender crossing and same-sex desire in modern Britain, the possibility of locating women within modern categories of sexual identity and affixing labels of sexual deviance would not become commonplace until about the 1940s.[15] Second, Gould and others assume that the "distasteful" or "threatening" appearance of mannish or masculine women stretched the moral boundaries of proper womanhood.[16] This important claim merits further consideration because, on a more modest scale, public displays of militarism and female masculinity captivated filmmakers, artists, photographers, and journalists, changing public perceptions of British femininities even before the war. As early as 1885, "three hundred uniformed women soldiers" of the Salvation Army marched to the House of Commons in support of a social purity campaign, and in 1909 members of the Girl Guide movement — athletic adolescent girls and young women — could be seen in the country's towns and cities sporting a distinctively military style of dress and marching outdoors in militarylike formations, suggesting that gender boundaries were already in flux without inviting the public to measure deviations against a checklist of symptoms in need of medical intervention.[17] To argue that "it was not uncommon" for some women to be branded "peculiar" or "immoral" is as deeply misleading as it is untenable (as is Gould's claim that there was general hostility toward such women), for such punishing strictures would have applied to countless women, since a journalist in the *Spectator* remarks (and obviously exaggerates) that "quite half the feminine world must be in uniform now."[18] Gould rightly observes how the body conveys social meanings to outside observers and is bound up with notions of selfhood, but the classification systems of early sexology often conflated gender and sexuality in relation to the somatic, so that the categories of gender inversion and sexual inversion sometimes overlapped in confusing and contradictory ways.

Finally, and most important for my argument here, the uncritical linkage of gender deviations with modern formulations of lesbianism (that is, same-sex erotic behaviors, relations, or identities between sexed female bodies) points to certain inadequacies in the tools currently at our disposal in understanding the war's impact on some women. This cultural moment — exceptional because change was so widespread — vividly illustrates the epistemological consequences of an overdetermined relation between gender and sexuality and suggests the potential for historical investigation in cultivating greater skepticism and mistrust of the clarity that categorization seems to promise. How can we reconfigure gender and sexuality as analytic categories to better grasp how they are mutually constitutive and how they intersect with other categories (such as age, class, nation, or race)?[19] Is it necessary, viable, or desirable to abandon categorization's ordering of the heterogeneity of human sexuality? As I discussed in part 1, the dangers of projecting current formulations retrospectively are now well known — even so, simply recognizing the importance of avoiding ahistoricism does not let us off the hook, since other epistemological problems linger as we endeavor to historicize the gendered and sexualized subject in relation to cultural categories. For ancestral genealogists in particular, whose primary interests lie in origins, the prospect of relinquishing categories we know as insufficient (or, in the case of queer genealogy, suspending conceptual investments in norms or binary structures known to us now) threatens to compromise any semblance of legibility — and the subsequent loss of resemblance seems to undermine the ability to fulfill the political objectives of the genealogical project. However, rethinking how categorization dictates and curtails the way the gendered and sexual past is made knowable highlights compellingly the need for interpretive leeway so that gender and sexuality can be positioned in relation to the multiple social differences of lived experience. Practicing sexual history differently, I would argue, calls for delineating other trajectories that the genealogical project obscures.

The first step in realizing this risky venture is to intensify our awareness of the epistemological repercussions of bringing into productive exchange discourses around gender *and* sexuality as taxonomizing systems — a strategy that seems obvious but has been surprisingly rare. Consider, on the one hand, some missed opportunities to engage with the sexual in recent historical work on gender and the First World War, such as Janet Watson's description of female ambulance drivers.[20] While acutely attentive to class, this historian's consideration of the cultural signifiers some early twentieth-century sexologists associated with sexual inversion — "'sporting' women, former tomboys . . . unwomanly" — focuses exclusively on "gender ambiguity."[21] Watson wisely refrains from making the same mistake as Gould and others who argue for direct and unequivocal links that might not have existed; nonetheless, it is troubling that sexuality — an equally crucial aspect of human experience and category of analysis — is nowhere on the horizon. Historians of lesbianism, on the other hand, frequently seize on any sign of gender variance as symptomatic of women who loved women. A good example of this is *Britannia's Glory: A History of Twentieth-Century Lesbians*, in which the author cites the "arresting 'masculine appearance'" of Barbara "Toupie" Lowther, the founder of an all-women ambulance unit, as primary evidence of her lesbianism.[22] Judith Halberstam's discussion of Lowther points to a set of traits notably similar to Watson's — "gallant demeanor"; "overtly masculine"; a sportswoman with mechanical knowledge of car engines — not to assert the category of lesbian, but to advocate on behalf of a different category, believing that Lowther manifests signs of an incipient transsexual identity.[23] These critical transactions, genealogically speaking, are invaluable, yet "what desires, what interests are served by the development of comprehensive schemes of categorization? What might we gain by accepting an irreducible dimension of opacity in our efforts to comprehend differences?"[24] In a study of Oscar Wilde, Morris Kaplan negotiates the conundrum of categories by shifting the onus of analysis to readers, who are free to make informed decisions based on the stories the subjects tell themselves. In the end, this tactic achieves mixed results, because our automatic reflex to classify is so entrenched, so overpoweringly irresistible, that we are only too eager to fill in the blanks on whether sexual subjects were this or that, thus replacing Kaplan's silence with a resounding "yes they were."[25] Kaplan's practice of interpretive restraint has been read as an abdication of the "historian's obligation to explain the past," though, while difficult questions persist, this interesting experiment is instructive in warning of the dangers in ignoring the impulse to classify.[26] Perhaps the more vexing problem of categories is that they are at once analytically enabling and disabling, depending on the purpose of the history making. Without them identity history would collapse, but at the same time we cannot ignore categorization as a knowledge apparatus that elucidates and constrains. Left to their own devices, some readers inevitably fall back on the reassuringly familiar, suggesting the helpfulness of other historiographical frameworks that scrupulously interrogate the usefulness of categories and expose their definitional inadequacies and boundaries. In the absence of private papers that allow us to secure identities, scholars can do little more than speculate, but these negotiations need not necessarily impel us to privilege one modern category over another or marshal historical detail only for identification, though these various historical projects enhance our understanding of cultural change. No single approach will adequately explain the complexity and ubiquity of the war's impact on gender, because the set of signifiers scholars often link to female sexual inversion, such as mechanical aptitude or a militaristic manner, were ubiquitous, for instance, among the ranks of women who served in ambulance units near the Western Front. As one wartime observer explains: "The war has shown . . . [that] a mechanical turn of mind . . . is not an exclusive attribute of the masculine brain."[27] Neglecting sexuality provides an account as partial as the positioning of the sexual subject in one category or another, which is the reason a practice informed by the judicious use of a queer critique open to uncertainty might effectively expose what categorization occludes.

Neither academic history nor queer theory has offered clear methodological guidance in mediating the limits of categorization as a structuring enterprise or as a tool that demands constant vigilance. Literary specialists and historians have explored those sexual subjects who slip between existing discourses and — consciously or unconsciously — resist being pegged down in their relationships and practices. Martha Vicinus, for instance, probes the ways some women refashioned their "intimate friendships and desires" through the "familial dynamics" of an eroticized "mother-daughter" relationship, and Julian Carter too points to "mother-love" to describe a "nonlesbian sexual relationship between women" in early twentieth-century American culture.[28] The two argue in different ways for a breakdown of narrower formulations of lesbian identity, but Carter prefers the term queer because it cannot be reduced to "any single consistent meaning."[29] Indeed, this refusal in queer theory to pin down the meaning of "queer" as a category has been both enabling and restricting. The very fluidity and openness of "queer" has attracted scholars who have discovered its usefulness in dealing with sexualities of the past and the present (and, at the same time, has confused and even angered some nonacademic LGBT audiences who yearn for a usable past).[30] Matt Houlbrook believes there are many good reasons for rejecting the "very categories of identity — 'gay' and 'straight,' 'homo' and 'heterosexual' — that have often been taken for granted since the 1970s."[31] Like Houlbrook, James Vernon turns to the discursive regimes of the law and the print media not to situate subjects in categories, but to examine, on the one hand, how individuals of the past understood sexuality and, on the other, how these understandings intersected with and acted on formations of self-understanding.[32] Whereas Houlbrook surveys a vast terrain of sexual subjectivities over several decades, Vernon focuses on a single sexual subject (Colonel Barker, known also as Valerie Arkell-Smith), a colorful figure who has captured the interest of historians of lesbianism, female masculinity, transvestism, and transgenderism. Such willingness to expand and multiply the range of available subject positions (unlesbian, genderqueer, and so on) effectively complicates earlier practices infused by the politics of identity — nonetheless, the impulse to classify goes unchallenged. Queer genealogists have exposed sexual subjectivities as fluid, ruptured, and indeterminate, but stepping outside some of the conceptual traps of an "old-style" lesbian and gay framework also entails problematizing the relational logic of similitude and alterity, normative and deviant.[33] Analytical dependence on oppositional relationalities is, of course, a legacy of sexology; as women's studies scholar Jennifer Terry elucidates, our protocols are derived from "taxonomies" that reduced "human diversity" to groups.[34] Despite good queer critiques of the sexological apparatus, far less attention has been paid to events or individuals resistant to this way of knowing—the system of classification itself.[35]

In this chapter I survey several of the responses of onlookers to wartime reconfigurations of gender. Uniformed women, remember, formed only a part of a larger female workforce mobilized for the war effort, and it would be unwise to generalize about all women war workers.[36] Furthermore, I will leave it to others to consider the uniformed female war worker as a statistical fact; my interest is in how she registered in public culture through the eyes of journalists, cartoonists, and photographers. I should also point out that this chapter does not mark my first foray into the subject of the uniformed woman of the First World War. Elsewhere I have examined flamboyant appropriations of the uniform in relation to women's attempts to gain the power of the law as policewomen, alongside the case of the masquerader Colonel Barker.[37] I return to this terrain to pursue a different set of historiographical questions because I believe there is no better site, in the context of modern Britain, to observe the cultural effects of gender reformulations regarded— then and now—as unprecedented. Others might argue that the extraordinary conditions of war skew our ability to differentiate between aberrant momentary shifts and permanent transformation. Any historically situated reading of gender and sexuality during the war will likely continue to haunt debates concerning the degree and extent of social and cultural change. As I have already indicated, the overexposure of uniformed women in the press seems to have greatly exceeded their actual numbers in service at home and near the zones of conflict, providing historians with a rich terrain in which to scrutinize permutations in the gender system. This chapter further calls attention to the ways historians of sexuality attempt to illuminate through categorization what in human experience is disordered, mutable, incoherent, and indeterminate. Ironically, our theoretical models have been most successful when they have been most determinate, that is, when we spot gendered and sexual subjects who most closely approximate our modern categories, however we choose to name them. Nevertheless, these investigatory habits sometimes let us down when those subjects fail to conform to our preconceptions and expectations. Negotiating the past in relation to gender and sexuality forces us to raise our tolerance for conceptual messiness as we engage in the pleasures of conjecturing about what may in the end prove unknowable and irresolvable.

A Race of Young Amazons

A tangible sign that the nation was engaged in total war was its transformation in becoming a "world of women — women in uniform."[38] This new state of affairs meant the British public had many opportunities to become acquainted with a new type of woman whose patriotism was marked on her body and in her clothing, actions, and manner. The tabloids frequently called such women Amazons, in reference to a mythical tribe of female warriors who for centuries have been associated with masculinity (in their virility, power, aggression, and military skills) as well as sexual aberration (in their ability to control sexual access and abstinence in their relations with men). With 1970s radical lesbian-feminists appropriating the term Amazon, it is not surprising that scholars looking at women represented as Amazons during the First World War sometimes conflate the categories of gender variance and sexual inversion, categories with overlapping meanings even in the sexological literature.[39] According to Vicinus, "gender inversion" in the late nineteenth and early twentieth centuries "continued as the major visible sign of lesbian desire" for "some number of social commentators, political and sexual activists, and sexologists."[40] Beyond the narrow circles of the educated elite, it is unclear if most ordinary citizens thought about the so-called amazonian woman as somehow unnatural or perverse.

As I mentioned in the introduction, scholars sometimes point to the publication dates of key works of sexology or examples of literary texts as evidence of a broad public understanding of the masculine woman as sexual invert, a type sufficiently legible to fuel anxieties we now term homophobic. A novel cited as illustrative of the existence of a wider reading public in the know about the gendering of female homosexuality is Rose Allatini's *Despised and Rejected* (1918).[41] A close reading of the novel indicates that Allatini accepted the theories of Edward Carpenter, whose concept of an "intermediate sex" (termed Uranians) understood sexuality and gender as intertwined. It is unlikely that a book almost immediately banned under the Defence of the Realm Act (DORA) for its pacifist sympathies would have been influential in shaping public opinion.[42] Also cited are allusions to female sexual perversity in the 1918 "cult of the clitoris" case, but the exotic and feminine appearance of the dancer Maud Allan problematizes rather than confirms possible associations between female masculinity and sexual inversion.[43] Just as accusations of sexual perversion seemed "dim" or "hazy," to cite the socialite Diana Manners's impression of what many people gleaned from the claims swirling around the courtroom during the Allan trial, so too is the possibility of any secure link between the masculine woman and the modern lesbian.[44] That there was no degree of association between the two can be neither affirmed nor denied; therefore, before the gradual consolidation around issues of sexuality in the postwar era, we can only adduce that coherence was elusive and notions of inversion, variance, or deviance in the realms of gender and sexuality were far more fluid and elastic than we have hitherto imagined. With social commentators such as Alec-Tweedie advancing the extravagant claim that in wartime Britain "every woman is a man," and with women stretching configurations of gender on an unprecedented scale, there are few better opportunities to dissect the categorization problem. Read as a kind of syllogism, we might infer that every woman is therefore a soldier — or, to put it less literally, every woman is doing her bit for the country; yet the statement could also be taken in other ways.[45]

On one level, the claim speaks to the general upheaval in British national life during the Great War. In response to the rapid changes in living and working conditions at home and in the war zones, both women and men had become something other than their prewar selves. In *Ladies' Field* Dr. Robertson Wallace writes admiringly of the war's dramatic effects on women: "The shock of war . . . electrified our lady of the shattered nerves, and made a woman . . . of her. . . . Woman has now put her nerves on a war footing. . . . Woman has a part to play in war, and she plays it nobly."[46] As gender historians have amply documented, beginning in the autumn of 1914, significant numbers of women gradually undertook employment that redefined the boundaries of class and gender, some filling the places left vacant by men who had enlisted to serve in the Great War.[47] As a result, women found themselves a topic of endless fascination in the national press and public debate, and the more unusual the job the greater the interest, as conveyed in a poem by Nina Macdonald:

> Girls are doing things
> They've never done before,
> Go as 'bus conductors,
> Drive a car or van,
> All the world is topsy-turvy
> Since the War began.[48]

Historians urge caution in accepting government figures, but the *Report from the War Cabinet Committee on Women in Industry* (1918) conjectured that approximately 7,310,500 women were doing some form of paid labor in industry, commerce, agriculture, transport, and national and local government, an increase of 23 percent over the total estimated four years earlier.[49] In addition to waged employment, women from more privileged backgrounds volunteered for organizations like the Red Cross or the Voluntary Aid Detachment (VAD) and accepted assignments at home or abroad. Some 60,000 women are estimated to have served in the armed forces or the Women's Land Army, and of these, perhaps as many as 25,000 worked near the Western Front.[50] Although the war drove a wedge through the women's suffrage movement, many supporters of the cause regarded the mobilization of female labor as a way to live feminism rather than just talk about it; as one leading supporter proclaimed, "War compels women to work. That is one of its merits."[51] We might therefore understand modern Britain at war as an exemplary site in exposing the cultural meanings of "man" and "woman" as paradoxical: "at once empty and overflowing categories."[52]

We no sooner refer to the stretching of the boundaries of class and gender than we stabilize categories that are useful only insofar as lived experience can be broadly generalized — and the gender system will never be as stable as our historical investigation requires. Historian Gail Braybon has accused scholars who write on the First World War and gender of bandying "about in a cavalier manner . . . terms [which] are loaded with existing meaning," a problem that can be redressed by turning to the queer theorist Judith Butler, who writes that

> gender is the apparatus by which the production and normalization of masculine and feminine take place along with the interstitial forms of hormonal, chromosomal, psychic, and performative that gender assumes. To assume that gender always and exclusively means the matrix of the "masculine" and "feminine" is precisely to miss the critical point that the production of that coherent binary is contingent, that it comes at a cost, and that those permutations of gender which do not fit the binary are as much a part of gender as its most normative instance. To conflate the definition of gender with its normative expression is inadvertently to reconsolidate the power of the norm to constrain the definition of gender.[53]

What becomes apparent in this examination of the uniformed woman is the considerable elasticity of so-called normalization. It is commonplace in historical work on gender and the First World War to characterize women's greater opportunities for employment or service as liberating in transcending "the more profound constraints imposed by traditional sex roles."[54] But nearly a century on, assessing the cultural significance of the range of permutations against a presumed norm has proved more difficult, owing to the greater pliancy in the physical embodiment of gender expression resulting from the temporary exigencies of war.

Recent queer historical work poses new challenges to analytical practices that have relied on the categories of gender and sexuality as polarized and fixed when — like all categories — these systems are actually always in flux and subject to any number of contradictory "alternative, denied, or suppressed definitions."[55] For example, at the Western Front, mothering could be performed by upper-class male officers who tended their men or by men of the lower ranks who attended to the needs of women ambulance drivers, as evinced by two FANYs who describe how their guide, "as naturally as a mother, took over our comfort and happiness under his personal care."[56] The recognition that domestic care — keeping the men or female drivers "warm, dry, clean, and well-fed" — was essential to morale and emotional survival problematizes the dominant paradigm of spatial configurations in First World War studies because, if there was always a "home front" in the trenches, the division between the two spheres so often characterized as "severe and uncompromising" was actually less rigid.[57] Understanding gender difference and cultural change (as registered, for instance, in shifting modes of employment or expanding forms of sartorial expression) invariably pivots around supposed norms, traditions, or conventions that lend a false coherence and stability to lived experience, for it is the nature of the category to fix, naturalize, and stabilize what is in fact "crafted in time" and therefore contingent.[58]

In Alec-Tweedie's "New Britain," the "world had discovered women," by which she meant that Britons, as a consequence of the war, had discovered the rapid expansion of social and cultural constructions of the gendered category of "woman."[59] On any given day, she elaborated, men bound for the army, on arriving at a railway station, might encounter a "blue-uniformed woman" who would ask to see their tickets, a female "railway porter" in "badges and belts" who would show them the way to the platform, and "brawny women" who would take care of any luggage. Had these men traveled by tram or bus to the station, their tickets would have been punched by female conductors, and their fellow passengers would have included "khaki-clad girls on business bent, or splendid, silver-buttoned policewomen" (fig. 1). If any of the male passengers had gazed out the window on their journey through the

Figure 1. Woman bus conductor, ca. 1916–19. Photographer unknown. © Transport for London Collection of London Transport Museum 2001/56599.

British Advance near Evesham

The above armed Amazons are not Hun-killers but weed-killers, marching out of Evesham to attack the farmers' enemy, which has taken advantage of the men's absence to overrun the land. Below is a group of "Blue Angels," as Tommy has nicknamed the ladies in sky-blue overalls who minister to his necessities, in the Soldiers' free Buffet at Euston, from six in the morning to midnight, catering for a thousand clients every day.

Figure 2. Amazons are not Hun-killers. © The British Library Board *War Budget,* July 13, 1916, 278 (LON 664).

countryside, they might have seen women "harvesting, fruit-picking, turnip-hoeing, plowing with great traction motors, cutting trees, milking cows, driving cattle to market" (fig. 2). What disturbs the equanimity of Alec-Tweedie's imaginary "traveling male" is less this panorama of an all-female workforce ("doing what, before the war, was essentially 'a man's job'") than the worry that happy, productive, and efficient female workers might displace men forever, as he explains with dismay: "Ye Gods! . . . the women have eliminated us. We shall soon be as extinct as the dodo."[60]

On another level, Alec-Tweedie's sense of topsy-turvydom in her anatomy of the nation could refer less to the expansion or stretching of gender boundaries than to the disturbing havoc the war (and the work of war) wreaked on the legibility of gender itself. The First World War had been transformative for women as well as men, changing "everything and everybody," possibly signaling permanent rupture. According to her formulation, male warriors, in defense of their nation, were learning that good soldiering entailed new forms of hypermasculinity (or, alternatively, that bad soldiering entailed the very opposite in the form of shell shock). Women, on the other hand, veered to the extremes, either the ultrafeminine (or patriotic maternal)[61] or the masculine, as they "found themselves" in possession of the necessary skills, talents, strengths, and abilities to perform men's jobs, thus revealing how, like sexuality, gender too is "an open mesh of possibilities."[62] While the press regularly raised questions concerning the long-term repercussions of these new gender expressions, the female war worker was often cast as heroic or self-sacrificing: "Nearly everything that has been written on the subject of women's fitness for doing the ordinary everyday work of men, has been written by men inspired by admiration of their courage and resourcefulness."[63] At the height of the war, the uniformed woman more often denoted "pluck and resource," as is evident in a report on the FANYs that appeared in the *War Budget* (1916): "No wonder the Tommies are proud of [them]. They have shown themselves to be brave, bright, and indomitable."[64] For these daughters of the "New Woman," the war was in effect a "crucible" where the "dross was purged away, and the pure gold of New Womanhood emerged."[65]

Finally, and most provocatively, to read Alec-Tweedie's proposition more literally and explore further how bold and unsettling reconfigurations in the cultural understandings of sex and gender emerged in the tumult of war, we confront some intriguing and as yet unanswered questions about the nature of the manhood or masculinity of what might be termed the "woman-man" implicit in this version of gender transformation. First, it is worth considering whether historians have tended to scrutinize the cultural implications for women of the loss of femininity rather than the implications of acquiring masculinity (or conveying it to others). Women, for instance, were sometimes regarded variously as manlike, mannish, or masculine, yet haziness descends in attempts to articulate incisively what kind of "man" these women became as a result of new freedoms in the movement of their bodies, the labor those bodies performed, and the way those bodies were represented to the reading public.

For this reason, gender crossing may be less helpful in understanding public perceptions of the uniformed woman than gender stretching, because the former secures fixity, as if the gendered subject travels from one coherent category to another to achieve a final destination. Also troubling is how the female as masculine primarily foregrounds how femininity was stretched, as if masculinity, once associated with the female body, was subsequently fixed in ways that lack differentiation. Alec-Tweedie's view that such trans-

Figure 3. *Punch*, November 1, 1916. © *Punch* Ltd. The Eternal Feminine. *Railway Amazon.* "Excuse me, Mam, but is my box on straight?"

formations were happening to all women (and to all men) misconstrues how gender operates in relation to the cultural expectations of other regimes of power, so that we need to exercise caution around any universalizing claim on behalf of "every woman." This problem has not been helped by our preoccupation with a sex/gender distinction that has made it difficult to construct a "concrete, situated, and materialist understanding of the body."[66] Alec-Tweedie's remarkable proposition suggests how the jarring concept of woman as temporary man exposes the limitations of analytical frameworks that overlook differences within masculinities. In tackling masculine jobs, many women were not self-consciously perfecting their performance of masculinity; their interest concerned how they, in their female bodies, could get the jobs done — jobs previously reserved for men (fig. 3).[67] In fact, some newspapers feminized (and reclassed) work originally done by men, such as ambulance driving: "The work is hard . . . but it is women's work, noble in character, and of immense importance to the empire."[68]

A second line of enquiry calls for further speculation on the variations and differences of the performance of "masculinity" by certain women and thereby complicates the operation of systems of sex and gender with reference to other categories, especially nation and class. To some observers, the emancipated "new New Woman" (associated in the popular imagination with the social elite) represented the quintessence of class-specific Englishness, simultaneously "eccentric . . . interesting . . . [and] mannish."[69] These women—"intelligent, highly educated [and] remarkably indifferent to the opinion of the outside world"—enrolled in the FANYs, VADs, and other organizations to make "Tommy's life in a foreign land agreeable."[70] The English upper-class woman (hat "pulled well over her ears" and dressed in a "thick, short grey woolen skirt, long cigarette invariably drooped from the corner of her pretty, but determined mouth" and walking "with a swinging, athletic stride") was a recognizable type and almost a regular feature subjected to gentle ridicule in the pages of *Punch*, the magazine credited with "knowing England."[71]

One 1917 cartoon captioned "After the War: The War-Work Habit" envisions a postwar society that continues to be run by strident and striding women, whose breeding has accustomed them to assuming authority and issuing orders to men beneath them in class position but whose wartime experiences have emboldened them still further to seize control of difficult situations with crisp military precision (fig. 4). Such women are reminiscent of an encounter by one "mere male member of the *Daily Graphic* staff" who, on visiting a FANY camp in 1909, "found himself in the presence of a busy band of aristocratic amazons in arms [in] picturesque uniforms"—the spectacle, in other words, was hardly disconcerting.[72]

Physically energetic, resourceful in problem solving, and knowledgeable about all things mechanical, this sporty breed of action women in their sensible clothing is depicted in *Punch* as exuding brazen self-assurance in repairing a mechanical breakdown or handling tools. This futuristic vision of postwar Britain spotlights female war workers as cultural oddities because, in peacetime, they have not broken the "war-work habit" and perform their tasks, routine and exceptional, with an excess of zeal and alacrity peculiar to their class and upbringing.[73] Cultural anxieties about the war-work habit intensified after the war, as seen in the comments of barrister Sir Ellis Hume-Williams in a 1922 divorce trial:

LADY GREEN-PARKER (LATE PLATOON-COMMANDER IN A WOMAN'S VOLUNTEER CORPS) STARTS HER GARDENERS AT WORK FOR THE DAY.

MRS. BROMPTON RHODES (WHO HAS BEEN WORKING ON THE LAND) FINDS IT IMPOSSIBLE TO ARRANGE THE FLOWERS ON HER DINING-TABLE WITHOUT DONNING HER SMOCK AND CORDUROYS.

LADY ALBERT HALL (FORMERLY A RED-CROSS AMBULANCE DRIVER) DEALS WITH A BREAK-DOWN OF HER CAR IN BOND STREET.

THE HON. MRS. KENSINGTON GORE (ONCE A MUNITION-WORKER) IS INFORMED THAT SOMETHING IS WRONG WITH THE TAP OF HER SCULLERY SINK.

Figure 4. *Punch's Almanack for 1917.* © *Punch* Ltd. After the War: The War-Work Habit.

The war had produced in women effects which would undoubtedly have astonished, and perhaps would have shocked, our ancestors. Women had done men's work during the war; they dressed like men and were working in conditions in which sex was subordinated and forgotten. That had had a profound effect on their manners. . . . No woman who had lived that kind of life during the war could entirely shed it when she came out of it.[74]

Newspapers such as the *Sheffield Daily Telegraph* urged women "to shed their army manners with the military uniforms," something the women in the *Punch* cartoon clearly fail to do.[75]

The ideological work of this cartoon highlights the curious inconsistencies of the class consequences of this strange breed of amazonian women who in two instances brush aside their servants rather than stand by helpless and passive. Thinking about these four women as either classed or gendered misses the complexity of the censure, since "a sexed human being (man or woman) is *more* than sex and gender . . . race, age, class, sexual orientation, nationality, and idiosyncratic experience are other categories that always shape the experience of being one sex or the other."[76] Working with Simone de Beauvoir's understanding of the "body" as "a situation," literary critic Toril Moi observes that "the meaning of a woman's body is bound up with the way she uses her freedom . . . [which is] not absolute, but situated."[77] In this notion of the situatedness of the body, we find another way to read this *Punch* cartoon to discover what kind of man these women became. On view are four examples of women from privileged class backgrounds performing jobs with particular gendered and classed associations — a full-page spread that conveys equally and succinctly the gains in situating the body in relation to, in this case, the London elite and the "idiosyncratic experience" gained as a result of war service.[78]

Crucially, the *Punch* cartoon produces a social critique of a favorite target: the upper-class woman, whose economic independence has enabled her to step outside bourgeois conventions; hence the assignment of names that zero in on an area of roughly one square mile associated with affluence and privilege (Green Park, Brompton Road, Albert Hall, and Kensington Gore). On the upper left, it is clear that life on a country estate goes topsy-turvy when Lady Green-Parker — a "late platoon-commander" in an unnamed "woman's volunteer corps" — issues marching orders to a hapless ragtag army of shuffling farm laborers, bearing "weapons" more suitable for gardening than military deployment. Here the cartoonist pokes fun at the highborn lady who imposes military discipline on her unsuspecting gardening staff (an elderly gentleman performing a similar role would be an instantly recognizable type); as the lady of the manor, Lady Green-Parker is entitled to exercise power over her male underlings regardless of the strictures of gender. Misunderstanding the correct time and place for a military parade and displaying a brisk, unladylike gait, she maintains her class privileges so that her well-cut, feminine uniform renders her antics harmless fun rather than a cultural threat. With the outbreak of war the legibility of class distinctions through clothing was simultaneously destabilized and reinscribed by the uniformity of the uniform, and here we see how the uniform works to redefine gender while reinscribing class. In contrast to Lady Green-Parker's slender womanliness, the practically dressed Mrs. Brompton Rhodes (once a land girl) registers differently as a gendered subject, though her task of overseeing the flower arranging would have been common to women of her background. On view is a woman whose ability to fulfill the cultural expectations of her upper-class status is undermined by the incongruity of her clothing and stance. Unlike Lady Green-Parker, Mrs. Brompton Rhodes interacts with her butler in a class-appropriate way, but her wartime habit of dressing in a sacklike smock and breeches (the outfit of the land girl) encourages the wrong posture. In other words, while she is correctly situated in terms of class, her violations of gender do not convey a reassuring performance of upper-class domesticity.

The more serious transgressions of the two women in the lower half of the layout relate to class. Lady Albert Hall (a onetime Red Cross ambulance driver in the war) has failed to reconcile herself with a postwar world in which women, once again, rely on men, so she pushes her chauffeur aside to deal with a breakdown herself, betraying the conventions of class by becoming not a gentleman who takes pleasure in operating his own motor vehicle, but a servant who deals with repairs and routine maintenance.[79] During the war a specialist knowledge of auto mechanics constituted a rite of passage in transforming a "little girl" into a "woman," capable of handling "mechanics, breakdowns, car-washing, engine-cleaning, tire-mending and general repairs."[80] Another article, from 1915, details the mechanical skills required by women military drivers in exceptionally active and robust terms: "The dismantling of an engine, the grinding-in of the valves, the removal of the wheels, the manipulation of tires, and minor repairs of all kinds, including soldering, vulcanizing, screw-cutting, the use of the hack-saw, and brazing."[81] Surely there were keen male automobilists of the upper classes who relished these dirty jobs, but their mechanical knowledge was more a hobby than a prerequisite for service in France, and therefore not an attempt by an aristocrat to take up a working-class occupation. Lady Albert Hall offers passers-by on Bond Street an opportunity to admire askance both her brilliant mechanical expertise and her well-rounded posterior.

Finally, we see perhaps the most interesting cartoon of all, as the Hon. Mrs. Kensington Gore (a former munitions worker) demonstrates an aptitude for all things mechanical by attempting to repair the scullery tap. Like the factory where she presumably assembled munitions, the kitchen is not a domain most upper-class women would have been acquainted with — "something is wrong," and it is obviously more than the tap. Unlike the three previous ladies, who at least had a tenuous claim to occupying a class-appropriate social space (the country house garden, the dining room of a great house, and an upmarket shopping district), Mrs. Kensington Gore bursts into an area of the house off limits even to some servants. Here the disconcerting sight of a woman in highly feminine attire performing a job that requires brawn and wielding all manner of tools points to an unwelcome by-product of war. It is no surprise that *Punch* regards women's "war-work habit" as one to be avoided; yet for this cartoonist, gender is more the veneer and class is the substance. The greater anxiety concerning the unpleasant habits such women have picked up relates to an "interesting tendency on the part of gentlewomen to take up various forms of domestic service."[82] These women have in no clear sense become men because, despite manifestations of "attributes" that "confirm the power and prestige of men" ("physical strength and practical competence," "calculative rationality and technical expertise"), their performance of hegemonic masculinity misses entirely its "central structuring principle," that is, "power over women."[83] These women have instead become something else, their imperfections an amusing light entertainment. Sometimes seen as behaving like men, female war workers were neither becoming men nor becoming like men (or masculine) — rather, they were becoming another sort of woman, creatures whose newness defied legibility. Shifting attention away from the inescapable binaries embedded in the concept of female masculinity toward a notion of the body as a "situation" (which, arguably, the dissonant phrase female masculinity signals) clarifies the specific and intersecting ways gendered, classed, and sexualized bodies experienced — and were represented as experiencing — new bodily and cultural freedoms. If women were actively redefining themselves through their war-work habits,

Figure 5. *Punch*, May 29, 1918. © *Punch* Ltd. *First Officer (in spasm of jealousy).* "Who's the knock-kneed chap with your sister, old man?" *Second Officer.* "My other sister."

they were becoming nothing like any particularized or culturally differentiated man.

Useful insights into the complexities of reading the uniformed body at this specific historical moment can also be found in another *Punch* drawing of 1918, which depicts two upper-class male officers observing two other figures in the distance (fig. 5). Although the men loom prominently in the foreground, the cartoon's real interest lies in the couple hovering in the background, one in a skirt (thus obviously female) and the other in jodhpurs (sex indeterminate without the caption). In response to the first officer's question: "Who's the knock-kneed chap with your sister, old man?" the bemused second officer retorts: "My other sister." Any temptation on our part to read the officer's query as an expression of sexual interest in the "knock-kneed chap" evaporates with the caption's parenthetical phrase "in spasm of jealousy," though, with "gross indecency" between men punishable under the law, it is highly unlikely that an instance of homoerotic desire would appear in a mainstream publication.[84] The second officer's speedy clarification of the indeterminate figure's biological sex is a relief to the first officer, who learns that he has no male rival in his pursuit of the woman in the skirt. That the mystery pair's relationship is sororal rather than amorous ends speculation about possible romantic entanglement, but fixing the biological sex of the apparently "cross-dressed" woman leaves other questions about gender and sexuality unresolved.

The drawing's representation of the uniformed woman invites our recognition of an act of *mis*recognition, but even when the figure's sex is revealed, the cultural significance of female mannishness cannot be reduced to a single effect and relies on available interpretive strategies, both then and now. Here, as at other moments in history, female mannishness might refer to one or several attributes, including, as Vicinus points out, "an estimable power of reasoning, or remarkable learning and knowledge, or an assertive patriotism in defense of one's country, or a dangerous aggressiveness in defying male privilege, or a too-overt interest in pursuing women as erotic objects."[85] In contrast to the men, who stroll through the garden seemingly with time on their hands, the two sisters, utterly unaware of being observed, are preoccupied with their serious, businesslike conversation; one points to the building in the background, and the other looks down at her papers. The last laugh in the cartoon is more at the expense of the perplexed male perceiver who has jumped to the wrong conclusion than of the perceived, who herself is not directly subject to censure or ridicule, despite the slighting reference to her knock-kneed stance by a male fearful of competition. Of course, were not some women in uniform at this time occasionally mistaken for men, *Punch* would hardly have been interested: the cartoon thus acknowledges the oddness in the temporary confusion over gender to convey the more comforting message that, left alone to go about their work, these uniformed sisters — female patriots obviously serving their country — pose no social threat.

We Became Soldiers from That Hour

To map in close historical detail the lives and experiences of actual women in uniform, I turn to ambulance drivers who served on or near the Western Front, not because their jobs in the war zones were more thrilling, glamorous, or dangerous than other forms of service (though this was a view often advanced in the popular press and by some of the women themselves) or because of the often assumed link between lesbianism and ambulance driving (though women famously associated with flamboyant lesbianism — Gertrude Stein, Dolly Wilde, and Joe Carstairs, for instance — drove, or were purported to have driven, ambulances near the front lines),[86] but because the labor is curiously unique in requiring physical strength, an aptitude for mechanical work, excellent driving skills, rudimentary nursing skills, and gentle attentiveness in carrying the wounded on stretchers. Unlike nursing, a profession regarded as almost instinctive to women, ambulance driving called for a new kind of modern woman whose exceptional traits and virtues, personal qualities, and mental and physical abilities had, before the war, been culturally located in men.[87] One driver warned potential recruits that they should not expect an adventure, for women had to endure "an extremely Spartan mode of living. . . . Therefore, it will be readily understood that the butterfly woman is absolutely out of her element. . . . The more solid and responsible woman, with plenty of grit and pluck, is the only type who is likely to 'stick it out.'"[88] Such delineations point to the elasticity of the category of woman and to its range of differentiation. Again, in contrast to nursing, the ambulance driver's job "to prepare and carry a stretcher" was not one in which many women would "find themselves immediately at home," for it required the stamina to "stand the work, for driving continuously in good and bad weather alike, cranking up, washing a car, fitting tires" (fig. 6).[89] Good nursing, on the other hand, called for different skills, as shown in this 1915 drawing from the *Ladies' Field* (fig. 7), in which the men are in charge of the physical conveyance of the wounded and the professional female nurse calmly dresses the wounds. One writer for the *Daily Mail* recognized that "not every able-bodied young woman is fitted to be a nurse. . . . [They] see that the particular type of drudgery required in a hospital is, for them, not the way. There have always been some women who could do . . . exceptional work requiring physical strength, steady nerves, and endurance."[90] These requirements were not the exception but the rule for any woman wishing "to drive an ambulance in France," which, according to Gladys de Havilland in *The Woman's Motor Manual* (1918), was the "chief ambition of the majority of women motorists."[91] Ambulance drivers were seen as a specimen apart from their compassionate nursing sisters, and potential recruits needed to demonstrate that they were sufficiently physically developed or hardened for strenuous work (fig. 8); such women were seen as "breaking the conventions with a vengeance," and the payoff for "their pluck and push" was that they could readily enter "every door of opportunity opened to them."[92]

Ambulance driving — in some respects, the female equivalent to flying — thus attracted a certain type of outgoing, risk-taking woman, as is evident in photographs that convey something of their allure, their tendency to swagger, their camaraderie (figs. 9 and 10).[93] F. Tennyson Jesse, a journalist writ-

Figure 6. FANYs carrying wounded Belgian soldier. © The British Library Board *War Budget*, January 16, 1915, 291 (LON 477).

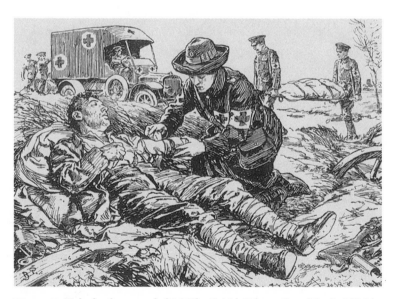

Figure 7. Help for the wounded!! © The British Library Board *Ladies' Field*, January 23, 1915, 350 (LON 194).

Figure 8. Snapshot of Nurse Dewar and FANY ambulance driver Bobby Bail-
lie, 1916. From the photograph album in the Grace McDougall collection
held by the Imperial War Museum, with permission of Desmond McDougall.

ing for *Vogue* who visited a FANY camp in France in the early months of
1918, echoed this sentiment when she exclaimed that the uniforms left the
women looking "like splendid young airmen," an elite form of masculinity.[94]
Jesse believed such dashing outfits lent the women of the ambulance corps
an attractive air of raffish manliness, as the group posed formally for a photographer in their khaki breeches, berets, heavy fur coats, and boots, a mode
of self-presentation not unsettling but highly practical, given the conditions,
and perhaps even vaguely seductive.[95]

Such panache was also noted by a French soldier: "'C'est chic, les
Anglaises.' . . . The admiration of the French trooper for the amazon-like
achievement of these Englishwomen knows no bounds. . . . Les Anglaises
are heroic," sentiments emblematized in a full-length portrait of the FANY
driver Muriel Thompson, whose courage under shell fire earned her the Order of Leopold II (fig. 11).[96] Class privilege too contributed to their glamour,
as the photographer Olive Edis comments in 1919: FANYs are "a very jolly
type of good-class English girl . . . some of a decidedly sporting and masculine stamp — but so fresh and healthy and attractive."[97]

This heady spectacle of masculine clothing on the female body, in tandem with a masculine demeanor, was likewise shrewdly noted by the nov-

Figure 9. A VAD about to start out with her motor ambulance, Etaples, June 27, 1917. Imperial War Museum (Q2439).

Figure 10. First Aid Nursing Yeomanry, Calais, January 1917. Imperial War Museum (Q4669).

Figure 11. Miss Muriel Thompson. ©The British Library Board *War Budget*, April 24, 1915, 291 (LON 477).

elist May Sinclair, who disclosed her own shock and awe in watching the ambulance driver Mairi Chisholm stroll "about the seat of War with her hands in her pockets, as if a battle were a cricket match . . . and yet there isn't a man in the Corps who does his work better or with more courage and endurance than this 18 year old child" (fig. 12).[98] Sinclair's conflicted response in finding Chisholm's boyishness at once charming and appalling indicates the availability of multiple readings of such women. Neither Sinclair nor the sophisticated journalist seems self-conscious about expressing intense, sometimes romantic, feelings toward these women as they go about their grim

Figure 12. Mairi Chisholm with Belgian officer, Pervyse, September 9, 1917. Imperial War Museum (Q2970).

work. Even when Jesse's reactions toward the FANYs border on the erotic, she locates her frisson as a response to the women's freedom from the social pressures of performing femininity:

> It is a sort of splendid austerity, that pervades their look and outlook . . . and in their bodies expresses itself in a disregard for appearances that one would never have thought to find in a human woman. It leaves you gasping. They come in, wind-blown, reddened, hot with exertion . . . they come in, toss their caps down, brush their hair back from their brow in the one gesture that no woman has ever permitted herself or liked in a lover — and they don't mind. It is amazing, that disregard for appearances.[99]

In a society magazine dedicated to fostering women's keen interest in cosmetics and up-to-date fashion, Jesse envies women who redefine femininity and openly admits that she is fascinated with the female drivers' insouciance about their appearance. Back home such neglect would be unthinkable, but the Western Front offers women a "blessed freedom," for this "is what it is to be as free as a man" (reinforcing, of course, a popular stereotype of the male as exempt from the pleasures of preening).[100]

Full of admiration for the women's youthful magnetism and their apparent coolness in the face of danger, Jesse notes that the drivers "were not pretty"—feminine, in other words—but she still swoons with pleasure, declaring the experience "all wonderful": "They made me feel, in the beautiful way they shepherded me, that I was a silly useless female, and that they were grave chivalrous young men; they watched over me with just that matter-of-fact care."[101] Jesse's invocation of the codes of chivalry suggests that the female ambulance driver's masculinity was gentlemanly, by exhibiting the noble virtue of protecting the weak, in this instance, a "silly useless female." She thinks less of how she has placed herself close to the same treacherous zones of conflict as the manly women she so admires. Although partaking in their soldierly courage, albeit for the duration of her short visit, Jesse distinguishes between her own gender stretching in undertaking a hazardous assignment near the front lines and that of the ambulance drivers engaged in lifting men onto stretchers and into waiting motor ambulances before speeding off to field hospitals or ambulance trains. This disconnect points to further permutations of gender performativity—and all this without a whisper that the women's breathtaking masculinity might also be perverse: "And I stood and listened and watched them, and I received an impression of extraordinary beauty."[102]

We will never know if Jesse understood her feelings toward the drivers as erotic, but she obviously is transported to a vaguely defined higher plane of transcendent, spiritual exaltation—such women "were touched with something finer, some quality of radiance."[103] This same quasi-religious language is also used by a FANY who delights in how the sight of women in their "manly Yeomanry uniform" was "a never-failing source of wonderment . . . [filling] the French inhabitants . . . with awe and admiration."[104] Similarly, soldiers reportedly used "madonna" and "angels of light and healing" to refer to the two women who collectively came to be known in the popular press as the "heroines of Pervyse," the Baroness de T'Serclaes (formerly Mrs. Elsie Knocker, who was nicknamed "Gipsy") and Mairi Chisholm (fig. 13).[105]

This discourse of saintliness—radiance, wonderment, awe, madonna—seems inappropriate for women outfitted for the harsh working conditions

Figure 13. Baroness T'Serclaes and Miss Mairi Chisholm, Pervyse, September 9, 1917. Imperial War Museum (Q2969).

at the front.[106] Neither motherlike nor ministering angels (the familiar stereotypes of the nursing sister tending the wounded and the dying behind the lines), these women in their khaki uniforms, puttees, and high leather boots left onlookers floundering to classify the unclassifiable. Absent in these commentaries is any sense that it was somehow unnatural for strong women to dress as soldiers or to carry the bodies of weak or damaged men; as an American visitor commented in 1918, "The British woman had found herself and her muscles."[107] Only when watching men being loaded "like fragile and precious parcels" does Jesse convey her unease: "And suddenly it seemed to me there was something profoundly shocking about the sight of a man lying flat and *helpless*. . . . It was a thing wrong in essence . . . I got an odd feeling that there was something unnatural about the mere posture."[108] Here outrage is directed not toward the masculinizing effects of war on women but the unnaturalness of a war that emasculates men. That a female ambulance driver shifts the bodies of the injured and dying more adroitly than the male stretcher bearer escapes Jesse's observation, though others note that soldiers "invariably pay" the women "the compliment of saying [they] bump them less and treat them more gently than" their male counterparts.[109]

By the mid- to late 1920s the unusual work and life experience of female ambulance drivers would attract writers such as Hall, who idealizes and glorifies their deeds in *The Well of Loneliness* as well as in an important short story written two years earlier, "Miss Ogilvy Finds Herself," exposing the bleak postwar prospects of a demobilized driver.[110] During the 1928 obscenity trial of the novel, the presiding magistrate singled out as particularly disturbing an episode depicting sexual love between some women who served in France during the First World War: "According to the writer of this book, a number of women of position and admirable character, who were engaged in driving ambulances in the course of the war, were addicted to this vice."[111] For Hall, familiar with the sexological literature, the ranks of the ambulance corps contained many "less orthodox sisters" who, like the invert-protagonist Stephen Gordon, were handsome, manly women drawn to feminine women.[112] Ambulance driving required "a sound and fairly muscular physique"—one similar, in fact, to sexologist Stella Browne's 1918 description of a female "invert" (case E) "of the most pronounced physical type," who was overly fond of "driving" and whose body was "tall, stiff, [and] rather heavily muscular."[113] The clear identification within literary representation of certain "types" of women (unequivocally sexually inverted in the sense we now recognize as lesbian, transgendered, or queer) who donned mannish uniforms and joined their female comrades to drive ambulances near the fighting at the front was slowly becoming a more straightforward affair, though such clarity (or, from another perspective, a loss of ambiguity) was notably absent in the diaries or later recollections of the women who had become temporary "men" in the topsy-turvydom of war.[114] As Alec-Tweedie forcefully maintained, the world had discovered women, and thus the masculine woman in military uniform was, as later cultural critics might surmise, "not always reduced to being a misfit or a figure of abject loneliness."[115] Wartime commentators were more apt to see "this new and glorious creature, truly emancipated by the stern hand of war" as a sign of Britain's "rich symbolism of promise."[116]

Under the extraordinary conditions of war, women workers (uniformed women in particular) were sometimes seen as masculine or masculinized or sometimes regarded themselves as "like men." Yet—in all if not most cases—this was less seen as a predicament to be deplored than accepted as a necessary effect of war. Moreover, uniformed women, "whatever their motivations," may have been seen as "fundamentally disturbing to wartime definitions of both femininity and masculinity," but not in relation to a classificatory system stable and fixed—gender norms are always in flux, though the pace of change too fluctuates.[117] Far from branding women in the military services, in Gould's terms, as "peculiar at least, if not downright immoral," there was the expectation that when it was all over more familiar configurations of gender would be largely restored, since "women would always love home . . . nothing could destroy her matronly instinct."[118] Newspapers and magazines speculated regularly on how the war produced new gender configurations, but not always with agitation or alarm. For the sake of wartime expediency, practicality, and safety, women rejected what was euphemistically described as a "sensible mean": "[Women] indignantly decline to be the 'pretty darlings.' . . . [O]n the other hand, the mannish idea of the late Mrs. Bloomer and the epicene horror of the ill-dressed, short-haired, aggressive spinster are both out of favor. The young woman of today likes to look her best; but she likes also to be capable, active, and self-supporting."[119] The *Light Car* conjectured that military service would "open the eyes and educate the mechanical side of many a woman. . . . The arduous service required . . . will mean that on the return of normal times the lady driver will resort less often to the assistance of the garage hands."[120] Charting the tolerance levels shown toward displays of female masculinity reveals all manner of response between 1914 and 1918, from occasional opprobrium to astonished amazement, but in accounts of these same displays published after the war, the tenor gradually shifts. In recollections of mannish military or military-like women published in the immediate aftermath of the war and well into the 1930s, there is almost a collective amnesia that women had been granted so much latitude in stretching the boundaries of gender. With the quelling of hostilities and the return to a labor market that privileged male workers, some commentators seemed to awaken startled and anxious that what the war had wrought might prove irrevocable. The terrible results, some fretted, of allowing women to become temporarily like men might not be contained, and some broadsheets and popular magazines contained murmurs about the unwelcome dangers of a third sex. In the weeks before the Armistice, *The Times* reported: "There were some people who felt that one ill-effect of the war would be the development of a definite third sex, something neither man nor woman."[121] Of far greater concern were fears that women might not give up their jobs to demobbed soldiers. While some people queried, "What's going to happen to all these girls, how will they settle down?" the response was for the most part pragmatic; as one (male) commanding officer put it: "I don't think there'll be any trouble whether they [female ambulance drivers] marry or not. They will have had their adventure."[122]

Categorization Has Its Place

In 2008 historian Lucy Noakes, author of several extensively researched studies of gender in both world wars, scrutinized the British public's response to "the sexualization of female soldiers in First World War Britain," based on one of the broadest surveys of the print media to date.[123] Even though the materials unearthed by this scrupulous and respected social historian lead overwhelmingly to her recognition that such women were considered the "very visible symbols of national unity and a shared patriotism . . . [and that] the service that many uniformed women were carrying out was usually praised," her conclusion follows in the footsteps of Gould's article some twenty years earlier: "'Mannish' lesbians" took "advantage of the opportunities the war offered to dress and act as men and to live in a homosocial world."[124] She contends further, "There existed a *less explicit belief* that many women had been drawn to military service because they were attracted by the masculine nature of the work and uniforms."[125] Just as Gould believed the association of militarism and masculinity "*must have* affected . . . the public's view" of masculine women, so too does Noakes rehearse the familiar argument that such women were thought "abnormal," "freakish," and "unnatural" — concepts inherited from sexology, which posited these links.[126] If such women were "usually praised," how was it that they were also regarded as mannish lesbians? Despite an evidentiary base suggesting otherwise, readers are informed that such women were "legible only through inference": "While this was not made explicit in any of the journalism I have looked at it was at times implied"; "again, while this was not made explicit in the contemporary press"; and "while none of the articles cited here explicitly called these militarized, 'masculine' women lesbians."[127] In other words, there must have been a shared cultural understanding — albeit tacit — that particular traits signaled specific sexual proclivities because, Noakes avers, these well-known linkages had somehow permeated the national consciousness. This assertion can be documented and established as a "fact" only about a decade or so after the war, specifically in Hall's *The Well of Loneliness* (1928) and an often cited memoir by the Marchioness of Londonderry, *Retrospect* (1938) — texts that "made what was implicit in much wartime writing explicit."[128] I want to argue that in these debates about the circulation of knowledge, or the relative interconnectedness of gender and sexual deviance, much more is at stake than mere quibbles over the nature and interpretation of historical evidence. The epistemological crux of the matter is this: Historians such as Gould and Noakes, or literary critics such as Sandra M. Gilbert, Susan Gubar, and David Trotter, reach these conclusions because, as for most of us, taxonomies structure epistemology and sharply curtail the limits of historical imagination, even when those taxonomies mislead, don't work, or are completely false.[129] Noakes and others have been let down by a history of sexuality that assumes the cultural meaning of uniformed women based on a secure link with notions about sexuality that evolves in British society later in the interwar period. The more significant challenge for historians and historically minded critics is to figure out how to scrutinize taxonomy as a system and not allow its structuring habits to overdetermine our accounts of the past.

Even if the links sexologists posit between the categories of gender inversion and sexual inversion were firmly consolidated and well known by members of the legal and medical professions in the early decades of the twentieth century, and even if those links were known to a few of the better-informed members of the general public, the numbers of women taking on men's jobs, and the habits and clothing necessary to perform those jobs, would surely have thrown certainties into disarray. Scholarly persistence in linking the uniformed woman to deviant sexual practices is evidence itself of the resilience and power of systems of categorization. Some masculine or mannish women, historians argue, may have been lesbian, lesbianlike, sapphist, genderqueer, or any other category we have yet to articulate, but what invariably goes unchecked in these scholarly negotiations (however mindful we are of the dangers of misrecognition or of reading retrospectively) is that first impulse to classify. We are, after all, subject to — and subjects of — the habits of our own time, and why should we not now partake of the pleasures of speculating about the sexual nature of these intriguing women who reveled in the opportunity to expand the conventions or rules of gender? I see no problem with looking at photographs of dashing manly women serving in the Great War either to delight in imagining the antecedents of modern lesbian subjectivities or to contribute to the genealogical project of lesbian, gay, and queer history, as long as we understand how these interests shape our understanding of the past in particular ways. For example, in a recent study of "lesbianism and war in early twentieth-century Britain," scholar Deborah Cohler cites "wartime gendered possibilities for women" as crucial in "the production of modern lesbian subjectivity," a project deeply informed by the structure of categorization.[130] Here is a good example of history making more interested in finding "us," which is by no means a bad thing — the problem is that this approach is less adept at denaturalizing current categories or tolerating messiness and illegibility. This kind of work, and here I include my own earlier genealogical sorties into the sapphic twenties, has political purpose and meaning but yields few surprises, because historicizing and denaturalizing the categories is never simply a matter of tracing similarities or differences across time and place. It is a project ill equipped for examining beings who come into existence as the result of transitory conditions of war, with no equivalences and therefore untranslatable.

To read these women's lives in historically situated ways, it is necessary to understand the cultural work that categorization achieves (or fails to achieve). One member of the Women's Army Auxiliary Corps (WAAC) recollects that the women who stayed at home divided the women who served abroad into two categories: "heroic martyrs carrying on our work under continual shell fire or bombardment from the air" or "the lowest type of womanhood," keen to get to France "solely" to pursue "men and pleasure."[131] The truth of the matter, in her view, was both simpler and more complex: "In reality few of us came under either category. We were just ordinary people who had drifted into foreign service more by accident than by good management."[132]

The work of history is to expose categories as inadequate and inaccurate — "empty," as Joan Scott understands the term — "because even when they appear to be fixed, they still contain within them alternative, denied, or suppressed definitions."[133] In peering again at the May 1918 *Punch* cartoon (fig. 5), *we* see a paradigm of how *we* currently go about negotiating categorization in writing history impelled by categories of identity. Like the curious officer, *we* also tend to look at individuals and jump to our own conclusions. Too often these critical acts gloss over the specificity of time and place, collapsing myriad possibilities into a simple match of what appears to be the most relevant label or connection between labels, thus imposing onto a past gendered and sexual subject a narrow range of connotations.[134] The *Punch* cartoon makes it glaringly obvious what is missing in these visual transactions: with the women's backs toward the male onlookers as well as the viewer, none of us as viewers/voyeurs have a clue to what these sisters think about their own self-presentation or its impact on others. The cartoon reveals that during the First World War some women were momentarily mistaken for men, and it shows further that *we* cannot know, in many instances, if such women thought about the sexual implications of their temporary female masculinity or if others might have reached any conclusions about the sexuality of women who appeared at first to be men.

Our systems of taxonomizing promise (and appear to deliver) legibility, but as queer critics have pointed out for well over a decade, no single category can ever satisfactorily be made "to signify monolithically."[135] Yet no matter how grossly inadequate or unstable, categorization remains the all too familiar route through which sexuality is explored "as a conjunction of strategies for ordering social relations, authorizing specialized knowledges, licensing expert interventions, intensifying bodily sensations, normalizing erotic behaviors, multiplying sexual perversions, policing personal expressions, crystallizing political resistances, motivating introspective utterances, and constructing human subjectivities."[136]

Halperin, How to Do ...

In exposing how the fissures of the classificatory apparatus close down intellectual inquiry, the queer critique seeks the assiduous unlearning of habits and assumptions, whether the tendency to assume that categories of the past worked the same way as categories of the present or the inclination to allow categories to overrule historical evidence.[137] Imagining a history of sexuality, or a history of gender and war, without modern categories of sexual identity could seem injudicious or impractical: What, we might ask, would be the point of investigating gender and sexuality without the very categories that have made these fields of enquiry possible in the first place? Whether we risk abandoning outright our reliance on categories of identity (thus dismantling the genealogical project) or, as I discuss in the following chapter, we disturb current practices by opening up alternative approaches in the way we analyze the manifold expressions of genders and sexualities of the past, it is necessary to denaturalize not only individual taxonomies but the *inclination* to taxonomize as an epistemological project—an impulse itself historically contingent. Ironically, this scrutiny of cultural topsy-turvydom in the early twentieth century—the utter confusion over gender—points with some clarity to the possibilities of a queer critical historiography that takes into account how gender and sexuality are intertwined in order to understand categorization itself as historical and historicized.

4 / "We Cannot Use That Word"
On the Habits of Naming,
Name Calling, and Self-Naming

It's remarkable that something which is so evidently mutable and plastic as an "identity" should be periodically invoked and hunted as if it had the hard permanence of diamonds.

DENISE RILEY (2000)

On July 31, 1931, the Rev. Dr. F. W. Norwood and six members of a committee of private citizens met with the attorney general, Sir William Jowitt, in his rooms in the House of Commons to discuss "facts not hitherto known to the Government" about the 1918 case of the Hon. Violet Blanche Douglas-Pennant (fig. 14).[1] According to her fervent supporters, Douglas-Pennant had suffered a great injustice when dismissed in a manner "short, sharp, and sudden" from her post as leader of the newly formed Women's Royal Air Force (WRAF) (DM, 44). She was told then that she lacked the requisite organizational skills, but it would emerge years later that the air minister, Lord Weir, had acted swiftly in ousting her from the job because he accepted as true advice he had received confidentially from others—secret and false allegations made against her "moral character" (DM, 6). Led by the Labour MP William J. Brown, this group of the titled and pedigreed hoped to persuade His Majesty's government that a new hearing on the causes of Douglas-Pennant's dismissal was warranted, since recent "sworn declarations" would contradict the official position that no "imputations" had ever questioned her personal integrity (DM, 4). Throughout the private meeting Jowitt, a highly skilled lawyer known for handling difficult cases "with great delicacy," offered friendly and helpful legal guidance and appeared in no way hostile or obstructionist.[2] Even so, while noting the merits of the case, Jowitt expressed serious concerns that obstacles remained: it was "critical" to substantiate the claim that unfounded rumors about sex were

134

Figure 14. The Hon. Violet Douglas-Pennant, November 1921. Photograph by Elliott and Fry, reproduced in *Under the Searchlight: A Record of a Great Scandal* (London: George Allen and Unwin, 1922).

"the underlying cause of her [Douglas-Pennant's] summary and grossly ir-regular dismissal from her Corps contrary to every principle of justice" (DM, 4). After some minutes of listening patiently to their arguments, Jowitt finally rejected the group's fresh information as nothing more than "idle gossip" — "mere tittle-tattle of what somebody said to somebody else and somebody else told somebody else" (DM, 14, 36). According to Jowitt, what stood be-tween success and failure in their campaign to exonerate the former leader was "real evidence" that addressed a "perfectly categorical question": Did "Miss A or B" go to Weir and say, "This woman is a lesbian" (DM, 39, 38)?

In this chapter I argue that our interest in how this question might be answered has sometimes distracted us from the cultural significance of the question itself, which represents a distinctive feature of sexual modernity in the West in assuming as naturalized the attaching of a name to a practice or an identity. Thinking about Douglas-Pennant as a woman named — or as a woman who named herself — offers important insights into how the questioner thought the sexual could be understood and discussed in 1931. Equally fascinating are the discursive exchanges of this remarkable meeting in showing the operations of sexual knowledge as multiple epistemological systems — competing and colliding around the table in ways unnoticed by participants then and by historians of sexuality now. By the early 1930s some "men of the world" — and a few women too — were beginning to cultivate labeling habits similar to our own (DM, 14–15). The attorney general (a product of the elite public school Marlborough and of New College, Oxford, and a man with social connections to Bloomsbury) sought to clarify all the murky ambiguities behind the accusation with a single word — an inclination undoubtedly useful, but one the historian must regard with caution. This naming of sexual practices and identities, a product of the "scientific" origins of late nineteenth-century sexology, evolved gradually and erratically through the twentieth century, eventually transforming the messy business of human erotic life into the "perfectly categorical." Queer theory would, of course, later restore the messiness by unsettling the identity categories on which ancestral genealogy is based.[3] In this project's earliest stage I envisioned this chapter building on lesbian, gay, and queer historiography by examining the interrelated transactions of naming, name calling, and self-naming, as well as the refusal, lack of interest, or inability to name or self-name in relation to the sexual — a familiar line of inquiry in a field long interested in semantic shifts in the classification of sexualities across time and place.

The history of modern lesbianism — a sexual practice (unlike male homosexuality) seldom the concern of legal regulation in Britain — has often been organized in relation to the name, as seen in the titles of published scholarly debates ("lesbian historiography before the name") or chapter titles ("physical intimacy and the erotics of unnaming").[4] Furthermore, access to the lexicons of sexology or psychiatry (discourses layered over terms and understandings that date back to antiquity) is routinely cited as a marker of sexual modernity, the newly self-aware sexual subject configured as endowed with the capacity to name and self-name. However, while the shift by queer genealogists *to name* some beings as "queer" unsettles fixity, the *habit* of naming escapes analysis. This is why I am interested in the analytical possibilities of a historiographical practice that does not take names or naming for granted. The payoff, I further argue, is that the suspension or defamiliarization of the habit illuminates certain blind spots in a genealogical project often inclined to insert its own names rather than to consider the epistemic consequences of naming. In short, I sometimes sense queer anxieties that without a name there is no sexuality to see; after all, the "empty placeholder" of queer designates queerness-as-being.[5] If, as David Halperin argues, "history is necessarily and inevitably framed by contemporary preoccupations and investments" and the historian "looks to the past for something lacking in the present, something that can offer new leverage against the contemporary problems with which the historian is engaged," it is incumbent on the maker of history to understand the past not simply on our terms alone.[6] The task of historicizing also demands that we endeavor to understand how the sexual may have been structured differently, even in the early half of the twentieth century.

My discovery of the verbatim report of this 1931 meeting (later deposited in the National Archives) indicated that, although the late nineteenth-century invention of the homosexual had given rise to new forms of subjectivity in some social circles, elsewhere enunciations of the individual as a sexual subject in a public setting were subject to factors such as gender, class, age, and education. This partly accounts for the adamant refusal of Jowitt's formulation by one committee member, Brigadier General Blakeney: "We cannot use that word" (DM, 42). This terse reply perplexed me for some time, until I realized that Jowitt and Blakeney were speaking at cross-purposes, with the question situated in the modern discourse of sexual identity and the response grounded in an older discursive framework that understood allegations of sexual transgression as pertaining to moral character (that is, a system of assessing ethical conduct in terms of virtue that assumes shared values on what constitutes right and wrong or in terms of alternative readings of the law in relation to a name).[7] In an early essay on historicizing sexuality, Halperin observes, "Sexuality generates sexual identity: it endows each of us with an individual sexual nature, with a personal essence defined (at least in part) in specifically sexual terms; it implies that human beings are individuated at the level of their sexuality, that they differ from one another in their sexuality and, indeed, belong to different types or kinds of being by virtue of their sexuality."[8] I accept that sexual identity is integral to our current conceptualization of sexuality, but in light of the queer critique, the time is long overdue to revisit an earlier historiographical dictum that differentiates premodern acts and modern sexual identities as an orderly transition. We also need to pause — as historians and historicists — and consider the habit of naming the sexual being as historically contingent. There are excellent tools at our disposal to discern the epistemic significance of Jowitt's perfectly categorical question; according to the *Oxford English Dictionary*, by 1925 the term lesbian denotes a "female homosexual." Jowitt's unequivocal formulation of the question, however, treats as axiomatic the attachment of a sexual act to a being that is "named." Moreover, his clumsy attempt to "clarify" actually makes matters worse: "You know what I mean, immorality with women" (DM, 42). The problem with this "explanation" is that the phrase "immorality with women" operates in a different discursive orbit than modern sexual knowledge, so Jowitt's shift from one epistemological structure to another represents a slippage between systems — the modern and the moral. Being "immoral with women" does not denote a "type" of woman whose "personal essence" can be identified and categorized, so the "you know what I mean" leaves us none the wiser about how the transgression and transgressor may have been understood in 1918.

Although it was detrimental to the members' own political interests, the committee insisted on framing past events within the conceptual parameters available at the time. In response to the attorney general's phrase ("made similar allegations of lesbian[ism] against some other women") Blakeney intervenes with the corrective "caused similar trouble with other women," stating that while Jowitt's question is "perfectly legitimate to ask," it is "extraordinarily difficult to answer" (DM, 42).[9] Figuring out how to make sense of this disconnect between the speakers seems to call for at least two analytical frameworks, inside and outside the genealogical project. Dealing with Jowitt's query in the context of identity (stable or fluid) appears to be ideal terrain for ancestral or queer genealogists — Blakeney's response, on the other hand, not only underlines a need for alternative historiographical approaches, but also outlines a rationale: the word lesbian is inappropriate on the grounds that it "was not actually used in the House of Lords enquiry" (DM, 42). This explanation helped me see that attentiveness to the uses of the word — in projecting or imposing modern conceptualizations of sexuality onto the past and, more crucially, the expectation that sexual knowledge generates a sexual identity — actually secures the structure of how we currently understand sexuality to be known. If we are serious about the possibilities of queerness-as-method extricated from queerness-as-being, these epistemological fissures between modern and residual knowledge regimes need to become more visible, although breaking the habit of identification might entail stepping back from an interest in sexual identity to investigate how the identity habit shapes historiographical practice.

Avoiding ahistoricism is an occupational hazard for historians of homosexuality, who have long debated the relative merits and drawbacks of applying "terminologies and typologies" that hold specific meanings in the present to characterize the past. Lesbian historians, in particular, have shown immense interest in thinking beyond the word itself; hence phrases such as lesbianlike or protolesbian.[10] No degree of semantic quibbling, however, can resolve the problems that arise from a conceptual investment in the structuring logic of a sexual knowingness that, first, observes and categorizes the other preliminary to attaching a label and, second, assumes the sexual as constitutive of self-identity. While there is no escaping the power and dynamism inherent in any given name, scrutiny of the habits of naming, name calling, and self-naming — as historically contingent processes determined by other power relations and social conditions — directs attention not only to cultural meaning but also to sexual identity as a *process* that has often eluded historicizing. The habit of naming the modern sexual subject — as lesbian or queer — makes salient what otherwise is invisible, but such historicizing inevitably occludes knowledge practices outside the logic of this framework, especially in the modern age. Because our conceptualizations of sexuality are so naturalized, the project of historicizing sexuality in the early decades of the twentieth century assumes as commonplace the distinctive conceptual moves that current intelligibility and legibility depend on, even though the habit does not appear widespread until late in the interwar era.

This examination of archival materials relating to women, work, and the First World War indicates that ordinary people did not generally name or self-name. The case studies I discuss in this chapter demonstrate that as late as the 1930s some women understood themselves and were perceived by others in relation to gender and class yet manifested little interest in, or seemed to have limited access to, the technologies or subjectivities of sexuality. This is why I position the Hon. Violet Douglas-Pennant at the center of the chapter, alongside a pair of women famous for their work as drivers and nurses near the Western Front: Elsie Knocker and Mairi Chisholm (known as "the two," or the "heroines of Pervyse").[11] Ancestral and queer work on twentieth-century sexuality has been most productive in tracing the construction of a personal identity by "women who *feel themselves* to be more masculine than feminine" or women who "self-consciously sought to understand their feelings, their actions, and their relationships apart from men."[12] The women I discuss here exhibit self-awareness that the war had changed their gendered selves or left them vulnerable to allegations of sexual impropriety. Yet there is scant evidence in their diaries or letters that, concerning sexuality, these women felt themselves to be anything, least of all a name. For them, gender variance or sexual promiscuity was observed without signaling an identity — outside an emergent "style of reasoning" that would link sexual identity to "impulses, tastes, aptitudes, satisfactions, and psychic traits," a conceptual apparatus that structures sexuality as order and disorder.[13]

empiricist?

In privileging either the technologies of selfhood (in the metaphysical sense of an inner essence or authentic self) or the frameworks of sexual subjectivity, modern sexuality is often seen as holding "the key to unlocking the deepest mysteries of the human personality" and as positioned "at the center of the hermeneutics of the self."[14] My case studies reveal that some women had little sense of sexual selfhood or subjectivity, a condition that has sometimes frustrated historians of lesbianism. Martha Vicinus, for instance, finds it troubling that scholars such as Judith M. Bennett and Leila Rupp argue "against using the word *lesbian* for women who did not use the word themselves."[15] While Bennett's preferred phrase, "lesbian-like," assists in destabilizing "the notion of a single sexual identity" and "avoids an ahistorical focus on identity," highlighting sexual behavior instead, Rupp opts for the phrase "same-sex sexuality."[16] Either solution, for Vicinus, is problematic in "uncomfortably concentrating on the unknowable, rather than the knowable" and is "vague."[17] For scholars of modern sexuality, the challenge of putting identity aside — or inside *and* outside the framework of historical investigation — seems a trickier maneuver, demanding perhaps that we reconsider the value of unknowability and vagueness as a way of knowing differently. This will to ignorance is an ideal site to consider names that cannot be written down, acts that cannot be named, and the unsaid as a way of knowing, for this ignorance "is a product of, implies, and itself structures and enforces a particular knowledge."[18] For this reason I will also consider the political uses and cultural effects of name calling, tittle-tattle, and above all gossip, a verbal transaction that "circulates widely among a social network, beyond the control of private individuals. . . . [It] circulates without the awareness of some people."[19] The evidence points to a wartime rumor mill in which some "sort of talk was going about" which did not generate identities related to sexuality (DM, 42).

Calculated to damage lives and reputations, rumors and whispers behind closed doors manifest a thoughtless disregard for the truth of the sexual self. The atmosphere of war, combined with gossip between people living and working in close quarters, meant that vague innuendos worked to great effect, acting like a "poison" in the "minds of those who hear them," leaving "a scar like vitriol" (DM, 7). Even the recollection of the hothouse of wartime sex talk incites Blakeney to implicate, perhaps recklessly, the women who attacked Douglas-Pennant as belonging to "some funny sort of Society. These secret Societies very often bring accusations of sex perversion in connection with them" (DM, 41). I propose to bring a different slant on the name game by examining how Douglas-Pennant and others navigated the limits of naming and self-naming, thereby problematizing sexual awareness as "something that has to be routinely created and sustained in the reflexive activities of the individual."[20] This is not to suggest that a queer critical historical approach divested of an identitarian framework offers a more authoritative analysis of shifts that occurred with the gradual dissemination of new discursive possibilities as a result of the popularization of sexology and psychiatry through sex education and marital advice literature. Rather, I am interested in exploring what different questions or problems emerge in the refusal to name or the unavailability of naming, terrain that suggests the value of a critical history practice interested in producing "an *undetermined history.*"[21]

Genealogists have productively speculated on the cultural meanings of the refusal to name. In what follows I argue that, in the case of Douglas-Pennant, this refusal to use the naming practices of 1931 to account for events in 1918 represents a significant historiographical intervention that goes beyond warning of the dangers of ahistoricism. This discursive collision suggests a need for a dialogue between, on the one hand, practitioners with genealogical interests in how the "diamonds" gained their "hard permanence" and, on the other, critical historians positioned outside the genealogical framework seeking to understand the cultural processes by which the sexual could be known. During the war and its immediate aftermath, sexuality seems to have been generally understood as neither a constituent part of a personal identity nor a naming process that situated acts or desires within systems of classification linking individuals to a group. Historicizing the name and naming need not culminate in a call for the "diamonds" to be discarded, but it does entail repositioning them to the edges of historical inquiry for the purpose of ascertaining, for instance, how formations of selves and self-formation sometimes operate as a dialogical process between name calling and self-naming. That the word lesbian was not used in 1918 is an important consideration, but the more urgent concern is to rethink the potential of a historiographical mode less tethered to, or enmeshed in, the habits of naming. I propose instead — by critically historicizing — to build on genealogical interest in the historicity of identity categories by examining a foundational premise in genealogical work: that individuals in the modern age routinely named or self-named by invoking the categories familiar to us now. This close analysis of a few individuals who were not preoccupied with, or had no access to, self-reflexive taxonomizing habits in the realm of sexuality suggests not resistance to known categories but an unwillingness to know the self or an unfamiliarity with the idea that the self might be known as a sexual category. As Douglas-Pennant commented, for instance, "It is odious to have to refer to anything which concerns me personally."[22] Grasping the manifold and conflicting ways modern sexuality evolves entails tracing shifts in the terms or expressions, but also cultivating conceptual distance from modern identity categories that clean away the "ambiguities" to give us a "perfectly clear apprehension" (DM, 61, 62).

Women Have Found Themselves

If, as Ethel Alec-Tweedie passionately believed, the war had transformed the status of women in British society, it had also served as a catalyst for self-reflection: "The world has discovered women, and women have found themselves."[23] However debatable its key assertion that women's talents, skills, and abilities were recognized and appreciated across the class spectrum, this statement nonetheless provokes a related question: *In what sense* did women find themselves? To chart how (or if) war work mobilized new modes of self-understanding in dialogue with the world, I turn to the wartime experiences of three individuals whose paths crossed briefly: the Hon. Violet Douglas-Pennant (1869–1945), Mrs. Elizabeth "Elsie" Knocker (1884–1978), and Miss Mairi Chisholm (1896–1981).[24] In May 1918 ill health and injury left Knocker and Chisholm unfit for overseas service, and on returning to England the pair were interviewed by Douglas-Pennant for jobs as WRAF officers and subsequently sent to Hurst Park Motor Depot.[25] My reading of their diaries, letters, transcripts of interviews, and published and unpublished work amply illustrates self-naming arising from interactions with family, colleagues, and friends. Evidence further indicates a sense of selfhood "forged by autonomous acts of individual will" in terms of class, nation, and, for the latter two women, gender — each self forged according to the "limited discursive resources available."[26]

I choose these women in particular because they represent a class of individuals free from the personal or financial constraints that sometimes inhibit self-reflection. Crucially, too, there is a rich archive of materials detailing how each came in contact with more open discussion of sexual behavior at a time when class-based rules of social respectability were under stress, suggesting the possibility of tracing interactions between sexual identity and self-creation. Knocker and Chisholm spent much of the war together nursing Belgian soldiers in the cramped quarters of a cellar room near the front lines in Pervyse, "far from the conventions of the civilized code, yet giving no hint of scandal to sharp-eared gossip," according to a visiting war correspondent referring to middle- and upper-class British women living and working without male chaperons.[27] There is no sense in this account or elsewhere of a friendship that exceeded the bounds of propriety.[28] Douglas-Pennant, meanwhile — once accused — became an accuser herself and conveyed her suspicions that others were leading "very improper lives," especially at the WRAF camps, where, according to the minister of labor, there had been "disquieting reports of slackness and indiscipline" and concerns about that most capacious of sexual categories — "immoral relations" — between male officers of the Royal Air Force and members of the WRAF.[29]

Looking first, briefly, at Knocker and Chisholm, I scrutinize how their "practical immersion in the interactions of day-to-day life" reconfigured their gendered embodiment in ways disassociated from the codes sexologists assigned to sexual inversion.[30] The writings of journalists and other visitors indicate that outsiders admired the women's camaraderie — and the women themselves depicted their sharing a bed as one hardship among many. In interviews a half century later, however, the topic of sexual deviance surfaces explicitly. I then consider the self-naming habits of Douglas-Pennant, a woman from an aristocratic family forced to negotiate the "narrative forms through which others had sought to render . . . [her] knowable," narratives triggered by sexual reverberations that she proved highly adept at evading but could never entirely dispel.[31] I recognize that this sampling of women disinclined or unable to identify as sexual subjects is small, but it is important to remember that the history of lesbianism in early twentieth-century Britain has tended to focus on an equally narrow section of British society (relative to the population), typically the educated elite or women associated with literary, artistic, or bohemian cultures.[32] In selecting Knocker, Chisholm, and

Douglas-Pennant I attempt to move outside these parameters to construct a history of sexuality beyond a few well-known individuals who wrote and thought about themselves as modern sexual subjects. Sexual history dependent on identity as a thing or "essence" acquired by self-reflexivity makes it difficult to think more expansively about those past individuals who may have been less attuned to modes of psychosexual interiority and who did not think to attach to themselves sexual labels or names.[33] For these three women, the circumstances of war reaffirmed prior understandings of selfhood and granted agency in developing new forms of introspection, but it also excluded a dimension of life we now consider central.

SIX WEEKS after Britain declared war on Germany, Elsie Knocker (nicknamed Gipsy) and Mairi Chisholm turned up at Victoria Station in "big khaki overcoats, high lace-up leather boots, and riding-breeches," on the first leg of their journey to Belgium to serve as drivers in Dr. Hector Munro's Ambulance Unit (the Flying Ambulance Column [FAC]).[34] A qualified nurse from a middle-class background and, in her own words, an "expert driver and mechanic," Knocker was twelve years older than Chisholm, the daughter of a well-to-do Scottish family.[35] Far from feeling out of place or ridiculous in their self-designed uniforms, the pair relished the way their appearance generated "excitement"—onlookers stood and stared, "scandalized" by their breeches.[36] Acknowledging that their self-fashioning "caused a degree of stir," these two women exhibit consciousness that the gendered "body is not just a physical entity which we 'possess,' it is an action-system."[37] The sight of women outfitted in uniforms of every description also captivated the press, which never tired of the novelty of "muscular femininity" and regularly featured images of women marching, driving, heaving, hoisting, pulling, fixing, cranking, and lifting as well as tending, cleaning, caring, feeding, nursing, and mothering.[38] As the most visible emblem of patriotism and national service, uniforms in every color and design threw "gender into sharp relief," though the military or militarylike uniform pushed gender boundaries the furthest, as discussed in chapter 3.[39] Female war workers knew that, whether at home or near the fighting, appearances mattered, and fashion magazines featured the new highly masculine military "look" as tasteful and elegant; in sporting such clothing, Knocker and Chisholm were not confirming aspects of a sexual identity: "Men's clothes," Knocker sensibly pointed out, "have this advantage over women's, they are at all events more practical."[40]

The women of Pervyse actively revised prewar British femininity and carried it off with panache, according to an impression of the pair by war correspondent Philip Gibbs, who greatly admired "the women in their field kit, so feminine though it included breeches . . . playing a man's part with a feminine pluck."[41] For about two months, each drove ambulances with the FAC under dangerous conditions and had the physical strength to cross into no-man's-land on foot with stretchers to carry the wounded back to ambulances up to three miles away—Knocker was even known to have hauled wounded soldiers on her back.[42] An adept wheeler-dealer, Knocker convinced the Belgian army of their importance to the war effort and soon relocated to an advanced dressing station known as the Cellar House in Pervyse, where she lived and worked in close quarters with the intrepid eighteen-year-old Chisholm. Relics of these women's legendary mission in Pervyse now reside in the Imperial War Museum (including Chisholm's breeches and the door to the cellar house), since the pair gained fame as "angels of light and healing" for nursing the wounded and dying.[43] Enduring harsh living conditions and—like soldiers—subjected to heavy shelling and gas attacks, Knocker and her "faithful companion" were kitted out to attend to casualties: "The two lived for months in a cellar twelve feet by ten; they slept on straw, and of necessity used foul water from a ditch. . . . [T]here was, of course, no possibility of changing clothes. When they wanted sleep they lay down as they were, and were often called up in the middle of the night to attend to ghastly wounds."[44] Once in the line of fire, they spent little time ruminating on or fretting about what onlookers deduced about the women's "unconventional" self-presentation.[45]

In 1916 these "two delicately-nurtured ladies"—"their hands . . . engrained with coarse work" and clothing "smeared with soup and cocoa, mud, and blood"—willingly lost the greatest asset of womanliness in cutting their hair short, "for it was impossible to retain long hair in such conditions."[46] Much was made in the press of the women's shorn locks—the *War Budget Illustrated* even published a photograph of them taken from behind, their heads bowed to display their napes to the camera (fig. 15). In a 1916 account loosely based on Knocker's diary extracts, the hair cutting is conveyed as transformative, suffused with personal significance:

They held each other's hands, and determined to thrust away all idea of fears, nerves, or feminine weaknesses. In the early grey light of the morning they consummated that heroic resolve with a real sacrifice. . . . Mairi

Figure 15. "'The Two' after having sacrificed their hair." Reproduced in *The Cellar-House of Pervyse: A Tale of Uncommon Things from the Journals and Letters of the Baroness T'Serclaes and Mairi Chisholm* (London: A. and C. Black, 1916).

cut and hacked and chopped until she had shorn her friend's dark silky hair . . . and then Gipsy did the same for the strong fair crop so unlike her own. They looked at it, laughing queerly. . . . Gipsy [said]: "We became soldiers from that hour."[47]

Such erotically charged terms of expression — hands held, resolve consummated, "dark silky hair," "strong fair crop" — invite the modern reader to speculate about what sort of queer sisterhood the women had formed, but it is a relationship cast in terms of comradeship, with no self-awareness of romance or erotic attraction. We learn that the women regarded this act of shearing their hair together as the ultimate sacrifice, constituting a rite of passage to a kind of female manhood, but whether it was a romantic friendship, a cross-age intimate friendship (to borrow Martha Vicinus's term),[48] or full-blown lesbianism (in other words, what we see now), based on materials produced during the war we can only establish that these women did not think of themselves in terms of sexual identity. In Pervyse the pair lived for nearly four years cheek by jowl, where they "retained their bedroom to themselves."[49] Portrayed in one biography as a hardship, these circumstances allowed the women an opportunity to sleep together, apparently huddling for warmth. Yet Chisholm's matter-of-fact description of how the pair "shared a big double bed whenever we happened to be in there," where they "snuggled up close," demonstrates a lack of sexual self-awareness that the sleeping arrangements for women of their class background might encourage others to read their relationship as sexual.[50] In one diary entry Chisholm notes, "In the evening G. [Gipsy] complained of being very tired so I offered to go and sleep with Dorothie which I forthwith proceeded to do. However G. wouldn't go to bed till I had come back so I had to go back."[51] Again, this passage might be read as suggesting the physical intimacy of lovers, but if Chisholm had thought her diary might invite readers to surmise a sexual relationship, it is hardly likely she would have deposited it in the Imperial War Museum.

What is clear from comments Chisholm made during a mid-1970s BBC interview is that she understood herself in terms of gender variance. As a young girl, she recalls, "I had absolutely no use for the feminine thing. . . . I spent my entire time in a spare stall in the stables . . . playing about with my brother, who was two years senior, with his motor bike. Stripping it down, grinding in valves, everything."[52] A self-described "tomboy" who never married, Chisholm shows no inhibition in confessing her desire for mechanical things, traits linked to sexual inversion in the sexological literature.[53] At a time of widespread public discussion of moral laxity, women like Knocker and Chisholm "found themselves" in terms other than names corresponding with categories of sexual identity. In other words, there is little evidence of an inclination to self-name or to assume that their friendship might be subject to naming by others.

IN APRIL 1918 Douglas-Pennant's name appeared on a list of six "gentlewomen and women of the world" in a letter sent by the social reformer and antisuffragist Violet Markham to Major General Sir Godfrey Paine, the man in charge of organizing the search for a new commandant of the WRAF.[54] For Markham, it was essential that any candidate seeking a high-level post in a military organization possess "the ideal combination of character, tact, and administrative experience."[55] By the time the war broke out, Douglas-Pennant had a long record of public service both as a volunteer in numerous organizations, especially related to youth, education, social welfare, and local government, and as a paid employee, including the post of national health insurance commissioner for South Wales, for which she reportedly earned an annual salary of £1,000, making her one of the most highly paid women in Britain.[56] Markham enthusiastically recommended Douglas-Pennant as "a very charming and tactful woman with much sound administrative capacity and experience"—the very same qualities others would judge her as lacking four months later when, in the eyes of her critics, she "proved herself utterly incapable temperamentally of holding her job."[57] She was ordered to step down from her command, and the counsel for the Air Ministry eventually concluded that Douglas-Pennant was "suffering from hallucinations, hallucinations run mad," while Dr. Letitia Fairfield, chief medical officer of the WRAF, declared that "the poor lady" suffered from "a form of delusional insanity."[58] For decades references by Douglas-Pennant's so-called enemies would discursively secure her reputation as a woman on the verge of madness, using words such as "hallucinations," "schizophrenia," "insanity," and "paranoia."[59] Although Douglas-Pennant seems not to have recorded her innermost thoughts in diaries, an examination of her personal correspondence, her public utterances, and her 1922 account of the case, *Under the Searchlight: A Record of a Great Scandal*, offers an opportunity to unravel the complex mental workings of a woman whose life was spiraling out of control, leaving her unable to make sense of either the initial explanations for her dismissal on the grounds of professional incompetence or the revelations a year later that the actual charges were, in the words of Tyson Wilson (chief whip of the Labour party), "impossible to tell ladies" (*US*, 216).

Of the available categories of identity, Douglas-Pennant understands best her class and family position. Born in 1869, this daughter of the Welsh peer George Sholto Gordon Douglas-Pennant, second Baron Penrhyn, appears to have had a fairly conventional late Victorian childhood of wealth and privilege.[60] When the general who fired her states, before a select committee of the House of Lords in 1919, that the commandant had "assured him that [her] station in life was considerably better than that of . . . other people," she insists that she would never have been "guilty of such unpardonable bad taste and pointless vulgarity" (*US*, 141). In the Lords select committee hearings, when Douglas-Pennant is once again asked under oath whether she had claimed to be a "lady," she responds ironically: "I am quite certain I did not. I never knew there was any doubt" (*US*, 323). Pushed further, she is asked whether she professed to *be* a lady and, although she obviously believes that some other women were not, she insists resolutely that she would "never [say] anything so rude" and dismisses such talk as "fantastic": "It had never occurred to me that it would fall to my lot to have to *defend* myself against charges of discourtesy and vulgarity"—to be a proper lady is never to assert one is a lady (*US*, 324, 325; emphasis mine). Douglas-Pennant emphatically denies social snobbery, but elsewhere in *Under the Searchlight* she tells readers she would never put WRAF girls "at the mercy of women Officers whose only experience of life had been gained on the music-hall stage of an inferior type or 'on the streets'" (*US*, 94). Douglas-Pennant also expresses fury that a young WRAF officer very much her junior had the ear of the leader of the Air Ministry, even though only a few months before this woman had been a mere clerk in a toy shop (*US*, 83). This sense of herself as a lady from a prominent family explains why, after the commandant's humiliating dismissal, she did not retire quietly, as confirmed in a confidential report prepared by Cecil Harmsworth, secretary to the prime minister, Lloyd George: "I do not think it will be possible to turn [Miss Douglas-Pennant] from her purpose. . . . [She] impresses me as a woman of remarkable determination. She believes that she has a duty to herself and a duty to the public to fulfil. The old Penrhyn spirit is there and I do not think there is any chance of dissuading [her]" from fighting to clear her name.[61]

Based on her meticulous gathering of the so-called facts about the case, Douglas-Pennant's desultory account of events becomes, in effect, a foundational text for a twenty-seven-year campaign to clear her name—a site of self-creation to expose her detractors' charges of inefficiency, incompetency, and unpopularity as groundless and to lob equally damaging counteraccusations (a tactic that led to heavy court fines for libel).[62] To the charge of inexperience, she lists in minute detail all her previous employment (running to four pages, single-spaced) (*US*, v–viii).[63] To the charge that she lacks tact, she insists that, even in the most difficult of situations, she was unfailing in her courtesy to individuals of all class backgrounds. To the charge that she was unpopular, she mentions countless letters of support from women who served with her (attached to an appendix in the book under the heading "Proofs of Public Opinion" [*US*, 455–63]). The very illustrations of the book work to support this claim, several bearing the caption "presented to Miss V. Douglas-Pennant by the WRAF Staff," implying that she enjoyed the organization's unquestioning loyalty save for a handful of disaffected women whose vindictiveness was little more than retribution for being passed over for promotion. The charges were all the more puzzling to the commandant since, frustrated with the slow pace of organizational change, she had offered the Air Ministry her resignation only weeks earlier but had been turned down because her services were then thought indispensable to the war effort (*US*, 134–35).

Such an about-face, in tandem with the lack of any credible evidence to support these flimsy complaints, gave rise to numerous wild and unsubstantiated rumors that she must have been a bully, a drug addict, a drunkard, or even a German spy (*US*, 169). Her heated disavowal of all the pernicious impugning of her character proves not only that Douglas-Pennant heeded the public criticism of her peers, but that her attempts to correct these apparently erroneous accounts are the product of a dialogical exchange with her foes. Strategically naming her self in relation to family and class to refute the alternative selves created by her detractors points to identity as "always articulated through concepts (and practices) . . . mediated by family, peers, [and] friends."[64] The former commandant's identity formation evolves less as an affirmation of similarity or sameness than as an assertion of dissimilitude, an adversarial dialogic that shatters any mirrorlike relationality to generate the self as a product of negativity, denial, contradiction, and distortion. The disjunction between her own self-construction and that of her opponents finally leads Douglas-Pennant to ruminate about a fictional character: Alice in Wonderland. Alice alone, Douglas-Pennant writes, would "sympathize with my position, closely akin to hers when she stepped through the looking-glass and found herself in a world where everything was reversed and distorted" (*US*, 301). In *The Logic of Sense* Gilles Deleuze describes this distortion as "a veritable becoming mad," noting how Alice's life reverses cause and effect so that she is "punished before having committed a fault"; the effect of such reversals, he continues, is nothing less than "the contesting of Alice's personal identity and the loss of her proper name."[65] Alice's sense of dislocation is mirrored in Douglas-Pennant's claim that the allegations were "fantastic," an "extraordinary tangle of inconsistencies and chameleon-like changes in the conflicting charges" (*US*, 324). For several pages she repeats the same litany of accusations over and over, as if the constant repetition might somehow render the meaning intelligible: "an insolent autocrat and a great overbearing bully," "a bad character," "a disreputable adventuress" (*US*, 218, 170, 223). Like Alice in her backward world, Douglas-Pennant struggles in an absurd state of topsy-turvydom where the honorable become dishonorable and the well-bred are undermined by those less than ladylike.

To counteract aspersions against her own honor and uprightness, Douglas-Pennant declared, "I have personally nothing to fear" and positioned herself as tireless in her efforts to "sweep away uncleanliness" in the WRAF camps, where conditions were intolerable ("a perfect mass of corruption"), owing to the "immorality which was going on."[66] Citing as particularly disturbing an incident at one WRAF camp, Hurst Park, she alleged that RAF officers had provided WRAF girls with night passes so they could go to London. These same girls were later seen returning to camp "drunk at 3 o'clock in the morning."[67] She believed her attempts to clean up the camps were being met with deceit, anger, and retaliation by male officers using every means to safeguard their sexual pleasure. Douglas-Pennant's efforts to maintain moral order were much admired by the provincial press as well as by some politicians and churchmen, convinced that the government's shabby treatment was the result of her zeal. The *North Wales Chronicle*, for instance, noted that "there were a large number of these camps — girls' camps — without one single woman supervisor over the girls. . . . Was [Douglas-Pennant] to suffer because of her high moral aspirations?"[68] In a speech summarized by some national newspapers, Lord Stanhope (Douglas-Pennant's cousin) alerted his fellow peers in the Lords to the "grave scandals" at a "large Royal Air Force depot near London."[69] Briefed by Douglas-Pennant, Stanhope stated his belief that the dismissal was related to Douglas-Pennant's discovery of an illicit affair between an RAF officer and a member of the WRAF, who were found "by their landlady in the same room, *in flagrante delicto*, at three o'clock in the morning. That is the sort of thing that was going on."[70] Perversely, Stanhope implied, there were no repercussions for the philandering couple, while the woman endeavoring to repress "scandalous conduct" was punished for "her sternness and vigor."[71] The *Montgomery County Times* speculated that, with Douglas-Pennant's removal, young women would now be lured by unscrupulous male officers: "We presume the 'appointments' [of these mistresses] have been made, and almost heavenly bliss reigns in the dovecote of the Women's Royal Air Force."[72] In comments reported by the *Morning Post*, the bishop of Bangor felt "the safety of women's character and the honor of the Air Force was involved in this matter [as] certain officers . . . wished to have mistresses maintained by the State in appointments worth £300 or £400 a year."[73] That Douglas-Pennant's version of events found a receptive audience points to the resilience of the moral regulation of sexual behavior.

Those allied to her cause saw the dismissal as retribution, as one fellow officer told her in a statement quoted in the *Evening Standard*: "You have to go not because you are inefficient but because you are too efficient."[74] In a book of press cuttings Knocker later presented to the Imperial War Museum, "efficient" is crossed out (presumably by Knocker) and replaced with "unpopular."[75] Knocker herself submitted a report on October 8, 1918, about the "discipline" of Hurst Park, which — before her inquiries — had been described as "exceedingly bad."[76] By then known as Baroness de T'Serclaes (a venturous and worldly modern woman, who had kept her prewar divorce under wraps), Knocker searched for evidence of scandal only to find "in most cases pure invention or exaggerations of perfectly harmless amusements . . . the worst enemy this camp has is the civilian who has nothing to do in this war but gossip."[77] A 1919 report subsequently issued by a select committee in the House of Lords on the alleged scandals in the WRAF camps concluded that Douglas-Pennant's attitude toward women's new sexual freedom was badly out of step with the times. In their view "it would be a matter of surprise" if "rumors of immorality" did not surface: "such is the world and such is the tendency of some natures to think and speak evil of others."[78] Judging Douglas-Pennant's moral system as old-fashioned, the Lords argued: "Men and women have during the war been so thrown into daily contact with each other in work and in healthy recreation that conventional notions of a certain reserve as between the sexes have been very largely modified."[79] Just as Douglas-Pennant manufactured stories to suggest that immorality was more extensive than it might have been, others cast her as prudish, staid, and out of touch — overinvested in the moral values of a bygone era. In a secret report commissioned by Lloyd George, Harmsworth refers to Douglas-Pennant's alacrity in getting to the bottom of the rumors and rooting out the wrong sort of women: "She believes that the purity of the public service is at stake."[80] Decades later some would recollect a woman with "pre-suffragette conceptions," a woman caught up in "a genuine clash between nineteenth and twentieth century ideas of relationships between the sexes," a woman "a little correct . . . most unprogressive."[81] However, in 1964 Fairfield flatly contradicted these views: "It was quite untrue that people [at the time] laughed at Miss Douglas-Pennant's maidenly standards. . . . These stories were all dated *after* she had been dismissed."[82] This counterargument highlights the difficulties that arise when two incompatible systems of morality — the Victorian and the modern — rub against each other, revealing how the mythologizing of Victorian prudery secures the "modern" at the expense of a historical explanation of how things were understood in the past.

By late spring 1919 a different story began to emerge about the former commandant's dismissal, charges more difficult to explain: "scurrilous" rumors had spread "like wildfire" behind her back, eventually to reach the air minister (US, 223, 227). "Total strangers," Douglas-Pennant writes with incredulity, intimated "serious irregularities of conduct and administration" (US, 224, 223). Remarkably, considering the gravity of the accusation of immorality compared with the earlier charges made against her, Douglas-Pennant's first reference to sexual misconduct appears simply as one charge among several: "I was a well-known immoral character, no decent women would serve under me, young girls were unsafe in my hands" (US, 168). The allegations then reoccur throughout Under the Searchlight with no further comment: "source of danger to women," "dishonorable woman," "a woman of bad reputation," a "very bad woman" forced to resign because "the women in the Air Force had threatened to mutiny as no decent woman could serve under me," a woman guilty of performing "certain obscene acts" (US, 224, 190, 219, 223). In the end, no actual charges relating to sexual misconduct were ever made against Douglas-Pennant either in eighteen sessions of the 1919 select committee in the House of Lords or in the report issued after those hearings.[83] And so, to the charge of sexual malpractice Douglas-Pennant is silent — deafeningly so, because, "if the facts were known [she] could never hold up [her] head again" (US, 216). The penultimate chapter of her book, "Unsolved Enigmas," reviews — one final time — each reason given for her dismissal, save the one most compromising to her moral character (US, 419–41). As happened to Alice, intelligibility is stretched to the limits when the very accusation in most urgent need of explanation — her alleged guilt in performing "certain obscene acts" — is mentioned only in passing, its unfathomability making it unavailable as a mode of self-understanding. For women of a certain generation, family background, or class standing, direct refutation is impossible — acknowledgment itself is tantamount to dishonor, compromising respectability and besmirching the family name. In the absence of a verbal utterance of the "stigma" or "frightful stain" on her character, there can be no defense — only social ostracism: the impact of the slander "has transformed me from a person with everyone's respect and confidence into a person to be shunned and ostracized. . . . I have not only been ostracized by those who do not know the truth, but financially ruined and unable to obtain any post of responsibility."[84]

Months before Douglas-Pennant's order from the air minister to stand down, another highly publicized case fueled by wartime rumor and innuendo (Maud Allan's alleged membership in the "cult of the clitoris") had shown the dangers for women of possessing sexual knowledge, and so it is unsurprising that the former leader does not conjecture on the meaning of the phrase "certain obscene acts" (*US*, 223).[85] Instead she presents her case as one of unfair dismissal, based on vague and unsubstantiated rumors circulated by the unscrupulous on behalf of a political agenda that makes no sense to her at all. Just as the specific acts were "impossible to tell ladies," it was impossible for ladies to tell (*US*, 216).

In Other Words

On July 3, 1931, the *Manchester Guardian* reported on a protest meeting held at the Central Hall Westminster, London, within short walking distance of the prime minister's residence and thus a venue ideal for capturing government and press attention. Restricted to adults only and attended by over one thousand people (predominantly women), the meeting disclosed an astonishing revelation concerning the Douglas-Pennant case. Organized by the Douglas-Pennant Committee (as a small group of her supporters called themselves), the event was prompted by new proof that the air minister had been swayed in his decision to dismiss the commandant by secret evidence pertaining to moral character and that, supporters alleged, successive governments had attempted to cover up. The credentials of the platform party could not have been more respectable — Rev. Dr. F. W. Norwood, pastor of City Temple (London) presided, joined by "representatives of the Church, the Army, the Law, [and] the Salvation Army" as well as ex-inspector John Syme, formerly of the Metropolitan Police, himself a victim of wrongful dismissal.[86] After several speeches, the assembly duly passed a resolution calling on the prime minister to reopen the case to allow Douglas-Pennant to respond to the new evidence and to make reparations to an innocent woman characterized as having endured great personal suffering. Particularly helpful in its promise to bring closure to a long campaign for justice was Tyson Wilson's admission that "he was wrong" and had been "misled" on first hearing the "vile" rumors of a "serious charge of personal impropriety" against Douglas-Pennant.[87] In an unusual departure from the euphemisms of other major newspapers, the *Guardian* quoted Douglas-Pennant's legal adviser J. J. Edwards verbatim: his client had been "accused of being immoral with women, *in other words*, of being a Sapphist."[88]

The brevity of this extraordinarily dramatic statement belies its immense epistemological significance in naming as "sapphist" a type of woman who has had sexual relations with other women; defining, in other words, an inner essence based on sexual object choice, the signature feature in the modern understanding of sexuality. Whereas in 1918 this highborn lady had been accused of *doing* something immoral — "a disgraceful act"—by 1931 it was possible for her to be apprehended by some individuals as *being* something (DM, 244).[89] Especially noteworthy in J. J. Edwards's speech is a seemingly unremarkable subordinate clause — "in other words"—linking the phrase to a name. It is precisely the epistemological consequence of this small gesture I seek to explore, for historians of modern sexuality do something similar every time a modern conceptualization is applied to sexual beings or relations in the past. Arguably, writing identity history without access to this shorthand would make it difficult if not impossible to historicize categories of identities. I am less interested in establishing this heuristic maneuver as anachronistic than in assessing its effect on how we historicize sexuality before fixing modern labels became habitual, whether sapphist, lesbian, or female homosexual. Reading as merely linguistic the movement from phrase to label or vice versa obfuscates significant epistemological shifts in the configuration of sexuality, as this discussion demonstrates in analyzing two moments in the early twentieth century.

Just days after the 1931 public announcement of the "true" cause of Douglas-Pennant's ouster, a contingent of her supporters was invited to meet with the attorney general to present "fresh evidence" about what Lord Weir had been told (DM, 3). The discursive exchanges in this meeting offer a compelling illustration of the epistemic repercussions in the "translation" of whispers and inferences about "sex perversion" in 1918 to a name associated with sexual identity in 1931, a slippage second nature to us now. Throughout the lengthy exchange, Jowitt repeatedly refers to "lesbian" or "lesbianism"— highly charged terms that, if accepted, would ratchet up the intensity and strengthen the group's cause. Yet no others use it (save one). Prevarication and circumnavigation are the order of the day, as evinced by the preference for clunky, imprecise expressions: "sex perversion," "personal immorality with women," "allegations against her moral character," "these kinds of allegations," "criminal immorality between Miss Douglas-Pennant and women of the Air Force," and so on (DM, 34, 19, 3, 7, 9). The one person in the group to acquiesce to Jowitt's term is the brigadier general, who claims his twenty-five years' experience in the Near East makes him an authority on dirty talk and political intrigue, for there "such allegations are frequently made" (DM, 7). However, Blakeney speaks the word aloud only to register the strongest objection to its use because, he explains, "lesbian" "was not actually used in" 1919 (DM, 42). He ascribes his "linguistic unease" to a desire to meet the highest standard of legal and historical accuracy.[90] To prove that Douglas-Pennant was the unknowing victim of mere gossip, the deputation insists on accounting for the events of 1918 — the way it was possible "to know" then — by using the formulations available at the time, despite Jowitt's repeated request for unambiguous language to pin down what the group think had actually been said. Asking for their "help" in clarifying the point that one accuser had "made similar allegations of lesbianism against some other women," Jowitt is swiftly corrected by Blakeney's more historically accurate phrase: "caused similar trouble with other women" (DM, 42). The military officer's stubborn insistence on not being drawn (Is there evidence that someone told someone else that she was a lesbian?) seems reminiscent of the familiar queer admonition to avoid "perverse presentism" that falsely represents the past by lapsing into the terms of the present.[91] If we read this exchange as mere quibbling about a name (what to call a being we already know and understand either in 1918 or 1931), however, we miss what is most interesting about this example of linguistic obstinacy. Framing an allegation of improper sexual conduct as the name of a sexual being does not so much misrepresent the past as relinquish the wonderful ambiguity, uncertainty, and indeterminacy of 1918 sex talk. Jowitt's word misrepresents the past not merely because people didn't say those words then: people didn't think like that then.

Blakeney's explanation for his refusal is illuminating for two reasons: first, it reveals the epistemological shift in the modernizing of sexuality as gradual and erratic and, second, it suggests a new starting point for historicizing sexuality outside the identity paradigm. The group informs Jowitt that "the matter was so serious" that respectable women and men could not be pressed "to repeat it verbally"[92] — and neither would they "write that" (DM, 39). The discursive efficiency of modern sexuality is inadequate in conveying the imprecision of "the real character of this sort of charge" (DM, 12). In 1918 an allegation was all the more damaging and powerful because it was "never formulated on paper. It goes from mouth to mouth, and you have extraordinary difficulty to track it down" (DM, 12). Sensing the group's unease with his word choice, Jowitt quickly softens its power by acknowledging its nastiness ("It is a very unpleasant word and a very unpleasant subject") before attempting another expression to bridge the epistemological gap between moral opacity and clinical precision: "You know what I mean. Immorality with women" (DM, 42). Here Blakeney finds common ground in conceding that the charge is generally "known" only by inference: "Nothing else could have been the cause [behind the dismissal]. . . . Then on top of it, we have the fact that Mr. Tyson Wilson went to the air ministry and urged that she should be dismissed" because "she was an immoral woman or something of a disgraceful character . . . then one realizes what the nature of the allegation was" (DM, 6, 7). His shift to the present tense and acceptance of Jowitt's term ("There is more to this than you think; it is lesbianism" [DM, 39]) points to a modern understanding of the label to denote a woman whose nature draws her to engaging in sexual acts with other women, a topic that could now be discussed with some frankness, however "unpleasant" (DM, 42).

By 1937, her solicitor's letter to a different prime minister, Stanley Baldwin, would describe Douglas-Pennant as fighting to clear her name of the "foul offence of lesbianism."[93] In 1918, however, while every kind of wickedness exists, one "particular form of immorality"—whatever that means—is unnamable.[94] No sexual identity coheres in those whispers; sexual knowledge is exchanged, but there is no guarantee that people are talking about the same thing. To adduce that the whispers concerned "lesbianism" is therefore to "nail down" a wider range of possible meanings to a single sexual type (DM, 11). What this exchange discloses is that, first, widespread rumors of some sort of sexual perversion circulated behind closed doors during the war, but retrospection involves guesswork and conjecture, since—before the modern habit of naming—name calling intimated not a being but nastiness. Second, it shows that the legibility of the lesbian in the early 1930s notwithstanding, whether due to embarrassment or a will to ignorance or as a result of the inhibitions of class or gender, most committee members were not inclined toward naming the sexual or, in the case of Douglas-Pennant herself, toward self-naming.

At a later hearing in 1932 in which Douglas-Pennant was in attendance, neither "lesbian" nor "lesbianism" is spoken. Reorienting the subject of historical investigation from an interest in a sexual being named or unnamed to an interest in the conditions of knowing the sexual offers a different perspective on how sexuality was known. For historians of lesbian or queer lives, to configure the past within the knowledge structure of the present suggests significant adumbrations of a lesbian subject, but a critical history practice works differently in clarifying how other knowledge systems operated. The latter practice points to the tremendous power of innuendo and inference— an opacity sufficient to devastate a reputation in 1918. Paradoxically, we move closer in understanding what some unscrupulous women insinuated about the former commandant if "we cannot use that word." It is not that other—

better—words might be used. What is lost in thinking about the problem of historicizing as opting for one word or the other are the distinctive calibrations of a moral knowledge of the sexual that regulates differently. The class-based Edwardian ideals of self-control and moral standards police sexual acts through guilt and shame, so as not to let down one's family or lose respectability. The regulatory force of modern sexual discourse also shames, but through a different norm that we know as the "normal," as I discuss in the following chapter.

Mis-taken Identities

The peculiarly sexual nature of the character assassination of Violet Douglas-Pennant is all the more fascinating in that it concerned a realm of human existence she seems not to have addressed—we know virtually nothing about her sexuality or what she herself thought or understood about the rumors in circulation. However, one unintended result of the accusations was that the former commandant was impelled toward self-reflexivity, allowing the historian of sexuality an opportunity to observe self-fashioning in action as an intricate and ever evolving process. Had she entered the public record for reasons other than the scandal of 1918, Douglas-Pennant's wartime service would have been little more than a footnote in any history of women's military organizations. Extensively reported in the national press for nearly twenty years, this political scandal (like the Allan/Billing case of 1918) has received little attention from social and cultural historians, even though it closely involved several prime ministers (including David Lloyd George, Stanley Baldwin, and Winston Churchill) and hundreds of government ministers and sundry officials, members of both houses of Parliament, officers (women and men) of the armed forces, and ordinary citizens and supporters.[95]

Scholarly neglect of this case of a woman who never stated publicly, or confided to anyone in private, anything related to her sexual identity, desires, or practices suggests a need for a historical analysis that proceeds outside as well as inside the framework of modern sexuality. Throughout her ordeal Douglas-Pennant responds in writing to her unhappy predicament with excruciating detail, both through persistent lobbying on her own behalf and through vague references to the sexual ("guilty of certain obscene acts"), always stopping short of speaking openly or explicitly when refuting the charges (US, 223). *Under the Searchlight*, a nearly five-hundred-page exposé of a "great scandal," presents her version of events as a case of unfair dismissal, and in the context of justice and fair play it matters less to know precisely what she had been accused of than to establish that she was a victim of pernicious lies. The multiple injustices inflicted first by her accusers and then by a government disinclined to rectify its mistakes propel the commandant toward constructing a "self" seemingly dialogical in nature, but always devoid of interest in providing proof of sexual normality. She builds her defense and various alternative selves in conversation with what others think they "know" about her, using the categories available to her. Tracking Douglas-Pennant's identificatory practices reveals little about sexual identity but a great deal about the making, unmaking, and remaking of selfhood in relation to other naming practices — processes in every way as illuminating to the historian of sexuality as Jowitt's pursuit of certainty. The extensive paper trail of this case points to the shaping of the self as imbricated within "webs of interlocution," to borrow a phrase from philosopher Charles Taylor.[96] If we resist the very modern urge to define sexuality as fundamental and as knowable through an elaboration of sexual taxonomies and labels, other questions about the practices of self-fashioning seem to emerge. Douglas-Pennant's route to self-understanding is strikingly circuitous, involving less a rejection of specific names or labels than an interactive, dynamic, and dialogical interplay with systems in which the self might be known. Moreover, if self-definition is relational and in dialogue with any number of social groupings, Douglas-Pennant undertakes the "project of self-making" under considerable duress, and her inability to respond to the sexual nature of the accusations offers a different path by which to investigate how sexuality might have been known.[97]

The transcript of the 1931 meeting points to certain advantages in stepping outside a genealogical framework (ancestral or queer) that, on the one hand, embraces the word as if it denoted "a *thing*—a single, stable object" or, on the other, understands the word as "a social and discursive production in its own right," two interrelated approaches in the history of sexuality shaped by knowingness in the present.[98] A queer critical historical practice takes an active interest in "the interlocutor who has or pretends to have the *less* broadly knowledgeable understanding of interpretive practice" as possessing the power to "define the terms of the exchange"[99]—an insight suggesting a need to reconfigure a modern sexual past outside identification by, for instance, paying attention to the structures of sexual ignorance. By the summer of 1931, that Douglas-Pennant's case involved accusations of "sex perversion" had been widely reported in the press. Still, in the meeting between Jowitt and the committee, reticence and discomfort prevailed, perhaps out of social embarrassment, prudishness, or modesty (the "psychological operations" sometimes projected "around 'ignorance'") (DM, 34).[100] Blakeney's summation of the underlying cause of Douglas-Pennant's unfortunate downfall is telling: "There is more in this case than you think" (DM, 39). Blakeney is quite correct to observe that aspects of this complex case were "extraordinarily difficult" to talk about. In posing his question as "perfectly categorical," Jowitt discovered quite by accident a lesson historians of sexuality are only now coming to terms with: that it is extraordinarily difficult to imagine the operations of alternative regimes of sexual knowledge in the age of sexology, since we proceed always by assuming that a modern epistemological structure maps onto the sexual past to clean away the "ambiguities" and offer a "perfectly clear apprehension" (DM, 61, 62).

Queer genealogy has been effective in loosening up and disturbing the names and in tracing the historical processes by which the names became hardened. Yet a critical positionality conditioned by the modern habit of identification—and an embarkation point that assumes a knowingness about the past—makes it hard to resist the habit of translating the unsaid into something we think we already know. Too often there lurks in our interpretive engagement with the "not said" or "not seen," in "fragmentary evidence, gossip, and suspicion," the assumption that we know what others didn't or that we know what they were unable to name.[101] From our present vantage point, the gossip and rumors that circulated in 1918 and 1919, ruining Douglas-Pennant's life and career, cut to the core of her inner being because, in modern Western societies, "To know a person's sexuality is to know that person."[102] Read in this context, the long—and ultimately unsuccessful—campaign waged by Douglas-Pennant and her supporters to uncouple her name from a fixed sexual identity (as shown by the inclusion in *The Lesbian History Sourcebook* of the news article originally published in the *Manchester Guardian*) becomes a constitutive part of a narrative about deviant sexuality and the law, oppression, and discrimination.[103] Paradoxically, the queer disavowal of identity—its problematizing of this "business of being called something" or "being positioned by that calling"—secures the terms of identification as a condition of sexual knowledge.[104] In the context of the historiography of identity, there is no better framework than queer genealogy to examine subjects prone to the "perils of 'excessive introspection,'" for an alertness to the "useful provisionality in the categories of social being" teases out alternative modes of naming and self-naming.[105] There are other cases, however, as seen in the examples of Douglas-Pennant, Knocker, or Chisholm, in which introspection on sexuality was absent, impossible, or unthinkable — an ignorance that itself constitutes a way of knowing. This means not that identity history is flawed but that other historical practices are required to address questions that would otherwise go unanswered about the complex discourses within which historical subjects made sense of their lives. What we can conclude is that life in Pervyse or London had much to offer women attracted to adventure and danger, with no time or inclination to reflect on how their relationships were read or construed by others familiar with emergent sexological discourses, though their memoirs and letters offer tantalizing glimpses of new self-understandings of gender. Dumbfounded by the sexual nature of the charges against her, Douglas-Pennant seems ignorant or utterly unaware of her "self" as a sexual being. Subsequently, her refusal or inability to name (or self-name) — as "structured by particular opacities" — necessitates a mode of historicizing that is not closed down by the word but acutely attuned to "a plethora of *ignorances*. . . . Insofar as ignorance is ignorance *of* a knowledge"[106]

By the early 1960s, when David Mitchell conducted interviews in preparation for a book on Douglas-Pennant, Knocker, and Chisholm, among others, it is evident that accusations and counteraccusations continued to flourish. According to two of Mitchell's informants, Douglas-Pennant was a "fine-looking woman, most attractive," but "too imperious" and lacking "a certain affable guile . . . all very proper and Victorian," perhaps the victim of "some jealous (possibly even lesbian) woman who stirred up trouble."[107] Knocker recalled Douglas-Pennant as a "gentle, scholarly woman" but was considerably less sympathetic about Chisholm, whom she characterized as "a raving lesbian who had tried to 'corrupt' her. [Chisholm] had been notoriously promiscuous during their few months in the WRAF — actually going with other WRAF lesbians to parties given by wealthy degenerates in London."[108] Chisholm, in turn, described Knocker as "a marvellous leader and get-things-doner — and lesbian," possibly "mentally unbalanced."[109] Dr. Letitia Fairfield stated that both Knocker and Chisholm had "a very bad reputation as lesbians" — they were "notorious lesbians."[110] There is no record of what Douglas-Pennant made of Knocker or Chisholm, but Chisholm believed Douglas-Pennant was "out of her depth" and "was super anxious that none of the girls should have any opportunity whatsoever to meet . . . men."[111] Douglas-Pennant's successor, Chisholm recalled, encouraged socializing at Hurst Park, and "if normal relations occurred that was a pity, but far far worse would be an outbreak of lesbianism. How right she was — I never realized what could happen until I found myself chased by them! They were an absolute menace."[112]

Constructing a story about Douglas-Pennant as "an honest, decent, clean woman" brought down by malicious gossip alleging lesbianism facilitates the retrieval of a lesbian past by tracing back in time "how the wartime nationalist homophobia" contributed to "an emergent rhetoric of female homosexuality," with important "consequences of citizenship for modern queer identities" (DM, 49).[113] An alternative story about the women of Pervyse that generates "a historical consciousness about past identities" assists in "evaluating the worth and efficacy of present-day discourses and politics."[114] Either way, a preoccupation with sexual identity — as a thing or a process — obscures the variations, deviations, and complications of actual lives of individuals who were unaccustomed to sexual self-reflexivity. If people during the First World War did not associate gender variance with sexual deviance or connect incidences of sexual immorality with typologies of sexual deviance, we need to see how the epistemic repercussions of saying "we cannot use that word" play out differently inside and outside genealogy. To see if "more interesting and difficult questions can be asked about friendship, intimacy, sexuality and spirituality than who had what kind of identity when" entails training a critical eye on individuals wholly unfamiliar with any sense of identity formation as a psychical process.[115]

What might be gained in developing a historiography of sexuality that — like the Douglas-Pennant Committee of 1931 — pauses and hesitates with an uncomfortable self-awareness of the historiographical consequences in matching (or, in this attempt, failing to match) a name to the sexual subject, and what different sort of historicizing becomes available in disrupting the processes of naming, name calling, and self-naming? The purpose of lesbian, gay, and queer historiography, Halperin explains, is, first, "to recover the *terms* in which the erotic experiences of individuals belonging to past societies were actually constituted" and, second, "to measure and assess the differences between those *terms* and the ones we currently employ."[116] Douglas-Pennant's long struggle to clear her name highlights how, between the 1910s and 1930s, the epistemology of sexuality both changes and remains the same as sexological knowledge practices disseminate unevenly alongside preexisting discourses shaped by the constraints of gender and class. Without question, the emphasis in queer thought on disrupting the power of fixed and stable labels and categories has chipped away at identity's "hard permanence," yet there remain in queer genealogical practices vestiges of an interest in, and engagement with, "diamondness." It is a tacit precondition of the critical impulse to blur, unsettle, or destabilize identity to configure the past dialogically *with* identity, which points to an advantage of a queer critical history interested in confronting how identity history overdetermines the processes of "being named and self-naming," which occur "from the outside as well as within any speaker, as exteriority as well as interiority."[117] Even in the age of the queer disavowal of identity, resistance to this "business of being called something" or "being positioned by that calling" can signify "psychological weaknesses" or failure "of authenticity or solidarity," making it all the harder to work out how to historicize the sexual subject as "something of a disgraceful character"—something outside the logic of a genealogical framework that takes the identity habit for granted (DM, 7).[118]

5 / Normal Soap and Elastic Hymens
Historicizing the Modern Norms of Sexuality

"Queer" . . . acquires its meaning from its oppositional relation to
the norm. Queer is by definition *whatever* is at odds with the normal,
the legitimate, the dominant.

DAVID HALPERIN (1995)

If you have missed life's shining goal
And mixed with sex perverts and dopes
For normal soap to cleanse your soul
Apply to Marie Stopes

NOËL COWARD (1922)

In late 1920 the national press published accounts of a hearing that
had taken place before the lord chief justice of the King's Bench Division
in London, in which a former British Red Cross nurse, Miss Florence Eva
Harley, "with a fine war record," alleged she had been the victim of "terrible"
slander (fig. 16).[1] The plaintiff's counsel informed the court that the defendant, Walter Cyril Carr, had damaged his client's good name with all manner of calumny, including a murky reference to "a charge of malpractices."[2]
Over several days the judge, the jury, and a packed public gallery listened
to the minute details of claims, disclaims, and counterclaims — the evidence
was considered "most unpleasant," the case "unsavoury" and "horrible," and
the plaintiff a woman whose reputation had been dragged "through the dirt
and mire" by "a cad of the lowest type."[3] The exact phrases used by the
plaintiff and defendant and, more crucially, the meanings ascribed to those
phrases were hotly disputed — both parties agreed only that on May 3, Carr,
accompanied by his fiancée Miss Decima Hawes (formerly a close friend
of Harley's but soon to become Mrs. Carr), visited Harley at her rooms in
Kensington, whereupon angry verbal exchanges took place (fig. 17). Accord-

164

Figure 16. Nurse Harley. ©The British Library Board *News of the World,* December 5, 1920, 2 (LD 43).

Figure 17. Mr. W. C. Carr and Mrs. Decima Carr (née Hawes). ©The British Library Board *Daily Mirror,* December 4, 1920, 16 (LD 4).

ing to Harley, Carr said: "You want all the joys of married life without being married," a statement that implied sexual promiscuity outside matrimony and thus invoked a moral code often associated with the Edwardian middle classes, but also — in linking marital relations with joy — resonant of an emergent discourse pioneered in a hugely successful advice manual credited by historians as ushering in a new age of sexual enlightenment: Marie Stopes's *Married Love* (1918).[4]

Presenting the facts of life with a rare combination of explicit and accurate clinical detail given in highly accessible, spiritual, and poetic language, Stopes dedicated her volume to "normal" readers "who are married or about to be married" and urged them to master the art of lovemaking to achieve "irradiating joy" in coital union.[5] After decades of weighty tomes and multivolume studies by experts interested in sexuality's "many human variations and abnormalities," here — finally — was a slender little book addressed not to medical and legal professionals but to the "great majority of people" like Walter Carr, hitherto unfamiliar with the organization and expression of sexuality in terms of normal and abnormal.[6] In a trial that sometimes devolved into a slanging match, Carr directed his "most grievous sense of indignation" toward an unmarried woman's desire for illicit sexual pleasure, telling the court that Harley's "practices" had corrupted a "young, innocent girl" who he "knew was pure in her morals."[7] The plaintiff too declared her grievous sense of indignation in a caustic remark that the ill-bred Carr "came from the gutter," to which Carr retaliated by calling Harley "a sexual pervert"—a phrase found nowhere in the pages of Stopes.[8] On view in these provocative exchanges concerning female friendship, courtship, marriage, chastity, and perversion is a sexual landscape of rival regulatory systems otherwise known as "norms," each with the authority to police and arbitrate according to its own rules, and subject to any number of intersecting configurations of power, such as gender, class, and national identity.

Conflicting discourses around sexual regulation reverberate too in the Violet Douglas-Pennant case where, caught up in the machinations of political intrigue, the former Women's Royal Air Force (WRAF) commandant, and those she in turn accused of immorality (including Miss Gwenda Mary Glubb), sought to establish the veracity of their accounts of sexual conduct. At a 1919 hearing of a select committee in the House of Lords, members heard expert testimony on the possibility of an elasticized hymen in which the bodily proof of proper moral conduct appears to evade medical certainty. This predicament of a gynecological inspection unable to confirm sexual morality finds an analogy in our expectation now that an inspection of any given social norm, especially that familiar construction called "the normal," produces a "truth" about the social regulation of sexuality. If, as Foucault asserts, the norm "is an element on the basis of which a certain exercise of power is founded and legitimized," and the norm's power is always historically contingent, attempts to understand the operations of "the normal"—the system we are currently most likely to rely on—need to be situated in relation to other systems active in the governance of sexuality.[9] All these systems are, of course, subject to negotiation and constant change, since norms are not static or fixed but sometimes zigzag erratically and chaotically in any given cultural moment across several discursive realms, for instance, from the medical to the moral and back to the medical again. Norms—at once coherent and incoherent—intensify and recede; exhibit pliancy and elasticity; tend to expand and contract rather than dissolve or break; and exert force unevenly.[10] These parliamentary discussions are less indicative of how, during the war and in its immediate aftermath, there were shifts in social tolerance toward "unconventional" or "modern" sexual behaviors than of how the placement of moral goalposts might have unanticipated consequences, as Douglas-Pennant would discover to her cost. While the 1919 inquiry into the reasons for her dismissal initially focused on the women and men Douglas-Pennant accused of sexual immorality, ultimately her own measure of a moral norm was mocked as prurient, old-fashioned, and naive. This is evident in the tone of the report that followed — a document that exudes smugness in its embrace of modern permissiveness (for example, sexual relations between women and men outside marriage), yet is also peppered with sly innuendo and euphemism.[11]

The disruptions of war placed middle-class women in unsupervised spaces with men, created plentiful homosocial living arrangements, and reconstituted relations between women, between men, and between women and men. However, interests in relaxing, for instance, a system of chaperonage designed to safeguard chastity coexisted alongside insistent claims (by both Harley and Douglas-Pennant) that younger women left to their own devices faced uncertain dangers. At any given moment, the norms of one system might be imperative for some individuals and disregarded by others; enforced one year only to vanish the next, perhaps resurfacing later; powerful in one location and absent elsewhere. Above all, what are often characterized as "dominant cultural expectations" or "conventional morality" were structures and relations subject to gender, class, age, and education.[12] Sexual impropriety might in some instances have been associated with dishonor, while elsewhere there were those who did not respect, acknowledge, or accept a value system that restricted sexual relations to the married, especially in a time of upheaval. Whatever changes took place in the public understanding of sexual morality as a result of the war defy generalization, because the regulatory systems we call norms — once set in motion — fluctuate and shift in unpredictable ways, each interacting with others in a complex web of power relations mediated by varying degrees of agency.

Attempts to analyze the terms and expressions of alleged sexual misconduct at a time when normality's "claim to power" was not yet secure suggest the mutual benefits of an exchange between queer studies and academic history.[13] Just as historical analysis shows how and when the normal begins to exert its considerable power, the "insatiable appetites and marvelous elasticity" of a queer analytical perspective can help in navigating the multivalent, overlapping, and conflicting layers of the social regulation of sexuality neatly encapsulated by the playwright Noël Coward, who advises sex perverts to scrub with "normal soap."[14] Coward, who met Stopes by chance on a transatlantic crossing in late 1921, constructs the modern sex guru as a purveyor of a product that, in its jarring dissonance and gleeful absurdity, brilliantly captures how purification and hygiene, for example, operate in different modalities, recognizing that sexual relations are governed by systems that collide and compete in a never-ending struggle for cultural dominance. Whether the perverts in question have missed out on normality or long for it, the transforming effects of "life's shining goal" (at once temporary and permanent) still await those with the wherewithal to cleanse. And while it seems obvious that souls and bodies are cleansed differently, scholars interested in cultural change in modern Britain have at present only the vaguest sense of how and when a new regulatory force we now call "normality" began to shape and influence how people thought about sexuality. This is why, of all the available theoretical frameworks to investigate the history of sexuality, queerness-as-method appears the most efficacious in explicating legal cases mired in obfuscation, contradiction, and misunderstanding, cases in which the agendas of questioner and respondent seem at cross-purposes and the ambiguities of phrases resist clarification. At the same time, however, queer analysis often neglects the epistemological consequences that arise in defining queer in terms of oppositionality ("at odds with") or deviation (especially as "deviant" and "normal"). This predicament is compounded by the multiple meanings of the word deviation itself, which, as the *Oxford English Dictionary* indicates, refers to both divergence from a rule (or norm) *and* a statistical measurement (such as standard deviation), a source of potential confusion.[15] Here is where I see certain advantages in a queer critical history practice interested in investigating the slippages from "deviation" to "deviant" or "normal." Queer critical history opts not to discover "so-called deviant sexualities" (a concern of queer genealogy) but to critique queer investments in "deviation" as a foundational premise in the epistemological structure of modern sexuality. To probe "that which deviates from" *any* norm and to calibrate "the force of that deviation" demands dismantling the logic of deviation across multiple norms as systems.[16]

My students are astounded when I inform them that the categories of the norm and normal in reference to social regulation emerged only in the mid-nineteenth century, whereupon a "new type of law came into being, analogous to the laws of nature, but pertaining to people" and "expressed in terms of probability."[17] Students find it hard to imagine a time when social relations were regarded neither as "normal," which the *OED* defines as "a type or standard; regular, usual, typical; ordinary, conventional" (in common use ca. 1840), nor as a statistical "norm," a word synonymous with "normal" but also denoting acceptable group behavior (ca. 1900).[18] Even more incredible to them is the realization that the cultural habit of measuring all aspects of sexuality against a reference point called "average" did not become widespread in Britain or North America until about the mid-twentieth century, in a shift that has had devastating effects on how we think about sexuality in that, confusingly, "normal" refers not only to a statistical average, but also to what is healthy or good. Early glimmers of the infiltration of this construction are easily observable in Stopes's use of a phrase so common now that we hardly give it a moment's thought: "In this little book average, healthy, mating creatures will find the key to the happiness which should be the portion of each."[19] The words in question — "average, healthy" — signal the beginning of this profoundly unsettling epistemological problem in the modern history of sexuality, for being average *and* healthy conflates two separate and distinct meanings of normal in denoting, first, a statistical average against which variation might be measured and, second, what is healthy or physically sound; as historian Ian Hacking perceptively explains: "The normal stands indifferently for what is typical, the unenthusiastic objective average, but it also stands for what has been, good health, and for what shall be, our chosen destiny. That is why the benign and sterile-sounding word normal has become one of the most powerful ideological tools of the twentieth century."[20] Linking the statistical average with good health would work against the ambitions of early sexologists who sought, through the rule of average, to remove sexuality from the domain of the moral and establish variance as a neutral value (though variance itself was sometimes also thought symptomatic of physical, emotional, and psychological ill health and anxiety).[21] By the 1940s another groundbreaking book in the domain of sexuality (American sexologist Alfred C. Kinsey's *Sexual Behavior in the Human Male*) would try — and fail — to expose problems inherent in aligning as inextricable the idea of normal as statistical average (quantitative) and normal as healthy (evaluative) across realms as diverse as morality and social hygiene.[22] Arguably (and perversely), queer studies — a field that often defines "queer" in relation to the normal — has devoted its considerable intellectual energies to opposing and destabilizing a category already intrinsically riddled with inconsistency, because, strictly speaking, "if normal just means within a common statistical range . . . to be fully normal is . . . impossible. Everyone deviates from the norm in some way."[23]

Thinking about the norm of "normal" as one of several regulatory systems (such as morality) is difficult because it is all too easy to elide normal and norm, as historian Anna Clark observes: "Modern discourses often employ the term 'normal' or 'natural' in opposition to the deviant or abject. But it is important for historians not to conflate prescriptive ideals, ethical norms, and common behaviors with 'normativity.'"[24] This uncritical habit of conflation, as seen in the work of either historians or queer studies specialists, is partly the consequence of sweeping generalization and simplification. For historians faced with the difficult job of presenting concise explanations of a slow cultural change as seismic as the development of the normal, it has sometimes been necessary to oversimplify. This tendency can be glimpsed in Jeffrey Weeks's helpful primer *Sexuality*, in which he explains that "Northern European and American societies . . . have *since the nineteenth century* at least been obsessively concerned whether a person is normal or abnormal, defined in terms of whether we are heterosexual and homosexual."[25] Others argue that "some historians have assumed that the sexologists' definitions of so-called deviant sexuality became increasingly dominant during the years 1880–1930"—when, in fact, the category of the normal starts to gather momentum in British and American public discourse only in about the 1930s or, at the very earliest, the late 1920s.[26] Situating the normative as oppositional to deviance frequently appears in queer historical work, which is the reason Sally Newman reminds practitioners of the dangers of implicitly imposing "normative status" on sexual subjects of the past.[27] Newman flags a valid concern in her important reconsideration of the status of evidence in historicizing lesbian desire, but it is equally important to historicize that "normative status." Still others assume that in 1900 people typically measured their sexual preferences or feelings not only against an axis of normal or abnormal, but against what they understood as the "majority" ("some men and women began to interpret their homosexual desires as a characteristic that distinguished them from the majority")—an impulse again that would become second nature about the middle of the twentieth century. Good historical work clarifies that in 1950s America it was not uncommon for "the deviant" to be brought "into conformity with the majority" or for deviants to be marginalized "in the interest of maintaining majoritarian social order," but our knowledge of similar shifts in a British context remains hazy.[28]

Meanwhile, scholars in queer studies too readily latch on to the normal as an easy and succinct way to define the analytical operations of queer. Consider, for instance, the definition of queer studies in an online "encyclopedia of gay, lesbian, bisexual, transgender, and queer culture," which depicts the field as engaged in a "political critique of anything that falls into normative and deviant categories."[29] In light of early queer enunciations of its political stance as against "the normalizing methodologies of modern social knowledge," the "normalization of behavior in the broadest sense," the "normal behavior of the social," and above all the "*idea* of normal behavior," it is little wonder that the definition of "queer" — often "constructed as a sort of vague and indefinable set of practices and (political) positions" — pivots relationally with the normal and "normative knowledge."[30] Queer theory is routinely characterized in short introductory volumes as "positioned abrasively toward notions of the normal — and specifically tendentious categories of 'normal sexuality'" or as an attempt to "frustrate . . . heteronormative knowledges and institutions."[31] Reading queer oppositionality strictly as "the name of a certain unsettling relation to heteronormativity" diminishes the power of queer to destabilize any number of norms.[32] Scholar Janet R. Jakobsen regards the "slippage between the statistically normal and the imperative power of moral norms" as a habit symptomatic of the modern, in which "norms themselves become organized according to what can be read as normal, and their constraining and productive power is tied to disciplinary apparatuses, technologies of government, and organized around" statistical norms.[33] Such slippages are commonplace in a field that, as Jakobsen notes, "defines itself" as a site of resistance to the "'the norm,' the 'normal,' or 'heteronormativity.'"[34] A major challenge for the practice of queer critical history is to articulate fully the particularized relational values of the norm, normal, and heteronormativity and demonstrate how the normal shapes, consolidates, and reifies the concepts of the average and healthy (in the medical and psychiatric spheres, for example) in highly specific ways that differ from a host of other discursive realms (such as natural/unnatural) and social institutions (such as the church). No single norm can or should be seen as equivalent to any other cultural mode of regulation, an argument forcefully articulated in a study of "medico-moral politics in England since 1850" by historian Frank Mort, who observes, with considerable alarm, the "reductionist" and "simplistic" queer movement "from identifying the structures of perversion to much more global pronouncements" that ignore "awkward questions of periodization, location, and verification."[35] As my historical case studies suggest, legal exchanges about sexual impropriety did not evince immediate references to normality, a distinctive discursive system that would seep into public consciousness throughout the twentieth century as an additional layer of sexual regulation.

Close inspection of the governance apparatus of "sexual normality" reveals too that its operations are not simply replicated in other domains, such as the moral, scientific, medical, juridical, religious, gender, or class, making it all the harder to disentangle either the power circuitries of the normal or the cultural consequences of its interactions with a plurality of residual and emergent regulatory systems.[36] As a result, the relationality between the "whatever" and the "normal" in David Halperin's now classic definition of queer as "*whatever* is at odds with the normal" has lacked differentiation.[37] How and why this is a problem can best be elucidated by historical example, where it becomes observable how each of Halperin's reference points — "the normal, the legitimate, the dominant" — is a regulatory apparatus in its own right, with relationalities that are not irreducible to the powerful modern dynamic of the normal as it has evolved in the realm of sexuality. Of Halperin's three examples of social regulation, queer analysis has been most preoccupied with the first, as if the normal (and of course its opposite — the deviant, abnormal, or pathological) were transhistorical, outside and beyond history. As queer theorist Michael Warner explains, queer "gets a critical edge by defining itself against the normal rather than the heterosexual"; therefore, "queer self-understanding" emerges from the experience of stigmatizing in every domain of social life, including "gender, the family, notions of individual freedom, the state, public speech, consumption and desire, nature and culture, maturation, reproductive politics, racial and national fantasy, class identity, truth and trust, censorship, intimate life and social display, terror and violence, health care, and deep cultural norms about the bearing of the body."[38] The normal/deviant binary is historically contingent, and it exerts its regulatory force across these cultural domains in specific ways very unlike, for instance, class-bound systems of morality.

Whether signifying a quantitative or an evaluative judgment, embedded in the activation of normal is the (tacit and unthinking) assumption that — say — one out of every ten individuals is deviant, since deviation and variation are conditions of the normal as a regulatory norm. However, the distinctive relationality of normal — as statistical measurement — is not endlessly reproduced or commensurate with other realms, such as morality, in which it is the cultural expectation that all individuals respect its laws. In theory, all citizens of wartime and postwar British society would have been subject to the shifting conventions of sexual morality as mediated by the privileges of gender or class, and thus its rules were observed, evaded, or disobeyed accordingly. The crucial point then is that, while there has always been a sense of right and wrong in human societies, the idea of normality, or the understanding of variations or deviations from a norm, represented a new habit of thought. Therefore the analytical force of "denormativizing" is delimited and curtailed in the absence of historical understanding of the regime of the normal as a discourse that—through the work of Stopes and many others—acquires its meaning gradually as another force governing sexuality.[39]

As in the previous two chapters in part 2, where I have attempted to clarify what the queer critique has to offer historical investigation, here also I wish to emphasize the usefulness of historical analysis for a queer studies sometimes unaware of the historicity of its own conceptual underpinnings. Reconsidering the normal as other than a discursive success story works to complicate the queer privileging of the normal as a norm and foreground the historical conditions in which it emerges and struggles to prevail. The queer troubles with normal cannot be resolved entirely by historical example, but the cases of *Harley v. Carr* and Douglas-Pennant are an excellent place to begin. The story of the rise of the normal/deviant binary as a descriptor of sexuality is less one of supersession or displacement of prior regimes than of accretion, and just as the regime of the normal can never guarantee statistical regularity or fixed ideals, so too systems of morality prove equally adroit in yielding and bending in response to scrutiny. By the middle of the twentieth century the normal would become so inextricably linked with the notion of the norm that these terms would become interchangeable, an elision best grasped by discerning what is at stake in measuring the normal's particular calibrations against the resilience of older norms.

Currents of Sympathy

In September 1917 Florence Eva Harley left Ypres to recover in England from injuries she received while on duty as an army nurse at a clearing station for wounded soldiers (fig. 18).[40] Employed temporarily with the National Health Committee of the Ministry of Health during her recovery, Harley first met Decima Hawes, who worked in the same office. Harley subsequently returned to the front but was ordered home a second time after sustaining even more serious wounds in an air raid at Etaples. As she convalesced, Hawes would "visit her, and by that time they had become fast friends."[41]

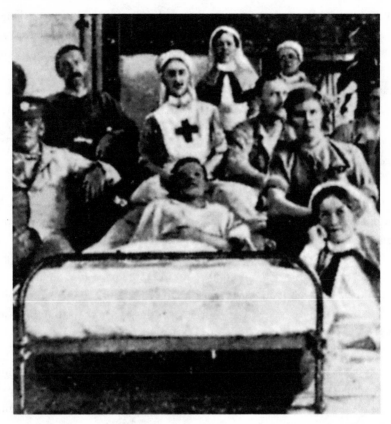

Figure 18. Nurse Harley with wounded soldiers. ©The British Library Board
Daily Mirror, December 4, 1920, 16 (LD 4).

The women's "pure and honorable" friendship was so "close" that they were inseparable — there was a "current of sympathy" between them, and though Hawes would eventually turn against her friend and characterize her as domineering and manipulative, she conceded that they were both "very happy at first."[42] On being discharged from the hospital, Harley felt she could not return to her nursing duties and leave Hawes, a woman who, in the witness box, admitted her nervous disposition and emotional instability. For the next two years, like countless other middle-class single women in England during the war and into the 1920s, the pair "occupied a room together" and lived "in perfect friendship and happiness" until the defendant, Walter Cyril Carr, arrived on the scene and everything changed.[43]

To prise apart these currents of sympathy, we must try to recapture the strangeness of how circuitries of desire were acted on, imagined, and felt between two women (Harley and Hawes) and a newly married couple (Carr and Hawes) and to gauge how others construed these relationships, based on reports of the trial in the press. Feigning indignation that this spectacular case exposed many innocent "women and girls" to some of the more bizarre aspects of sexuality, the lurid headlines of the *Empire News* tantalized readers with promises to reveal the secrets contained in a "mysterious phrase in a letter," which told "an amazing story of a girl's love for another girl"—an unsettling topic possibly unfit for public discussion and "for the general moral good of the community"—but too sensational to ignore.[44] For scholars adept at reading modern lesbian desire between the lines, this courtroom drama seems to highlight the unhappy consequences for women whose love for other women leaves them vulnerable to what is now called homophobic attack. With all the predictable elements of a same-sex love affair gone wrong, it features a familiar cast of characters in the form of a slightly older jealous and domineering predatory lesbian, her once innocent and now corrupted younger female lover, and the scheming opportunist and alleged fraudster and bigamist who drugged Hawes before coercing her into marriage.[45] Yet situating this narrative within the genealogical project offers only a partial explanation of the charge deemed most baffling in 1920: moral perversion. Working outside the epistemological framework of taxonomies and identities carves a conceptual space in which to unpack the logics and codes of regulatory systems both familiar (like morality) and unfamiliar (like class-bound conventions of respectability). Open to the fundamental strangeness of the sexual past, queer critical history—like queer genealogy—acknowledges what is permanently unclear and irresolvable. But—unlike queer genealogy—it notes the organization of sexuality as a complex interplay of several regulatory systems, each rubbing against the next.

Believing Carr was "a cad and a cur," Harley confided to one friend that she would like to see the defendant's face when "confronted" in court "by all the Mrs. Carrs and all the little Carrs."[46] The defendant's supposed philandering was ruining Hawes's life, and because of the likelihood that he would continue to harm other women, Harley claimed it was her duty, first, to protect a dear friend incapable of looking after herself and, second, to stop Carr by threatening to write to his employer (at the Ministry of Health) to expose his "true" character and, later, by ordering her solicitor "to send him to hell—not to the gates of hell, but inside."[47] Carr, in the meantime, presented himself as a man suffering the relentless harassment of a "moral pervert" (a phrase never clarified during the proceedings), based on information he obtained from the unstable Hawes.[48] With one outrageous claim pitched against another, the plaintiff and defendant sought both to prove and to disprove allegations concerning their actions and character — a difficult task for Carr, who acknowledged he little understood the nature of affection between women. Harley argued that Carr's statements were so injurious to her "good name and reputation" ("the jewel of her soul which she wanted to possess untarnished") that he left her little choice but to "smash him" by bringing an action against him in the courts. And, as with Douglas-Pennant, her indifference to expense and to possible negative publicity offers an indication of her social rank and privilege.[49] Whether Harley was intent on retribution against an impudent man who had stolen away her friend or on justice against slander, the result came to the same thing. Unlike Harley, Carr, as a "young man 22 years of age, a clerk by calling," had little money and, after losing both his counsel and solicitor because he lacked funds, he was forced to defend himself (while also counterclaiming for alleged slander and libel).[50] Locating Carr's class position is difficult, since clerking — a "socially amphibious" profession — was poorly paid but demanded reasonable educational qualifications and secretarial skills.[51] While he may have come from the respectable working classes or the lower middle class, he nevertheless exhibited, in the eyes of one admiring journalist, an "uncanny knowledge" of "strict judicial procedure" in every way as expert as Harley's distinguished barrister's.[52]

In fact, the *Empire News* shaped this "dramatic contest" as a kind of David and Goliath struggle in which Carr — a young amateur — found himself in the ring with "one of the most famous fighters at the bar of England," Sir Ernest Wild, KC.[53] Knowing full well the defendant stood almost no chance of outfoxing his formidable opponent, the newspaper painted Carr as a man with innate legal talent, as if "clever dissection, lucidity, and common sense" would triumph.[54] At issue in the twists and turns of the case was who had the right to act chivalrously in defending an innocent and vulnerable, even unbalanced, twenty-two-year-old woman: the female plaintiff (at six years Hawes's senior, a plausible chaperone) or the male defendant? Harley portrayed Carr as lacking gentlemanly manners and argued that his actions sullied Hawes's honor by enticing her to join him on an illicit excursion to Epsom (to satisfy his own craven sexual needs).[55] Carr, on the other hand, fended off accusations that his intentions toward Hawes were improper by arguing that he had acted only out of concern that Harley "wanted this young girl for her own purposes."[56] On trial, therefore, was not simply the veracity of each of Miss Hawes's would-be defenders, but the question of what constituted the proper behavior of a lady and gentleman in the immediate postwar period, since the rules that had previously governed systems of social propriety and moral conduct seemed to many observers to have been profoundly shaken by the war. Cleverly pitching the slander case as a "battle for honor," the *Empire News* recognized that the gendered experience of war sometimes reversed power relations in unexpected ways, allowing women to take on the role of chivalrous protector.[57]

Wild's opening statement highlighting Harley's distinguished career as a nurse was calculated to undermine Carr and establish Harley's credibility and respectability as a fervent patriot who, through the most socially acceptable work undertaken by middle-class women, served with distinction and honor at home and near the war zones. This tactic achieved the desired effect, with headlines reading "Mons Nurse's Honor Vindicated" (*Empire News*), "War Heroine's Slander Action" (*Daily Telegraph*), "Mons Nurse Upholds Her Honor — Fights for Reputation" (*Sunday Chronicle*), and "Nurse Wins Fight for Her Honor" (*Evening Standard*).[58] As the first fight of the war between the British Expeditionary Force (BEF) and the German army, the battle (and retreat) at Mons held particular symbolic value, with resonances of volunteerism, the rush to colors, heroism, and personal sacrifice.[59] Newspapers linked Harley not merely with the womanly work of nurturing wounded and dying soldiers, but also with the travails of battle itself. Although at the time of the trial the two key players were employed as ordinary government clerical staff (Harley in the Ministry of Munitions and Carr in the Ministry of Health), newspaper photographs of Harley in uniform placed her literally and physically on a higher plane than Mr. and Mrs. Carr, who, in civilian dress, appear to have evaded dangerous war work.[60] Harley volunteered to go to the front as a nursing sister (with the Queen Alexandra Imperial Military Nursing Service Reserve) on August 8, 1914, and served in one organization or another until late 1918, receiving the Mons medal.[61] *The Times* reported that Harley "was sent to France and was wounded and received burns [at Ypres]. . . . [S]he was again wounded during an enemy air raid at Etaples, and was on that occasion partially buried. She was sent home to hospital in a critical condition, suffering from open wounds."[62] The *Daily Mirror* added that the former nurse still had "a German bullet under her heart."[63] With her war experiences presented as being as harrowing and courageous as those of any Tommy fighting on the Western Front, press attention on the war-scarred body positioned Harley as a hero in another kind of battle, which transformed her from a passive female victim of a male slanderer into a decorated war hero forced to take "singular slander action" in defense of her honor.[64] Carr's own record shows that he signed up with the Royal Navy for the twelve-year stint of a regular contract in March 1912 but was not called for further service after December 1919.[65] During his seven-year career at sea he served on several ships and was disciplined at least once for willful disobedience, with a thirty-day detention.[66] Carr's career hardly compared with the nurse's frequent exploits of bravery and valor, indicating the greater cultural capital of a woman wounded in the line of duty compared with the undistinguished career of an ordinary seaman.

One of Carr's great miscalculations was to call Harley's account of her exploits "untrue" and insist she had been "sent away for misconduct."[67] He attacked her service record, claiming she had spent only a few weeks in France, had never been wounded, and had picked up her Mons medal in a stall on the Edgware Road—each charge flatly refuted.[68] Documents held in London's National Archives confirm that Harley did indeed arrive in France as part of the BEF campaign on August 8, 1914.[69] Moreover, in recognition of her "special proficiency and good conduct," she was entitled to wear the 1914 Mons Star, a point she clarified to the judge, who mistakenly believed the Distinguished Service Order (DSO) was given only to men.[70] Later, as a nursing sister with the Royal Red Cross, Harley was awarded the British Women's War Medal Emblems, an honor noted in the *British Journal of Nursing:* "The King has conferred decorations as follows. . . . The Royal Red Cross (First Class) . . . [to] Miss Florence Harley."[71] British Red Cross records affirm that she enrolled with their organization in October 1914 and was discharged in 1918, during which time she worked in five hospitals in England and, toward the end of the war, at a military hospital in France (May to November 1918).[72] Another medal card indicates that Harley also worked as a VAD (Voluntary Aid Detachment), though she was turned down for a British War and Victory Medal because the case for this decoration was not thought sufficiently strong.[73] Harley may have exaggerated the length of her time in France (since each time she received injuries she was sent back to England), but there is no doubt that during her intermittent assignments near the front lines she suffered physical injury more than once.

Persistently asked by Carr whether she had been dismissed from any posting under a cloud or forced to resign—charges she vehemently denied—Harley, under oath, confessed that there was only a single blemish in her otherwise impeccable record, a fact previously known only to Hawes, whom she had sworn to secrecy. In a registered letter Harley sent to Hawes, the former nurse wrote: "Did you realize when telling your secret [to Carr] that you betrayed my honor which you have pledged, and which was not yours to give away. Our secret should have been ours to the grave."[74] When asked by the judge to explain the meaning of that "secret," the plaintiff asserted it pertained to her status as an absentee from the British Red Cross, because she had failed to return to base when summoned: "Do you mean to tell me," the lord chief justice asked, "that this secret referred simply to your breaking the Army regulations?"[75] Harley affirmed that this was indeed the case: "It was the only time I smirched my honor," a word that, in the context of distinguished national service, adds other meanings to a woman's sexual probity.[76] The judge's tone of incredulity indicates that, although plausible in its consistency with the actions of a woman passionate about protecting her reputation, other interpretations could be ascribed to the "secret," as well as to another troubling phrase: "Do you remember our final mating?" (reported variously as "meeting").[77]

Wild pounced on Carr's admission that he found this phrase mystifying, discovering an opportunity, first, to expose the defendant's ignorance of the ways the emotional intensities of female friendships might be completely harmless and innocent ("he did not know that young women were often extravagant in their language") and, second, to insinuate that Carr was responsible for planting a more unsavory interpretation of Harley's intentions in the mind of the impressionable and sheltered Hawes.[78] In other words, the barrister scored a double victory. On the one hand, Wild argued, Carr implied that the word honor referred not to Harley's "Army honor but to the secret practices she was afraid Miss Hawes would reveal."[79] On the other hand, Wild noted that Hawes did not provide Carr with "details at first, but she did later," a sequence of knowledge transfer implicating Carr as a man who had instructed her on how to interpret what might have been perfectly clean and pure: "During their friendship the plaintiff had made indecent suggestions to [Hawes]. She did not know at the time what the suggestions meant, but she did later. She also said that the plaintiff had committed malpractices upon her."[80] Once armed with Carr's lessons in sex education, Hawes allegedly attempted to call off her engagement because she refused to enter into an unsound marriage (declaring, "Cyril, I am not fit to marry you"—a statement evocative of eugenics).[81] By carefully establishing that Carr "began to talk about dirty things" before their engagement (a notably different register than the sexual knowledge of the normal), the accomplished barrister questioned Carr's own respectability.[82] Carr was also thought guilty of over-reading Harley's words by twisting them to mean what they did not ("A great deal more often can be made of the language by a critic than the writer suggested"), a rather unfair chastisement, since even early sexologists were perplexed about how to differentiate between unnatural practices and a "vague sensual pleasure" derived from "'sentiments of exalted sympathy.'"[83] Wild's greatest success was in turning the tables on Carr by arguing that Hawes saw nothing "wrong" about her relations with Harley until Carr's salacious inferences — he, therefore, was the corruptor.[84]

Carr's predicament was a catch-22. Everything he "knew" about Harley was mediated by Hawes, which meant he had to ignore the judge's caution not to put his own wife on the stand. Once in the witness box, Hawes "admitted that she suffered from neurasthenia and hysteria," introducing late nineteenth-century medical discourses associated with nervous diseases and linked by scholars to gender, class, modernization, and above all the emotional trauma of war.[85] No further proof of Hawes's emotional or mental instability was necessary after she freely admitted she was prone to hallucinations that "sometimes took the form of seeing little nigger boys dancing on the moon," injecting fantasies of imperial lunacy into the proceedings.[86] In his summation, the judge emphasized that Hawes "had strange ideas, and thought things had happened which, in fact, had never happened."[87] Hawes's admissions and Wild's attack on Carr's alleged knowledge of sexual matters meant that knowledge was a dangerous business — and if Hawes's imagination was as vivid as she confessed in the courtroom, her testimony was as unreliable and tainted as Carr's sexual knowledge. Far from corroborating Carr's claims and counterclaims, Hawes's obvious mental fragility rendered Harley's faithful and patient care more a virtue than a vice. In fact, Harley testified that she had been informed by a physician that separation "would imperil" Hawes's life, explaining why Harley did not return to her nursing duties.[88] *Harley v. Carr*, then, was largely conveyed to the reading public as a tale of competing chivalries between a woman and man in which class and war service were more significant determinants than gender and sexuality. As a professional nurse, decorated war hero, and woman of some means (or a woman with friends or relations who could assist her by paying the fees of "one of the most famous barristers at the bar of England"),[89] Harley appeared better positioned to protect Hawes than a man of uncertain character and rapidly diminishing resources. Yet still in the balance were the results of a medical examination to determine if anything was "wrong" about Harley's friendship with Hawes.

The Test of Virginity

According to Sir Ernest Wild, the defendant's exclamation "you are not a virgin" constituted impugning his client's chastity, subject to prosecution under the Women's Slander Act of 1891, "which rendered slanders on women actionable without proof of special damage."[90] In summing up, the judge instructed the jury to consider whether Carr's statement referred "to immorality in the ordinary sense" (presumably, sexual intercourse with a man) or "something different"—an interesting choice in pitting a shared understanding of sexual morality against something that resists specificity.[91] One route to proving the "ordinary sense" was to submit to the ordeal of gynecological scrutiny where the condition of the hymen, a thin membrane attached to the walls of the vagina, would either confirm or deny the medical condition of virginity in a court of law. Harley's specialist was Dr. Jane Walker, a distinguished physician with "a private practice at her home in Harley Street, London" (a further indication of class status), who informed the court that "the plaintiff was distinctly a virgin."[92] Unaware that an ocular probe of the female orifice might trigger debates about what constitutes legal proof of an unmarried woman's chastity, the inexperienced Carr failed to push Walker further about her findings, even though the previous year this conundrum about the moral and legal ramifications of a potentially flawed medical examination had been extensively discussed in a well-publicized hearing conducted by a select committee in the House of Lords, involving Glubb and Douglas-Pennant. Like Harley, Glubb responded to the former commandant's allegations of sexual misconduct by submitting to a test of virginity by a physician who subsequently reported that his patient's membrane was "unbroken."[93] In attempting to insert his little finger and then his forefinger into his patient's vagina, Dr. Alexander McGregor Shart observed that Glubb "showed signs that she was suffering pain."[94] The expert witness then seized the opportunity to present a brief tutorial on the intricacies of the female anatomy, since even some physicians at this time were "surprisingly ignorant" of the basic "physiological facts," and concluded there was "no definite test" to guarantee female virginity.[95] When asked by peers of the realm for clarification on whether his examination could absolutely affirm that Glubb had never had "sexual intercourse with a man," the doctor restated his opinion that the hymen was intact, but then he appeared to undermine his own medicolegal authority by stating that no test existed to establish virginity beyond all reasonable doubt, for there were always exceptions to any rule or general principle.[96] Medical opinion on the physical state of virgo intacta would never represent anything more than a "fairly sure guide" of virginity, because "three possibilities" existed "where a hymen would not be ruptured: the first is where the aperture is large; the second is where the male organ is very small; and the third is where the hymen is very elastic so that it would stretch."[97] Since Glubb's hymen was not elastic, nor was her aperture large, conditions that would allow some women to cheat the system, it remained a possibility that she had been penetrated by a very small male organ. However, unsurprisingly, the anatomy of her alleged male lover was not subjected to the medical gaze.

While the results of a gynecological examination were accepted in both cases as legal proof of the women's moral character, in reality the burden of establishing reliable norms in the realm of medicine was as elusive and insecure as other regulatory systems. In Glubb's case the integrity of the test of virginity was thought compromised, since the physician hedged his bets. In *Harley v. Carr* the plaintiff was declared virgo intacta, but her physician's findings that there could be no imputation on her chastity "in the narrow sense" went unchallenged.[98] Carr elected not to "attack the woman doctor's evidence, which, it turned out, was another colossal miscalculation on his part since, according to Wild, Carr "knew" that Walker's "medical evidence killed his case."[99] Yet Carr's decision not to cross-examine the physician could also be read as an honest mistake, since he believed the practices "carried out by Miss Harley," as described to him by his informant (Hawes), "did not affect her in a way that the doctor's examination would disclose."[100] Dr. Walker, when queried by the judge, asserted that "had there been habitual malpractices there would have been evidence of them, and she found nothing of the kind. There was no evidence of her being a sexual pervert."[101] Probing further, the judge stretched the medical measure of a moral norm and the legal meaning of the physicality of virginity to its limits: "Supposing there had been habitual unnatural practices, would you have expected to find some signs of it?" The physician, without commenting on how she understood "unnatural practices" or the importance of frequency, replied in the affirmative.[102] The hymen might be elastic, but so too is the medical test itself, which, as this exchange shows, might be deployed to prove anything. In accusing Harley of addiction to "filthy, abominable, and unnatural practices with womankind," Carr located things that "ought to scorch the paper on which it was printed" within the discursive field of religious morality.[103] The devil was in the details — and Carr was markedly reluctant to clarify in court what he thought those "practices" entailed, although in his particulars for the trial he explicitly stated that the plaintiff was "a sexual pervert," whatever that might mean.[104]

Carr's silences were filled by Wild, who spoke of "dirty things" and a "wrong thing" — even asking Hawes outright why she stayed with a friend who did "filthy things" to her, to which the witness replied, "She told me that they were right and holy."[105] This invocation of the spiritual suggests an intimacy between the women akin to matrimony, but whatever took place between them, Carr was literally at a loss for words. That "something different" one woman might do with another woman was not a criminal act subject to legal regulation. Carr's defense was that he was justified in making claims against Harley since in his view (contrary to the court's view) sexual relations between women, first, compromised a woman's virginity and, second, constituted sexual perversion. The defendant never denied that he had spoken the words "you are not a virgin" to Harley, insisting instead that he never meant she had experienced sexual relations with a man. Harley, on the other hand, had to demonstrate that Carr had spoken a slander that was injurious to her reputation. In the eyes of the court, nothing Harley did with Hawes could be as serious as "immorality in the ordinary sense," equivalent to the grave violation of sexual penetration outside marriage. Again Wild forcefully argued that Carr "had misconstrued something" in the contents of a letter Harley sent to Hawes and "suggested something nasty to his neurasthenic sweetheart which she had adopted as a fact."[106] In alluding to nastiness, Wild sought to associate Carr with moral depravity, though this tactic was undermined by his own client, whose recollection of Carr's phrases ("that is really what you are suffering from" and "I can tell it by your face")[107] shifted the register to the medical, as if the defendant was proffering an unwanted diagnosis of a sick patient. Noting signs in the plaintiff's face of "dissipation," Carr concluded that Harley suffered from an ailment related to sexual frustration, her desire for marital joy thwarted by her spinsterhood.[108] Yet at this juncture the defendant floundered, as Wild's coup de grâce turned the visual evidence of the alleged slander on its head: "Was there ever a woman who looked less like a sexual pervert than the plaintiff?"[109] This invitation to read Harley's appearance in relation to the most ill-defined category of all was a brilliant tactic, for Wild's rhetorical question was impossible to answer.

The more knowledge Carr betrayed in asserting the legibility of the marks of dissipation, the more he undermined his own case. Discursive slippages worked to obscure rather than illuminate the nature of unnatural practices, since, despite the greater dissemination of works by Stopes and others, in the legal realm it remained a precondition of sexual knowledge to pervert the knower. Harley's credibility, on the other hand, was enhanced by the jury's acceptance of her argument that she found Carr's slanders unintelligible; reticence about sexual matters secured her position within the boundaries of proper womanhood, thought at the time to transcend class. The presiding judge himself confirmed that it was difficult to persuade a woman, "in even a court of law, to give details of indecency because of the *natural* modesty that she possesse[s]. That [is] the case even with girls of the poorest class and humble education."[110] In a court of law the inability to understand the meanings of words ("filthy, abominable, and unnatural practices with wom-ankind") was an asset, since speaking freely about sexual matters was judged transgressive (as Maud Allan had discovered) and culturally unacceptable.

That Stopes's *Married Love* contributed to expanding what was once a specialist knowledge to a wider public might not have been an altogether welcome change in a world where ignorance about sex worked to one's legal advantage. In 1920 possessing sexual knowledge was associated with taint—the more partial and imperfect one's understanding of sexual acts between women, or between women and men, the greater the likelihood of exoneration or vindication. According to the judge, knowledge compromised virtue: no decent woman would speak of such matters, "yet Mrs. Carr, after only a few weeks' acquaintance with the man she eventually married, told him the whole history of her secret."[111] The value of not-knowing was a lesson Carr failed to learn.

Labeling Harley a sexual pervert exposes the limits of Carr's sexual knowl-edge, since he was unable to explain his meaning. This predicament points to a need for an analytical framework outside the context of sexology, because the snippets of information Carr seems to have gleaned during his time in the navy or back home in the office did not produce a sexual subject through an articulation of acts or identities. One newspaper asserted that the nature of Carr's allegation "at first baffled even one of the greatest lawyers the Realm possesses," the plaintiff's own counsel.[112] Wild's profession of ignorance was obviously calculated to sway the jury, since, a few months later, during the debates on proposals to criminalize gross indecency between females, he proclaimed to his fellow parliamentarians in the House of Commons that he was well informed and highly experienced in such matters.[113] In expressing in court his relief that "he did not know what those malpractices were," Wild shrewdly portrayed the enlightened Carr as doubly corrupt, first, in instructing his wife that Harley's suggestions were "indecent" and, second, in besmirching Harley's reputation.[114] To the judge's question to the jury whether Carr implied that Harley was "guilty" of being unchaste (defined as "meaning sexual connection between the plaintiff and a man or men") or "only guilty of the malpractices described," the foreman responded "only malpractices," a charge the jury disbelieved and dismissed.[115] With the twelve men of the jury returning a verdict in Harley's favor, the judge awarded damages to the plaintiff of £1,000 with costs (and further ordered the defendant to pay costs on his counterclaim against the plaintiff), acknowledging the plaintiff's arguments that expressions of one "girl's love for another girl" were harmless, malpractices of a different order — "something different," not subject to juridical regulation.[116]

Harley's other claims against Carr — that he had been involved in a "pernicious friendship with Miss Hawes" and had done "all sorts of things"[117] — required no expert witness; in her view, these actions spoke for themselves. The former nurse claimed the moral high ground because the class codes governing how a gentleman should treat a lady, though stretched during the war, had not snapped. Some gentlemen invited ladies to go away for a night "on a two days' acquaintance" or kept ladies out late at night, and some ladies accepted such invitations, unconcerned or unaware that their behavior might compromise the class-bound rules of respectability.[118] In a court of law, Harley convinced the jury that Carr's violations endangered the reputations of both the woman he courted and her female friend. Carr's accusations against Harley, on the other hand, ran the gamut of available regulatory systems — from the moral (she is no virgin) to the medical (she is suffering from something) to the modern (she wants the joy of married life), though not sexology or psychoanalysis. Ironically, next to an announcement of the verdict of *Harley v. Carr* in the *Daily Mail* ("a paper," according to Lord Salisbury, "written by clerks for clerks") was an article headlined "Sex Side of New 'Science,'" expressing anxieties about a sudden surge of interest in a "medical theory" called "psychoanalysis": this "popular craze . . . is passing out of the hands of doctors into the hands of all sorts of practitioners, including young women."[119] Like sexology, psychoanalysis was considered dangerous because of its national origin (Germany), its frankness about sexuality, and the fact that it was "practiced outside the medical profession."[120]

Through the interwar period ordinary people would become increasingly familiar with normal or abnormal as descriptors of sexual types — polarities that added discursive layers to the epistemology of modern sexuality rather than displacing older ones.

She Did Not Know at the Time

Florence Harley's slander action was brought before the lord chief justice and a special jury because the plaintiff sought to "smash" the man whose accusations, if left unchallenged, would ruin her reputation.[121] Reported extensively in the national press, *Harley v. Carr* was depicted as "remarkable."[122] Photographs of the former nurse in uniform — her chest emblazoned with the red cross of selfless service — emphasized the womanly work she had done on behalf of soldier-patients. Here was a story of the vindication of a heroic nurse wrongly accused of doing terrible things with another woman and the downfall of her unscrupulous male accuser, a clerk financially ruined as "bit by bit his money had gone."[123] For different reasons, the case remains just as remarkable for historians of sexuality and practitioners of queer studies, because it demands contextualization inside and outside the logic of the genealogical project.

The issue before the jury was whether Carr's remarks constituted "words spoken and published which impute unchastity or adultery to any woman or girl."[124] Wild had only to prove the plaintiff's innocence in the "ordinary sense," ostensibly measurable and verifiable via a virginity test. Carr's defense strategy, on the other hand, required the jury to accept that he had never impugned Harley's virginity or acted with malice or recklessness, that like any future husband in his position, he acted to protect his fiancée from a woman who "wanted this young girl for her own purposes," a woman whose face bore the "marks . . . of her dissipation."[125] Harley's loss of virginity, the defendant claimed, was not the result of carnal knowledge but of malpractices with Hawes. Crucially, however, reading the marks of moral dissipation represents a different procedure than the taxonomizing of a sexological case study to affix a label based on acts, identities, or desires. Carr's preoccupation with Harley's facial appearance references not sexological typologies but Victorian physiognomy, which "still had wide purchase after the war": "Virginity would certainly be considered transparent or at least detectable, as would sexual depravity."[126] Sexual knowledge too, in Carr's eyes, was not a modern science to banish "sex-ignorance" but a corrupting force.[127] In exposing Harley as the source of Hawes's "sexual knowledge," Carr sought to assign guilt, for here was "a young and pure girl, and if she had sexual knowledge to whom was it to be attributed but to the plaintiff?"[128] *Harley v. Carr*, then, presents a case in which "none of the bicameral rubrics through which we routinely process" modern sexuality (normal versus abnormal, deviant, or pathological) "provide us with much analytical purchase on the sexual and knowledge relations."[129] The normal, invoked obliquely in the slander ("joys of married life"), hovered on the margins of a legal process in which other indexes of sexual regulation circulated: pure/impure, chaste/unchaste, virtuous/unvirtuous, clean/filthy, right/wrong, honorable/dishonorable, natural/unnatural, or respectable/unrespectable.

Within this densely imbricated network of emergent and residual discourses—some barely mobilized pushing against others tried and tested over centuries—the jury deliberated on the meaning of Carr's allegations impugning Harley's chastity, a charge in every way as damaging in some social circles in early twentieth-century Britain as references to "sexual perversion," which might have meant anything. As we have seen, situating this trial or its outcome in the context of an ancestral history invested in the "tired trope" of the incomprehensibility of lesbian sexuality does not get us far.[130] Queer critical history seeks to understand the conditions of how the sexual was constituted across space and time and—like queer genealogy—knows that privileging "modern norm-speak" obscures the workings of other systems.[131] The difficulty for the queer genealogist in analyzing this case is the absence of sexuality as ontological, the realm of queerness-as-being. Of paramount concern throughout the trial was the problem of inexplicable terms and phrases: "sexual perversion and malpractices"; "final mating"; or "our secret should have been ours to the grave."[132] Calling on his own wife to take the stand, Carr asked Hawes to explain what Harley meant in promising to "show . . . the crowning gift of love," to which she responded that she "did not know at the time."[133] This explanation—she did not know at the time—is hugely significant, since it indicates that sexual knowledge rather than sexual identity was paramount. We will never know what physical acts constituted "malpractices" or what anyone then imagined such relations entailed. What can be established is this: the alleged goings-on between two women did not produce a sexual subject; the court determined that "something different" between women constituted a lesser offense; and the truthfulness of Carr's alleged proficiency in reading virginity on the body ("you are not a virgin") was subject to expert medical scrutiny to prove or disprove his claim.

A major challenge for the historian of modern sexuality is how to enter this stranger realm of the past and account for other configurations of sexual knowledge, one in which the normal might be seen as jostling against (rather than "shattering") existing discourses of morality and class-inflected notions of respectability.[134] Women and men were caught up in the dilemma of how to speak about sexual matters without compromising respectability, as the judge remarked during the hearing, since "even common girls" possessed a "modesty" that forced them "to shrink from expressing themselves on a subject of that kind."[135] Hawes told the court that when Harley promised to show her friend "the crowning gift of love," she "did not know at the time whether it was a mental or physical state, but later on the plaintiff showed her"—an admission that would have compromised the virtue of a woman not suffering from "hallucinations."[136] In a culture that valued unknowing, the only clarity to emerge is that, beyond a small educated elite, beyond the pockets of the bohemian or privileged classes, the broader British public did not think about human sexuality as we do now, though change was in the air. Between the wars sex education and more open discussions of "sexual questions" would slowly gain respectability, and modern sexual enlightenment would be associated with the demarcation of prescribed and reliable boundaries around the construction of the normal.[137] However—as with all regulatory systems—its power is tenuous, and in the constant struggle for dominance it sometimes loses. In Harley's and Glubb's medical examinations, normative values (that is, those derived "from observation, compilation, measurement, and comparison") surface briefly—but the cultural significance of the medical test of virginity was not primarily understood outside medical circles as a scientific mechanism of categorization and enumeration or as a condition registered within an economy of the average or healthy.[138] In the end, scrutiny of the hymen proved less than conclusive in measuring either personal moral conduct or sexual peculiarities. Other discourses were also invoked as plausible ways of knowing, such as class, gender, or citizenship, each operating in accordance with its own rules and cultural imperatives. Equally important, too, were "tactful silences" that worked not to "preserve hetero privilege" or signal "variations from the norm," but to create a space for willful unknowing, since there were things some people did not want to know and things that assigned guilt through the knowing.[139]

The case studies investigated in this chapter expose as a fiction what is often called conventional morality, its borders permeable and open to evasion and negotiation. Returning to the bizarre exchanges in the Lords' select committee, the expert physician responds with exasperation to a lawyer's last attempt to recuperate the test as a definitive indicator that Miss Glubb's "vagina and hymen" were "ordinary" and "normal" rather than elastic.[140] After a lengthy and nuanced explanation of the test of virginity, the physician's clinical discourse of modern medical knowledge and scientific testing merges with the language of the moral: "I would say this girl is a virgin," shifting with ease from one discourse to another.[141] Unfortunately for Carr, no mechanism existed to detect activity apart from penetration — Harley's innocence hinged on a test that even her accuser knew was useless. There was, however, a different sort of test to reassure the jury that women were safe with Harley, as provided by her landlady, Mrs. Ann Creber. Under oath the landlady informed the court that her husband, "with full knowledge of the slander had permitted" his wife to sleep with Harley: "There was only one breath of fresh air in that foetid case," Harley's barrister announced with bravado, "and that was when Mrs. Creber said that for two months, with her husband's consent, she had allowed the plaintiff to share her bed."[142] By the middle of the twentieth century, the prospect of two women sleeping together would not provide a breath of fresh air — such arrangements would be closely scrutinized and likely judged as abnormal, depending on the extenuating circumstances, reaffirming that "the abnormal of today" may have been "the normal of yesterday."[143]

These cases reveal that at a time when even physicians disagreed about what constituted a bodily act of sex, notions such as perversion, malpractice, or neurasthenia floated freely as not quite empty or loose signifiers, useful in suggesting rather than specifying. Systems of social regulation — at once interdependent and mutually exclusive — were constantly variable and highly mutable. Incompatibilities notwithstanding, systems governed in accordance with their own internal logics, values, beliefs, ideals, principles, knowledges, and understandings. Yet people seemed generally not to notice, unperturbed by the inconsistencies generated by their movements between one regulatory system and another. Above all, historical analysis reveals that the point of view of "the normal" had hardly begun to infiltrate, infuse, or saturate modern sexuality — a concept that remained for many an utterly unambiguous "whatever." Thanks to the producers of marital advice literature, sexual knowledge would gradually be revealed to a wider reading public. Stopes, for example, sought to illuminate the mysteries of sexuality by addressing "the married and . . . those about to marry, provided they are normal in mind and body and not afraid of facing facts."[144] At the same time, her exposition of the "joys of married love" also muddied the waters because the new discourse in the regulation of sexuality she helped to create — clinical, precise, accurate, and normalizing — would never prove powerful enough to obliterate or dislodge earlier understandings. This is how modern sexual knowledge emerged in interwar Britain — as a complex, multilayered, and multifaceted site that had not yet achieved the standard of identificatory efficiency of the late twentieth century.

Whatever Is at Odds

The "logic of the sexual order" is "deeply embedded" in modern consciousness, but not in a logical way.[145] Complicating genealogies of modern homosexuality by introducing other analytical categories — such as "citizenship, empire, and nation" — represents an important development in identity history.[146] At the same time, we cannot overlook the infrastructure and logic of sexological thought itself, underpinned as it is by the values of "normative or deviant" (a phrase that appears repeatedly in Deborah Cohler's study of lesbianism and the First World War).[147] Queer critical history shifts attention away from "competing models of female homosexuality" to explore unimaginable terrain.[148] As I have suggested, this predicament does not point to inherent weaknesses in the genealogical project, for its purpose is to provide accounts of homosexual emergence. Historical work locked into the logic of identity, however, struggles to detect and explicate the intricacies of other regulatory systems. For example, in a close reading of the 1921 parliamentary debates concerning the addition of a clause to regulate indecency between females, Cohler translates as "homosexual acts" what one supporter of the bill describes as a "moral" weakness in violation of "the dictates of Nature and morality," a register significantly different from sexological discourse.[149] There are few more convincing examples than this parliamentary debate to observe the leaps and circuitous navigations across discursive structures, ranging from eugenic anxieties about race suicide to morality to medicine — regulatory systems hardly reducible to the normative as normal.

Since its inception, the primary cultural work of queering has been to oppose, destabilize, undo, or challenge norms — and while it has sometimes achieved analytically dazzling results through "displacement" and through "knock[ing] signifiers loose, ungrounding bodies, making them strange," historians express amazement that queer studies has too often sidestepped the historicity of the normal.[150] It seems counterintuitive that a critical practice well versed in the methods of defamiliarizing and denaturalizing would be so conceptually overinvested in one cultural mode of regulation either, on the one hand, to scrutinize the logic of the relationalities of normal and deviant or, on the other, to deconstruct its distinctive workings in relation to other regulatory systems. Some practitioners of queer studies approach the sexual past in highly strategic ways in conjunction with their interests, for example, in the etiology of deviance, in contrast to historians of modern sexuality who place utmost value on the careful dissection of the confluences of the moral, ethical, religious, secular, scientific, or medical. The popularization of a new discourse of sexual regulation in the form of marital advice literature added another discursive layer — the normal — which means that Halperin's "whatever" needs to be analyzed with utmost care, the calibrations of each domain — "the normal, the legitimate, the dominant" — anatomized and assessed.

The important job of putting the normal into historical perspective has begun in queer studies in some periods and contexts (notably, medieval, early modern, and American); even so, the temporal logic of queer thought persistently pulls away from its historicity.[151] Note, for instance, a telling phrase in Judith Halberstam's approving endorsement of Karma Lochrie's skills in taking "her readers on an astonishing tour of the 'prenormative past.'"[152] From the perspective of the critical historian, Lochrie's "when normal wasn't" effectively conveys the disorderly diachronic and synchronic evolution of a concept we can no longer do without. Part of the success of this formulation, it seems to me, is that it frustrates and thwarts the queer impulse to read the past from the perspective of the present — what Halberstam elsewhere calls "the trap of simply projecting contemporary understandings back in time."[153] Pitting a slippery and elastic queer against a coherent, all-powerful normal makes it difficult for queer scholars to provide explanations for students who ask, as mine have, what normal was called before it was invented. As simple as this question sounds, it is one that queer studies has only recently begun to address, though queer scholars, attuned to contradiction and paradox, would surely appreciate Hacking's explanation of normality as in some sense "both timeless and dated."[154] It "has been with us always," but it "can in a moment adopt a completely new form of life."[155]

The queer faith in the power of the normal to control and govern sexuality is actually a testament to the success of a relatively recent ideological system that has effectively masked the incoherencies of a time when normal wasn't. Historical investigation of the systems that regulate sexuality in modern Britain suggests not the secure reign of the normal but a mishmash of regulatory structures, each exerting authority or influence in one realm or another, unevenly, unpredictably, and erratically. In the early decades of the twentieth century individuals might have navigated any number of power structures — the law, media, government, military, family, church, or medical establishment — through the differentiations of nation, empire, race, class, age, gender, and education. The configuration of normal versus pathological (or deviant) in the domain of sexuality changed cultural understandings of sexual relations while leaving other norms, with different ethical or moral imperatives, largely undisturbed. Queer studies has been effective in exposing the social realm as shot through with "normalizing methodologies," a critique that has elucidated the relational dynamics of oppositionality ("whatever is at odds").[156] In dialogue with historical practice, queer historicizing holds the potential to expand the queer fascination with dissidence, abnormality, and the pathological, transgressive, subversive, or perverse, first, to unpack the cultural dynamics of oppositionality across the registers of a nexus of diverse regulatory systems and, second, to situate oppositionality as one mode in tension with other relationalities of social differentiation. This is by no means a simple transaction, but that does not mitigate its urgency. Queer reassessment of identity politics is already well under way, as scholars wrestle with theorist Lee Edelman's controversial call for a "queer oppositionality . . . that would oppose itself to the logic of opposition."[157] It is difficult to overstate the disturbing implications of this provocative statement that cuts to the conceptual core of the queer project. Edelman's challenge, unsettling and enlivening, has breathed new life into a field often thought moribund.[158] Resistance to the unrelenting undertow of the normal, underwritten by the logic of oppositionality, allows a conceptual space in which to suspend, even if momentarily, the urge to locate and privilege the normal so as to consider the multiple technologies of power.

This is why queer critical history is committed to stepping outside the epistemological apparatus of modern sexuality to determine, for instance, the relational logics of other regulatory systems (pure/impure or chaste/unchaste) less familiar now; the degrees of intersectionality between systems; the repercussions of collisions between the residual and emergent; and the significance of the absence of the privileged reference point of "average."[159] Normal soap and elastic hymens suggest that making sense of the sexual past means exploring the silences of willful unknowing, the gradations and shadings of nuances and innuendo, the shreds of information and misinformation, in tandem with polarities familiar and less familiar and relations that resist polarization — and even this provides only a "fairly sure guide" to what is always a messier affair.[160]

EPILOGUE

We have to produce something that doesn't yet exist and of which
we can have no idea of what it will be.
MICHEL FOUCAULT (1980)

In 1919 Florence Harley and Decima Hawes lodged together in
Campden Hill Square, Kensington, renting rooms not far from the Old
House at 13 Holland Street, Violet Douglas-Pennant's address in the 1920s,
or 37 Holland Street, where between 1924 and 1929 Radclyffe Hall lived with
her partner Una Troubridge.[1] Strolling through this genteel neighborhood
today, it is not difficult to bridge the distance between then and now. Thanks
to political activists in the lesbian and gay movement, national institutions
such as English Heritage recognize the value of cultural inclusiveness, as
seen in its placing a blue plaque to commemorate the historical significance
of Hall's former residence.[2] Standing on the pavement outside, it feels possible to touch the lesbian past — its materiality representing the "concretion
of identity" that enables the individual to establish social, political, emotive,
and psychic connections with a group.[3] The heritage experience invites visitors to imagine, all those decades ago, Hall sitting at her oak desk, fingers
stained with nicotine and ink. By putting pen to paper to write *The Well
of Loneliness* (1928) in support of her passionate belief that sexual inverts
deserved the same rights as everyone else, this established novelist risked losing everything — her literary reputation, economic security, friends, even her
beautiful Kensington home. Fully aware of the danger of controversy, Hall
approached the famous sexologist Havelock Ellis to ask for his blessing — to
no avail: *The Well* was swiftly prosecuted for obscene libel, the presiding
magistrate singling out as especially disturbing its portrayal of female ambulance drivers during the Great War as "addicted to this vice."[4] On hearing

195

this damaging accusation, Hall rose to her feet and shouted "I protest" in an effort to protect the reputation of the drivers as honorable, subsiding only when a police sergeant approached to silence her.[5] This highly charged exchange over the ownership of how these drivers' war was to be remembered reveals the making of cultural memory as a process of construction or contestation rather than preservation, a site in which multiple pathways to the past become entangled and blurred, crosscut with history, myth, and heritage.

Perhaps the most usable of usable pasts, heritage configures a practical past that binds groups through shared memories, legitimizes identity, affirms the political rights of citizenship, and contributes to a sense of belonging — effects, values, and objectives not wholly dissimilar from some ancestral and queer genealogical practices. This book has shown that queer expressions of "an overwhelming desire to *feel historical*" manifest the unmistakable affective registers of a mode of historicizing that induces the pleasures (and invokes the disruptive force) of nostalgia and fosters pride in the rituals and habits of collective remembrance of good times and bad.[6] Meanwhile, other queer scholars dismiss the lesbian and gay heritage trail as "a linear, triumphalist view of history," mistaking the earlier iterations of social history for the state of academic history now (a discipline, in actuality, committed to any number of ideological imperatives and forms of historiographical critique).[7] In an evocative discussion of "historical emotion," literary critic Christopher Nealon describes his response to "the strangeness of *witnessing* that dreamed-of collectivity realized long after the fact, in the archive: a history of mutually isolated individuals, dreaming similar dreams, *arrayed before me* in the aftermath of collective struggles and new identities."[8] Here is an excellent example of the queer penchant to devise what history is and how it works, the historical past as already constituted. Imagined memory is not, however, as Walter Benjamin reminds us, "an instrument for exploring the past but its theatre."[9] For Nealon the archive is less a site of critical historical analysis than a stage on which a queer fantasia of pastness is projected. This strand of queer genealogy — like heritage itself — sometimes "exaggerates and omits, candidly invents and frankly forgets," and in so doing it carves out a new conceptual space to ponder "the sensing of history and of the historic."[10]

Yet if the objective of queer genealogy is, first, to shape and transform the "destinies of queer community" and, second, to open "doors to futures we might not otherwise have been able to imagine," it is crucial, I believe, to grasp the effects of critically historicizing.[11] Queer genealogists must maintain a lively conversation with identity and identification, since the appeal to history assists in envisioning an enduring queer kinship across space and time, animating a politics of transformation, and explaining the historical conditions that have given rise to the formation of modern homosexuality. There can be no doubt that the genealogical project makes good on its first objective in delivering community, which is the reason queer deconstructionists who inveigh against queer genealogists for committing the cardinal sin of being teleological rather miss the point. To desist from that conversation is to self-destruct, because "a queer genealogy that does not attempt to account for, much less credit, the existence of the category of 'modern homosexuality' is . . . a contradiction in terms. Whatever the incoherencies of modern identity categories — and there are many — this does not obviate their force as palpable social constructions."[12] Palpable now, that is to say, for a specific reason and, if identity history's foundational premises are rooted in the logic of lineage, it is the price of securing "dreamed-of collectivity" and needs no defense or apology.[13] As for the second ambition, it is less clear whether ancestral or queer genealogy currently achieves all it desires: the fly in the ointment is that it is a condition of its project that achieving the first goal complicates (perhaps even compromises) the second. This is because its histories are constructed more like the present and thereby reinscribe the terms and conditions of the structure of modern sexual knowledge.

Historiography primarily interested in the homosexual or queer object as either "starkly different from the present" or "uncannily similar" secures and legitimizes the queerness of the present, whether practiced by the professional historian who meets the discipline's rigorous standards for meticulous research and careful argumentation or by the historically minded queer critic who is freed from the tyranny of evidence and thus the strictures of academic history.[14] Questions remain not only unanswered but unanswerable, since we did not think to ask. The challenge to *all* scholars engaged in genealogical work — ancestral or queer, inside and outside academic history — is to determine and assess the efficacy of individual practices vis-à-vis the purpose of historicizing and, for queer genealogists specifically, to ascertain if the demands made of history can be fully met by the pathways currently traversed — paths that so-called mainstream history sometimes regards, to a greater or lesser extent, with unease or assigns marginal status. Queer engagements with temporality and memory tend to render the discipline of history at best irrelevant and, worse still, useless in contributing toward the goal of transformative futures.[15] Equally disturbing are the difficulties faced by lesbian, gay, or queer historians in departments of history, who often labor productively in crafting narratives of a sexual past unnoticed by an academic history that perceives as tangential or insubstantial historicizing operationalized by an interest in homosexual or queer lives.[16]

This is why I envisage a new practice, a queer critical history that seeks to understand the multiple, contradictory, and overlapping configurations of the sexual that are unmappable within the epistemological apparatus of modern sexuality. The payoff lies not in its potential to satisfy queer yearnings for collective belonging but in its alertness to other *structures of knowing,* including residual knowledges now vanished. The needle of the compass of queer critical history does not point toward queer objects in the past as continuous or discontinuous or recurring in relation to current categories but spins in any direction. Modern sexuality is both knowable and unknowable through classification and identification; attuned to variations from a norm called "normal" but also to other relationalities and modes of social regulation. The orientations of queer genealogy and this new practice, then, could not be more different, for one is sutured to the logic of traceability (whether secure or broken) and the other is not; one traces the histories of queer beings, while the other seeks to know the conditions of knowledge. Their shared tool kit notwithstanding — both recognize the evolution of the epistemological premises of modern sexuality as uneven, unpredictable, and erratic and seek to clarify what is historically contingent and specific (rather than transcendent or universal) — they produce different accounts of the sexual past because their questions and purposes are not the same. Queer critical history differentiates between the purposes of collective memory and history to understand, for instance, how modern sexual knowledge sometimes jostled against older knowledge regimes, opaque or incoherent knowledge practices that escape the notice of an ancestral and queer genealogy activated by queerness-as-being. As demonstrated by my case studies, ordinary Britons in the early decades of the twentieth century seem not to have viewed sex or sexuality as we do now; sex talk buzzed all around, legible to some and baffling to others — the aware, self-aware, and unaware gathered around a table to converse on a topic at once present and unfathomable. To construct how the sexual was known, partially known, and not known necessitates another starting point: a queer critical history eager to use queer methods in constructing representations of past sexualities grounded in the materiality of the archive.

Recounting Hall's rise to fame, sacrifice for a cause, and retreat to self-imposed exile nourishes a sense of community with a common political purpose, revealing the power of myth, memory, and heritage. What is more difficult to discern, difficult perhaps because as yet untried, is the inescapable fact that any historiographical project in dialogue with identity or identification—whether marching forward from darkness into light or backward "from light into darkness"[17]—operates within similar epistemological constraints. Invented legacies, critical history reminds us, will always tell us more about ourselves—our categories, our identities, our oppositional binaries—than about how sexuality was made knowable in the past. And genealogical conversations will incur paralysis by preventing movement outside the conditions of that discourse, a predicament best confronted not by spoiling identity history or abandoning it entirely but by anatomizing its workings and accepting its limitations—and above all understanding how its purposes and discourses shape our knowledge of the sexual past. Ancestral and queer genealogists have been slow to acknowledge how their particular interests necessarily shape the boundaries of their collective enterprise, leaving to other investigatory modes, such as critical history, the task of pursuing related questions to gain unexpected insights about how sexuality was understood, partially understood, and misunderstood. At the same time, there is no reason the intellectual energies animated across these exploratory trajectories should not work productively alongside other practices, mutually informing one another.

The future of the history of sexuality may surprise us all, a future in which unforeseen hybrid practices evolve to capitalize on the strengths of current approaches now seen as incompatible. New queer historical practices disaggregated from ontology illuminate the intricate interplay between gender and sexuality, the usefulness and uselessness of identity, the historicity of key concepts such as the normal, and the cultural meanings of inference, innuendo, even incomprehensibility. In short, the sexual past is likely to be far stranger than meets the genealogical eye.

NOTES

PRIMARY SOURCES

Churchill Archives Centre, Cambridge
    Papers of William Douglas Weir, First Viscount Weir WEIR
House of Lords Record Office, London
    David Lloyd George Papers LG
Imperial War Museum, London IWM
    Department of Documents DD
    Department of Printed Books DPD
    Sound Archive
    Women at War Collection
The Museum of London
    David Mitchell Papers DM
The National Archives, London TNA PRO
    Home Office Records HO
    Prime Minister's Papers PREM
    Royal Air Force Records AIR
    Treasury Document Records TS
University of Glasgow Archives
    William Douglas Weir Papers DC
University of Leeds Library, Women's Catalogue
    Peter Liddle 1914–1918 Personal Experience Archives PL

PREFACE

1. This case is discussed in greater detail in chapter 4. See also Violet Douglas-Pennant, *Under the Searchlight: A Record of a Great Scandal* (London: George Allen and Unwin, 1922).

2. See "Author's Forenote" in Radclyffe Hall, *Miss Ogilvy Finds Herself* (London: William Heinemann, 1934), n.p.

3. Jenny Gould, "Women's Military Services in First World War Britain," in *Behind the Lines: Gender and the Two World Wars*, ed. Margaret Randolph Higgonet et al. (New Haven, CT: Yale University Press, 1987), 121; George Robb, *British Culture and the First World War* (Basingstoke, UK: Palgrave, 2002), 60 and 56; Radclyffe Hall, *The Well of Loneliness*, reprint ed. (New York: Anchor Books, 1990). The term lesbian appears in scare quotes to signal the possibility of other categorizations of the novel, such as transsexual; see, for instance, Jay Prosser, *Second Skins: The Body Narratives of Transsexuality* (New York: Columbia University Press, 1998).

4. Gertrude Stein, *The Autobiography of Alice B. Toklas* (New York: Harcourt, Brace, 1933), 135; Kate Summerscale, *The Queen of Whale Cay: The Eccentric Story of "Joe" Carstairs, Fastest Woman on Water* (London: Fourth Estate, 1997), 25–26; Emily Hamer, *Britannia's Glory: A History of Twentieth-Century Lesbians* (London: Cassell, 1996), 52–54. In her semiautobiographical novel *Two Selves* (Paris: Contact, 1923), Bryher (the pen name of Winifred Ellerman) writes that she considered ambulance driving but dismissed the idea because she was "no good at steering" (246). The literary critic Jane Marcus describes the ambulance unit depicted in Radclyffe Hall's novel *The Well of Loneliness* as a "hotbed of lesbian lovers"; see Jane Marcus, "Corpus/Corps/Corpse: Writing the Body in/at War," in *Arms and the Woman: War, Gender, and Literary Representation*, ed. Helen M. Cooper, Adrienne Munich, and Susan Merrill Squier (Chapel Hill: University of North Carolina Press, 1989), 154.

5. Lee Edelman, *No Future: Queer Theory and the Death Drive* (Durham, NC: Duke University Press, 2004), 17.

6. The cultural critic Annamarie Jagose considers this paradox at length, observing that "lesbian invisibility is precisely, if paradoxically, a strategy of representation" and therefore contributes (perversely) to increasing knowability; see Annamarie Jagose, *Inconsequence: Lesbian Representation and the Logic of Sexual Sequence* (Ithaca, NY: Cornell University Press, 2002), 2.

7. Robyn Wiegman refers to "identity knowledges to reference the many projects of academic study that were institutionalized in the U.S. university in the twentieth century for the study of identity"; see Robyn Wiegman, *Object Lessons* (Durham, NC: Duke University Press, 2012), 1.

8. An entry on William Douglas Weir can be found in the *Oxford Dictionary of National Biography* (DNB) *Online*; see http://www.oxforddnb.com/view/article/36818, accessed March 10, 2011.

9. David Mitchell, *Women on the Warpath: The Story of the Women of the First World War* (London: Jonathan Cape, 1965), 234. For a *DNB* entry on Sybil Margaret Thomas (née Haig), Viscountess Rhondda see http://www.oxforddnb.com/view/article/58913, accessed March 10, 2011.

10. A letter from W. A. Robinson (then permanent secretary at the Air Ministry) to

Lord Weir confirms that a meeting took place between Weir and Lady Rhondda on August 26, 1918. Papers of Lord Weir, Glasgow University Archives, DC96/22/23.

11. Papers of Lord Weir, Glasgow University Archives, DC96/18/148.

12. It was not uncommon during the war for women to present men of military age dressed in civilian clothing with a white feather to taunt them into enlisting. For a discussion of this practice see "The Order of the White Feather," in Nicoletta F. Gullace, *"The Blood of Our Sons": Men, Women, and the Renegotiation of British Citizenship during the Great War* (New York: Palgrave Macmillan, 2002), 73–97.

13. The historian Jill Liddington uses this phrase to describe how the diaries of Anne Lister (an early nineteenth-century Yorkshire diarist often called the first modern lesbian) confirm her sexual identity. See http://www.jliddington.org.uk/anne lister.html, accessed March 9, 2011.

14. I am grateful to Laura Gowing for this observation.

15. The historian Dipesh Chakrabarty discusses the need of marginal groups for *"affective* narratives of human belonging"; see Dipesh Chakrabarty, *Provincializing Europe: Postcolonial Thought and Historical Difference* (Princeton, NJ: Princeton University Press, 2008), 71; emphasis in original.

1 6. Laura Doan, *Fashioning Sapphism: The Origins of a Modern English Lesbian Culture* (New York: Columbia University Press, 2001).

17. Pierre Nora, "Between Memory and History: *Les Lieux de Mémoire,*" *Representations* 26 (1989): 7–24.

18. Ibid., 8.

19. The literary specialists Carolyn Dinshaw and Valerie Traub configure queer historiography as "touching" and "recurring," respectively; see Carolyn Dinshaw, *Getting Medieval: Sexualities and Communities, Pre- and Postmodern* (Durham, NC: Duke University Press, 1999), 1; Valerie Traub, "The Present Future of Lesbian Historiography," in *A Companion to Lesbian, Gay, Bisexual, Transgender, and Queer Studies*, ed. George E. Haggerty and Molly McGarrity (London: Blackwell, 2007), 125.

20. Joan Scott, "History-Writing as Critique," in *Manifestos for History*, ed. Keith Jenkins, Sue Morgan, and Alun Munslow (London: Routledge, 2007), 24.

21. Hayden White, "Afterword," in *Manifestos for History*, ed. Keith Jenkins, Sue Morgan, and Alun Munslow (London: Routledge, 2007), 224.

INTRODUCTION

1. Deputation of Members of the Douglas-Pennant Committee with Dr. Norwood to the Attorney General (July 31, 1931), 9 and 49. TNA PRO PREM 1/205.

2. A vigorous critique of lesbian and gay history appears, for instance, in Scott Herring, *Queering the Underworld: Slumming, Literature, and the Undoing of Lesbian and Gay History* (Chicago: University of Chicago Press, 2007). Queer history — indeed, the workings of academic history itself — has been sharply criticized by queer

deconstructionists, as discussed later in this book; see especially Carla Freccero, *Queer/Early/Modern* (Durham, NC: Duke University Press, 2006).

For introductions to queer theory and queer studies, see Donald E. Hall, *Queer Theories* (Basingstoke, UK: Palgrave Macmillan, 2003); Annamarie Jagose, *Queer Theory: An Introduction* (New York: New York University Press, 1996); Nikki Sullivan, *A Critical Introduction to Queer Theory* (New York: New York University Press, 2003); William B. Turner, *A Genealogy of Queer Theory* (Philadelphia: Temple University Press, 2000).

At present there is no short introductory volume on critical history, a practice I discuss further in this introduction as well as in later chapters. The historian Joan Scott's explanation provides a useful starting point: critical history "suggests that the point of doing . . . history is to critically engage some conceptual or theoretical or taken-for-granted notion about why things are the way they are, and how they got to be the way they are"; see "Secularism . . . A Really Interesting Problematic: A Conversation with Joan Scott" (March 2010), http://blogs.ssrc.org/tif/wp-content/uploads/2010/11/RitesResponsibilities.JoanWallachScott.TIF.pdf, accessed September 7, 2011.

See also Joan Scott, "Finding Critical History," in *Becoming Historians*, ed. James M. Banner and John R. Gillis (Chicago: University of Chicago Press, 2009).

3. Foucault writes: "One has to dispense with the constituent subject, to get rid of the subject itself, that's to say, to arrive at an analysis which can account for the constitution of the subject within a historical framework. And this is what I would call genealogy, that is, a form of history which can account for the constitution of knowledges, discourses, domains of objects, etc., without having to make reference to a subject which is either transcendental in relation to the field of events or runs in its empty sameness throughout the course of history"; see Michel Foucault, *Power/Knowledge: Selected Interviews and Other Writings, 1972–1977* (Hemel Hempstead, UK: Harvester Press, 1980), 117. In "What Is Enlightenment?" Foucault argues for a mode of "historical investigation" of "events that have led us to constitute ourselves and to recognize ourselves as subjects of what we are doing, thinking, [and] saying"; see Michel Foucault and Paul Rabinow, *The Foucault Reader* (New York: Pantheon, 1984), 32–50, especially 46. Finally, in an interview Foucault states that "recourse to history . . . is meaningful to the extent that history serves to show how that-which-is has not always been; i.e., that the things which seem most evident to us are always formed in the confluence of encounters and chances, during the course of a precarious and fragile history"; see Michel Foucault, *Politics, Philosophy, Culture: Interviews and Other Writings of Michel Foucault*, edited with an introduction by Lawrence D. Kritzman (London: Routledge, 1988), 37.

4. Details of the trial are summarized in Deborah Cohler, *Citizen, Invert, Queer: Lesbianism and War in Early Twentieth-Century Britain* (Minneapolis: University of Minnesota Press, 2010), 128–43.

5. Ibid., 128. More information on this novel appears in chapter 3.

6. Jodie Medd, "'The Cult of the Clitoris': Anatomy of a National Scandal," *Modernism/Modernity* 9, no. 1 (2002): 25.

7. Cohler, *Citizen, Invert, Queer*, 128 and 146; Medd, "'Cult of the Clitoris,'" 25, 31, and 44.

8. Arthur Marwick, *The Deluge: British Society and the First World War* (New York: Norton, 1970), 258; Gerard J. De Groot, *Blighty: British Society in the Era of the Great War* (London: Longman, 1996), 193 and 236; George Robb, *British Culture and the First World War* (Basingstoke, UK: Palgrave 2002), 59; Adrian Gregory, *The Last Great War: British Society and the First World War* (Cambridge: Cambridge University Press, 2008), 241.

9. Cohler, *Citizen, Invert, Queer*, 146; Medd, "'Cult of the Clitoris,'" 34. *Oxford English Dictionary Online*, accessed February 12, 2012.

10. Hayden White, "Afterword," in *Manifestos for History*, ed. Keith Jenkins, Sue Morgan, and Alun Munslow (London: Routledge, 2007), 228.

11. Alan Megill, "History, Memory, Identity," *History of the Human Sciences* 11, no. 3 (1998): 36–62, especially 57.

12. Joan Scott, "The Evidence of Experience," *Critical Inquiry* 17 (1991): 777.

13. Deputation of Members of the Douglas-Pennant Committee with Dr. Norwood to the Attorney General (July 31, 1931), 12 and 44. TNA PRO PREM 1/205. The barrister in *Harley v. Carr* spoke of "dirty things" (cf. chapter 5); *The Times*, December 3, 1920, 5.

14. Psychoanalysis was, of course, an equally powerful force in the discursive construction of twentieth-century understandings of sexuality and selfhood, gaining influence in Britain in the 1930s. My interest in foregrounding the importance of sexology throughout this book is to highlight its role in shaping the "sexual" as a classificatory project, thus paving the way for the development of what Foucault calls a "reverse discourse," reclaiming pathologized terms for political purposes; see Michel Foucault, *The History of Sexuality*, vol. 1, *An Introduction* (London: Penguin, 1976), 101.

15. Jeffrey Weeks, *Sexuality* (London: Routledge, 2003), 7.

16. Foucault, *Politics, Philosophy, Culture*, 37. Several examples of the methods and concerns of critical history can be found in Keith Jenkins, Sue Morgan, and Alun Munslow, eds., *Manifestos for History* (London: Routledge, 2007). See also the online journal *History of the Present: A Journal of Critical History*, http://www.history ofthepresent.org, accessed September 3, 2011.

17. Foucault, *Power/Knowledge*, 117.

18. Joanna Bourke, "Foreword," in *Manifestos for History*, ed. Keith Jenkins, Sue Morgan, and Alun Munslow (London: Routledge, 2007), xii.

19. Jeffrey Weeks, "Queer(y)ing the 'Modern Homosexual,'" *Journal of British Studies* 51, no. 3 (2012): 523–39.

20. White, "Afterword," 228. See also Chakrabarty's incisive critique of "the discourse of 'history' produced at the institutional site of the university" (particularly its "deep

collusion" with "the modernizing narrative[s] of citizenship, bourgeois public and private, and the nation-state") in Dipesh Chakrabarty, *Provincializing Europe: Post-colonial Thought and Historical Difference* (Princeton, NJ: Princeton University Press, 2008), 71. Examples of queer specialists who engage with Chakrabarty's work include Lauren Berlant and Elizabeth Freeman; see Lauren Berlant, "Thinking about Feeling Historical," *Emotion, Space, and Society* 1 (2008): 4–9; Elizabeth Freeman, *Time Binds: Queer Temporalities, Queer Histories* (Durham, NC: Duke University Press, 2010).

21. White, "Afterword," 228.

22. Dominick LaCapra, "Resisting Apocalypse and Rethinking History," in *Manifestos for History*, ed. Keith Jenkins, Sue Morgan, and Alun Munslow (London: Rout-ledge, 2007), 166.

23. Dipesh Chakrabarty, "History and the Politics of Recognition," in *Manifestos for History*, ed. Keith Jenkins, Sue Morgan, and Alun Munslow (London: Routledge, 2007), 77.

24. Michael Oakeshott, *On History and Other Essays* (Indianapolis, IN: Liberty Fund, 1999), 38. These definitions of Oakeshott's formulations appear in an unpublished paper by Hayden White titled "The Practical Past" (2010). I am grateful to him for sharing this work.

25. Freeman, *Time Binds*, xiii, xxii, xxiii, and xi.

26. Ibid., 11 and ix.

27. Ibid., xiii; Eric Partridge and Paul Beale, A *Dictionary of Slang and Unconventional English: Colloquialisms and Catch Phrases, Fossilised Jokes and Puns, General Nicknames, Vulgarisms and Such Americanisms as Have Been Naturalised*, 8th ed. (London: Routledge, 1984), 823. In common use today in the ancient sport of road bowling, *Fág a' bealach* (pronounced Faug on bal och) is well known in Ireland, meaning "leave/get out of/clear/the way." According to scholar Katherine O'Donnell, the phrase became "the battle cry on the foundation of the Royal Irish Fusiliers when they were mustered in the 1790s to fight against the French with the British," and was also taken up by other Irish regiments. Personal correspondence with Katherine O'Donnell, November 2011.

28. White, "Practical Past" (2010).

29. Ibid.

30. Ibid.

31. Robert A. Rosenstone, "Space for the Bird to Fly," in *Manifestos for History*, ed. Keith Jenkins, Sue Morgan, and Alun Munslow (London: Routledge, 2007), 17.

32. Arnold I. Davidson, *The Emergence of Sexuality: Historical Epistemology and the Formation of Concepts* (Cambridge, MA: Harvard University Press, 2001), 21.

33. New historical work on the consolidation in the mid-twentieth century of modern sexual knowledge as fixed labels includes Leif Jerram, *Streetlife: The Untold Story of Europe's Twentieth Century* (Oxford: Oxford University Press, 2011), especially chapter 4, "Sex and the City," 247–316; Margot Canaday, *The Straight State:*

Sexuality and Citizenship in Twentieth-Century America (Princeton, NJ: Princeton University Press, 2009); Simon Szreter and Kate Fisher, Sex before the Sexual Revolution: Intimate Life in England, 1918–1963 (Cambridge: Cambridge University Press, 2010). I am grateful to my colleague Leif Jerram for sharing his project at proof stage.

34. See, for instance, Lucy Bland and Laura Doan, eds., Sexology in Culture: Labelling Bodies and Desires (Chicago: University of Chicago Press, 1998); Lucy Bland and Laura Doan, eds., Sexology Uncensored: The Documents of Sexual Science (Chicago: University of Chicago Press, 1998).

35. David M. Halperin, How to Do the History of Homosexuality (Chicago: University of Chicago Press, 2002), 104.

36. H. G. Cocks and Matt Houlbrook, Palgrave Advances in the Modern History of Sexuality (Basingstoke, UK: Palgrave Macmillan, 2006), 3.

37. Geoff Eley, A Crooked Line: From Cultural History to the History of Society (Ann Arbor: University of Michigan Press, 2005), 252n19. Eley cites Robert A. Padgug, "Editors' Introduction to 'Sexuality in History,'" Radical History Review 20 (1979): 3–23; Jeffrey Escoffier, Regina Kunzel, and Molly McGarry, "Editors' Introduction to 'the Queer Issue,'" Radical History Review 62 (1995): 1–6; John C. Fout and Maura D. Shaw, American Sexual Politics: Sex, Gender, and Race since the Civil War (Chicago: University of Chicago Press, 1993); and Kathy Lee Peiss, Christina Simmons, and Robert A. Padgug, Passion and Power: Sexuality in History (Philadelphia: Temple University Press, 1989).

A more representative list of work in the field might include George Chauncey, Gay New York: Gender, Urban Culture, and the Makings of the Gay Male World, 1890–1940 (New York: Basic Books, 1994); Davidson, The Emergence of Sexuality; John D'Emilio and Estelle B. Freedman, Intimate Matters: A History of Sexuality in America (Chicago: University of Chicago Press, 1988); Jennifer Terry, An American Obsession: Science, Medicine, and the Place of Homosexuality in Modern Society (Chicago: University of Chicago Press, 1999); Thomas Laqueur, Solitary Sex: A Cultural History of Masturbation (New York: Zone Books, 2003); Thomas Laqueur, Making Sex: Body and Gender from the Greeks to Freud (Cambridge, MA: Harvard University Press, 1990); Martha Vicinus, Intimate Friends: Women Who Loved Women, 1778–1928 (Chicago: University of Chicago Press, 2004); and Jeffrey Weeks, Making Sexual History (Cambridge: Polity Press, 2000).

38. There are passing references to Foucault in relation to sexuality in Peter Burke, History and Social Theory, 2nd ed. (Ithaca, NY: Cornell University Press, 2005), 53; Ludmilla Jordanova, History in Practice, 2nd ed. (London: Oxford University Press, 2006), 75–76; and Willie Thompson, Postmodernism and History (Basingstoke, UK: Palgrave Macmillan, 2004), 85–86. Queer theory in relation to history surfaces briefly in Robert Gildea and Anne Simonin, eds., Writing Contemporary History (London: Hodder Education, 2008), 88–89, and Simon Gunn, History and Cultural Theory (Harlow, UK: Pearson Longman, 2006), especially 146–49.

Examples of recent historiographical work that does not discuss sexuality include Michael Bentley, *Modern Historiography: An Introduction* (London: Routledge, 1999); Stefan Berger, Heiko Feldner, and Kevin Passmore, eds., *Writing History: Theory and Practice* (London: Arnold, 2003); Mary Fulbrook, *Historical Theory: Ways of Imagining the Past* (London: Routledge, 2002); John Lewis Gaddis, *The Landscape of History: How Historians Map the Past* (Oxford: Oxford University Press, 2002); Georg G. Iggers, *Historiography in the Twentieth Century: From Scientific Objectivity to the Postmodern Challenge* (Hanover, NH: Wesleyan University Press, 1997); Keith Jenkins, *Re-thinking History* (London: Routledge, 1991); David Lowenthal, *The Past Is a Foreign Country* (Cambridge: Cambridge University Press, 1985); Alun Munslow, *Deconstructing History*, 2nd ed. (New York: Taylor and Francis, 2006); and Roger Spalding and Christopher Parker, *Historiography: An Introduction* (Manchester, UK: Manchester University Press, 2007).

39. Eley, *Crooked Line*, 171. See also Laura Lee Downs, "From Women's History to Gender History," in *Writing History: Theory and Practice*, ed. Stefan Berger, Heiko Feldner, and Kevin Passmore (London: Arnold, 2003), 262–81.

40. The early modern historian Cynthia Herrup offers a compelling argument for the importance of sexuality in understanding, for example, "the relation of felonious sex to other sexual behaviors, to public awareness of the law, to social hierarchies, and to the nuances of the public and the private" (263). She further identifies what she terms the "paradox of triviality" in that "if we attempt to co-opt the status of being peripheral by creating (however temporarily) a discrete subfield, we validate the significance of work on sex, but in a way that makes it difficult to convince or even to address anyone who is not already persuaded of the subject's importance"; see Cynthia Herrup, "Finding the Bodies," *GLQ: A Journal of Lesbian and Gay Studies* 5, no. 3 (1999): 263 and 257.

41. Peter N. Stearns, *Sexuality in World History* (London: Routledge, 2009), 1–2.

42. Joanne J. Meyerowitz, "Transnational Sex and U.S. History," *American Historical Review* 114, no. 5 (2009): 1276.

43. Lisa Duggan, "The Discipline Problem: Queer Theory Meets Lesbian and Gay History," *GLQ: A Journal of Lesbian and Gay Studies* 2, no. 3 (1995): 180. Lisa Duggan was among the first to decry the marginalizing of sexuality as well as the charge of triviality in academic history, as I discuss at length in chapter 1.

44. Meyerowitz, "Transnational Sex and U.S. History," 1276. In the same issue Margot Canaday characterizes the history of sexuality as "still a relatively new field," and though "the situation has improved markedly in the past two decades, historians of sexuality continue to be at least somewhat marginalized by the broader discipline"; see Margot Canaday, "Thinking Sex in the Transnational Turn: An Introduction," *American Historical Review* 114, no. 5 (2009): 1251.

45. In a special issue on "feminine sexual pathologies," historians of sexuality Peter Cryle and Lisa Downing write: "This research does not seek to contribute to debates in identity politics (for example, by establishing a 'lesbian history')"; see Peter

Cryle and Lisa Downing, "Feminine Sexual Pathologies," *Journal of the History of Sexuality* 18, no. 1 (2009): 7.

Excellent new historical work on other sexualities includes Steven Angelides, *A History of Bisexuality* (Chicago: University of Chicago Press, 2001); Joanne J. Meyerowitz, *How Sex Changed: A History of Transsexuality in the United States* (Cambridge, MA: Harvard University Press, 2002); Elizabeth Reis, *Bodies in Doubt: An American History of Intersex* (Baltimore: Johns Hopkins University Press, 2009).

46. *Journal of the History of Sexuality* can be accessed electronically: http://www .utexas.edu/utpress/journals/jhs.html.

Early sexual science also privileged "homosexuality"; for instance, the first volume to appear in Havelock Ellis's massive *Studies in the Psychology of Sex* in 1897 was titled *Sexual Inversion*; see Havelock Ellis and John Addington Symonds, *Sexual Inversion*, reprint ed. (New York: Arno, 1975).

In Cocks and Houlbrook's *Palgrave Advances in the Modern History of Sexuality*, references to homosexuality outnumber references to heterosexuality four to one. Of the approximately one hundred articles published by the *JHS* between 2002 and 2008, more than half looked at some aspect of homosexuality (fifteen on homosexuality and the law, four on gay rights, seventeen on male homosexuality, sodomy, or homoeroticism, six on same-sex relations, and eleven on lesbianism). During this same period, one article addressed heterosexuality; see James A. Schultz, "Heterosexuality as a Threat to Medieval Studies," *Journal of the History of Sexuality* 15, no. 1 (2006): 14–29.

47. I use the phrase lesbian, gay, and queer to signal fields concerned with the history of modern homosexuality. Historians of other sexual identities (such as bisexual, trans, or heterosexual) may also find aspects of this study of identity-based history relevant to their interests.

48. Gabrielle M. Spiegel, "History, Historicism, and the Social Logic of the Text in the Middle Ages," *Speculum* 65, no. 1 (1990): 80 and 79; emphasis in original.

49. Ibid., 79.

50. See, for example, Jeffrey Weeks, *Coming Out: Homosexual Politics in Britain from the Nineteenth Century to the Present* (London: Quartet Books, 1977); Lillian Faderman, *Surpassing the Love of Men: Romantic Friendship and Love between Women from the Renaissance to the Present* (London: Women's Press, 1981).

51. For a clear overview of these debates, see "Mary McIntosh and the 'Homosexual Role,'" in Weeks, *Making Sexual History*, especially 53–74. Also, for a prehistory of the influential work of McIntosh, see Chris Waters's "The Homosexual as a Social Being in Britain, 1945–1968," *Journal of British Studies* 51, no. 3 (2012): 685–710.

52. Lillian Faderman, "Who Hid Lesbian History?" *Frontiers* 4, no. 3 (1979): 74–76. Alternatives to "lesbian" include "proto-lesbian" and "lesbian-like." The former term appears in Eve Kosofsky Sedgwick, *Tendencies* (Durham, NC: Duke University Press, 1993), 79. The latter was coined in 1990 by historian Judith Bennett to refer to "women whose lives might have particularly offered opportunities for

same-sex love; women who resisted norms of feminine behavior based on hetero-sexual marriage; women who lived in circumstances that allowed them to nurture and support other women"; see Judith Bennett, *History Matters: Patriarchy and the Challenge of Feminism* (Philadelphia: University of Pennsylvania Press, 2006), 110. For a sophisticated analysis of the emotional and psychic investments of this mode of lesbian history, see Valerie Traub, *The Renaissance of Lesbianism in Early Modern England* (Cambridge: Cambridge University Press, 2002), especially 326–54.

53. *Empire News*, December 5, 1920, 2.

54. See Annamarie Jagose, *Inconsequence: Lesbian Representation and the Logic of Sexual Sequence* (Ithaca, NY: Cornell University Press, 2002); Traub, *Renaissance of Lesbianism in Early Modern England.*

55. Halperin, *How to Do the History of Homosexuality*, 107; Foucault, *History of Sexuality*, vol. 1. Pierre Nora also comments on critical history's "suspicions" of "collective memory," even suggesting that history's "true mission" is "to suppress and destroy it"; see Pierre Nora, "Between Memory and History: *Les Lieux de Mémoire*," *Representations* 26 (1989): 9 and 7.

Thanks to Amelia Jones, who clarified the different forms of identity politics in recent queer theoretical interventions, and to Jonathan D. Katz, who shared his ongoing critique of historiography.

56. Halperin, *How to Do the History of Homosexuality*, 107.

57. Michel Foucault, "Entretien avec Michel Foucault," in his *Dits et écrits II, 1976–1988* (Paris: Gallimard, 2001), 896, cited by Joan Scott, "History-Writing as Critique," in *Manifestos for History*, ed. Keith Jenkins, Sue Morgan, and Alun Munslow (London: Routledge, 2007), 29.

58. Matt Houlbrook, *Queer London: Perils and Pleasures in the Sexual Metropolis, 1918–1957* (Chicago: University of Chicago Press, 2005), 265.

59. For early examples, see Jonathan Goldberg, *Sodometries: Renaissance Texts, Modern Sexualities* (Stanford, CA: Stanford University Press, 1992); Jonathan Goldberg, ed., *Queering the Renaissance* (Durham, NC: Duke University Press, 1993); David M. Halperin, *One Hundred Years of Homosexuality: And Other Essays on Greek Love* (New York: Routledge, 1990).

60. Susan McCabe, "To Be and to Have: The Rise of Queer Historicism," *GLQ: A Journal of Lesbian and Gay Studies* 11, no. 1 (2005): 120 and 121.

61. Valerie Traub, "The Present Future of Lesbian Historiography," in *A Companion to Lesbian, Gay, Bisexual, Transgender, and Queer Studies*, ed. George E. Haggerty and Molly McGarrity (London: Blackwell, 2007), 131.

62. Joan Scott, "Fantasy Echo: History and the Construction of Identity," *Critical Inquiry* 27, no. 2 (2001): 284. Nora also critiques what he terms "the repetition of the ancestral"; Nora, "Between Memory and History," 7.

63. Carla Freccero, "Queer Times," *South Atlantic Quarterly* 106, no. 3 (2007): 487. An example of the elision from "lesbian and gay" to "queer" can be seen in Matt Cook's explanation of "a conceptual separation of family from homosexuality

which has tended to inform historical approaches to both male and female queer lives in the past"; see Matt Cook, "Families of Choice? George Ives, Queer Lives, and the Family in Early Twentieth-Century Britain," *Gender and History* 22, no. 1 (2010): 1. Deborah Cohler, on the other hand, configures queer as a catch-all term for fluid identities that fit uneasily into existing categories; Cohler, *Citizen, Invert, Queer*.

64. LaCapra, "Resisting Apocalypse and Rethinking History," 161.

65. Duggan, "Discipline Problem." For concise overviews of the queer turn in the history of sexuality, see Brett Beemyn and Mickey Eliason, eds., *Queer Studies: Lesbian, Gay, Bisexual, and Transgender Anthology* (New York: New York University Press, 1996); Robert J. Corber and Stephen Valocchi, eds., *Queer Studies: An Interdisciplinary Reader* (Oxford: Blackwell, 2003); and Donald E. Morton, ed., *The Material Queer: A LesBiGay Cultural Studies Reader* (Boulder, CO: Westview, 1996).

66. Kenneth Plummer, *Sociology: The Basics* (New York: Routledge, 2010), 172. Thanks to Jeff Geiger for this reference.

67. Terry Castle, ed., *The Literature of Lesbianism: A Historical Anthology from Ariosto to Stonewall* (New York: Columbia University Press, 2003), 48.

68. Rebecca Jennings, "From 'Woman-Loving Woman' to 'Queer': Historiographical Perspectives on Twentieth-Century British Lesbian History," *History Compass* 5, no. 6 (2007): 1904; Alison Oram, "'Friends, Feminists, and Sexual Outlaws': Lesbianism and British History," in *Straight Studies Modified: Lesbian Interventions in the Academy*, ed. Gabriele Griffin (London: Cassell, 1997), 179; Martha Vicinus, "Lesbian History: All Theory and No Facts or All Facts and No Theory?" *Radical History Review* 60 (1994): 66.

David Halperin suggests that "whatever else the current and ongoing explorations of lesbian history have to offer us, one of their most startling benefits will be a much-enhanced understanding of the different historicities of female and male homosexuality"; see Halperin, *How to Do the History of Homosexuality*, 80.

69. Cohler, *Citizen, Invert, Queer*, xx.

70. Havelock Ellis, *Essays in War-time* (London: Constable, 1916), 53.

71. "The New Woman: An Historical Note," *The Times*, January 6, 1916, 11.

72. Robb, *British Culture and the First World War*, 59; David Trotter, "Lesbians before Lesbianism: Sexual Identity in Early Twentieth-Century British Fiction," in *Borderlines: Genders and Identities in War and Peace, 1870–1930*, ed. Billie Melman (New York: Routledge, 1998), 195.

73. Robb, *British Culture and the First World War*, 59.

74. Cohler, *Citizen, Invert, Queer*, 112.

75. Angela Woollacott, "Sisters and Brothers in Arms: Family, Class, and Gendering in World War 1 Britain," in *Gendering War Talk*, ed. Miriam Cooke and Angela Woollacott (Princeton, NJ: Princeton University Press, 1993), 143.

For space considerations it is not possible to provide an exhaustive historiography of gender and the First World War in the context of Britain. Relevant work includes Gail Braybon and Penny Summerfield, *Out of the Cage: Women's Experiences in Two World Wars* (London: Pandora, 1987); Susan R. Grayzel, *Women's Identities at War: Gender, Motherhood, and Politics in Britain and France during the First World War* (Chapel Hill: University of North Carolina Press, 1999); Nicoletta F. Gullace, *"The Blood of Our Sons": Men, Women, and the Renegotiation of British Citizenship during the Great War* (New York: Palgrave Macmillan, 2002); Lucy Noakes, "Demobilizing the Military Woman: Constructions of Class and Gender in Britain after the First World War," *Gender and History* 19, no. 1 (2007): 143–62; Lucy Noakes, *Women in the British Army: War and the Gentle Sex, 1907–1948* (London: I. B. Tauris, 2006); Janet S. K. Watson, *Fighting Different Wars: Experience, Memory, and the First World War* (Cambridge: Cambridge University Press, 2004); and Angela Woollacott, *On Her Their Lives Depend: Munitions Workers in the Great War* (Berkeley: University of California Press, 1994).

76. Florence Tamagne, "The Homosexual Age, 1870–1940," in *Gay Life and Culture: A World History*, ed. Robert Aldrich (London: Thames and Hudson, 2006), 176.

77. Chakrabarty, *Provincializing Europe*, 71; emphasis in original. Radclyffe Hall's short story "Miss Ogilvy Finds Herself" (written in 1926 but not published until 1934) depicts the bleak postwar life of the leader of an all-female ambulance unit on demobilization. The preface to the collection refers to "congenital sexual inversion" and to the "hundreds of sexually inverted women," but it remains unclear whether Hall understood sexual inversion in terms of gender variance or sexual object choice (n.p.). Hall's 1928 novel *The Well of Loneliness* also includes an episode near the Western Front as the protagonist, Stephen Gordon, volunteers as a driver. Both characters feel themselves to be men trapped in female bodies. See Radclyffe Hall, *Miss Ogilvy Finds Herself* (London: William Heinemann, 1934); Radclyffe Hall, *The Well of Loneliness*, reprint ed. (New York: Anchor Books, 1990).

78 Violet Douglas-Pennant, *Under the Searchlight: A Record of a Great Scandal* (London: George Allen and Unwin, 1922).

79. David Halperin, *Saint Foucault: Towards a Gay Hagiography* (Oxford: Oxford University Press, 1995), 62; emphasis in original.

80. See especially Halperin, *How to Do the History of Homosexuality*; Valerie Traub, *Making Sexual Knowledge: Thinking Sex with the Early Moderns* (Philadelphia: University of Pennsylvania Press, 2013).

81. Halperin, *How to Do the History of Homosexuality*, 107.

CHAPTER ONE

1. This shift in academic history (known also as the linguistic turn) is commonly thought to have begun in the 1980s and will be discussed more extensively in chapter 2. For a lucid overview, see Geoff Eley, *A Crooked Line: From Cultural History to the History of Society* (Ann Arbor: University of Michigan Press, 2005). See also

Steven Maynard, "'Respect Your Elders, Know Your Past': History and the Queer Theorists," *Radical History Review* 75 (1999): 56–78; Joyce Oldham Appleby, Margaret C. Jacob, and Lynn Hunt, *Telling the Truth about History* (New York: Norton, 1994); Victoria E. Bonnell, Lynn Hunt, and Richard Biernacki, *Beyond the Cultural Turn: New Directions in the Study of Society and Culture* (Berkeley: University of California Press, 1999); John Toews, "Intellectual History after the Linguistic Turn: The Autonomy of Meaning and the Irreducibility of Experience," *American Historical Review* 92 (1987): 879–907.

2. Historian Mary Fulbrook discusses in detail the various metaphors ("window, mirror, and magnifying glass") frequently associated with a practice "deemed to be a transparent or reflective means" to gaze on the "real"; see Mary Fulbrook, *Historical Theory: Ways of Imagining the Past* (London: Routledge, 2002), 28. Lisa Duggan too refers to social history's "empirical strategies," which "treat documentary sources as transparent windows onto the 'real' experience of populations"; see Lisa Duggan, "The Discipline Problem: Queer Theory Meets Lesbian and Gay History," *GLQ: A Journal of Lesbian and Gay Studies* 2, no. 3 (1995): 182.

3. Queer theory cannot be easily defined or neatly summarized; as historian William B. Turner observes, the field, which is associated with the work of Judith Butler, Michel Foucault, Eve Kosofsky Sedgwick, Gayle Rubin, Teresa de Lauretis, Michael Warner, Lauren Berlant, and Lee Edelman, among others, "remains conceptually slippery . . . it is even difficult to summarize what queer theory is about in a sentence, or even a paragraph." See William B. Turner, *A Genealogy of Queer Theory* (Philadelphia: Temple University Press, 2000), 3.

4. Christopher S. Nealon, *Foundlings: Lesbian and Gay Historical Emotion before Stonewall* (Durham, NC: Duke University Press, 2001), 8. See also Lauren Berlant, "Thinking about Feeling Historical," *Emotion, Space, and Society* 1, no. 1 (2008): 4–9.

5. Nealon, *Foundlings*, 13; emphasis in original. Nealon cites Fredric Jameson, *The Political Unconscious* (Ithaca, NY: Cornell University Press, 1981).

6. Duggan, "Discipline Problem."

7. Historians of sexuality, as I discuss in the introduction, believe their field remains marginalized in academic history.

8. Fulbrook, *Historical Theory*, 39; Duggan, "Discipline Problem," 181.

9. Historian Allan Bérubé, for instance, expressed unease with queer theory's abstraction; see Maynard, "'Respect Your Elders, Know Your Past,'" 58.

10. Martha Vicinus, "Lesbian History: All Theory and No Facts or All Facts and No Theory?" *Radical History Review* 60 (1994): 57–75.

11. Duggan, "Discipline Problem," 181.

12. To avoid confusion in this chapter on disciplinarity and interdisciplinarity, I will refer to "lesbian and gay social history" (rather than "ancestral genealogy") and "queer history" (rather than "queer genealogy").

13. Michael Warner, ed., for Social Text Collective, *Fear of a Queer Planet: Queer*

Politics and Social Theory (Minneapolis: University of Minnesota Press, 1993), xi and xii.

14. Vicinus, "Lesbian History," 61.

15. A sampling of queer work by literary and cultural critics with interests in history and historicity includes Joseph Allen Boone, *Libidinal Currents: Sexuality and the Shaping of Modernism* (Chicago: University of Chicago Press, 1998); Glenn Burger and Steven F. Kruger, *Queering the Middle Ages* (Minneapolis: University of Minnesota Press, 2001); Ed Cohen, *Talk on the Wilde Side: Toward a Genealogy of a Discourse on Male Sexualities* (New York: Routledge, 1993); Carolyn Dinshaw, *Getting Medieval: Sexualities and Communities, Pre- and Postmodern* (Durham, NC: Duke University Press, 1999); Jonathan Dollimore, *Sexual Dissidence: Augustine to Wilde, Freud to Foucault* (Oxford: Clarendon Press, 1991); Carla Freccero, *Queer/Early/Modern* (Durham, NC: Duke University Press, 2006); Diana Fuss, *Inside/Out: Lesbian Theories, Gay Theories* (New York: Routledge, 1991); Jonathan Goldberg, *Sodometries: Renaissance Texts, Modern Sexualities* (New York: Fordham University Press, 2010); George E. Haggerty, *Men in Love: Masculinity and Sexuality* (New York: Columbia University Press, 1999); Judith Halberstam, *Female Masculinity* (Durham, NC: Duke University Press, 1998); Annamarie Jagose, *Queer Theory: An Introduction* (New York: New York University Press, 1996); Karma Lochrie, *Heterosyncrasies: Female Sexuality When Normal Wasn't* (Minneapolis: University of Minnesota Press, 2005); Marlon B. Ross, *Manning the Race: Reforming Black Men in the Jim Crow Era* (New York: New York University Press, 2004); Alan Sinfield, *The Wilde Century: Effeminacy, Oscar Wilde and the Queer Movement* (London: Cassell, 1994); Valerie Traub, *The Renaissance of Lesbianism in Early Modern England* (Cambridge: Cambridge University Press, 2002); Ruth Vanita, *Queering India: Same-Sex Love and Eroticism in Indian Culture and Society* (London: Routledge, 2001).

16. Ann Cvetkovich, *An Archive of Feelings: Trauma, Sexuality, and Lesbian Public Cultures* (Durham, NC: Duke University Press, 2003); Elizabeth Freeman, "Time Binds, or Erotohistoriography," *Social Text* 23, no. 3–4 (2005): 59; Heather Love, *Feeling Backward: Loss and the Politics of Queer History* (Cambridge, MA: Harvard University Press, 2007), 24; Halberstam, *Female Masculinity*, 53; Freccero, *Queer/Early/Modern*, 79. Heather Love also refers to an "affective historiography" on p. 37.

17. See, for instance, Love, *Feeling Backward*; Scott Bravmann, *Queer Fictions of the Past: History, Culture and Difference* (Cambridge: Cambridge University Press, 1997); Scott Herring, *Queering the Underworld: Slumming, Literature, and the Undoing of Lesbian and Gay History* (Chicago: University of Chicago Press 2007).

18. Fredric Jameson, *Postmodernism, or The Cultural Logic of Late Capitalism* (London: Verso, 1991), 279. See also F. R. Ankersmit's *Sublime Historical Experience* (Stanford, CA: Stanford University Press, 2005).

19. Love, *Feeling Backward*, 37; Vicinus, "Lesbian History," 62. Steven Maynard also

describes queer studies as "ahistorical" and argues that "queer theory lacks historical perspective and appreciation"; see Maynard, "'Respect Your Elders, Know Your Past,'" 60 and 59.

20. Hayden White, "Afterword," in *Manifestos for History*, ed. Keith Jenkins, Sue Morgan, and Alun Munslow (London: Routledge, 2007), 224.

21. Simon Gunn, *History and Cultural Theory* (Harlow, UK: Pearson Longman, 2006), 22. The supposed passing of the "queer moment" was almost contemporaneous with its inception, as Annamarie Jagose comments: "Almost as soon as queer established market dominance as a diacritical term, and certainly before consolidating itself in any easy vernacular sense, some theorists were already suggesting that its moment had passed"; see Jagose, *Queer Theory*, 127. A decade later Janet Halley and Andrew Parker observed that queer, "if not already passé, was rapidly approaching its expiration date," which led them to question "whether or how this rumor might be true." See Janet Halley and Andrew Paker, "Introduction," *South Atlantic Quarterly* 106, no. 3 (2007): 421. With new queer work appearing each year, predictions of its demise seem unfounded. Lee Edelman's provocative intervention on queer futurity, for example, has galvanized and reenergized the field; see Lee Edelman, *No Future: Queer Theory and the Death Drive* (Durham, NC: Duke University Press, 2004). See also the recent "Cluster on Queer Modernism" in *PMLA* 124 (2009): 744–816, and Lynne Huffer, *Mad for Foucault: Rethinking the Foundations of Queer Theory* (New York: Columbia University Press, 2010). In January 2012 Duke University Press discontinued its influential Series Q, reigniting speculation on the state of the field; see Michael Warner, "Queer and Then? The End of Queer Theory?" *Chronicle of Higher Education*, January 1, 2012, http://chronicle.com/article/QueerThen-/130161, accessed January 3, 2012.

22. Jeffrey Escoffier, Regina Kunzel, and Molly McGarry, "Editors' Introduction to 'the Queer Issue,'" *Radical History Review* 62 (1995): 3, hereafter referred to as *RHR*.

23. Donna Penn, "Queer: Theorizing Politics and History," *Radical History Review* 62 (1995): 24–42; Martha M. Umphrey, "The Trouble with Harry Thaw," *Radical History Review* 62 (1995): 9–23.

24. Penn, "Queer," 30.

25. Annamarie Jagose, *Inconsequence: Lesbian Representation and the Logic of Sexual Sequence* (Ithaca, NY: Cornell University Press, 2002), 8.

26. Queer history is discussed in greater detail in the next chapter, but in the context of North America and the United Kingdom some examples include Steven Angelides, *A History of Bisexuality* (Chicago: University of Chicago Press, 2001); John Howard, *Men Like That: A Southern Queer History* (Chicago: University of Chicago Press, 1999); Seth Koven, *Slumming: Sexual and Social Politics in Victorian London* (Princeton, NJ: Princeton University Press, 2004); and Joanne J. Meyerowitz, *How Sex Changed: A History of Transsexuality in the United States* (Cambridge, MA: Harvard University Press, 2002).

27. Escoffier, Kunzel, and McGarry, "Editors' Introduction to 'the Queer Issue,'" 3.

28. Ibid.

29. Love, *Feeling Backward*, 130.

30. Joan Wallach Scott, "Gender: A Useful Category of Historical Analysis?" in her *Feminism and History* (Oxford: Oxford University, 1996), 166.

31. Carolyn J. Dean, "Intellectual History and the Prominence of 'Things That Matter,'" *Rethinking History* 8, no. 4 (2004): 542.

32. Jeffrey Weeks, *Coming Out: Homosexual Politics in Britain from the Nineteenth Century to the Present* (London: Quartet Books, 1977), 11.

33. Jeffrey Weeks, *Making Sexual History* (Cambridge: Polity Press, 2000); Jeffrey Weeks, *Sexuality* (London: Routledge, 2003).

34. Notable exceptions include Alkarim Jivani, *It's Not Unusual: Gay and Lesbian History in the 20th Century* (London: Michael O'Mara, 1997); Robert Aldrich, *Gay Life and Culture: A World History* (London: Thames and Hudson, 2006).

35. Hugh David, *On Queer Street: A Social History of British Homosexuality, 1895–1995* (London: HarperCollins, 1997); James Gardiner, *A Class Apart: The Private Pictures of Montague Glover* (London: Serpent's Tail, 1992); James Gardiner, *Who's a Pretty Boy, Then? One Hundred and Fifty Years of Gay Life in Pictures* (London: Serpent's Tail, 1997); Graham Robb, *Strangers: Homosexual Love in the 19th Century* (London: Picador, 2003); Neil Bartlett, *Who Was That Man? A Present for Mr Oscar Wilde* (London: Serpent's Tail, 1988); Morris B. Kaplan, *Sodom on the Thames: Sex, Love, and Scandal in Wilde Times* (Ithaca, NY: Cornell University Press, 2005); Sinfield, *Wilde Century*; Matt Cook, *London and the Culture of Homosexuality, 1885–1914* (Cambridge: Cambridge University Press, 2003); Harry Cocks, *Nameless Offences: Homosexual Desire in the 19th Century* (London: I. B. Tauris, 2009); Matt Houlbrook, *Queer London: Perils and Pleasures in the Sexual Metropolis, 1918–1957* (Chicago: University of Chicago Press, 2005).

36. In his review article, Chris Waters refers to Hugh David's *On Queer Street* as "dubious"; Chris Waters, "Distance and Desire in the New British Queer History," *GLQ: A Journal of Lesbian and Gay Studies* 14, no. 1 (2007): 142. For a complete list of work published by Diana Souhami, see http://www.dianasouhami.co.uk, accessed October 10, 2009, and Emily Hamer, *Britannia's Glory: A History of Twentieth-Century Lesbians* (London: Cassell, 1996).

37. Lesbian History Group, *Not a Passing Phase: Reclaiming Lesbians in History, 1840–1985* (London: Women's Press, 1989); Lillian Faderman, *Surpassing the Love of Men: Romantic Friendship and Love between Women from the Renaissance to the Present* (London: Women's Press, 1981); Martha Vicinus, *Intimate Friends: Women Who Loved Women, 1778–1928* (Chicago: University of Chicago Press, 2004); Terry Castle, *The Apparitional Lesbian: Female Homosexuality and Modern Culture* (New York: Columbia University Press, 1993); Nicky Hallett, *Lesbian Lives: Identity and Auto/Biography in the Twentieth Century* (London: Pluto Press, 1999); Alison Oram, *Her Husband Was a Woman! Women's Gender-Crossing in Modern*

British Popular Culture (London: Routledge, 2007); Rebecca Jennings, A Lesbian History of Britain: Love and Sex between Women since 1500 (Westport, CT: Greenwood, 2007); Rebecca Jennings, Tomboys and Bachelor Girls: A Lesbian History of Post-war Britain, 1945–71 (Manchester, UK: Manchester University Press, 2007); Sally Newman, "Sites of Desire: Reading the Lesbian Archive," Australian Feminist Studies 25, no. 64 (2010): 147–62; Leila J. Rupp, A Desired Past: A Short History of Same-Sex Love in America (Chicago: University of Chicago Press, 1999); Maryanne Dever et al., The Intimate Archive: Journeys through Private Papers (Canberra: National Library of Australia, 2009).

38. Carolyn J. Dean, "Queer History," History and Theory 38, no. 1 (1999): 127. This is a review of Scott Bravmann's book, which she regards as a lost opportunity both in its failure to define or clarify the meaning of "history" and in its representation of academic history as driven by empiricism and overly invested in the metanarrative. Historian Patrick Joyce writes that "it is the discipline that regulates the practice of history, and still defines the identity of the historian"; see Patrick Joyce, "The Gift of the Past: Towards a Critical History," in Manifestos for History, ed. Keith Jenkins, Sue Morgan, and Alun Munslow (London: Routledge, 2007), 90.

39. Dean, "Queer History," 130 and 127. Some of the important work Dean refers to here includes Allan Bérubé, Coming Out under Fire: The History of Gay Men and Women in World War Two (New York: Plume, 1991); George Chauncey, Gay New York: Gender, Urban Culture, and the Makings of the Gay Male World, 1890–1940 (New York: Basic Books, 1994); John D'Emilio, Sexual Politics, Sexual Communities: The Making of a Homosexual Minority in the United States, 1940–1970 (Chicago: University of Chicago Press, 1983).

40. Vicinus is not a "literary theorist" but a specialist in literary studies and women's studies, particularly Victorian studies; see Dean, "Queer History," 124 and 128. For a good discussion on "the familiar groove of the bipartisan divide between 'historians' and 'their colleagues in other fields,'" see Ann Rigney, "Being an Improper Historian," in Manifestos for History, ed. Keith Jenkins, Sue Morgan, and Alun Munslow (London: Routledge, 2007), 149–59.

41. Foucault himself had wide-ranging intellectual interests exemplary of how historical work can also resist and exceed disciplinary boundaries. Historians' relationship with Foucault is complicated. Regarded as one of the most influential theorists (or philosophers) on the practice of history, especially for historians of sexuality, he "has not been without his critics. He has been lambasted for his empirical shoddiness, for writing a history without identifiable historical agents, for reducing the history of sexuality to a history of the classifications or representations of sexuality, for viewing the individual as little more than the passive victim of sexological discourse"; see Chris Waters, "Sexology," in Palgrave Advances in the Modern History of Sexuality, ed. H. G. Cocks and Matt Houlbrook (Basingstoke, UK: Palgrave Macmillan, 2006), 54. Historians such as Ludmilla Jordanova warn that describing Foucault as a historian is "seriously misleading," while Michael Bentley writes, "It

is not that Foucault was a historian himself or, if he were, he was a very bad one"; see Ludmilla Jordanova, *History in Practice*, 2nd ed. (London: Hodder Arnold, 2006), 74, and Michael Bentley, *Modern Historiography: An Introduction* (London: Routledge, 1999), 141. Jeffrey Weeks contends that "Foucault's history is of a curious sort"; see Weeks, *Making Sexual History*, 109. For examples of critics who describe Foucault as a historian, see Jagose, *Queer Theory*, 10; Alan Bray, *Homosexuality in Renaissance England* (New York: Columbia University Press, 1995), 9; and Sara Ahmed, *Queer Phenomenology: Orientations, Objects, Others* (Durham, NC: Duke University Press, 2006), 69.

42. Keith Jenkins, *Refiguring History: New Thoughts on an Old Discipline* (London: Routledge, 2003), 3. On p. 36 Jenkins borrows the term tribe from Michael Roth's *The Ironist's Cage* (New York: Columbia University Press, 1995).

43. Hayden White believes that "postmodernist experimentation" will "get us beyond the distinction"; see White, "Afterword," 231. Rigney issues a fierce retort to historians who would rebuke disciplinary outsiders as "improper historians"; see Rigney, "Being an Improper Historian," 150.

44. Bruce Robbins, "Oppositional Professionals," in *Consequences of Theory*, ed. Jonathan Arac and Barbara Johnson (Baltimore: Johns Hopkins University Press, 1991), 1.

45. Ibid., 2.

46. Robbins cites Richard Rorty, *Consequences of Pragmatism: Essays, 1972–1980* (Minneapolis: University of Minnesota Press, 1982). See Robbins, "Oppositional Professionals," 3.

47. William Hamilton Sewell, *Logics of History: Social Theory and Social Transformation* (Chicago: University of Chicago Press, 2005), 192.

48. Eley, *Crooked Line*, xvii.

49. Ibid.; emphasis mine. Rigney also comments on history as "governed . . . by the ethos of a rather exclusive club whose members are committed" to preserving history as distinct from other disciplines; see Rigney, "Being an Improper Historian," 150.

50. My own career trajectory is a case in point — after completing doctoral training in cultural history at the University of Chicago I moved from a department of interdisciplinary humanities to English to women's and gender studies to sociology and back to English. Another traveling scholar is David Halperin, who moved from classics to sociology and finally to English, and many others (such as Martha Vicinus and Valerie Traub) hold joint appointments.

51. Eley, *Crooked Line*, 163.

52. Ibid., 192.

53. Rigney, "Being an Improper Historian," 149 and 150.

54. Lynn Hunt, "The Objects of History: A Reply to Philip Stewart," *Journal of Modern History* 66 (1994): 546.

55. Ibid.

56. Joan Scott, "History-Writing as Critique," in *Manifestos for History*, ed. Keith Jen-

kins, Sue Morgan, and Alun Munslow (London: Routledge, 2007), 24. The shared intellectual investments of queer studies and critical history will be discussed further in chapter 2.

57. White, "Afterword," 224–25.

58. Ibid., 224.

59. Sewell, *Logics of History*, 3; Dean, "Queer History," 125.

60. White, "Afterword," 224.

61. Dean, "Queer History," 124 and 125.

62. Bravmann, *Queer Fictions of the Past*, x. Bravmann's PhD supervisor was Hayden White in the History of Consciousness program at the University of California, Santa Cruz.

63. Ibid., ix.

64. Examples include Koven, *Slumming*; Howard, *Men Like That*; Houlbrook, *Queer London*; and Regina G. Kunzel, *Criminal Intimacy: Prison and the Uneven History of Modern American Sexuality* (Chicago: University of Chicago Press, 2008).

65. Eley, *Crooked Line*, xvii.

66. John Howard, "Review," *American Historical Review* 103, no. 5 (1998): 1567.

67. Bravmann, *Queer Fictions of the Past*, x.

68. Ibid., ix–x.

69. Ibid., 45. Carolyn Dinshaw's discussion of postmodern history in the context of queer historical studies, for example, has been influential; see especially the introductory chapter of Dinshaw, *Getting Medieval*, 1–54.

70. Dean, "Queer History," 124–25.

71. Carolyn Dinshaw et al., "Theorizing Queer Temporalities: A Roundtable Discussion," *GLQ: A Journal of Lesbian and Gay Studies* 13, no. 2–3 (2007): 178.

72. Laura Doan, *Fashioning Sapphism: The Origins of a Modern English Lesbian Culture* (New York: Columbia University Press, 2001).

73. Diana Souhami, for instance, writes that Hall's "clothes asserted masculine authority. She wore neckties, sapphire cufflinks, and a monocle and had her hair barbered fortnightly"; see Souhami's introduction to the 2008 reprint of Radclyffe Hall's 1928 novel *The Well of Loneliness* (London: Virago), ix.

74. Escoffier, Kunzel, and McGarry, "Editors' Introduction to 'the Queer Issue,'" 3. For a discussion on the "new British queer history," see Waters, "Distance and Desire in the New British Queer History." See also a special issue of the *Journal of British Studies* on "British queer history": 51, no. 3 (2012).

75. Maynard, "'Respect Your Elders, Know Your Past,'" 59; Duggan, "Discipline Problem," 181.

76. Carla Freccero describes the "pieties of the discipline that would require the solemn, even dour, marshalling of empirical evidence to prove its point"; see Freccero, *Queer/Early/Modern*, 3. Empiricism can be defined as "the philosophical standpoint which maintains that knowledge cannot legitimately go beyond the

analysis of concrete facts"; see Willie Thompson, *Postmodernism and History* (Basingstoke, UK: Palgrave Macmillan, 2004), 130.

77. Duggan, "Discipline Problem," 188.

78. Ibid., 181.

79. Scott, "Gender,"166.

80. Dinshaw, *Getting Medieval*, 14.

81. Georg G. Iggers, *Historiography in the Twentieth Century: From Scientific Objectivity to the Postmodern Challenge* (Hanover, NH: Wesleyan University Press, 1997), 145. Positivism "has been the subject of much misunderstanding" in modern historiography. The term is associated with the French thinker Auguste Comte, who thought that "the only true knowledge was scientific knowledge, and that scientific knowledge could be defined as that which could be induced from observation and, where possible, experiment." Empiricism, on the other hand, is linked to the "observational side of positivism," using "our sensory perception to acquire knowledge"; see Roger Spalding and Christopher Parker, *Historiography: An Introduction* (Manchester, UK: Manchester University Press, 2007), 9–10.

82. Lisa Duggan, "Commentary: Dreaming Democracy," *New Literary History* 31, no. 4 (2000): 853.

83. Scott, "History-Writing as Critique," 22; Appleby, Jacob, and Hunt, *Telling the Truth about History*, 237 and 261.

84. Scott, "History-Writing as Critique," 22.

85. Appleby, Jacob, and Hunt, *Telling the Truth about History*, 255; Dean, "Intellectual History and the Prominence of 'Things That Matter,'" 538.

86. Dominick LaCapra, "Resisting Apocalypse and Rethinking History," in *Manifestos for History*, ed. Keith Jenkins, Sue Morgan, and Alun Munslow (London: Routledge, 2007), 165.

87. White, "Afterword," 226. Scott also points out that the "'discovery' of new materials is actually an interpretive intervention"; see Joan Scott, "After History?" *Common Knowledge* 5, no. 3 (1996): 25.

88. White, "Afterword," 227.

89. LaCapra, "Resisting Apocalypse and Rethinking History," 171; Iggers, *Historiography in the Twentieth Century*, 145; emphasis mine.

90. LaCapra, "Resisting Apocalypse and Rethinking History," 165; Joyce, "Gift of the Past," 95. Joyce explains that history is theoretical "because it is alert to how history is always structured by different sorts of intellectual framework" and empirical "because it is concerned with developing theory through practice, and regenerating and refining practice through theory."

91. Scott, "After History?" 25.

92. Duggan, "Commentary," 854.

93. Ibid., 853.

94. Robert A. Rosenstone, "Space for the Bird to Fly," in *Manifestos for History*, ed. Keith Jenkins, Sue Morgan, and Alun Munslow (London: Routledge, 2007), 17.

95. For a good discussion of the current intense interest in the historical past, see also Jerome de Groot, *Consuming History: Historians and Heritage in Contemporary Popular Culture* (London: Routledge, 2009).

96. For introductions to queer theory, see Jagose, *Queer Theory*; Nikki Sullivan, *A Critical Introduction to Queer Theory* (Edinburgh: Edinburgh University Press, 2003); Donald E. Hall, *Queer Theories* (Basingstoke, UK: Palgrave Macmillan, 2003); and Turner, *Genealogy of Queer Theory*. For edited collections on queer studies, see Brett Beemyn and Mickey Eliason, eds., *Queer Studies: Lesbian, Gay, Bisexual, and Transgender Anthology* (New York: New York University Press, 1996); Robert J. Corber and Stephen Valocchi, eds., *Queer Studies: An Interdisciplinary Reader* (Oxford: Blackwell, 2003); Donald E. Morton, ed., *The Material Queer: A LesBiGay Cultural Studies Reader* (Oxford: Westview Press, 1996); and Donald Hall and Annamarie Jagose, eds., *The Routledge Queer Studies Reader* (New York: Routledge, 2012).

97. Fuss, *Inside/Out*, 1.

98. Ibid.; Robyn Wiegman, *Object Lessons* (Durham, NC: Duke University Press, 2012), 1. Wiegman offers an incisive critique of the current state of queer studies. Queer studies also "developed out of—and continues to be understandable in terms of—feminist knowledges"; see Jagose, *Queer Theory*, 119.

99. David M. Halperin, *Saint Foucault: Towards a Gay Hagiography* (New York: Oxford University Press, 1995), 62.

100. Escoffier, Kunzel, and McGarry, "Editors' Introduction to 'the Queer Issue,'" 3.

101. Eve Kosofsky Sedgwick, *Epistemology of the Closet* (Berkeley: University of California Press, 1990), 44; emphasis in original; White, "Afterword," 224.

102. David M. Halperin, *How to Do the History of Homosexuality* (Chicago: University of Chicago Press, 2002), 13; Sedgwick, *Epistemology of the Closet*, 48.

103. Sedgwick, *Epistemology of the Closet*, 45; emphasis in original.

104. Houlbrook, *Queer London*, xiii; Jonathan Ned Katz, *Love Stories: Sex between Men before Homosexuality* (Chicago: University of Chicago Press, 2001), 6; Jagose, *Queer Theory*, 15.

105. Foucault's essay "What Is Enlightenment?" appears in Michel Foucault and Paul Rabinow, *The Foucault Reader* (New York: Pantheon, 1984), 46.

106. Sedgwick, *Epistemology of the Closet*, 44 and 46.

107. Michel Foucault, *The History of Sexuality*, vol. 1, *An Introduction* (London: Penguin, 1976), 43; Halperin, *How to Do the History of Homosexuality*, 46.

108. Halperin, *How to Do the History of Homosexuality*, 11.

109. White, "Afterword," 224.

110. Halperin, *How to Do the History of Homosexuality*, 11.

111. Ibid., 11 and 12.

112. Ibid., 109.

113. Jason Edwards, *Eve Kosofsky Sedgwick* (London: Routledge, 2009), 11.

114. Cited by Maynard, "'Respect Your Elders, Know Your Past,'" 73.

115. Cvetkovich, *Archive of Feelings*; Love, *Feeling Backward*; Herring, *Queering the Underworld*.

116. Herring, *Queering the Underworld*, 23.

117. Joanna Bourke, "Foreword," in *Manifestos for History*, ed. Keith Jenkins, Sue Morgan, and Alun Munslow (London: Routledge, 2007), xii.

118. Herring, *Queering the Underworld*, 20.

119. Ibid., 3–4. This call for undoing is echoed in the title of a chapter in Carla Freccero's 2006 book *Queer/Early/Modern*, "Undoing the Histories of Homosexuality," 1–50.

120. Joan Scott, "The Evidence of Experience," *Critical Inquiry* 17 (1991): 773–97.

121. Ibid., 778. Chapter 2 looks more extensively at the queer critique of visibility in historical work, especially the contributions of Annamarie Jagose and Valerie Traub.

122. Cvetkovich, *Archive of Feelings*, 268.

123. Pierre Nora, "Between Memory and History: *Les Lieux de Mémoire*," *Representations* 26 (1989): 8; Cvetkovich, *Archive of Feelings*, 8.

124. Eley, *Crooked Line*, 10.

125. Cvetkovich, *Archive of Feelings*, 269.

126. Ibid., 268; emphasis mine.

127. Ibid.

128. Ibid., 166.

129. Ibid. Students in history learn early in their careers to be wary of the "cult of the archive," since its "'raw' materials" are quite seductive; see Jordanova, *History in Practice*, 161–63.

130. Carolyn Steedman, *Dust: The Archive and Cultural History* (Manchester, UK: Manchester University Press, 2001), 68; emphasis in original.

131. I thank Matt Houlbrook for reminding me that "all artifacts can be incorporated into institutional forms of memory." Even the notion of "raw materials" needs to be problematized, since these are subject to selection and ordering (personal communication, July 2010).

132. Kaplan, *Sodom on the Thames*, 7.

133. Cvetkovich, *Archive of Feelings*, 268; Scott, "Evidence of Experience," 778.

134. Cvetkovich, *Archive of Feelings*, 268; Jacques Derrida, *Archive Fever: A Freudian Impression* (Chicago: University of Chicago Press, 1996).

135. Steedman, *Dust*, 68.

136. Steedman draws here on the work of theorist Jean Laplanche; see Jean Laplanche, *Life and Death in Psychoanalysis*, trans. with intro. Jeffrey Mehlman (Baltimore: Johns Hopkins University Press, 1976). Steedman, *Dust*, 38 and 77; emphasis in original.

137. Steedman, *Dust*, 77; emphasis mine.

138. Love, *Feeling Backward*, 24.

139. Cvetkovich, *Archive of Feelings*, 8 and 3.

140. Scott, "Evidence of Experience," 777.

141. Houlbrook, *Queer London*, 271; Love, *Feeling Backward*, 29.

142. Love, *Feeling Backward*, 129.

143. Scott, "Evidence of Experience," 778.

144. Nealon, *Foundlings*, 17.

145. Love, *Feeling Backward*, 33.

146. Ibid., 21; White, "Afterword," 224; emphasis in original.

147. White, "Afterword," 225 and 224.

148. Sedgwick, *Epistemology of the Closet*, 22.

149. Eve Kosofsky Sedgwick, *Tendencies* (Durham, NC: Duke University Press, 1993), 8; emphasis in original.

150. Ibid., xii.

151. Harriette Andreadis, *Sappho in Early Modern England: Female Same-Sex Literary Erotics, 1550–1714* (Chicago: University of Chicago Press, 2001), 21. This reference to possible new directions in queer studies appears in "Affect Theory Roundtable Questions, MLA 2012"; see http://supervalentthought.com/category/affect-theory, accessed January 21, 2012.

152. Sedgwick, *Tendencies*, xii.

153. Scott, "History-Writing as Critique," 22.

154. Ibid.

155. These phrases appear in the *Times Literary Supplement* in reviews by Richard Davenport-Hines (November 27, 2009) and Jonathan Clark (January 15, 2010). The "Books of the Year" exercise is instructive in gauging what some historians regard as excellence in the field. The November 2009 issue also includes Ferdinand Mount's assessment of a new book on the First World War that notes its "gripping narrative and sober analysis," while Linda Colley lists books that examine "familiar themes through rather different lenses." Reviews in other learned journals (such as *Past and Present, Radical History Review, History and Theory, History Workshop Journal, American History Review,* or *Cultural and Social History*) might, of course, assess historical work differently.

156. Sewell, *Logics of History*, 4.

157. Confirmation of the status of high theory in queer studies can be seen in the recent publication of a study celebrating the perverse virtues of "low theory"; see Judith Halberstam, *The Queer Art of Failure* (Durham, NC: Duke University Press, 2011).

158. Hayden White, *Tropics of Discourse: Essays in Cultural Criticism* (Baltimore: Johns Hopkins University Press, 1978), 126.

159. Ibid., 127.

160. Howard, *Men Like That*, 30. See also Paul R. Deslandes's use of queer theory in *Oxbridge Men: British Masculinity and the Undergraduate Experience, 1850–1920* (Bloomington: Indiana University Press, 2005).

161. Houlbrook, *Queer London*, 231; Kunzel, *Criminal Intimacy*, 102.

162. Aldrich, *Gay Life and Culture*, 12.

163. Sedgwick, *Epistemology of the Closet*, 23; emphasis in original.

164. The single mention of queer theory appears in Gert Hekma, "The Gay World: 1980 to the Present," in *Gay Life and Culture: A World History*, ed. Robert Aldrich (London: Thames and Hudson, 2006), 356.

165. Howard, *Men Like That*, 6.

166. Houlbrook, *Queer London*, xiii.

167. Note that Cocks draws on important work of queer literary critics as well, such as D. A. Miller, Alan Sinfield, and Ed Cohen; Cocks, *Nameless Offences*, 3.

168. Kaplan, *Sodom on the Thames*, 269.

169. Ibid., 265. The problem, as Sewell sees it, is that historians believe the "concepts don't quite fit" and "need to be adjusted, nuanced, or combined with concepts from other, apparently incompatible, theoretical discourses in order to be useful in historical research. In this sense, our use of theory is, practically speaking, critical"; see Sewell, *Logics of History*, 5.

170. See Scott, "History-Writing as Critique," 22.

171. Lest this distinction seem overdrawn, I should acknowledge that most period-based work by literary and cultural critics, especially those influenced by new historicism, is scrupulous about proper contextualization. In my work on the First World War, literary critics typically do not differentiate between fiction published during the war and work appearing a decade later.

172. For an excellent example of an interdisciplinary project that includes both historians and literary scholars, see Kenneth Borris and G. S. Rousseau, eds., *The Sciences of Homosexuality in Early Modern Europe* (London: Routledge, 2008).

173. Herring, *Queering the Underworld*, 209. Judith Halberstam's comment appears in Carolyn Dinshaw et al., "Theorizing Queer Temporalities: A Roundtable Discussion," *GLQ: A Journal of Lesbian and Gay Studies* 13, no. 2–3 (2007): 182.

174. Jordanova, *History in Practice*, 170–71.

175. Duggan, "Discipline Problem," 182.

176. Duggan's definition of a "queer methodology" is drawn from the work of Judith Halberstam. See Lisa Duggan, "Down There: The Queer South and the Future of History Writing," *GLQ: A Journal of Lesbian and Gay Studies* 8, no. 3 (2002): 383; Halberstam, *Female Masculinity*.

177. See Hunt, "The Objects of History: A Reply to Philip Stewart"; Catherine Gallagher and Stephen Greenblatt, *Practicing New Historicism* (Chicago: University of Chicago Press, 2000), 31.

178. Sarah Maza, "Stephen Greenblatt, New Historicism, and Cultural History, or What We Talk about When We Talk about Interdisciplinarity," *Modern Intellectual History* 1, no. 2 (2004): 258.

CHAPTER TWO

1. Carla Freccero, "Queer Times," *South Atlantic Quarterly* 106, no. 3 (2007): 490.
2. Carolyn Steedman, *Landscape for a Good Woman: A Story of Two Lives* (London: Virago, 1986), 21.
3. David M. Halperin, *How to Do the History of Homosexuality* (Chicago: University of Chicago Press, 2002), 106 and 107; emphasis mine.
4. Ibid., 107; emphasis mine.
5. Louise Fradenburg and Carla Freccero, *Premodern Sexualities* (London: Routledge, 1996), xix.
6. Valerie Traub, "The New Unhistoricism in Queer Studies," *PMLA* (2013), forthcoming. I am grateful to her for sharing early drafts of her work.
7. For an elaboration on the subject of the "queer historical impulse" as a desire to touch across time, see Carolyn Dinshaw, *Getting Medieval: Sexualities and Communities, Pre- and Postmodern* (Durham, NC: Duke University Press, 1999), 1–54. Valerie Traub writes, "There exist certain recurrent explanatory meta-logics that accord to the history of lesbianism over a vast temporal expanse a sense of consistency and, at times, uncanny familiarity"; see Valerie Traub, "The Present Future of Lesbian Historiography," in *A Companion to Lesbian, Gay, Bisexual, Transgender, and Queer Studies*, ed. George E. Haggerty and Molly McGarrity (London: Blackwell, 2007), 125.
8. Personal correspondence with Annamarie Jagose, August 2010.
9. Joanna Bourke, "Foreword," in *Manifestos for History*, ed. Keith Jenkins, Sue Morgan, and Alun Munslow (London: Routledge, 2007), xi; emphasis mine. For a discussion of "critical history" (variously called history as critique, a history of the present, or genealogy), see the previous chapter.
10. Joan Scott, "History-Writing as Critique," in *Manifestos for History*, ed. Keith Jenkins, Sue Morgan, and Alun Munslow (London: Routledge, 2007), 30. Scott cites Foucault's assertion that "nothing in man — not even his body — is sufficiently stable to serve as the basis for self-recognition or for understanding other men"; see Michel Foucault, "Nietzsche, Genealogy, History," in *Language, Counter-memory, Practice: Selected Essays and Interviews by Michel Foucault*, ed. with intro. Donald F. Bouchard (Ithaca, NY: Cornell University Press, 1977), 153.
11. Joan Scott, "Finding Critical History," in *Becoming Historians*, ed. James M. Banner and John R. Gillis (Chicago: University of Chicago Press, 2009), 48.
12. Valerie Traub similarly observes that "reflections on historiographic method often seem silently embedded in our scholarship, present implicitly in the mode of argumentation"; see Traub, "Present Future of Lesbian Historiography," 124.
13. Gordon S. Wood, "No Thanks for the Memories," *New York Review of Books*, 2011, xvii; David Lowenthal, *The Heritage Crusade and the Spoils of History*, 2nd ed. (Cambridge: Cambridge University Press, 1998).
14. Disciplinary cultures of individual departments of history are, of course, subject to

change, and therefore it would be unwise to attempt to name institutions known specifically for queer historical work, though my colleagues in the United Kingdom often comment that such work in a North American context flourishes. For further discussion see Marc Stein, "Committee on Lesbian and Gay History Survey on LGBTQ History Careers," June 2001, http://www.historians.org/perspectives/issues/2001/0105/0105affi.cfm.

15. The elisions that result from such estrangement can be seen in queer discussions of temporality; see, for instance, Carolyn Dinshaw et al., "Theorizing Queer Temporalities: A Roundtable Discussion," in GLQ: A Journal of Lesbian and Gay Studies 13, no. 2–3 (2007): 177–96.

16. Carla Freccaro comments on how "after a period of emphatically alterist history in the field of sexuality studies, the trend seems to be *moving toward* a reconsideration, in updated terms, of John Boswell's early and scandalous claims about the transhistoricity of same-sex unions"; see Carla Freccero, "We 'Other Victorians,'" GLQ: A Journal of Lesbian and Gay Studies 14, no. 1 (2008): 159; emphasis mine.

17. Reviewer Paul Bailey, for example, described Matt Houlbrook's Queer London as "written in the jargon favored by sociologists. I don't know where Houlbrook got 'performativity' from, but I advise him to give it back"; see "Sex and the City," Sunday Times, September 4, 2005.

18. Geoff Eley, A Crooked Line: From Cultural History to the History of Society (Ann Arbor: University of Michigan Press, 2005), 7.

19. Halperin, How to Do the History of Homosexuality, 17.

20. The authors of Telling the Truth about History argue that "postmodernists" define "'subaltern' groups" as including "workers, immigrants, women, slaves, and gays"; see Joyce Oldham Appleby, Margaret C. Jacob, and Lynn Hunt, Telling the Truth about History (New York: Norton, 1994), 217. See also Geoff Eley's explanation of subaltern as a term developed by Antonio Gramsci "for subordinate social groups lacking organized political autonomy"; Eley, Crooked Line, 142. For a good overview of the development of subaltern studies, see Simon Gunn, History and Cultural Theory (Harlow, UK: Pearson Longman, 2006), 166–73.

21. Ludmilla Jordanova, History in Practice, 2nd ed. (London: Hodder Arnold, 2006).

22. According to Matt Houlbrook, academic history has yet to come to terms with its unease around identity politics, perceiving "differences of class, gender, or race as somehow more 'real,' 'concrete,' or 'tangible' than those of sexuality." Personal correspondence, April 2010.

23. Evidence to support this claim about the marginalizing of the history of homosexuality in historiography is detailed in chapter 1.

24. Elizabeth Freeman, "Time Binds, or Erotohistoriography," Social Text 23, no. 3–4 (2005): 57–68; Elizabeth Freeman, Time Binds: Queer Temporalities, Queer Histories (Durham, NC: Duke University Press, 2010); Valerie Rohy, "Ahistorical," GLQ: A Journal of Lesbian and Gay Studies 12, no. 1 (2006): 61–83; Valerie Rohy,

Anachronism and Its Others (Albany: State University Press of New York, 2009); Traub, "Present Future of Lesbian Historiography."

25. Gabrielle M. Spiegel, "The Task of the Historian," *American Historical Review* 114, no. 1 (2009): 2. See also Nancy Partner, "Narrative Persistence: The Post-postmodern Life of Narrative Theory," in *Re-figuring Hayden White*, ed. Frank Ankersmit, Ewa Domanska, and Hans Kellner (Stanford, CA: Stanford University Press, 2009), 82; Eley, *Crooked Line*, 127–29.

26. Joan Scott, "After History?" *Common Knowledge* 5, no. 3 (1996): 9. Scott's discussion of the nature of historical practice is influenced by Michel de Certeau, *The Writing of History*, trans. Tom Conley (New York: Columbia University Press, 1988).

27. Scott, "After History?" 9.

28. Annamarie Jagose, *Inconsequence: Lesbian Representation and the Logic of Sexual Sequence* (Ithaca, NY: Cornell University Press, 2002), 8; Carla Freccero, *Queer/Early/Modern* (Durham, NC: Duke University Press, 2006), 48.

29. In the 1990 preface to the second edition of *Coming Out*, sociological historian Jeffrey Weeks emphasizes that "the history of homosexuality is not the story of the progressive unfolding of some essence of homosexual being, belonging to a constant minority throughout history. On the contrary, the idea of 'the homosexual' as a distinct sort of being has not always existed. It is an invention of the modern world. It is historically and socially constructed"; see Jeffrey Weeks, *Coming Out: Homosexual Politics in Britain from the Nineteenth Century to the Present* (London: Quartet Books, 1977), x. See also Chris Waters, "The Homosexual as a Social Being in Britain, 1945–1968," paper presented at the New British Queer History conference, 2010.

30. Dipesh Chakrabarty finds this phrase of philosopher Charles Taylor's useful for historical analysis; see Dipesh Chakrabarty, "History and the Politics of Recognition," in *Manifestos for History*, ed. Keith Jenkins, Sue Morgan, and Alun Munslow (London: Routledge, 2007), 77.

31. Lillian Faderman, *Surpassing the Love of Men: Romantic Friendship and Love between Women from the Renaissance to the Present* (London: Women's Press, 1981).

32. Ibid., 15.

33. Ibid., 15–16; emphasis mine; Lillian Faderman, *Odd Girls and Twilight Lovers: A History of Lesbian Life in Twentieth-Century America* (New York: Columbia University Press, 1991).

34. Freccero, "Queer Times," 485–87.

35. Frances Doughty, "Lesbian Biography, Biography of Lesbians," *Frontiers* 4, no. 3 (1979): 76.

36. In an often-cited passage Halberstam writes: "I want to argue for a perversely presentist model of historical analysis, a model, in other words, that avoids the trap of simply projecting contemporary understandings back in time, but one that can

apply insights from the present to conundrums of the past"; see Judith Halberstam, *Female Masculinity* (Durham, NC: Duke University Press, 1998), 52–53.

37. The early feminist critique of sexological formulations by scholars such as Sheila Jeffreys has since undergone substantial reevaluation; see Sheila Jeffreys, *The Spinster and Her Enemies: Feminism and Sexuality, 1880–1930* (London: Pandora, 1985). For an excellent overview of the origins of modern discourses of sexuality, see Chris Waters, "Sexology," in *Palgrave Advances in the Modern History of Sexuality*, ed. H. G. Cocks and Matt Houlbrook (Basingstoke, UK: Palgrave Macmillan, 2006). See also Harry Oosterhuis, *Stepchildren of Nature: Krafft-Ebing, Psychiatry, and the Making of Sexual Identity* (Chicago: University of Chicago Press, 2000); and Lucy Bland and Laura Doan, eds., *Sexology in Culture: Labelling Bodies and Desires* (Chicago: University of Chicago Press, 1998).

38. Lesbian History Group, *Not a Passing Phase: Reclaiming Lesbians in History, 1840–1985* (London: Women's Press, 1989).

39. Lillian Faderman, "Who Hid Lesbian History?" *Frontiers* 4, no. 3 (1979): 74.

40. Martha Vicinus, "Lesbian History: All Theory and No Facts or All Facts and No Theory?" *Radical History Review* 60 (1994): 57–75. The Lesbian History Group underscored this point as well, arguing that the "lesbian perspective" would "illuminate the history of women and of male power"; see Lesbian History Group, *Not a Passing Phase*, 229.

41. Vicinus, "Lesbian History," 58. Overviews include Emily Hamer, *Britannia's Glory: History of Twentieth-Century Lesbians* (London: Cassell, 1995); Rebecca Jennings, *A Lesbian History of Britain: Love and Sex between Women since 1500* (Westport, CT: Greenwood, 2007); Alkarim Jivani, *It's Not Unusual: Gay and Lesbian History in the 20th Century* (London: Michael O'Mara, 1997); and Leila J. Rupp, *A Desired Past: A Short History of Same-Sex Love in America* (Chicago: University of Chicago Press, 1999).

42. See Terry Castle, *The Apparitional Lesbian: Female Homosexuality and Modern Culture* (New York: Columbia University Press, 1993).

43. Terry Castle, ed., *The Literature of Lesbianism: A Historical Anthology from Ariosto to Stonewall* (New York: Columbia University Press, 2003), xx and 47.

44. Ibid., 1 and 11. The last quotation is italicized in the original.

45. Ibid., 6 and 11.

46. Valerie Traub, *The Renaissance of Lesbianism in Early Modern England* (Cambridge: Cambridge University Press, 2002), 352; Scott, "After History?" 19.

47. Weeks, *Coming Out*, 11. A good example of later work in this vein is Matt Cook's *London and the Culture of Homosexuality, 1885–1914* (Cambridge: Cambridge University Press, 2003).

48. Eley, *Crooked Line*, 128 and 196. Important examples of social history and new cultural history with particular interests in male and female homosexuality in a North American context include John D'Emilio, *Sexual Politics, Sexual Com-*

munities: The Making of a Homosexual Minority in the United States, 1940–1970 (Chicago: University of Chicago Press, 1983); John D'Emilio and Estelle B. Freedman, *Intimate Matters: A History of Sexuality in America* (Chicago: University of Chicago Press, 1988); Elizabeth Lapovsky Kennedy and Madeline D. Davis, *Boots of Leather, Slippers of Gold: The History of a Lesbian Community* (New York: Routledge, 1993); Carroll Smith-Rosenberg, *Disorderly Conduct: Visions of Gender in Victorian America* (New York: Alfred K. Knopf, 1985); and Martha Vicinus, *Independent Women: Work and Community for Single Women, 1850–1920* (Chicago: University of Chicago Press, 1985).

49. Nayan Shah, "Sexuality, Identity, and the Uses of History," in *A Lotus of Another Color: An Unfolding of the South Asian Gay and Lesbian Experience*, ed. Rakesh Ratti (Boston: Alyson, 1993), 128; Weeks, *Coming Out*, xi.

50. Judith Bennett, *History Matters: Patriarchy and the Challenge of Feminism* (Philadelphia: University of Pennsylvaia Press, 2006), 119. See also Laura Doan and Jay Prosser, eds., *Palatable Poison: Critical Perspectives on "The Well of Loneliness"* (New York: Columbia University Press, 2001).

51. As I mentioned in the introduction, in contemporary historiography there is little more than passing acknowledgment of LGBT or queer history.

52. Carolyn Steedman, *Dust: The Archive and Cultural History* (Manchester, UK: Manchester University Press, 2001), 77. For a thoughtful discussion of advocacy in historical writing, see Eley, *Crooked Line*, especially 6–8.

53. Lesbian History Group, *Not a Passing Phase*, 230.

54. Alison Oram and Annmarie Turnbull, eds., *The Lesbian History Sourcebook: Love and Sex between Women in Britain from 1780 to 1970* (London: Routledge, 2001), 1.

55. Traub, *Renaissance of Lesbianism in Early Modern England*, 335 and 352; emphasis in original.

56. Examples include Robert Aldrich, *Gay Life and Culture: A World History* (London: Thames and Hudson, 2006); Tom Ambrose, *Heroes and Exiles: Gay Icons through the Ages* (London: New Holland, 2010); Matt Cook et al., eds., *A Gay History of Britain: Love and Sex between Men since the Middle Ages* (Westport, CT: Greenwood World, 2007); Jennings, *Lesbian History of Britain*; and Leila J. Rupp, *Sapphistries: A Global History of Love between Women* (New York: New York University Press, 2009). See also the recent special issues of the *Journal of Lesbian Studies* on lesbian history; 13, no. 4 (2009), and 14, no. 4 (2010).

57. Robert A. Rosenstone, "Space for the Bird to Fly," in *Manifestos for History*, ed. Keith Jenkins, Sue Morgan, and Alun Munslow (London: Routledge, 2007), 17.

58. For an important example of recent British lesbian social history, see Rebecca Jennings, *Tomboys and Bachelor Girls: A Lesbian History of Post-war Britain, 1945–71* (Manchester, UK: Manchester University Press, 2007).

59. Pierre Nora, "Between Memory and History: Les Lieux de Mémoire," *Representations* 26 (1989): 8. For a theoretical discussion of the work of LGBT histories and

public culture, see Robert Mills, "Queer Is Here? Lesbian, Gay, Bisexual, and Transgender Histories and Public Culture," *History Workshop Journal* 62 (2006): 253–63.

60. Chakrabarty, "History and the Politics of Recognition," 77. See also Charles Taylor, "The Politics of Recognition," in *Multiculturalism: Examining the Politics of Recognition*, ed. Amy Gutman (Princeton, NJ: Princeton University Press, 1994).

61. Chakrabarty, "History and the Politics of Recognition," 77.

62. Wendy Brown, *States of Injury: Power and Freedom in Late Modernity* (Princeton, NJ: Princeton University Press, 1995), 60; Chakrabarty, "History and the Politics of Recognition," 77–78; emphasis in original.

63. The novels of Sarah Waters, for instance, have been highly successful in inventing past lesbian lives; see www.sarahwaters.com.

64. Heather Love, *Feeling Backward: Loss and the Politics of Queer History* (Cambridge, MA: Harvard University Press, 2007), 45 and 4.

65. Ibid., 173n9. See E. P. Thompson, *The Making of the English Working Class* (1963; Harmondsworth, UK: Penguin, 1968).

66. The "turn to affect" in queer cultural criticism has been characterized as "an open-ended or exploratory trajectory, a distrust and avoidance of yes/no structures, luxuriantly sensuous writing . . . and an intense focus on political and psychic dysphoria," according to Janet Halley and Andrew Parker in their introduction "After Sex? On Writing since Queer Theory," in a special issue of *South Atlantic Quarterly* 106, no. 3 (2007): 421–32, especially 428. See also Lauren Berlant, "Thinking about Feeling Historical," *Emotion, Space, and Society* 1 (2008): 4–9; and Ann Cvetkovich, *An Archive of Feelings: Trauma, Sexuality, and Lesbian Public Cultures* (Durham, NC: Duke University Press, 2003).

67. Love, *Feeling Backward*, 129.

68. Ibid., 5 and passim.

69. Hayden White, "Afterword," in *Manifestos for History*, ed. Keith Jenkins, Sue Morgan, and Alun Munslow (London: Routledge, 2007), 228.

70. Ibid.

71. Ibid.

72. Chakrabarty, "History and the Politics of Recognition," 83.

73. White, "Afterword," 228.

74. Jagose, *Inconsequence*, 13 and 9. See also Emma Donoghue, *Passions between Women: British Lesbian Culture, 1668–1801* (London: Scarlet Press, 1993).

75. For a cogent critique of queer temporalities see Traub, "Present Future of Lesbian Historiography," especially 135.

76. Chakrabarty, "History and the Politics of Recognition," 83.

77. Ibid. Included in this group are Carlo Ginzburg, Natalie Davis, Lynn Hunt, Lawrence Stone, and Eric Hobsbawm.

78. Ibid.

79. Brown, *States of Injury*, 73–74.

80. Traub, *Renaissance of Lesbianism in Early Modern England*, 350; emphasis in original.

81. Lesbian History Group, *Not a Passing Phase*, 230.

82. Scott, "After History?" 18. Scott's argument is informed by Brown's *States of Injury*.

83. Jagose, *Inconsequence*, 8.

84. Ibid., 8 and 2.

85. Ibid., 9 and 8.

86. Ibid., 13 and x.

87. Ibid., x.

88. Ibid., xi.

89. Ibid., 8; emphasis mine.

90. Halperin, *How to Do the History of Homosexuality*, 43.

91. Traub, *Renaissance of Lesbianism in Early Modern England*, 350.

92. Ibid., 353.

93. Traub, "Present Future of Lesbian Historiography," 138.

94. Alison Oram, *Her Husband Was a Woman! Women's Gender-Crossing in Modern British Popular Culture* (London: Routledge, 2007); Martha Vicinus, *Intimate Friends: Women Who Loved Women, 1778–1928* (Chicago: University of Chicago Press, 2004).

95. Oram, *Her Husband Was a Woman!* 157.

96. Hayden White, *Tropics of Discourse: Essays in Cultural Criticism* (Baltimore: Johns Hopkins University Press, 1978), 234; Vicinus, *Intimate Friends*.

97. Foucault, "Nietzsche, Genealogy and History," 154.

98. Halperin, *How to Do the History of Homosexuality*, 43; emphasis in original.

99. Traub, "Present Future of Lesbian Historiography," 139n1.

100. Traub, *Renaissance of Lesbianism in Early Modern England*, 32.

101. Matt Houlbrook, *Queer London: Perils and Pleasures in the Sexual Metropolis, 1918–1957* (Chicago: University of Chicago Press, 2005), 13.

102. Ibid., xiii.

103. Harry Cocks, *Nameless Offences: Homosexual Desire in the 19th Century* (London: I. B. Tauris, 2009); Sean Brady, *Masculinity and Male Homosexuality in Britain, 1861–1913* (Basingstoke, UK: Palgrave Macmillan, 2005).

104. Houlbrook, *Queer London*, 91; Richard Quentin Donald Hornsey, *The Spiv and the Architect: Unruly Life in Postwar London* (Minneapolis: University of Minnesota Press, 2010), 200.

105. Houlbrook, *Queer London*, 265; Morris B. Kaplan, *Sodom on the Thames: Sex, Love, and Scandal in Wilde Times* (Ithaca, NY: Cornell University Press, 2005), 7.

106. Scott Herring, *Queering the Underworld: Slumming, Literature, and the Undoing of Lesbian and Gay History* (Chicago: University of Chicago Press, 2007); Freccero, *Queer/Early/Modern*, 31; Julian Carter, "Gay Marriage and Pulp Fiction:

Homonormativity, Disidentification, and Affect in Ann Bannon's Lesbian Novels," *GLQ: A Journal of Lesbian and Gay Studies* 15, no. 4 (2009): 656. See also Judith Butler, *Undoing Gender* (New York: Routledge, 2004).

107. Peter Cryle and Lisa Downing, "Feminine Sexual Pathologies," *Journal of the History of Sexuality* 18, no. 1 (2009): 7. It is beyond the scope of this book focused on the relation between identity history and critical history to carefully examine the relations between the history of sexuality outside the framework of identity and critical history, an endeavor equally crucial.

108. Julian Carter, "On Mother-Love: History, Queer Theory, and Nonlesbian Identity," *Journal of the History of Sexuality* 14, no. 1–2 (2005): especially 107–8. Vicinus refers to mother love as "the strongest, the most troubling, and the most fundamental of all emotions for women and men" of the Victorian era; see Vicinus, *Intimate Friends*, 141.

109. Herring, *Queering the Underworld*, 20.

110. Ibid., 20–21 and 3–4.

111. Ibid., 209.

112. Partner, "Narrative Persistence," 91.

113. Keith Jenkins, *Refiguring History: New Thoughts on an Old Discipline* (London: Routledge, 2003), 29 and passim; emphasis in original.

114. Spiegel, "The Task of the Historian," 2 and 3; Eley, *Crooked Line*, 128.

115. This phrase is derived from Victoria E. Bonnell, Lynn Hunt, and Richard Biernacki, *Beyond the Cultural Turn: New Directions in the Study of Society and Culture* (Berkeley: University of California Press, 1999).

116. Spiegel, "Task of the Historian," 3n15; Joan Scott, "Unanswered Questions," *American Historical Review* 113 (2008): 1427.

117. For a discussion of historians' interest in sexuality and queer theory in general terms, see Joanne J. Meyerowitz, "A History of 'Gender,'" *American Historical Review* 113 (2008): 1352. Geoff Eley writes, "The cultural turn enabled a theoretical understanding of gender whose effects transformed the ground of thinking about history. . . . Only with the conceptual shift from the history of women to the history of gender did the protected central precincts of the discipline start to give way"; see Eley, *Crooked Line*, 126–27.

118. Scott, "After History?" 22.

119. Ibid.

120. Ibid., 24 and 23.

121. Ibid., 23. For a sustained engagement with questions relating to the future of identity politics, see the special issue of *New Literary History* ("Is There Life after Identity Politics?"), especially Robyn Wiegman's "Feminism's Apocalyptic Futures," *New Literary History* 31 (2000): 805–25. See also Wiegman's *Object Lessons* (Durham, NC: Duke University Press, 2012).

122. Scott, "History-Writing as Critique," 29–30.

123. Eve Kosofsky Sedgwick, *Epistemology of the Closet* (Berkeley: University of California Press, 1990), 33; emphasis in original. For an important critique of identity knowledges and intersectionality, see Wiegman, *Object Lessons*.

124. Sedgwick, *Epistemology of the Closet*, 30.

125. According to Joanne Meyerowitz, "In U.S. women's — and now gender — history . . . [historians] *brought in* race, sexuality, and nationality as equally useful categories of historical analysis, and they borrowed from postcolonial, critical race, queer, and political theory"; see Meyerowitz, "History of 'Gender,'" 1352; emphasis mine.

126. Sedgwick, *Epistemology of the Closet*, 31; emphasis in original.

127. Ibid.; Scott, "Unanswered Questions," 1422.

128. Lynn Hunt, "Where Have All the Theories Gone?" *Perspectives [of the American Historical Association]* 40 (2002): 5–7.

129. Bennett, *History Matters*, 14. In this passage Bennett considers aspects of Joan W. Scott, "Gender: A Useful Category of Historical Analysis?" in her *Feminism and History* (New York: Oxford University Press, 1996), 152–80. Scott argues that history is "inherently political"; see Joan Scott, "History in Crisis: The Others' Side of the Story," *American Historical Review* 94, no. 3 (1989): 681.

130. Scott, "Gender," 155.

131. Scott, "Unanswered Questions," 1427.

132. Jordanova, *History in Practice*, 89.

133. Halperin, *How to Do the History of Homosexuality*, 107.

134. Ibid.

135. Jagose, *Inconsequence*, 8–9.

136. For a discussion of Adorno's influence on critical history, see Scott, "History-Writing as Critique," especially 24–25.

137. Love, *Feeling Backward*, 32; Jenkins, *Refiguring History*, 29.

138. Jenkins, *Refiguring History*, 29.

139. Freccero, *Queer/Early/Modern*, 49 and 48. Joan Scott, for instance, points to similar methodological difficulties in her attempts to differentiate between women's history and gender history.

140. Traub, *Renaissance of Lesbianism in Early Modern England*, 28.

141. Freccero, *Queer/Early/Modern*, 3. For a more sustained examination of the work of Freccaro, Goldberg, and Menon that rethinks queer historiography, see Traub's forthcoming *Making Sexual Knowledge*. See also Freccero, "Queer Times"; Jonathan Goldberg and Madhavi Menon, "Queering History," *PMLA* 120, no. 5 (2005): 1608–17; and Jonathan Goldberg, "After Thoughts," *South Atlantic Quarterly* 106, no. 3 (2007): 501–10.

142. See Rohy, "Ahistorical"; Goldberg and Menon, "Queering History"; Freccero, *Queer/Early/Modern*; and Berlant, "Thinking about Feeling Historical."

143. Goldberg and Menon, "Queering History," 1609; Fradenburg and Freccero, *Pre-*

modern Sexualities, viii; Traub, *Renaissance of Lesbianism in Early Modern England*, 7.

144. Lynne Huffer characterizes the present moment as a "postqueer age" and "postsexual," citing the special issue "After Sex?" of *South Atlantic Quarterly* 106, no. 3 (2007), ed. Janet Halley and Andrew Parker; see Lynne Huffer, *Mad for Foucault: Rethinking the Foundations of Queer Theory* (New York: Columbia University Press, 2010), x and 305n105.

145. Traub, "Present Future of Lesbian Historiography," 133.

146. Halperin, *How to Do the History of Homosexuality*, 107.

147. Spiegel, "Task of the Historian," 4; emphasis in original.

148. Traub, *Renaissance of Lesbianism in Early Modern England*, 354; Jenkins, *Refiguring History*, 11.

149. Lowenthal, *Heritage Crusade and the Spoils of History*, xvii.

150. White, "Afterword," 224; Halperin, *How to Do the History of Homosexuality*. Valerie Traub attempts to mediate between the impulses of "transhistorical continuities" and "historical alterity"; see Traub, "Present Future of Lesbian Historiography," especially 127 and 132.

151. Spiegel, "Task of the Historian," 4.

152. Freccero, *Queer/Early/Modern*, 48–49.

153. Freccero, "Queer Times," 491.

154. Lee Edelman, *No Future: Queer Theory and the Death Drive* (Durham, NC: Duke University Press, 2004), 4.

155. Ibid., 4 and 10.

156. Ibid., 6.

157. Freccero, "Queer Times," 490.

158. As I point out in the introduction, my purpose is to scrutinize the genealogical project rather than to flesh out in detail the workings of a queer critical history practice.

159. James Vernon, "'For Some Queer Reason': The Trials and Tribulations of Colonel Barker's Masquerade in Interwar Britain," *Signs: Journal of Women in Culture and Society* 26, no. 1 (2000): 38. For another fascinating example of the good use of queer theory by a historian, see Seth Koven, *Slumming: Sexual and Social Politics in Victorian London* (Princeton, NJ: Princeton University Press, 2004).

160. Sharon Marcus, *Between Women: Friendship, Desire, and Marriage in Victorian England* (Princeton, NJ: Princeton University Press, 2007), 21 and 19.

161. Scott, "After History?" 21.

162. Freccero, *Queer/Early/Modern*, 69–104; Rohy, "Ahistorical"; Spiegel, "Task of the Historian," 4.

163. Traub, *Renaissance of Lesbianism in Early Modern England*, 331.

164. Traub, "Present Future of Lesbian Historiography," 131.

165. Scott, "Unanswered Questions," 1424.

166. Jagose, *Inconsequence*, 8.

167. Chris Waters, "Distance and Desire in the New British Queer History," *GLQ: A Journal of Lesbian and Gay Studies* 14, no. 1 (2007): 146, emphasis in original; Traub, "Present Future of Lesbian Historiography," 136.

168. Lisa Carstens, "Unbecoming Women: Sex Reversal in the Scientific Discourse on Female Deviance in Britain, 1880–1920," *Journal of the History of Sexuality* 20, no. 1 (2011): 62–94.

169. Ibid., 65.

170. Ibid., 79.

171. Ibid., 83. See also Laura Doan, *Fashioning Sapphism: The Origins of a Modern English Lesbian Culture* (New York: Columbia University Press, 2001), 35.

172. Spiegel, "Task of the Historian," 1; Carstens, "Unbecoming Women," 83.

173. Scott, "History-Writing as Critique," 25; emphasis in original.

174. Halperin, *How to Do the History of Homosexuality*, 107.

175. See Traub's forthcoming *Making Sexual Knowledge*.

CHAPTER THREE

1. Ethel Alec-Tweedie, *Women and Soldiers* (London: John Lane, 1918). For a brief account of Mrs. Alec-Tweedie's life and accomplishments, see Elizabeth Baigent, "Tweedie, Ethel Brilliana (1862–1940)," *Oxford Dictionary of National Biography Online*.

2. The historiography on women, work, and the First World War is immense; for an excellent introduction to the debates, see Penny Summerfield, "Women and War in the Twentieth Century," in *Women's History: Britain, 1850–1945; An Introduction*, ed. June Purvis (London: UCL Press, 1995), 307–32. See also Deborah Thom, "Women and Work in Wartime Britain," in *The Upheaval of War: Family, Work, and Welfare in Europe, 1914–1918*, ed. Richard Wall and Jay Winter (Cambridge: Cambridge University Press, 1988), 297–326.

3. Alec-Tweedie, *Women and Soldiers*, 5.

4. Delia Wilkin, "The War and Social Changes," *Ladies' Field*, November 11, 1916, 405. According to Havelock Ellis, "The Great War, which has changed so many things, has nowhere affected a greater change than in the sphere of women's activities.... Europe has ... become a great experimental laboratory for testing the aptitudes of women. The result of these tests, as they are slowly realized, cannot fail to have permanent effects on the sexual division of labor"; see Havelock Ellis, *Essays in War-time* (London: Constable, 1916), 35.

5. This statement was made in July 1916. Cited in Helen Fraser, *Women and War Work* (New York: Shaw, 1918), 124.

6. In a richly detailed study of women and war work in Britain, historian Deborah Thom finds it perplexing that "we still do not know for certain how many women worked in some occupations during the war.... [T]he simple question of how many women worked in jobs where they replaced men, and how many supple-

mented the existing numbers of workers, is itself fraught with difficulty"; see Deborah Thom, *Nice Girls and Rude Girls: Women Workers in World War I* (London: I. B. Tauris, 1998), 13. This topic is also discussed in Gerard J. De Groot, *Blighty: British Society in the Era of the Great War* (London: Longman, 1996), 126–39.

7. Gender historians such as Janet Watson tend to emphasize public "distrust" of uniformed woman; see, for example, Janet S. K. Watson, "Khaki Girls, VADs, and Tommy's Sisters: Gender and Class in First World War Britain," *International History Review* 19, no. 1 (1997): 51.

My examination of a broad cross-section of the national press indicates that public attitudes were never monolithic but were constantly shifting. In the years when women's labor was deemed crucial to the war effort, "the woman out of uniform became suspect. By the last half of the war, the patriotism of the women in uniform was even more insistently contrasted with the lack of that of the shameful 'slacker in petticoats'"; see Susan R. Grayzel, *Women's Identities at War: Gender, Motherhood, and Politics in Britain and France during the First World War* (Chapel Hill: University of North Carolina Press, 1999), 199–200.

8. "The Ex-Army Girl," *Sheffield Daily Telegraph*, June 12, 1919, as cited by Lucy Noakes, "Demobilizing the Military Woman: Constructions of Class and Gender in Britain after the First World War," *Gender and History* 19, no. 1 (2007): 148.

9. Jenny Gould, "Women's Military Services in First World War Britain," in *Behind the Lines: Gender and the Two World Wars*, ed. Margaret Randolph Higgonet et al. (New Haven, CT: Yale University Press, 1987), 121; emphasis in original. Jennifer Margaret Gould completed her PhD in history at University College, London, in 1988, with a thesis titled "The Women's Corps: The Establishment of Women's Military Services in Britain."

10. Ibid.; emphasis mine.

11. George Robb, *British Culture and the First World War* (Basingstoke, UK: Palgrave, 2002), 60 and 59.

12. Janet Lee, *War Girls: The First Aid Nursing Yeomanry in the First World War* (Manchester, UK: Manchester University Press, 2005), 51. Susan Grayzel also speculates that scandals concerning "heterosexual behavior" among the "rank and file overseas" may "in some way [have been] a means of combating possible suggestions of lesbianism or 'mannishness' in the women's army"; see Grayzel, *Women's Identities at War*, 199.

13. Robb, *British Culture and the First World War*, 60; Deborah Cohler, "Sapphism and Sedition: Producing Female Homosexuality in Great War Britain," *Journal of the History of Sexuality* 16, no. 1 (2007): 71; Deborah Cohler, *Citizen, Invert, Queer: Lesbianism and War in Early Twentieth-Century Britain* (Minneapolis: University of Minnesota Press, 2010). Rebecca Jennings also contends that during the war "female same-sex desire" was regarded as "a threat to the nation and the war effort"; see Rebecca Jennings, *A Lesbian History of Britain: Love and Sex between Women since 1500* (Oxford: Greenwood, 2007), 94.

14. See especially my chapter "Passing Fashions: Reading Female Masculinities in the 1920s," in Laura Doan, *Fashioning Sapphism: The Origins of a Modern English Lesbian Culture* (New York: Columbia University Press, 2001), 95–125.

15. Alison Oram, *Her Husband Was a Woman! Women's Gender-Crossing in Modern British Popular Culture* (London: Routledge, 2007).

16. Noakes, "Demobilizing the Military Woman," 159.

17. Frank Mort, *Dangerous Sexualities: Medico-moral Politics in England since 1830*, 2nd ed. (London: Routledge, 2000), 81. See also Deborah Lafferty, "'Guides, All Guides': Anglo-American Girlhood and Transnational Identity in the Girl Scout and Guide Movement, 1907–1926" (PhD thesis, King's College, London, 2010). There is a substantial body of scholarship on scouting and militarism. For a good overview see Martin Dedman, "Baden-Powell, Militarism, and the 'Invisible Contributors' to the Boy Scout Scheme, 1904–1920," *Twentieth Century British History* 4, no. 3 (1993): 201–33.

18. Gould, "Women's Military Services in First World War Britain," 121; *Spectator*, June 15, 1918, iv. While *Ladies' Field* (July 13, 1918, 149) notes that the British woman in military garb was thought to be a "familiar" sight "on our streets," *Autocar* observes that "the khaki-clad feminine driver, with her naval sister in blue, was everywhere accepted as a natural and welcome sign of the times" (January 31, 1920, 214). Similarly, the *Manchester Evening News* reported: "Walking with fine military precision, the WAACs were . . . a fine body of women, and were enthusiastically received. 'The Lassies are massing for the Spring offensive' was the inscription on [one] banner—further evidence of the great part women were playing in the war" (May 13, 1918, 7).

19. For an important feminist reconsideration of "intersectionality," see Robyn Wiegman, *Object Lessons* (Durham, NC: Duke University Press, 2012).

20. Janet S. K. Watson, *Fighting Different Wars: Experience, Memory, and the First World War* (Cambridge: Cambridge University Press, 2004).

21. Ibid., 114 and 115.

22. Emily Hamer, *Britannia's Glory: A History of Twentieth-Century Lesbians* (London: Cassell, 1996), 52.

23. Judith Halberstam, *Female Masculinity* (Durham, NC: Duke University Press, 1998), 84 and 85. Halberstam bases her reading of Lowther's sexual identity on her association, from 1920, with Radclyffe Hall.

24. Morris B. Kaplan, *Sodom on the Thames: Sex, Love, and Scandal in Wilde Times* (Ithaca, NY: Cornell University Press, 2005), 270.

25. Chris Waters, "Distance and Desire in the New British Queer History," *GLQ: A Journal of Lesbian and Gay Studies* 14, no. 1 (2007): 146.

26. Ibid.

27. Edith M. Barton, *Eve in Khaki: The Story of the Women's Army at Home and Abroad* (London: T. Nelson, 1918), 187.

28. Martha Vicinus, *Intimate Friends: Women Who Loved Women, 1778–1928* (Chi-

cago: University of Chicago Press, 2004), xxv; Julian Carter, "On Mother-Love: History, Queer Theory, and Nonlesbian Identity," *Journal of the History of Sexuality* 14, no. 1–2 (2005): 107.

29. Carter, "On Mother-Love," 112.

30. See, for example, Carla Freccero, *Queer/Early/Modern* (Durham, NC: Duke University Press, 2006); Jonathan Goldberg and Madhavi Menon, "Queering History," *PMLA* 120, no. 5 (2005): 1608–17.

31. Matt Houlbrook, *Queer London: Perils and Pleasures in the Sexual Metropolis, 1918–1957* (Chicago: University of Chicago Press, 2005), 265.

32. James Vernon, "'For Some Queer Reason': The Trials and Tribulations of Colonel Barker's Masquerade in Interwar Britain," *Signs: Journal of Women in Culture and Society* 26, no. 1 (2000): 37–62.

33. Carter, "On Mother-Love," 112.

34. Jennifer Terry, *An American Obsession: Science, Medicine, and the Place of Homosexuality in Modern Society* (Chicago: University of Chicago Press, 1999), 29. The foundational critique of categorization is, of course, Michel Foucault, *The Order of Things: An Archaeology of the Human Sciences* (New York: Routledge, 2007), especially 136–79.

35. In a now classic essay, historian George Chauncey interrogates the structure of categorization of military men at the Newport Naval Training Station in 1919: "The very terms 'homosexual behavior' and 'identity,' because of their tendency to conflate phenomena that other cultures may have regarded as quite distinct, appear to be insufficiently precise to denote the variety of social forms of sexuality we wish to analyze"; George Chauncey, "Christian Brotherhood or Sexual Perversion? Homosexual Identities and the Construction of Sexual Boundaries in the World War One Era," *Journal of Social History* 19, no. 2 (1985): 205.

An important early critique of sexological categorization appears in Judith Halberstam's *Female Masculinity*, which endeavors to expand the range of "models and taxonomies and classifications for future endorsement or rejection" by examining how inverts themselves "developed their own identities, sexual categories, self-understandings, and gender aesthetics." Halberstam continues, "I am well aware of the damaging history of taxonomies within the history of sexuality, but I think the main problem with taxonomizing was first that it was left to the sexologists, and second that we have not continued to produce ever more accurate or colorful or elaborate or imaginative or flamboyant taxonomies"; see Halberstam, *Female Masculinity*, 48 and 47.

36. While it is difficult to determine how many British women served as ambulance drivers on or near the Western Front in France and Belgium between 1914 and 1918, my research suggests there were a few hundred, based on my work in London and Leeds (the Department of Documents at the Imperial War Museum [IWM-DD]), London; the Peter Liddle 1914–1918 Personal Experience Archives at the University of Leeds; and the National Army Museum, London). Citing a docu-

ment in the FANY Archive, scholar Janet Lee puts the number of FANY nurses and driver-mechanics at 450; see Lee, *War Girls*, 2. The types of organizations were extremely varied and included ad hoc groups that ranged from the Dr. Hector Munro Ambulance Unit and the Hackett-Lowther Ambulance Unit to the better-organized FANY, founded before the war.

37. See chapter 3 in Doan, *Fashioning Sapphism*, 64–94.

38. *Manchester Evening News*, May 13, 1918, 7.

39. Karma Lochrie, *Heterosyncrasies: Female Sexuality When Normal Wasn't* (Minneapolis: University of Minnesota Press 2005), 104.

Publications such as *Everyweek* and *War Budget* routinely used the term Amazon, as seen in a caption that reads, "Some of the young British Amazons, whose pluck and perseverance have won the applause and gratitude of the whole nation" (May 2, 1918, n.p.). In addition to Lochrie's chapter ("Amazons at the Gates," 138), see also Leila J. Rupp, *Sapphistries: A Global History of Love between Women* (New York: New York University Press, 2009), and Valerie Traub, *The Renaissance of Lesbianism in Early Modern England* (Cambridge: Cambridge University Press, 2002), 65–67. For a discussion of radical lesbian-feminism in a British context, see Jennings, *Lesbian History of Britain*, especially 175–76.

40. Vicinus, *Intimate Friends*, 173.

41. *Despised and Rejected* was originally published by C. W. Daniel under the pseudonym A. T. Fitzroy.

42. See Edward Carpenter, *The Intermediate Sex: A Study of Some Transitional Types of Men and Women* (1908; reprint, London: George Allen and Unwin, 1916). An early important discussion of Carpenter's work and ideas can be found in Jeffrey Weeks, *Coming Out: Homosexual Politics in Britain from the Nineteenth Century to the Present* (London: Quartet Books, 1977). See also Sheila Rowbotham, *Edward Carpenter: A Life of Liberty and Love* (London: Verso, 2008).

43. The scholarship on the "cult of the clitoris" trial is too extensive to detail here; for an excellent introduction to the case, see Lucy Bland's essay "Trial by Sexology? Maud Allan, *Salome*, and the 'Cult of the Clitoris' Case," in Lucy Bland and Laura Doan, eds., *Sexology in Culture: Labelling Bodies and Desires* (Chicago: University of Chicago Press, 1998), 183–98. See also Judith R. Walkowitz, "The 'Vision of Salome': Cosmopolitanism and Erotic Dancing in Central London, 1908–1918," *American Historical Review* 108, no. 2 (2003): 337–76.

44. May 31, 1918, in Artemis Cooper, ed., *A Durable Fire: The Letters of Duff and Diana Cooper* (London: Collins, 1983), 66; cited in Bland, "Trial by Sexology?" 194–95.

45. In a letter to *Autocar* (December 14, 1918, 590) a WAAC remarks, "We almost felt like soldiers."

46. Dr. Robertson Wallace, *Ladies' Field*, March 20, 1915, 210.

47. There is a significant historiography on the impact of the First World War on gender in Britain, and the scholarly interest shows no sign of abating; see Gail Bray-

bon and Penny Summerfield, *Out of the Cage: Women's Experiences in Two World Wars* (London: Pandora, 1987); Gail Braybon, *Women Workers and the First World War* (London: Routledge, 1989); Grayzel, *Women's Identities at War*; Nicoletta F. Gullace, *"The Blood of Our Sons": Men, Women, and the Renegotiation of British Citizenship during the Great War* (New York: Palgrave Macmillan, 2002); Susan Kent, *Making Peace: The Reconstruction of Gender in Interwar Britain* (Princeton, NJ: Princeton University Press, 1993); Thom, *Nice Girls and Rude Girls*; Angela Woollacott, *On Her Their Lives Depend: Munitions Workers in the Great War* (Berkeley: University of California Press, 1994).

48. "Sing a Song of War-time" first appeared in *Wartime Nursery Rhymes: Dedicated to DORA* [Defence of the Realm Act] (London: Routledge, 1918) and has been reprinted in Catherine W. Reilly, ed., *The Virago Book of Women's War Poetry and Verse: An Omnibus Edition of "Scars upon My Heart" and "Chaos of the Night"* (London: Virago, 1997), 69.

49. Cited in Gill Thomas, *Life on All Fronts: Women in the First World War* (Cambridge: Cambridge University Press, 1989), 9. Thom argues that these figures are unreliable; see Thom, *Nice Girls and Rude Girls*, 13.

50. Summerfield, "Women and War in the Twentieth Century," 315; Thomas, *Life on All Fronts*, 30.

51. Harriot Stanton Blatch writes, "Great Britain is not talking about feminism, it is living it"; see Harriot Stanton Blatch, "Mobilizing Woman-Power" (1918), http://www.gutenberg.org/files/10080/10080-h/10080-h.htm#FNanchor2.

For further discussion of the response of women suffragists to the war, see Gullace, *"The Blood of Our Sons"*; Sandra Stanley Holton, *Feminism and Democracy: Women's Suffrage and Reform Politics in Britain, 1900–1918* (Cambridge: Cambridge University Press, 1986), especially 116–33; Angela K. Smith, *Suffrage Discourse in Britain during the First World War* (Aldershot, UK: Ashgate, 2005); and Kent, *Making Peace*.

52. Joan Wallach Scott, "Gender: A Useful Category of Historical Analysis?" in her *Feminism and History* (Oxford: Oxford University Press, 1996), 174.

53. Gail Braybon, "Winners or Losers: Women's Symbolic Role in the War Story," in *Evidence, History, and the Great War: Historians and the Impact of 1914–18*, ed. Gail Braybon (New York: Berghahn, 2003), 99; Judith Butler, *Undoing Gender* (London: Routledge, 2004), 42. Toril Moi argues, "Whether it is to reaffirm or to deconstruct the concept, most feminist theories today rely on a universalized and reified concept of 'femininity'"; see Toril Moi, *What Is a Woman? And Other Essays* (Oxford: Oxford University Press, 1999), 8.

54. Sandra M. Gilbert, "Soldier's Heart: Literary Men, Literary Women, and the Great War," in *Behind the Lines: Gender and the Two World Wars*, ed. Margaret Randolph Higgonet et al. (New Haven, CT: Yale University Press, 1987), 216.

55. Scott, "Gender," 174. A good recent example of queer historical work that rethinks sexuality in relation to gender is Sharon Marcus, *Between Women: Friendship,*

Desire, and Marriage in Victorian England (Princeton, NJ: Princeton University Press, 2007).

56. Gladys de Havilland, *The Women's Motor Manual* (London: Temple, 1918), 75. The author also recalls an orderly known as Poppa "who mothers all the chauffeuses!" (80).

57. Michael Roper, *The Secret Battle: Emotional Survival in the Great War* (Manchester, UK: Manchester University Press, 2009). The division between the home front and the Western Front is discussed by Paul Fussell, *The Great War and Modern Memory* (New York: Oxford University Press, 1975), 86. Susan Kent offers an extensive and perceptive account of the blurring of gender lines in relation to the spheres of war; see Kent, *Making Peace*. Other important work reassessing masculinity in the context of the First World War includes Joanna Bourke, *Dismembering the Male: Men's Bodies, Britain and the Great War* (London: Reaktion Books, 1996); Ana Carden-Coyne, *Reconstructing the Body: Classicism, Modernism, and the First World War* (Oxford: Oxford University Press, 2009); and Santanu Das, *Touch and Intimacy in First World War Literature* (Cambridge: Cambridge University Press, 2005).

58. Butler, *Undoing Gender*, 13.

59. Alec-Tweedie, *Women and Soldiers*, 5. All citations in this paragraph are from this passage.
   This social phenomenon of women's taking on men's work was a frequent topic in the press, often illustrated. Further examples can be found in *Punch* (June 28, 1916), 427, in an unusually serious article titled "Women in War-time." As Mr. Punch strolls about London he notices women in their "various incarnations, everywhere," most visibly in work related to public transportation, but also as drivers of all manner of vehicles, including motorcycles. Women are also seen doing heavy lifting — their uniforms are described as "trim" and "businesslike," with no hint that a "manly" appearance is unsettling. Even "dressed in khaki," she poses no threat: "Never does she look so masterful as then, for she marches . . . like a real commander." On November 11, 1916, *Ladies' Field Supplement* notes this range of employment, even jobs that demand the physical "stamina characteristic of strong men" (2).

60. *Autocar*, March 16, 1918, 260.

61. Grayzel thoughtfully comments that "rather than completely undermining specific assumptions about gender . . . the war, from its outset, paradoxically both expanded the range of possibilities for women and curtailed them by, among other things, heightening the emphasis on motherhood as women's primary patriotic role and the core of their national identity"; see Grayzel, *Women's Identities at War*, 3. An equally insightful discussion of "patriotic motherhood" can be found in Gullace, *"Blood of Our Sons,"* especially 53–69. Others argued that while women's work had changed, the women themselves had not, as evinced in an article that appeared in the *Manchester Evening News*, entirely dismissing the notion that women were be-

ing masculinized by the new jobs they were performing: "The war has shown how completely unjustified was the belief that woman was becoming more masculine. In Red Cross work, and in a hundred and one ways, the woman of today is proving herself to be as 'womanly' as in the peaceful seclusion of the early Victorian era" (February 17, 1915, 3). See also *The Times* (May 18, 1916, 9): "The new woman of 1915–16 is . . . still womanly. She has kept her softer qualities for all that she has stepped into man's place. . . . The new woman has kept her womanliness."

62. Alec-Tweedie, *Women and Soldiers*, 2; Eve Kosofsky Sedgwick, *Tendencies* (Durham, NC: Duke University Press, 1993), 8.

63. *Ladies' Field*, November 25, 1916, 65. Similarly, *War Budget* observed, "I wonder how the poetic chronicler . . . would eulogize women today. 'Ministering angel' is now but one facet in the Jewel of Creation. . . . First she outshines her male in the mere externals, the trappings of war. Accustomed to think of her as a pediment of frills and fluffs . . . he is rubbing his eyes at the sight of her in regiments. . . . But the uniform is merely an outward sign of an inward experience. Women's hearts are dyed khaki, and their cheeks flushed with honorable pride. They are out to win this war" (November 4, 1915, 371). Hostile criticism of women's work during the war is rare, as seen in the wartime issues of *Ladies' Field*, *Manchester Evening News*, *Punch*, *The Times*, and *War Budget Illustrated*.

64. *War Budget*, March 30, 1916, 217.

65. "The New Woman: An Historical Note," *The Times*, January 6, 1916, 11.

66. Moi, *What Is a Woman?* 31. For a concise introduction to feminist debates on the differentiation of sex and gender in the context of queer theory, see Annamarie Jagose, "Feminism's Queer Theory," *Feminism and Psychology* 19, no. 2 (2009): 157–74.

67. Historian Laura Downs has shown how industrialists "created the category of 'female labor,' with its particular functions and characteristics, despite the facts which contradicted this naturalization of women's work, and the ways they organized production through this category which survived long after the war. . . . [E]mployers invented the category of factory superintendent, who, in short, reassured management because they were middle-class in origin but presented women workers with a semblance of female solidarity." This summation of Downs's work appears in J. M. Winter and Antoine Prost, *The Great War in History: Debates and Controversies, 1914 to the Present* (Cambridge: Cambridge University Press, 2005), 142. See also Laura Lee Downs, *Manufacturing Inequality: Gender Division in the French and British Metalworking Industries, 1914–1939* (Ithaca, NY: Cornell University Press, 1995).

68. *The Times*, April 20, 1917.

69. Lt. Col. F. McKelvey Bell directed medical services for the Canadian armed services. This quotation appears in his memoir, *The First Canadians in France: The Chronicle of a Military Hospital in the War Zone* (Toronto: McClelland, Goodchild and Stewart, 1917), 209. I am grateful to Ana Carden-Coyne for this reference.

70. Ibid.

71. Ibid.; Blatch, "Mobilizing Woman-Power."

72. *Daily Graphic*, February 25, 1909, 7.

73. An image captioned "Home Leave, 1930" depicts a uniformed woman, smoking, in front of one poster that reads "Women wanted for the Royal Corps," while another urges "Women do your duty"; *Graphic*, November 24, 1917, 658.

74. *The Times*, July 21, 1922, 5. I am indebted to Lucy Bland for this reference; for a discussion of this case (*Russell v. Russell*), see Lucy Bland, *Sexual Transgression in the Age of the Flapper: Treacherous Women on Trial* (Manchester, UK: Manchester University Press, forthcoming).

75. *Sheffield Daily Telegraph*, June 12, 1919, 3.

76. Moi, *What Is a Woman?* 35; emphasis mine.

77. Ibid., 65–66.

78. Ibid., 35.

79. *Autocar* notes that "until recent years motoring was the hobby of the well-to-do. . . . They are not mechanically fastidious and . . . consider it almost vulgar to comprehend mechanism" (July 13, 1918, 38). *Ladies' Field* notes: "Men have usually risen from a lower rank to that of chauffeur whereas women usually descend . . . from quite a different class of society" (March 4, 1916, 54).

80. "Le Volant: A French Appreciation for English Motor Women's Work in France," *Autocar*, May 5, 1917, 463. *The Times* observed that there was "an enormous demand for the feminine motor-car driver who can do running repairs" (July 29, 1915, 9). *Autocar* later notes "the existence of a huge new type of chauffeur, i.e. women who can drive, women of all classes and sorts and tastes" (September 14, 1918, 254).

81. "Chauffeuse-Companion: Increasing Demand for Women Drivers," *The Times*, December 11, 1915, 11.

82. *The Times*, July 29, 1915, 9.

83. Stefan Dudink, Karen Hagemann, and John Tosh, "Hegemonic Masculinity and the History of Gender," in *Masculinities in Politics and War: Gendering Modern History*, ed. Stefan Dudink, Karen Hagemann, and John Tosh (Manchester, UK: Manchester University Press, 2004), 47, 48, and 51.

84. The masculinity on view is part of the familiar stereotype of the English upper-class gentleman, as seen in the casually confident, slightly back tilted stance of the second officer, his wounded arm as suggestive of damaged manhood as of heroic sacrifice.

85. Vicinus, *Intimate Friends*, xxiii.

86. For accounts of these women's experiences of driving on the Western Front, see Gertrude Stein, *The Autobiography of Alice B. Toklas* (New York: Harcourt, Brace, 1933); Joan Schenkar, *Truly Wilde: The Unsettling Story of Dolly Wilde, Oscar's Unusual Niece* (London: Virago Press, 2000); and Kate Summerscale, *The Queen of Whale Cay: The Eccentric Story of "Joe" Carstairs, Fastest Woman on Water* (London: Fourth Estate, 1997).

87. For an extended discussion on female ambulance drivers during the First World War, see Laura Doan, "Primum Mobile: Women and Auto/Mobility in the Era of the Great War," *Women: A Cultural Review* 17, no. 1 (2006): 26–41.

88. De Havilland, *Women's Motor Manual*, 72.

89. Ibid., 5.

90. *Daily Mail*, August 18, 1915, 4. This article was written by Elizabeth Robins.

91. De Havilland, *Women's Motor Manual*, 69. Mrs. L. C. Cowper (a British Red Cross ambulance driver) recollected in 1974 that "for a woman to get out to France was something wonderful" (27); IWM-DD PP/MCR/191.

92. *War Budget Illustrated*, March 30, 1916, 217.

93. Lady Baden-Powell noted, "Girls who are thrown together . . . day in, day out, form friendships with each other, as binding and as helpful as those between comrades in a regiment"; *Ladies' Field*, March 30, 1918, 144.

94. F. Tennyson Jesse, "A Night with a Convoy: An Eyewitness's Account of the Work of the Voluntary Aid Detachment in France," *Vogue* 51, no. 11 (1918): 72.

95. FANY driver Pat Beauchamp recalls how "the Parisians are very interested to see a girl dressed in khaki, and discussed each item of my uniform. . . . [Of] my field boots . . . they would exclaim: 'Look at them, she wears the big boots of a man. It is chic'"; see Pat Beauchamp [P. B. Waddell, later Washington], *FANNY Goes to War* (London: John Murray, 1919), 80. Elsewhere, a diary entry by Miss Ethel Harker states, "Everyone here wears stacks of clothing — it's just like camp life and the girls go about like Polar explorers"; see Miss E. Harker (British Red Cross Ambulance Convoy), 1918. IWM-DD 77/58/1.

96. *The Times*, December 27, 1915. Novelist Sarah Macnaughtan also writes of her admiration: "One was inclined to call them masqueraders in their knickerbockers and puttees and caps, but I believe they have done excellent work. It is a queer sight of war to see young, pretty English girls in khaki and thick boots, coming in from the trenches . . . wonderful little Walküres [*sic*] . . . I lift my hat to you"; see Sarah Macnaughtan and Mrs. Betty Salmon, *My War Experiences in Two Continents . . . Edited By . . . Mrs. Lionel Salmon . . . with a Portrait* (London: John Murray, 1919), 25.

97. Olive Edis, "The Record of a Journey to Photograph the British Women's Services Overseas Begun on Sunday March 2, 1919," 5; Miss O. Edis, IWM-DD 89/19/1. Edis was an official photographer for the Imperial War Museum. Janet Watson also comments on this passage in Edis's narrative, arguing that "'Healthy' seems to have been a frequent polite synonym for 'masculine,' or at least 'unfeminine'"; see Watson, *Fighting Different Wars*, 116.

98. David Mitchell, *Women on the Warpath: The Story of the Women of the First World War* (London: Jonathan Cape, 1965), 129.

99. F. Tennyson Jesse, "First Aid Nursing Yeomanry," *Vogue* 51, no. 10 (1918): 70.

100. Ibid.

101. Jesse, "First Aid Nursing Yeomanry," 70, and "Night with a Convoy," 72.

102. Ibid.

103. Jesse, "First Aid Nursing Yeomanry," 70. In *Intimate Friends* Vicinus notes the tendency in the eighteenth and nineteenth centuries to "spiritualize" same-sex friendships; see xviii–xix.

104. Beauchamp, *FANNY Goes to War*, 16. In his introduction to this volume, Major-General H. N. Thompson, director of medical services, British Army of the Rhine, writes (in reference to the FANYs) of his "wonder . . . almost adoration — which has from time to time overwhelmed me" (v).

105. Mairi Chisholm, Sound Archive. IWM-DD 000771/04 (interview conducted at the Imperial War Museum ca. 1975); *War Budget*, January 4, 1917, 242. On November 1, 1917, *War Budget Illustrated* printed two large photographs of Knocker and Chisholm under the heading "Two Angels of Mercy in Flanders," 267. According to biographer Diane Atkinson, the pair discarded tin hats in Pervyse on learning they might be mistaken for soldiers and targeted by German snipers; see Diane Atkinson, *Elsie and Mairi Go to War* (London: Preface, 2009). In Germany nurses were similarly idealized as motherly or saintly, resembling "nuns, angels or the Madonna"; see Bianca Schönberger, "Motherly Heroines and Adventurous Girls: Red Cross Nurses and Women Army Auxiliaries in the First World War," in *Home/Front: The Military, War, and Gender in Twentieth-Century Germany*, ed. Karen Hagemann and Stefanie Schüler-Springorum (Oxford: Berg, 2002).

106. In 1915 Louise Mack writes, "As for fear, there was none, not any at all, not a particle. Instead, there was something curiously akin to rapture"; see *A Woman's Experiences in the Great War* (London: T. F. Unwin, 1915), 27.

107. Blatch, "Mobilizing Woman-Power." A WAAC driver in France between 1914 and 1917, Mrs. R. I. Leared recalls that women's "muscles adapted themselves to the heavy work"; IWM-DD 73/34/1.

108. Jesse, "Night with a Convoy," 72.

109. *Ladies' Field*, November 25, 1916, 54.

110. See Radclyffe Hall, *The Well of Loneliness* (1928; reprint, New York: Anchor Books, 1990), and Radclyffe Hall, "Miss Ogilvy Finds Herself" (1926), reprinted in *The Literature of Lesbianism: A Historical Anthology from Ariosto to Stonewall*, ed. Terry Castle (New York: Columbia University Press, 2003), 635–48. Readings of Hall's work in relation to the Great War appear in essays by Sally R. Munt, Susan Kingsley Kent, Jodie Medd, and Trevor Hope in "The Well's Wounds"; see Laura Doan and Jay Prosser, eds., *Palatable Poison: Critical Perspectives on "The Well of Loneliness"* (New York: Columbia University Press, 2001), 199–273. Critical work on Hall's short story includes Laura Doan, "'Miss Ogilvy Finds Herself': The Queer Navigational Systems of Radclyffe Hall," *ELN: English Language Notes* 45, no. 2 (2007): 9–22; and Richard Dellamora, *Radclyffe Hall: A Life in the Writing* (Philadelphia: University of Pennsylvania Press, 2011), 214–27.

111. Sir Chartres Biron's judgment is cited in full in Doan and Prosser, *Palatable Poison*, 39–49.

112. Hall, *Well of Loneliness*, 271.

113. De Havilland, *Women's Motor Manual*; F. W. Stella Browne, "Studies in Feminine Inversion," in *Sexology Uncensored: The Documents of Sexual Science*, ed. Lucy Bland and Laura Doan (Chicago: University of Chicago Press, 1998), 64. Published in 1923, Browne's paper was presented to the British Society for the Study of Sex Psychology in 1918; see Lesley A. Hall, *The Life and Times of Stella Browne: Feminist and Free Spirit* (London: I. B. Tauris, 2011), 75.

114. Beauchamp recalls overhearing a local Belgian comment, "Truly, until one hears their voices, one would say they were men." The inclusion of the episode in her memoir suggests she was not insulted by the mistake or concerned over any unsavory associations with "deviant" sexuality, and this from a woman who recalls in an interview, "I longed to be a boy!" See *FANNY Goes to War*, 261; two-page typescript, Peter Liddle 1914–1918 Personal Experience Archives, University of Leeds, Women's Catalogue.

115. Halberstam, *Female Masculinity*, 85. This observation is made in reference to Toupie Lowther.

116. *The Times*, January 6, 1916, 11.

117. Watson, *Fighting Different Wars*, 57.

118. Gould, "Women's Military Services in First World War Britain," 121; Jesse, "First Aid Nursing Yeomanry," 54.

119. "Woman's New Place in the World," *The Times*, August 25, 1916, 9.

120. *Light Car*, January 2, 1918.

121. "Women True to Type: No Sex War after the War," *The Times*, November 2, 1918, 3.

122. Jesse, "First Aid Nursing Yeomanry," 54.

123. Lucy Noakes, "'A Disgrace to the Country They Belong To': The Sexualization of Female Soldiers in First World War Britain," *Revue LISA/LISA e-journal* 6, no. 4 (2008).

124. Ibid.

125. Ibid.; emphasis mine.

126. Gould, "Women's Military Services in First World War Britain," 121; Noakes, "'Disgrace to the Country They Belong To.'"

127. Noakes, "'Disgrace to the Country They Belong To.'" Deborah Cohler argues for legibility "through inference" as one interpretive possibility in reading the phrase "distaste for husbands" as denoting sexual desire between women. The phrase (in reference to a comment made in 1910 by suffragist Evelyn Sharp), Cohler believes, might also suggest an "absent mother" or the suffragist as "frigid," but — in the domain of assertion — any imagined interpretation is as good as any other. Legibility through inference points to how we construct the historical subject we claim only to seek; see Cohler, *Citizen, Invert, Queer*, 46.

128. Noakes, "'Disgrace to the Country They Belong To'"; Marchioness of Londonderry, *Retrospect* (London: Frederick Muller, 1938).

129. Sandra M. Gilbert and Susan Gubar, *No Man's Land: The Place of the Woman*

Writer in the Twentieth Century, vol. 2, *Sexchanges* (New Haven, CT: Yale University Press, 1988), 299; David Trotter, "Lesbians before Lesbianism: Sexual Identity in Early Twentieth-Century British Fiction," in *Borderlines: Genders and Identities in War and Peace, 1870–1930*, ed. Billie Melman (New York: Routledge, 1998), 195. See also Claire Buck, "British Women's Writing of the Great War," in *The Cambridge Companion to the Literature of the First World War*, ed. Vincent Sherry (Cambridge: Cambridge University Press, 2005), 103.

130. Cohler, *Citizen, Invert, Queer*, ix.

131. Mrs. R. I. Leared, IWM-DD 73/34/1.

132. Ibid.

133. Scott, "Gender," 174.

134. The task of the cultural historian, Halperin notes, is to "recover" the "sexual categories and identities" of "individuals belonging to past societies" and then "measure and assess the differences between those terms and the ones we currently employ"; see David M. Halperin, *One Hundred Years of Homosexuality: And Other Essays on Greek Love* (New York: Routledge, 1990), 29.

135. Sedgwick, *Tendencies*, 8. In 1998 Halberstam thoughtfully elaborated on Sedgwick's reference to "nonce taxonomies," "classifications of desire, physicality, and subjectivity that attempt to intervene in hegemonic processes of naming and defining. Nonce taxonomies are categories that we use daily to make sense of our worlds but that work so well that we actually fail to recognize them"; see Halberstam, *Female Masculinity*, 8.

136. David M. Halperin, *How to Do the History of Homosexuality* (Chicago: University of Chicago Press, 2002), 88.

137. Jonathan Ned Katz summarizes this point succinctly: "Using the vocabulary of the present to describe the past is not always or necessarily a mistake. Looking backward, we can often find good evidence of what we now call homosexual, bisexual, and even heterosexual relationships. But from a historical viewpoint, that retrolabeling is not informative. It begs too many questions about the sexual desires and acts of people from the past *in their original context*"; see Jonathan Ned Katz, *Love Stories: Sex between Men before Homosexuality* (Chicago: University of Chicago Press, 2001), 333; emphasis in original.

CHAPTER FOUR

1. Transcript of the shorthand notes of the Deputation of Members of the Douglas-Pennant Committee with Dr. Norwood to the Attorney General (July 31, 1931), 2, TNA PRO PREM 1/205 (hereafter, page numbers appear parenthetically in the text, following DM). The deputation included William J. Brown (Labour MP for Wolverhampton); Brigadier General R. B. D. Blakeney, CMG, DSO; Sir Robert Gresley, Bart.; Major Gordon Home; The Hon. Hilda Douglas-Pennant (Violet's sister); the Lady Maud Warrender; and the Rev. F. W. Norwood.

2. *Oxford Dictionary of National Biography Online*.

3. See also the work of social psychologists, such as Lisa M. Diamond, *Sexual Fluidity: Understanding Women's Love and Desire* (Cambridge, MA: Harvard University Press, 2008).

4. Elizabeth A. Castelli, "Lesbian Historiography before the Name?" *GLQ: A Journal of Lesbian and Gay Studies* 4, no. 4 (1998): 557–630; Harriette Andreadis, *Sappho in Early Modern England: Female Same-Sex Literary Erotics, 1550–1714* (Chicago: University of Chicago Press, 2001), 11.

5. David M. Halperin, *Saint Foucault: Towards a Gay Hagiography* (New York: Oxford University Press, 1995), 112.

6. David M. Halperin, *How to Do the History of Homosexuality* (Chicago: University of Chicago Press, 2002), 23.

7. For an insightful discussion of the gradual shift from "character" to "identity" in the context of twentieth-century America, see Philip Gleason, "Identifying Identity: A Semantic History," *Journal of American History* 69, no. 4 (1983): 926. See also Gary Watson, "On the Primacy of Character," in *Identity, Character, and Morality: Essays in Moral Psychology*, ed. Owen J. Flanagan and Amélie Oksenberg Rorty (Cambridge, MA: MIT Press, 1990).

8. David M. Halperin, "Is There a History of Sexuality?" *History and Theory* 28, no. 3 (1989): 259.

9. In the transcript of the Deputation of Members (cf. note 1 above), the last three letters of the word lesbianism are crossed out.

10. Valerie Traub, "The Present Future of Lesbian Historiography," in *A Companion to Lesbian, Gay, Bisexual, Transgender, and Queer Studies*, ed. George Haggerty and Molly McGarrity (London: Blackwell, 2007), 124.

11. A photograph of Knocker and Chisholm captioned "The Two" appears in "British Women in the Heat of Battle: Thrilling Adventures with the Belgian Army," *War Budget Illustrated*, January 4, 1917, 242; "For Gallantry and Devotion to Duty," *Ladies' Field*, December 15, 1917, 152.

12. Judith Halberstam, *Female Masculinity* (Durham, NC: Duke University Press, 1998), xi; emphasis mine; Martha Vicinus, *Intimate Friends: Women Who Loved Women, 1778–1928* (Chicago: University of Chicago Press, 2004), xix. For other good examples of work focused on British culture, see Rebecca Jennings, *Tomboys and Bachelor Girls: A Lesbian History of Post-war Britain, 1945–71* (Manchester, UK: Manchester University Press, 2007); and Alison Oram, *Her Husband Was a Woman! Women's Gender-Crossing in Modern British Popular Culture* (London: Routledge, 2007). For work on American lesbian subcultures, see Elizabeth Lapovsky Kennedy and Madeline D. Davis, *Boots of Leather, Slippers of Gold: The History of a Lesbian Community* (New York: Routledge, 1993), and Nan Alamilla Boyd, *Wide-Open Town: A History of Queer San Francisco to 1965* (Berkeley: University of California Press, 2003).

13. Arnold I. Davidson, *The Emergence of Sexuality: Historical Epistemology and the Formation of Concepts* (Cambridge, MA: Harvard University Press, 2001), 35.

14. David M. Halperin, *One Hundred Years of Homosexuality: And Other Essays on Greek Love* (New York: Routledge, 1990), 26.

15. Vicinus, *Intimate Friends*, xxi; emphasis in original.

16. Judith M. Bennett, "'Lesbian-like' and the Social History of Lesbianisms," *Journal of the History of Sexuality* 9, no. 1–2 (2000): 1; Vicinus, *Intimate Friends*, xxi; Leila J. Rupp, "Toward a Global History of Same-Sex Sexuality," *Journal of the History of Sexuality* 10, no. 2 (2001): 287.

17. Vicinus, *Intimate Friends*, xxi and xxii.

18. Eve Kosofsky Sedgwick, *Tendencies* (Durham, NC: Duke University Press, 1993), 25. Martha Vicinus also observes that "ignorance now and in prior times can be willed"; see Martha Vicinus, "Lesbian History: All Theory and No Facts or All Facts and No Theory?" *Radical History Review* 60 (1994): 58.

19. Michael Warner, "Publics and Counterpublics," *Public Culture* 14, no. 1 (2002): 59.

20. Anthony Giddens, *Modernity and Self-Identity: Self and Society in the Late Modern Age* (Cambridge: Polity, 1991), 52.

21. Joan Scott, "History-Writing as Critique," in *Manifestos for History*, ed. Keith Jenkins, Sue Morgan, and Alun Munslow (London: Routledge, 2007), 25; emphasis in original.

22. Letter from Violet Douglas-Pennant to Sir John Anderson, March 3, 1927, TNA PRO PREM 1/205. Before her appointment with the WRAF, Douglas-Pennant worked with Anderson at the National Health Insurance Commission.

23. Ethel Alec-Tweedie, *Women and Soldiers* (London: John Lane, 1918), 2.

24. There are substantial entries for each of these three women in the *Oxford Dictionary of National Biography Online*.

25. Baroness de T'Serclaes, *Flanders and Other Fields: Memoirs of the Baroness de T'Serclaes* (London: George G. Harrap, 1964), 103 and 104.

26. James Vernon, "'For Some Queer Reason': The Trials and Tribulations of Colonel Barker's Masquerade in Interwar Britain," *Signs: Journal of Women in Culture and Society* 26, no. 1 (2000): 59.

27. Philip Gibbs, *The Soul of War* (London: William Heinemann, 1915), 210.

28. Romantic friendship has long been of interest to historians of lesbianism. For a sophisticated reading of these relationships over a significant time span, see Vicinus, *Intimate Friends*. More recently, Victorian specialist Sharon Marcus has reframed debates on romantic friendships between women, suggesting that homoerotic bonds between women were not forbidden but "actively promoted"; Sharon Marcus, *Between Women: Friendship, Desire, and Marriage in Victorian England* (Princeton, NJ: Princeton University Press, 2007), 26.

29. *Report from the Select Committee of the House of Lords on the Women's Royal Air Force: Inquiry on Miss Violet Douglas-Pennant, with Two Appendices* (London: His

Majesty's Stationery Office, 1919), 10. (A copy of this publication is held in the Imperial War Museum, IWM P372 JLDF4); *The Times*, October 16, 1919, newspaper cutting, TNA PRO AIR 2/11903; "Statement by Wing Commander (Lieut. Col.) G. T. Brierley, RAF," September 24, 1919, TNA PRO AIR T528/3. In 1918 Brierley worked for the Discipline Branch of the Royal Air Force.

30. Giddens, *Modernity and Self-Identity*, 99.

31. Vernon, "'For Some Queer Reason,'" 59.

32. The material evidence available to historians of lesbianism in modern Britain privileges the upper and upper-middle classes, and women associated with literary culture. A good example of an attempt to expand this evidentiary base by focusing on working-class cultures is Oram, *Her Husband Was a Woman!*

33. Stuart Hall, "Cultural Identity and Diaspora," in *Colonial Discourse and Postcolonial Theory: A Reader*, ed. Patrick Williams and Laura Chrisman (New York: Columbia University Press, 1994), 395.

34. T'Serclaes, *Flanders and Other Fields*, 37.

35. Ibid., 36.

36. Women at War Collection, vol. 1, IWM 3072, 12.

37. Ibid.; Giddens, *Modernity and Self-Identity*, 99.

38. "Muscular Femininity," *War Budget Illustrated*, September 23, 1915, 173. See also "Outraging the Decencies of Nature: Uniformed Female Bodies," in Laura Doan, *Fashioning Sapphism: The Origins of a Modern English Lesbian Culture* (New York: Columbia University Press, 2001), 64–94.

39. Denise Riley, "Some Peculiarities of Social Policy concerning Women in Wartime and Postwar Britain," in *Behind the Lines: Gender and the Two World Wars*, ed. Margaret Randolph Higgonet et al. (New Haven, CT: Yale University Press, 1987), 260.

40. G. E. Mitton, ed., *The Cellar-House of Pervyse* (London: Black, 1916), 3.

41. Gibbs, *Soul of War*, 208–9 and 210.

42. Mairi Chisholm, Sound Archive, IWM-DD 000771/04 (interview conducted at the Imperial War Museum, ca. 1975).

43. *War Budget Illustrated*, January 4, 1917, 243. The IWM online catalog lists several artifacts; see http://www.iwm.org.uk/collections/item/object/30090509, accessed January 29, 2012.

44. *Universe*, July 20, 191[last number unclear] in Baroness de T'Serclaes, Book of Press Cuttings, IWM-DD P404; *War Budget Illustrated*, January 4, 1917, 242.

45. A press cutting from an unnamed newspaper (undated) reports: "Mrs. Knocker's dress was quite unconventional. She wore a short brown tunic, riding breeches, top boots, and a round dark blue cap with the brass letters"; Baroness de T'Serclaes, Book of Press Cuttings, IWM-DD P404.

46. *War Budget Illustrated*, January 4, 1917, 243 and 242.

47. Mitton, *Cellar-House of Pervyse*, 113–14.

48. Vicinus, *Intimate Friends*, passim.

49. Mitton, *Cellar-House of Pervyse*, 75.

50. Women at War Collection, vol. 1, IWM 3072, 17; diary entry, October 29, 1914, Miss Mairi Chisholm, IWM-DD 67/107/1 20731. Jonathan Ned Katz similarly notes that "men's bed sharing" in nineteenth-century America "was not then often explicitly understood as conducive to forbidden sexual experiments"; see Jonathan Ned Katz, *Love Stories: Sex between Men before Homosexuality* (Chicago: University of Chicago Press, 2001), 6.

51. Diary entry, December 13, 1914, Miss Mairi Chisholm, IWM-DD 67/107/1 20731.

52. Women at War Collection, vol. 1, IWM 3072, 2.

53. Ibid. In a recent biography of the pair, Knocker too was described as "tomboyish" in her youth; see Diane Atkinson, *Elsie and Mairi Go to War* (London: Preface, 2009), 12.

   Stella Browne's case D exhibited a "decided turn for . . . mechanics and executive manual work," a cross-gendered identification she associated with sexual inversion; see Stella Browne, "Studies in Feminine Inversion," in *Sexology Uncensored: The Documents of Sexual Science*, ed. Lucy Bland and Laura Doan (Chicago: University of Chicago Press, 1998), 64.

54. Letter from Violet Markham to General Sir Godfrey Paine, April 9, 1918, TNA PRO AIR 2/11880. Anne Summers described Markham as an antisuffragist; see Anne Summers, *Angels and Citizens: British Women as Military Nurses, 1854–1914* (London: Routledge and Kegan Paul, 1988), 274.

55. Letter from Violet Markham to General Sir Godfrey Paine, April 9, 1918, TNA PRO AIR 2/11880.

56. David Mitchell, *Women on the Warpath: The Story of the Women of the First World War* (London: Jonathan Cape, 1966), 230. This salary is confirmed by a debate in the Commons on the salary of national insurance commissioners; see *Hansard HC Deb*, June 20, 1916, vol. 83, cc43–109.

57. Letter from Violet Markham to General Sir Godfrey Paine, April 9, 1918, TNA PRO AIR 2/11880. Similarly, in a letter from Sir Godfrey Paine, master general of personnel, to Lord Rothmere, secretary of state for air, Douglas-Pennant is thought "undoubtedly" to possess "the qualities we require, and is spoken of very highly indeed by all who know her"; see April 19, 1918, TNA PRO AIR 2/11890. Weir's criticism of Douglas-Pennant was conveyed to the prime minister by his aide, Sir Ronald Waterhouse; see letter from Sir Ronald Waterhouse, KCB, to the Prime Minister, Rt. Hon. Ramsay Macdonald, April 1, 1924, TNA PRO PREM 1/205.

58. Violet Douglas-Pennant, *Under the Searchlight: A Record of a Great Scandal* (London: George Allen and Unwin, 1922), 444. Hereafter page numbers appear parenthetically in the text, preceded by US. Letter from Dr. J. L. D. Fairfield, CBE, to S. K. Ratcliffe, January 4, 1919. IWM-DD JLD F1. Biographical details on Dr. Fairfield can be found in the *Oxford Dictionary of National Biography Online*. In a 1964 interview with David Mitchell, Fairfield claimed "people thought there was something odd about [Douglas-Pennant], but could not publicly say they thought

she was mad." Douglas-Pennant, Fairfield continued, manifested "clinical signs of paranoic delusions, combined with schizophrenic detachment from the realities of the situation she was in," and she concluded that the former leader was "round the bend" and "mentally deranged"; see September 11 and 14, 1964, DMP/ML. In undated handwritten comments on David Mitchell's manuscript, Fairfield writes that Douglas-Pennant was "definitely psychotic" and had "a diseased imagination"; DMP/ML.

59. *The Times*, October 23, 1919. Newspaper cutting, TNA PRO AIR 2/11903; Molly Izzard, *A Heroine in Her Time: A Life of Dame Helen Gwynne-Vaughan, 1879–1967* (London: Macmillan, 1969), 190. Speech by Lord Buckmaster in the House of Lords on the Case of Miss Douglas-Pennant, 1919. Papers of Lord Weir, Glasgow University Archives, DC 96/22/23.

60. *Oxford Dictionary of National Biography Online*.

61. Report of Mr. C. Harmsworth to Prime Minister — Dismissal of Miss Douglas-Pennant Secret, November 7, 1918. Lloyd George Papers, LG/F/87/15/46, House of Lords Record Office.

62. According to the *Sunday Pictorial*, Douglas-Pennant was ordered to pay two hundred pounds plus court costs in one case. Newspaper cutting, n.d., Papers of Lord Weir, Glasgow University Archives, DC 96/30/3. See also Mitchell, *Women on the Warpath*, 242.

63. The *New English Weekly* also listed the full extent of the former commandant's employment history from 1899 to 1918, noting that "Douglas-Pennant had shown a special aptitude for public work"; see "Personalities in the Douglas-Pennant Mystery," April 26, 1924; newspaper cutting, Papers of Lord Weir, Glasgow University Archives DC 96/30/10.

64. Kwame Anthony Appiah, *The Ethics of Identity* (Princeton, NJ: Princeton University Press, 2005), 20.

65. Gilles Deleuze and Constantin V. Boundas, *The Logic of Sense* (London: Continuum, 2004), 3 and 5.

66. Letter from Violet Douglas-Pennant to Lloyd George, December 9, 1918, Lloyd George Papers, LG/F/87/16/12, House of Lords Record Office; *North Wales Chronicle*, April 17, 1919, newspaper cutting, TNA PRO AIR 2/11898; unsigned letter from "WRAF" to Lord Weir, March 14, 1919, TNA PRO AIR 2/11898; *Report from the Select Committee of the House of Lords on the Women's Royal Air Force*, 10. Douglas-Pennant also discusses this and other incidents at the camps in *Under the Searchlight*, 400.

67. *Report from the Select Committee of the House of Lords on the Women's Royal Air Force*, 10.

68. *North Wales Chronicle*, April 17, 1919, newspaper cutting, TNA PRO AIR 2/11898.

69. *Report from the Select Committee of the House of Lords on the Women's Royal Air Force*, 15.

70. Ibid.

71. *Daily News and Leader*, July 31, 1919, newspaper cutting, TNA PRO AIR 2/11903.

72. *Montgomery County Times*, March 22, 1919, newspaper cutting, TNA PRO AIR 2/11898.

73. *Morning Post*, April 2, 1919, newspaper cutting, TNA PRO AIR 2/11898. The bishop of Asaph too called for the government to ensure the safety of women entering the services; see *Bangor Paper*, undated, newspaper cutting, TNA PRO AIR 2/11898.

74. *Evening Standard*, January 8, 1919, newspaper cutting, TNA PRO AIR 2/11903.

75. Baroness de T'Serclaes, Book of Press Cuttings, IWM-DD P404.

76. Report by the Baroness de T'Serclaes. Douglas-Pennant Inquiry. Misc Papers. October 8, 1918, TNA PRO AIR 2/11903.

77. Ibid. Dr. Fairfield similarly dismissed such reports: "There was no foundation for general charges of immorality against the camps"; see *Report from the Select Committee of the House of Lords on the Women's Royal Air Force*, 13.

78. Ibid., 15.

79. Ibid., 13.

80. Report of Mr. C. Harmsworth to Prime Minister — Dismissal of Miss Douglas-Pennant Secret, November 7, 1918, TNA PRO AIR 2/11898.

81. Letter from David Mitchell to Mairi Chisholm, July 31, 1964, DMP/ML; Baroness de T'Serclaes, *Flanders and Other Fields*, cutting from the book, undated, DMP/ML; Sir Harold Morris interview with David Mitchell, October 3, 1964, DMP/ML.

82. Dr. Letitia Fairfield's undated handwritten comments on David Mitchell's manuscript, DMP/ML; emphasis in original.

83. *Report from the Select Committee of the House of Lords on the Women's Royal Air Force.*

84. References to character appear on page 6 in the transcript of the Deputation of Members of the Douglas-Pennant Committee with Dr. Norwood to the Attorney General (July 31, 1931), 2, TNA PRO PREM 1/205; letter from Violet Douglas-Pennant to Sir John Anderson, April 9, 1927, TNA PRO PREM 1/205.

85. In a letter to Sir Stanley Unwin (the publisher of *Under the Searchlight*), David Mitchell writes: "I also get the impression that [the Douglas-Pennant] scandal was not dissimilar . . . to the Pemberton-Billing case [the 'cult of the clitoris' scandal]," September 3, 1964, DMP/ML. In a 1925 letter to Lord Weir, Vivian E. Hosking draws parallels between the Douglas-Pennant case (with its "suggestion of a sinister kind implying or invoking something in the nature of moral turpitude") and the case of Florence Eva Harley ("whose moral character was cleared and vindicated by the court"). Hosking believed Harley's case had "a distinct bearing upon that of Miss Pennant"; see Churchill Archives Center, Papers of William Douglas Weir, 1st Viscount Weir, WEIR 2/6. For information on the case of Maud Allan, see above, chapter 3, at n. 43.

86. *Daily Telegraph*, July 3, 1931, newspaper cutting, TNA PRO PREM 1/205; "The Douglas-Pennant Scandal," *Truth*, May 27, 1931, 858. John Syme was a police of-

ficer who believed he had been wrongfully dismissed by the Metropolitan Police; see *Oxford Dictionary of National Biography Online*.

87. *Daily Telegraph*, July 3, 1931, newspaper cutting, TNA PRO PREM 1/205.

88. Alison Oram and Annmarie Turnbull, eds., *The Lesbian History Sourcebook: Love and Sex between Women in Britain from 1780 to 1970* (London: Routledge 2001), 170; emphasis mine.

89. In the early 1930s categories of sexual identity seem not to be widely understood within a framework of normal or deviant—a shift that evolves still later. Little is known about how and when the decidedly nonclinical term sapphist enters common parlance in modern Britain, but two OED entries from the 1920s suggest linkages to Bloomsbury (citing Virginia Woolf and Roger Fry).

90. Denise Riley, *The Words of Selves: Identification, Solidarity, Irony* (Stanford, CA: Stanford University Press, 2000), 2.

91. Halberstam, *Female Masculinity*, 53.

92. Deputation of Members of the Douglas-Pennant Committee to the Attorney General, June 22, 1932, 19, TNA PRO PREM 1/205.

93. Letter from J. J. Edwards and Co. Solicitors to Rt. Hon. Stanley Baldwin, February 4, 1937, TNA PRO PREM 1/205; emphasis mine.

94. Deputation of Members of the Douglas-Pennant Committee to the Attorney General, June 22, 1932, 10, TNA PRO PREM 1/205.

95. The Douglas-Pennant case is mentioned briefly by social historian George Robb, *British Culture and the First World War* (Basingstoke, UK: Palgrave, 2002), 60. The case has largely been taken up by popular writers on the First World War such as Katherine Bentley Beauman, *Partners in Blue: The Story of Women's Service with the Royal Air Force* (London: Hutchinson, 1971), 11–28; Beryl E. Escott, *Women in Air Force Blue: The Story of Women in the Royal Air Force from 1918 to the Present Day* (Wellingborough, UK: Stephens, 1989), 74–83; Izzard, *Heroine in Her Time*, 180–214; and Mitchell, *Women on the Warpath*, 229–43.

96. Charles Taylor, *Sources of the Self: The Making of the Modern Identity* (Cambridge, MA: Harvard University Press, 1989), 36.

97. Appiah, *Ethics of Identity*, 23.

98. Halperin, *How to Do the History of Homosexuality*, 57; emphasis in original.

99. Sedgwick, *Tendencies*, 23; emphasis in original.

100. Ibid., 25.

101. Vicinus, "Lesbian History," 58.

102. Davidson, *Emergence of Sexuality*, 21.

103. Oram and Turnbull, eds., *The Lesbian History Sourcebook*, 169–70.

104. Riley, *Words of Selves*, 2 and 1.

105. Chris Waters, "The Perils of Excessive Introspection: Psychoanalysis, Sexuality, and Selfhood in Britain in the 1920s," paper presented at the North American Conference on British Studies, 2006; Riley, *Words of Selves*, 1.

106. Sedgwick, *Tendencies*, 25; emphasis in original.

107. Interview conducted by David Mitchell with Sir Harold Morris, October 3, 1964, DMP/ML; letter from Sir Stanley Unwin to David Mitchell, September 4, 1964, DMP/ML.

108. Excerpts from Baroness de T'Serclaes, *Flanders and Other Fields*, cut from the book, n.d., DMP/ML; interview conducted by David Mitchell with John Barclay (Knocker's business manager), January 27, 1965, DMP/ML.

109. Ibid.

110. Interview conducted by David Mitchell with Dr. Letitia Fairfield, September 11, 1964, DMP/ML.

111. Letter from Mairi Chisholm to David Mitchell, n.d., DMP/ML.

112. Ibid.

113. Deborah Cohler, *Citizen, Invert, Queer: Lesbianism and War in Early Twentieth-Century Britain* (Minneapolis: University of Minnesota Press, 2010), 146, 148, and 149.

114. David Halperin and Valerie Traub, "Beyond Gay Pride," in *Gay Shame*, ed. David Halperin and Valerie Traub (Chicago: University of Chicago Press, 2009), 37.

115. Vicinus, *Intimate Friends*, xxiii.

116. Halperin, *How to Do the History of Homosexuality*, 63; emphasis mine.

117. Riley, *Words of Selves*, 112.

118. Ibid., 2 and 1.

CHAPTER FIVE

1. "Mons Nurse's Honor Vindicated," *Empire News*, December 5, 1920, 2. Matt Houlbrook first alerted me to this case, and this chapter is dedicated to him.

2. *The Times*, December 4, 1920, 4.

3. *Empire News*, December 5, 1920, 2; *The Times*, December 4, 1920, 4.

4. *Empire News*, December 5, 1920, 2. Marie Stopes's *Married Love* was published in March 1918 and sold 2,000 copies in the first two weeks — by 1923, there were 406,000 copies in print; see Ross McKibbin, "Introduction," in Marie Stopes, *Married Love*, ed. Ross McKibbin (Oxford: Oxford University Press, 2004), xxxvi; Cate Haste, *Rules of Desire: Sex in Britain, World War I to the Present* (London: Chatto and Windus, 1982), 60. Famously describing *Married Love* as having "crashed English society like a bombshell," Stopes reveals the "terrible price" she had paid for "sex-ignorance" and wrote of her determination to spare others a similar fate; see Marie Stopes, *Marriage in My Time* (London: Rich and Cowan, 1935), 44.

Although influenced by the work of Havelock Ellis and others, Stopes's project was also strikingly different. The *British Medical Journal* (May 4, 1918, 510) described this "physiological treatise on the Tree of Knowledge, written from the woman's point of view in popular language" as a refreshing shift away from the obsessive interest in "sexual aberrations beloved of German writers and their English and American imitators." Aspects of Stopes's work seem strange and unfashionable now, but with its florid expression and curious pseudoscientific references to the cyclical nature of the female "love-tide," we still recognize the origins of a sexual practice that would soon become widely known as heterosexuality; see Stopes, *Married Love*, 32. Decades later, feminist historians would assess Stopes's work as both radical (in breaking the silence around sexual knowledge) and reactionary (in its assertion of middle-class values in the context of racial instinct), yet even her fiercest critics acknowledge her great achievement in emphasizing a woman's equal right to sexual pleasure with a man to whom she is joined in matrimony; see Margaret Jackson, *The Real Facts of Life: Feminism and the Politics of Sexuality ca. 1850–1940* (London: Taylor and Francis, 1994).

Marie Stopes was not alone in her effort to popularize sexual knowledge, and her work should be seen as only a key example of marital advice literature. Excerpts of representative work can be found in "Heterosexuality, Marriage, and Sex Manuals," in *Sexology Uncensored: The Documents of Sexual Science*, ed. Lucy Bland and Laura Doan (Chicago: University of Chicago Press, 1998). See also Lesley A. Hall, ed., *Outspoken Women: An Anthology of Women's Writing on Sex, 1870–1969* (London: Routledge, 2005).

5. Stopes, *Married Love*, 10 and 82.

6. Ibid., 10.

7. *Evening Standard*, December 3, 1920, 1.

8. *Morning Post*, December 3, 1920, 10. "Sexual perversion" refers to such a huge range of sexual behaviors that the phrase is virtually meaningless. Over the centuries the phrase has been used in reference to, for instance, gender transgression, transvestism, sodomy or tribadism, masturbation, rape, pedophilia, and sadomasochism. For a thorough overview, see Julie Peakman, *Sexual Perversions, 1670–1890* (Basingstoke, UK: Palgrave Macmillan, 2009). A concise discussion of "perversion" in psychoanalytic discourse can be found in Claire Pajaczkowska, *Perversion* (Cambridge: Icon, 2000).

9. Michel Foucault, *Abnormal: Lectures at the Collège de France, 1974–1975*, ed. Valerio Marchetti and Antonella Salomoni (New York: Picador, 1999), 50.

10. In the context of Victorian Britain, Sharon Marcus perceptively comments on the "elasticity, mobility, and plasticity" of "institutions, customs, and relationships" between women and between women and men; see Sharon Marcus, *Between Women: Friendship, Desire, and Marriage in Victorian England* (Princeton, NJ: Princeton University Press, 2007), 22.

11. *Report by the Select Committee: Alleged Immorality at Hurst Park* (London: His Majesty's Stationery Office, 1919), 337, TNA PRO AIR 2/11900. Here is an example of such insouciance: "Rumors of immorality . . . did exist. It would be matter of surprise if they did not. Such is the world and such is the tendency of some natures to think and speak evil of others. . . . Equally it may well be — and we should be surprised if it were not the case — that some acts of immorality were committed" (11).

12. For a sociological discussion of the instabilities of "dominant ideology," see Nicholas Abercrombie, Stephen Hill, and Bryan S. Turner, *The Dominant Ideology Thesis* (London: Allen and Unwin, 1980).

13. Foucault, *Abnormal*, 50.

14. Carla Freccero, "Queer Times," *South Atlantic Quarterly* 106, no. 3 (2007): 490. Coward's poem is cited in Annette Kuhn, *Cinema, Censorship, and Sexuality, 1909–1925* (London: Routledge, 1988), 75.

15. There are now several good accounts of the epistemological turn toward the statistical norm; see Ian Hacking, *The Taming of Chance* (Cambridge: Cambridge University Press, 1990); Mary Poovey, *Making a Social Body: British Cultural Formation, 1830–1864* (Chicago: University of Chicago Press, 1995); and Karma Lochrie, *Heterosyncrasies: Female Sexuality When Normal Wasn't* (Minneapolis: University of Minnesota Press, 2005), especially 1–25.

16. Carla Freccero, *Queer/Early/Modern* (Durham, NC: Duke University Press, 2006), 18.

17. Hacking, *Taming of Chance*, 1. See also Ian Hacking, *The Emergence of Probability: A Philosophical Study of Early Ideas about Probability, Induction and Statistical Inference* (Cambridge: Cambridge University Press, 2006).

18. *Oxford English Dictionary Online*, accessed May 5, 2010.

19. Stopes, *Married Love*, 11.

20. Hacking, *Taming of Chance*, 169. See also Waltraud Ernst, ed., *Histories of the Normal and Abnormal: Social and Cultural Histories of Norms and Normativity* (London: Routledge, 2007).

21. I am grateful to Matt Houlbrook for this point.

22. Alfred C. Kinsey, *Sexual Behavior in the Human Male* (Philadelphia: W. B. Saunders, 1948).

23. Michael Warner, *The Trouble with Normal: Sex, Politics, and the Ethics of Queer Life* (Cambridge, MA: Harvard University Press, 1999), 54.

24. Anna Clark, "Twilight Moments," *Journal of the History of Sexuality* 14, no. 1–2 (2005): 141.

25. Jeffrey Weeks, *Sexuality* (London: Routledge, 2003), 28–29; emphasis mine.

26. Martha Vicinus, *Intimate Friends: Women Who Loved Women, 1778–1928* (Chicago: University of Chicago Press, 2004), 176.

27. Sally Newman, "The Archival Traces of Desire: Vernon Lee's Failed Sexuality and the Interpretation of Letters in Lesbian History," *Journal of the History of Sexuality* 14, no. 1–2 (2005): 60.

28. John D'Emilio and Estelle B. Freedman, *Intimate Matters: A History of Sexuality in America* (Chicago: University of Chicago Press, 1988), 227; Jennifer Terry, *An American Obsession: Science, Medicine, and the Place of Homosexuality in Modern Society* (Chicago: University of Chicago Press, 1999), 157. Thanks to the efforts of historians of sexuality such as Jennifer Terry and Julian Carter, there are excellent accounts of the history of the normal in twentieth-century American culture.

29. See http://www.glbtq.com/social-sciences/gay_lesbian_queer_studies,2.html, accessed September 10, 2010.

30. Michael Warner, "Introduction," in Warner, *Fear of a Queer Planet: Queer Politics and Social Theory* (Minneapolis: University of Minnesota Press, 1993), xxvii; Nikki Sullivan, *A Critical Introduction to Queer Theory* (Edinburgh: Edinburgh University Press, 2003), 43–44.

31. Donald E. Hall, *Queer Theories* (Basingstoke, UK: Palgrave Macmillan, 2003), 149.

32. Freccero, "Queer Times," 485.

33. Janet R. Jakobsen, "Queer Is? Queer Does? Normativity and the Problem of Resistance," *GLQ: A Journal of Lesbian and Gay Studies* 4, no. 4 (1998): 517–18.

34. Ibid., 512.

35. Frank Mort, *Dangerous Sexualities: Medico-moral Politics in England since 1830*, 2nd ed. (London: Routledge, 2000), xx.

36. For an explication of "residual and emergent" discourses, see Raymond Williams, "Base and Superstructure in Marxist Cultural Theory," *New Left Review* 82 (1973): especially 10–11.

37. David Halperin, *Saint Foucault: Towards a Gay Hagiography* (Oxford: Oxford University Press, 1995), 62; emphasis in original.

38. Warner, "Introduction," xxvi and xiii.

39. Freccero, "Queer Times," 490.

40. These details were presented to the court by Harley's barrister; see *The Times*, November 27, 1920, 4.

41. Ibid.

42. Ibid.; *Daily Telegraph*, November 27, 1920, 14; *Daily Mirror*, December 3, 1920, 2.

43. *Daily Mail*, November 27, 1920, 7; *The Times*, November 27, 1920, 4.

44. *Empire News*, December 5, 1920, 2.

45. Harley's age was variously reported as twenty-eight and thirty (*The Times*, November 27, 1920, 4, and *Daily Telegraph*, November 27, 1920, 14, respectively). Hawes was described as being twenty-two years of age and Carr twenty-four (*Daily Herald*, November 28, 1920, 12; *Daily Mail*, December 3, 1920, 8).

46. *The Times*, December 3, 1920, 5.

47. Ibid. Harley also conveyed her concerns in a letter to the branch of the Public Services Temporary Clerks' Association of which Carr was chairman, but he obtained an injunction to prevent its circulation (*Daily Mail*, November 27, 1920, 7; *The Times*, December 3, 1920, 4).

48. *Empire News*, December 5, 1920, 2.

49. *The Times*, December 4, 1920, 4; *The Times*, December 3, 1920, 5. Ironically, Harley's decision to take action against Carr meant that a slander allegedly uttered in private would be reported in numerous newspapers, including the *Daily Graphic*, *Daily Herald*, *Daily Mail*, *Daily Mirror*, *Daily Telegraph*, *Empire News*, *Evening Standard*, *Morning Post*, *News of the World*, *People*, *Reynolds's Newspaper*, *Scotsman*, *Sunday Chronicle*, and *The Times*.

Information on the social and class backgrounds of Harley, Carr, and Hawes is sparse. At the time of the incident Harley and Hawes lived in rooms at Campden Hill Square, Kensington, and Carr resided a mile away in Chesterton Road, North Kensington. During the trial, a reference to the fact that Harley's cousin was Sir John Harley Scott suggested important family connections. There is evidence that Scott corresponded with the prime minister David Lloyd George in December 1920 on matters unrelated to the case. The record held in the Parliamentary Archives describes Scott as a high sheriff in Cork as well as the secretary of the Galway County Council; Lloyd George Papers, LG/F/95/2/58, House of Lords Record Office. Harley was described as the daughter of a captain in the Merchant Service. In 1920 the plaintiff had taken rented rooms in Campden Hill Square, Kensington, in the home of the daughter of General H. Brackenbury (*The Times*, November 27, 1920, 4; *Daily Mail*, November 27, 7). Background details on Hawes are even scarcer, except that she attended a day school from ages six to seventeen and then went to Clark's Training College before becoming a clerk for the National Health Committee of the Ministry of Health in 1918 (*The Times*, November 27, 1920, 4). *The Times* mentioned Harley's suspicions that Carr was guilty of claiming extra separation allowances for service at sea and that he had illegitimate children (December 3, 1920, 5).

50. *Empire News*, December 5, 1920, 2.
51. B. A. Waites, "The Effect of the First World War on Class and Status in England, 1910–20," *Journal of Contemporary History* 11, no. 1 (1976): 29. See also Geoffrey Crossick, *The Lower Middle Class in Britain, 1870–1914* (London: Croom Helm, 1977); Jonathan Wild, *The Rise of the Office Clerk in Literary Culture, 1880–1939* (Basingstoke, UK: Palgrave Macmillan, 2006).
52. *Empire News*, December 5, 1920, 2. Carr, Harley, Hawes, another witness (Miss Frances Elizabeth Coxhill), and the husband of Harley's new roommate at the time of the trial (Mr. Creber) were all members of either the men's or women's branch of the Public Services Temporary Clerks' Association.
53. Ibid.
54. Ibid.
55. *The Times*, November 27, 1920, 4.
56. *The Times*, December 4, 1920, 4.
57. *Empire News*, December 5, 1920, 2.
58. Ibid.; *Daily Telegraph*, December 3, 1920, 3; *Sunday Chronicle*, December 5, 1920, 7; *Evening Standard*, December 3, 1920, 1.
59. For a discussion of the mythic status of Mons in the collective memory, see David Clarke, "Rumors of Angels: A Legend of the First World War," *Folklore* 113, no. 2 (2002): 151–73.
60. This information appears in *Evening Standard*, December 2, 1920, 8, and *The Times*, December 3, 1920, 5. For examples of the photographic layout see *Empire News*, December 5, 1920, 2, and *Daily Mirror*, December 4, 1920, 16.

61. *The Times*, November 27, 1920, 4.

62. Ibid.

63. *Daily Mirror*, December 4, 1920, 15.

64. *Reynolds's Newspaper*, December 5, 1920, 5.

65. TNA PRO ADM 188 680: Walter Cyril Carr. Harley's barrister never inquired about Carr's service record, and the defendant produced no witnesses to attest to his good character.

66. Ibid.

67. *The Times*, December 3, 1920, 5.

68. Ibid.

69. TNA PRO WO 372 23: Florence E. Harley.

70. *The Times*, December 3, 1920, 5.

71. TNA PRO WO 372 23: Florence E. Harley; *British Journal of Nursing*, January 10, 1920, 19.

72. I am grateful to London's British Red Cross Museum and Archives for this information.

73. TNA PRO WO 372 23: Florence E. Harley.

74. *Empire News*, December 5, 1920, 2.

75. Ibid.

76. *The Times*, December 3, 1920, 5.

77. The following reported "mating": *The Times*, December 3, 1920, 5; *Daily Graphic*, December 4, 1920, 3; *Daily Telegraph*, December 3, 1920, 3; and *Daily Mail*, December 4, 1920, 8. The *Daily Herald* reported "meeting," December 3, 1920, 2.

78. *The Times*, December 3, 1920, 5.

79. *Daily Mail*, December 3, 1920, 8.

80. *The Times*, December 3, 1920, 5.

81. *Daily Mirror*, December 3, 1920, 2.

82. *The Times*, December 3, 1920, 5.

83. *Daily Mirror*, December 4, 1920, 15; August Forel, *The Sexual Question*, trans. C. F. Marshall (New York: Rebman, 1905), 251.

84. *The Times*, December 3, 1920, 5.

85. For a concise overview of the vast literature on nervous diseases, and historical analysis of neurasthenia in early twentieth-century American culture, see Julian B. Carter, *The Heart of Whiteness: Normal Sexuality and Race in America, 1880–1940* (Durham, NC: Duke University Press, 2007), especially 42–74.

86. *The Times*, December 3, 1920, 5; *Empire News*, December 5, 1920, 2.

87. *Sunday Chronicle*, December 5, 1920, 7.

88. *The Times*, November 27, 1920, 4. The *Daily Telegraph* also noted that "a separation of the friends would affect the girl's health" (November 27, 1920, 14).

89. *Empire News*, December 5, 1920, 3.

90. *The Times*, December 4, 1920, 4.

91. Ibid.

92. *Oxford Dictionary of National Biography Online*, accessed April 8, 2010; *The Times*, December 3, 1920, 5.

93. *Report by the Select Committee*, 337, TNA PRO AIR 2/11900.

94. Ibid.

95. Stopes, *Married Love*, 54; *Report by the Select Committee*, 337, TNA PRO AIR 2/11900.

96. *Report by the Select Committee*, 337, TNA PRO AIR 2/11900. According to one legal scholar, "If the practice of medical jurisprudence had simply been about establishing and deriving certain knowledge from the presence or absence of . . . physical signs, then doctors could have been the 'purveyors of indisputable medical truths' that some historians have argued they claim to be. As texts described the practice of medical jurisprudence, however, the path from identifying signs to achieving certain knowledge about whether a woman had been raped or had intercourse was obstructed by the variety of meanings that these physical signs could have"; see Stephen Robertson, "Signs, Marks, and Private Parts: Doctors, Legal Discourses, and Evidence of Rape in the United States, 1823–1930," *Journal of the History of Sexuality* 8, no. 3 (1998): 364. The status of medical evidence in jurisprudence, Robertson argues, has been underinvestigated by historians of medicine (349). See also John Ayrton Paris and John Samuel Martin Fonblanque, *Medical Jurisprudence* (London: Phillips, 1823).

97. *Report by the Select Committee*, 337, TNA PRO AIR 2/11900.

98. *The Times*, December 4, 1920, 4.

99. *Daily Mail*, December 3, 1920, 8; *Scotsman*, December 4, 1920, 11.

100. *Daily Mail*, December 3, 1920, 8.

101. *The Times*, December 3, 1920, 5.

102. Ibid.

103. *The Times*, November 27, 1920, 4; *Daily Telegraph*, November 27, 1920, 14.

104. *The Times*, November 27, 1920, 4.

105. *The Times*, December 3, 1920, 5; *Reynolds's Newspaper*, December 5, 1920, 5.

106. *The Times*, December 4, 1920, 4.

107. *The Times*, November 27, 1920, 4.

108. *The Times*, December 4, 1920, 4.

109. Ibid.

110. *Daily Mail*, December 4, 1920, 8; emphasis mine. See also Havelock Ellis's discussion of modesty in women in *Studies in the Psychology of Sex: The Evolution of Modesty, the Phenomena of Sexual Periodicity, Auto-eroticism*, 3rd ed., rev. and enl. (Philadelphia: F. A. Davis, 1931).

111. *Daily Graphic*, December 4, 1920, 3.

112. *Empire News*, December 5, 1920, 2.

113. See Laura Doan, *Fashioning Sapphism: The Origins of a Modern English Lesbian Culture* (New York: Columbia University Press, 2001), especially 56–59.

114. *The Times*, November 27, 1920, 4; *Empire News*, December 5, 1920, 2.

115. The judge put several questions to the jury: "Were the words: 'You are not a virgin. I can tell it by your face' spoken?—Yes. Did the words mean that the plaintiff was guilty of unchastity . . . or only guilty of the malpractices described?—Only malpractices. Are the words true?—No. Was the defendant actuated by malice?— Yes. . . . On the counterclaim: Did the plaintiff publish the solicitor's letter?—Yes. Without malice?—Yes . . . Did the words impute critical offenses? No." *The Times*, December 4, 1920, 4.

116. *Empire* News, December 5, 1920, 2; *The Times*, December 4, 1920, 4. The financial implications for a man dependent on a clerk's salary would have been devastating. While there is no record detailing the fee paid to Wild in this case, an equally distinguished barrister (Sir Edward Marshall Hall) received 652 guineas for the brief in the 1923 case involving Madam Fahmy (a case that Lucy Bland discusses at length in her forthcoming *Sexual Transgression in the Age of the Flapper*); see Edward Marjoribanks, *The Life of Sir Edward Marshall* (London: Victor Gollancz, 1929), 435. The average pay for a male clerk in the early 1920s was approximately £320; see Guy Routh, *Occupation and Pay in Great Britain, 1906–1979* (London: Macmillan, 1980), 120. I am grateful to Lucy Bland for this information.

117. *Daily Graphic*, December 4, 1920, 3; *Daily Herald*, December 4, 1920, 3.

118. *The Times*, November 27, 1920, 4.

119. Peter Bailey, "White Collars, Gray Lives? The Lower Middle Class Revisited," *Journal of British Studies* 38, no. 3 (1999): 287; *Daily Mail*, December 4, 1920, 8. Terry notes that in the United States "the 1920s marked an important shift in popular and scientific thinking about sexuality"; see Terry, *American Obsession*, 154.

120. *Daily Mail*, December 4, 1920, 8.

121. *Evening Standard*, December 3, 1920 1.

122. Ibid.

123. *The Times*, December 4, 1920, 4.

124. Women's Slander Act of 1891, cap. 51, sec. 1. UK Statute Law Database, Office of Public Sector Information, accessed April 13, 2010.

125. *The Times*, December 4, 1920, 4.

126. Personal communication with Sharrona Pearl, April 2010; for further discussion of the uses of physiognomy, see Pearl's *About Faces: Physiognomy in Nineteenth-Century Britain* (Cambridge, MA: Harvard University Press, 2010).

127. Stopes, *Marriage in My Time*, 44.

128. *The Times*, December 4, 1920, 4.

129. Valerie Traub, "The Joys of Martha Joyless: Queer Pedagogy and the (Early Modern) Production of Sexual Knowledge," in *The Forms of Renaisssance Thought*, ed. Leonard Barkan, Bradin Cormack, and Sean Keilen (Basingstoke, UK: Palgrave Macmillan, 2008), 180.

130. Ibid., 173.

131. Lochrie, *Heterosyncrasies*, xxiii.

132. *The Times*, November 27, 1920, 4; *The Times*, December 3, 1920, 5; *Empire News*, December 5, 1920, 2.

133. *The Times*, December 3, 1920, 5.

134. In a recent study of the role of legal discourse in shaping the "social construction of modern sexuality," historian Sharon R. Ullman writes, "These courtroom conflicts became a mechanism that drove the shift in sexual attitudes. When sexual practice appeared before the bar, consternation abounded, and cases often ended in chaos. As individuals talked about their experiences, new values emerged and older ones were shattered"; see Sharon R. Ullman, *Sex Seen: The Emergence of Modern Sexuality in America* (Berkeley: University of California Press, 1997), 8. My reading of *Harley v. Carr* suggests that emergent discourses added to, rather than displaced, older understandings, even if contradictory.

135. *The Times*, December 4, 1920, 4.

136. *The Times*, December 3, 1920, 5.

137. Lesley Hall, *Sex, Gender and Social Change in Britain since 1880* (Basingstoke, UK: Macmillan, 2000), 126. See also Angus McLaren, *Twentieth-Century Sexuality: A History* (Oxford: Blackwell, 1999).

138. Lochrie, *Heterosyncrasies*, xxiii.

139. Warner, *Trouble with Normal*, 193. The "cult of the clitoris" case offers another example of the linkage of guilt with sexual knowledge; see chapter 3, n. 43.

140. *Report by the Select Committee*, 337, TNA PRO AIR 2/11900.

141. Ibid.

142. *News of the World*, December 5, 1920, 2; *The Times*, December 4, 1920, 4. Mrs. Ann Creber was a dining-room proprietess and wife of the general secretary of the Temporary Clerks' Association. When Miss Brackenbury (Harley's previous landlady) closed the house in Campden Hill Square to go abroad, Harley moved into lodgings with the Crebers. The court was told that Mrs. Creber and Harley "had been sleeping" together "for the past two months"; *Daily Telegraph*, December 3, 1920, 3.

143. Georges Canguilhem, *The Normal and the Pathological*, trans. Carolyn Fawcett (New York: Zone Books, 1991), 174.

144. *British Medical Journal*, May 4, 1918, 510.

145. Warner, "Introduction," xiii.

146. Deborah Cohler, *Citizen, Invert, Queer: Lesbianism and War in Early Twentieth-Century Britain* (Minneapolis: University of Minnesota Press, 2010), xvii.

147. Ibid., xiii.

148. Ibid.

149. Cohler, *Citizen, Invert, Queer*, 144; *Hansard, Commons*, 5th ser., 14 (1921): 1804. One of the cosponsors of the clause, Sir Ernest Wild, informed his colleagues, "This vice does exist, and it saps the fundamental institutions of society. In the first place it stops child-birth, because it is a well-known fact that any woman who

indulges in this vice will have nothing to do with the other sex. It debauches young girls, and it produces neurasthenia and insanity." Wild had done his homework, and he named two of the most famous sexologists in his speech (Krafft-Ebing and Ellis) as if to lend greater authority to his arguments. However, no sooner were these names mentioned than the usefulness of a knowledge practice invested in the normal and abnormal was swiftly dismissed: "My own feeling is simply to refer to the Lesbian love practices between women, which are common knowledge"; *Hansard, Commons*, 5th ser., 14 (1921): 1803.

150. Carolyn Dinshaw, *Getting Medieval: Sexualities and Communities, Pre- and Post-modern* (Durham, NC: Duke University Press, 1999), 151.

151. See especially Terry, *American Obsession*, and Carter, *Heart of Whiteness*.

152. Halberstam's comments appear on the back cover of Lochrie, *Heterosyncrasies*.

153. Judith Halberstam, *Female Masculinity* (Durham, NC: Duke University Press, 1998), 52.

154. Hacking, *Taming of Chance*, 160.

155. Ibid.

156. Warner, "Introduction," xxvii; Halperin, *Saint Foucault*, 62.

157. Lee Edelman, *No Future: Queer Theory and the Death Drive* (Durham, NC: Duke University Press, 2004), 4. For examples of the queer critical engagement with Edelman, see José E. Muñoz, *Cruising Utopia: The Then and There of Queer Futurity* (New York: New York University Press, 2009); Michael D. Snediker, *Queer Optimism: Lyric Personhood and Other Felicitous Persuasions* (Minneapolis: University of Minnesota Press, 2008); Kathryn Bond Stockton, *The Queer Child, or Growing Sideways in the Twentieth Century* (Durham, NC: Duke University Press, 2009).

158. As Annamarie Jagose observes, "There is no shortage of people claiming that queer theory is finished, washed-up, and over"; see Annamarie Jagose, "Feminism's Queer Theory," *Feminism and Psychology* 19, no. 2 (2009): 158.

159. Warner, "Introduction," xiii.

160. *Report by the Select Committee*, 337, TNA PRO AIR 2/11900.

EPILOGUE

1. *News of the World*, November 27, 1920, 2. Violet Douglas-Pennant lived at the Old House, 13 Holland Street, London W8, at the time of her dismissal through to (at least) the early 1930s, as can be seen by the address on a letter published in *Under the Searchlight: A Record of a Great Scandal* (London: George Allen and Unwin, 1922) (408) and a letter from her sister, Hilda Douglas-Pennant, to WCB, March 6, 1934, 4629/1/1934/7, Shropshire Archives.

2. The plaque reads, "RADCLYFFE HALL 1880–1943 Novelist and Poet lived here 1924–29." See http://openplaques.org/plaques/198, accessed August 28, 2011.

3. Jan Assmann and John Czaplicka, "Collective Memory and Cultural Identity," *New German Critique* 65 (1995): 128.

4. Sir Chartres Biron, "Judgment," in *Palatable Poison: Critical Perspectives on "The Well of Loneliness,"* ed. Laura Doan and Jay Prosser (New York: Columbia University Press, 2001), 49.

5. Ibid., 45. According to biographer Michael Baker, Radclyffe Hall "was especially sensitive to the section of *The Well* dealing with the women at the front. . . . Therefore, any aspersions on the fictional unit could be construed as a slur on the real women. [Hall's] strong sense of loyalty was outraged by such a notion. But it went deeper than this. To [Hall] there was something sacrosanct about those who had served at the battlefront during the Great War"; see Michael Baker, *Our Three Selves: The Life of Radclyffe Hall* (New York: William Morrow, 1985), 243–44. Another biographer, Diana Souhami, notes that "in a public lecture some two months later," Hall characterized the courtroom outburst as a response to the magistrate's "slur" on the women ambulance drivers; see Diana Souhami, *The Trials of Radclyffe Hall* (London: Weidenfeld and Nicolson, 1998), 210.

6. Christopher S. Nealon, *Foundlings: Lesbian and Gay Historical Emotion before Stonewall* (Durham, NC: Duke University Press, 2001), 8; emphasis in original. Nostalgia need not necessarily be seen "as a passive, wishy-washy, rose-tinted yearning for the past"—it is also "a vital force, passionate, [and] active"; Jeffrey Richards, *Films and British National Identity: From Dickens to Dad's Army* (Manchester, UK: Manchester University Press, 1997), 365.

7. Heather Love, *Feeling Backward: Loss and the Politics of Queer History* (Cambridge, MA: Harvard University Press, 2007), 3. Love writes: "Although many queer critics take exception to the idea of a linear, triumphalist view of history, we are in practice deeply committed to the notion of progress; despite our reservations, we just cannot stop dreaming of a better life for queer people. Such utopian desires are at the heart of the collective project of queer studies and integral to the history of gay and lesbian identity."

8. Carolyn Dinshaw et al., "Theorizing Queer Temporalities: A Roundtable Discussion," *GLQ: A Journal of Lesbian and Gay Studies* 13, no. 2–3 (2007): 179; emphasis mine.

9. Walter Benjamin, *"One Way Street" and Other Writings* (London: Verso, 1985), 314.

10. David Lowenthal, *The Heritage Crusade and the Spoils of History* (Cambridge: Cambridge University Press, 1997), 121; Lauren Berlant, "Thinking about Feeling Historical," *Emotion, Space, and Society* 1, no. 1 (2008): 4.

11. Dinshaw et al., "Theorizing Queer Temporalities," 187; Joan Scott, "History-Writing as Critique," in *Manifestos for History*, ed. Keith Jenkins, Sue Morgan, and Alun Munslow (London: Routledge, 2007), 35.

12. Valerie Traub, "The Present Future of Lesbian Historiography," in *A Companion*

to Lesbian, Gay, Bisexual, Transgender, and Queer Studies, ed. George Haggerty and Molly McGarrity (London: Blackwell, 2007), 136.

13. Dinshaw et al., "Theorizing Queer Temporalities," 179.

14. Sharon Marcus, *Between Women: Friendship, Desire, and Marriage in Victorian England* (Princeton, NJ: Princeton University Press, 2007), 5.

15. There are, of course, important exceptions. Elizabeth Freeman, for instance, thoughtfully considers points of congruence between temporality and historiography; see Elizabeth Freeman, *Time Binds: Queer Temporalities, Queer Histories* (Durham, NC: Duke University Press, 2010). Queer critic Jonathan Goldberg also argues that "future possibility in the present might mean that our sense of the past needs to be rethought"; see Jonathan Goldberg, "After Thoughts," *South Atlantic Quarterly* 106, no. 3 (2007): 510.

16. I am pleased to note important exceptions to this claim, such as Margot Canaday's impressive and award-winning study of "federal interest in *what becomes* homosexuality by midcentury." Here is an example of historical work that traces "backward in time" but also is concerned more with "a process . . . than a thing"; see Margot Canaday, *The Straight State: Sexuality and Citizenship in Twentieth-Century America* (Princeton, NJ: Princeton University Press, 2009), 11.

17. Matt Houlbrook, *Queer London: Perils and Pleasures in the Sexual Metropolis, 1918–1957* (Chicago: University of Chicago Press, 2005), 271. For discussions of the interrelation between history, memory, and identity, see Martin O. Heisler, "Challenged Histories and Collective Self-Concepts: Politics in History, Memory, and Time," *Annals of the American Academy of Political and Social Science* 617 (2008): 199–211; Andreas Huyssen, *Twilight Memories: Making Time in a Culture of Amnesia* (New York: Routledge, 1995); Wulf Kansteiner, "Finding Meaning in Memory: A Methodological Critique of Collective Memory Studies," *History and Theory* 41 (2002): 179–97; Kerwin Lee Klein, "On the Emergence of Memory in Historical Discourse," *Representations* 69 (2000): 127–50; Pierre Nora, "Between Memory and History: Les Lieux de Mémoire," *Representations* 26 (1989): 7–24; and Allan Megill, "History, Memory, Identity," *History of the Human Sciences* 11, no. 3 (1998): 37–62.

INDEX

academic history, xi, 9, 17, 29–31, 34, 55, 57, 64, 81, 102–3, 198, 203–4n2; as craft, 36; and critical history practice, 62; and cultural turn, 8, 39, 75; departments of, and lesbian, gay, or queer historians, 197–98; and empiricism, 88; and genealogical project, 62; historical evidence, as tethered to, 35; and historiography, 6; and identity politics, 226n22; lesbian and gay history, status of in, 28; as "old discipline," 35; politically motivated outsiders, suspicion toward, 9; professional historian, notion of, 36; professional training, high value on, 9; as professionalized, 35, 53; and queer studies, 6, 8, 167; queer studies, distance between, 27, 44, 56, 62–63, 86; queer theory, marginalization of in, 33; and sexuality, 12; sexuality, as indifferent to, 28; "tribe," as members of, 35. *See also* history; proper history

Adorno, Theodor, 37, 85

ahistoricism, 89; and homosexuality, 139

AIDS, 39

Alec-Tweedie, Ethel Brilliana, 97, 106, 108, 110–12, 128, 142

Allan/Billing trial, 3, 22, 91, 106, 158, 253n85. *See also* Noel Pemberton Billing

Allan, Maud, 3, 105, 153, 184

Allatini, Rose, 3, 105

alterity/continuism, 78, 90

Amazon, 105, 113, 115, 122; as term, 239n39

ambulance drivers, viii, 21, 101–2, 108, 112–13, 124, 195, 212n77, 238–39n36, 265n5; and class privilege, 122; codes of chivalry, 126; lesbianism, assumed link between, vii, 119; literary representation of, 127–28; modern woman, call for, 120; nursing, contrast with, 120; quasi-religious language, use of toward, 126–27; requirements of, 120; risk-taking woman, attraction to, 120, 122; social pressures of gender, freedom from, 125–26; as specimen apart, 120; on Western Front, 119, 126, 238–39n36

America, 18, 66, 170. *See also* United States

ancestral genealogy, 2–3, 16, 19, 23, 58–59, 61–62, 65, 84, 86, 101, 138, 159, 197–99; and ancestral work, 72; as archival source, 71; before and after narrative and, 73; as eclectic, 71; exclusion, rectifying of, 15; and genealogical project, 88; historical memory, as collective act of, 69, 196; identity, fixing of in, 74–75; as late ancestral genealogy, 72; lesbian or gay past, methodologies of, 87; likeness and resemblance, tracing of in, 73; lineage, enduring interest in, 75–76; literary expression, receptivity to, 68; origins, fascination with, 15; purpose of, as foundational, 71; queer genealogy, affinities between, 60, 63, 67; queer genealogy, undoing of, 79; and queer theory, 136; as recuperative, 73; resilience of, 70; value

Cowper, Mrs. L. C., 244n91
Coxhill, Frances Elizabeth, 259n52
Creber, Ann, 189, 263n142
critical history, 2, 38–39, 43–46, 61, 72, 75, 80–81, 86, 192, 204n2; and academic history, 62; discontinuity, privileging of, 90; and genealogical project, 89; and historiography, 6; and invented legacies, 199; past, as radically unknowable, 60; present, as history, 51; and queer genealogy, 84, 87; queer history, alliances between, xii, 16; and queer studies, 62; and retrospective identifications, 16; value of, and undetermined history, 92; universals, rejection of, 88. *See also* Foucauldian genealogy; queer critical history
cross-dressing women, 77
"Cult of the Clitoris." *See* Allan/Billing trial
cultural history, 48
cultural studies, 33, 41
cultural turn, 39, 65, 67, 86, 232n117; and academic history, 8, 75; and archival materials, 48; and discipline problem, 17; and historiography, 72; and history, 37, 65, 81, 86; and homosexuality, relation to, 81; impact of, debate over, 81; and lesbian and gay social history, 27; and queer history, 27; and queer methodology, 56, 70; and queer theory, 41; results of, 37, 48; theoretical implications of, 38
Cvetkovich, Ann, 46–50

Daily Mail (newspaper), 120, 185
Daily Mirror (newspaper), 177
Daily Telegraph (newspaper), 177
David, Hugh, 33
Dean, Carolyn J., 34–35, 37–39, 217n38
de Beauvoir, Simone, 115
de Certeau, Michel, 85
deconstruction, 74, 85
Defence of the Realm Act (DORA), 105
de Havilland, Gladys, 120
de Lauretis, Teresa, 213n3
Deleuze, Gilles, 150
D'Emilio, John, 34
Derby, Lord, 98
Derrida, Jacques, 85; and "archive fever," 49
Despised and Rejected (Allatini), 3, 105
de T'Serclaes, Baroness. *See* Elsie Knocker
Dickens, Charles, 75
Dickinson, Emily, 66
Dinshaw, Carolyn, 41–42, 52, 203n19, 219n69

disciplinarity, 34, 36, 53, 55–57, 86
"discipline problem," 29, 31, 41–43, 51, 55, 65; and homosexuality, 69
"The Discipline Problem: Queer Theory Meets Lesbian and Gay History" (Duggan), 17, 28
Donoghue, Emma, 73
Douglas-Pennant Committee, 154, 162
Douglas-Pennant, George Sholto Gordon, 148
Douglas-Pennant, Violet, 15, 22, 139, 142, 173, 181, 195, 252n62, 253n85, 264n1; as accuser, 143; allegations or accusations against, vii–viii, 141, 149–62, 166; background of, 148–49; career of, 147–48; clearing name, attempts to by, 149, 154, 157–60, 162; dismissal of, vii, ix, 21, 134–35, 148, 151–55; as highly regarded, 251n57, 252n63; as mentally ill, accusations of, 148, 251–52n58; naming and, 141; as old-fashioned, 152, 167; public humiliation of, vii; public service record of, 147–48; self, unawareness of, 161; and selfhood, 159; self-making of, 159; and self-naming, 141, 143, 157; sexual identity of, as unknown, 21, 141, 158–59; social snobbery, denial of, 149; supporters of, 134; and wartime sex talk, 141; women's new sexual freedom, attitude toward, 152
Downs, Laura, 242n67
Duggan, Lisa, 13, 29, 31–32, 42–43, 56, 208n43, 213n2; and "discipline problem," 17, 28, 41, 51; social history, critique of, 51, 213n2
Duke University Press, 215n21
du Maurier, Daphne, 75

Edelman, Lee, viii, 1, 192, 213n3, 215n21; and queer negativity, 88
Edis, Olive, 122, 244n97
Edwards, J. J., 154–55
Eley, Geoff, 12, 36, 226n20; on cultural turn, 232n117
Ellis, Havelock, 11, 19, 195, 255–56n4, 263–64n149
Empire News (newspaper), 175–76
empiricism, 56, 217n38; and academic history, 88; as defined, 219–20n76; and positivism, 220n81
England, 18, 66, 171, 174; upper-class gentleman, stereotype of, 243n84; upper-

England (*continued*)
class woman in, as recognizable type, 113. *See also* Britain
erotohistoriography, 29
essentialism, 67
eugenics, 179
Europe, 11, 235n4
Evening Standard (newspaper), 151, 177
Everyweek (newspaper), 239n39

Faderman, Lillian, 34, 66, 68–69, 73, 75
Fahmy, Madam, 262n116
Fairfield, Dr. Letitia, 148, 152, 161, 251–52n58, 253n77
family history, 2
Fashioning Sapphism: The Origins of a Modern English Lesbian Culture (Doan), x–xi
Feeling Backward: Loss and the Politics of Queer History (Love), 72
female homosexuality. *See* lesbianism
female masculinity, 119, as abnormal, 130; classify, impulse to and, 131; concept of, 117; female homosexuality, linkages between, 19–20; gender boundaries, stretching of, 129; gender inversion, 99, 105; lesbianism, assumed linkages to, 130–31; and militarism, 99–100; reactions to, 130; as threatening, 99; tolerance levels toward, 129. *See also* gender variance; lesbian; lesbianism
Female Masculinity (Halberstam), 238n35
female war workers, 242n67; as cultural oddities, 113; cultural anxieties over, 113, 115; female masculinity, concept of, 117; as heroic, 111; notion of body, as "situation," 117; occupations of, uncertainty of, 235–36n6. *See also* uniformed women; women
feminism, 19; lesbianism, association with, 98
First Aid Nursing Yeomanry (FANY), 99, 108, 111, 113, 122, 125–26, 238–39n36, 245n104
First World War, 18–19, 195; bad soldiering, and shell shock, 110–11; British society, impact on, 1, 3; disruptive effects of, 20; emergent homosexual subcultures, assumed as crucial for, 19, 21, 99; and female homosexual identity, 20; female labor during, unfamiliar configurations of, 98; female masculinity and female homosexuality, linkages between, 19–20;

female war workers during, as heroic, 111; gendered experience of, 20; gender expressions during, long-term repercussions of, 111; gendering effects of, as class differentiated, 20–21; gender relations, effects of on, 83; gender stratification, in labor market, 97; good soldiering, and hypermasculinity, 110; homosocial arrangements during, vii; men, effects on, 110, 127; men, emasculating of during, 127; norms, in flux during, 167; sexual relations between women and men, changes in, 20, 167, 177; sex talk during, 5, 10–11, 22, 141; third sex, fear of, 129; topsy-turvydom during, 97, 110; as transformative time, 110; as turning point, and homosexuality, 21; women, and auto mechanics, knowledge of, as rite of passage, 116; women, effects on, 1, 106, 110–11, 127–30, 235n4, 241–42n61; women, and gender and class, 117. *See also* female war workers; uniformed women; Western Front; women
Flying Ambulance Column (FAC), 144–45. *See also* Hector Munro's Ambulance Unit
Foucauldian genealogy, 59, 65–66, 75–76, 82, 84–86, 90. *See also* critical history
Foucault, Michel, 2, 12, 15–16, 20, 31, 34–35, 47, 52, 70, 75–76, 78, 82, 85, 92, 166, 195, 204n3, 213n3, 225n10; criticism of, 217–18n41; critique, notion of, 37; Great Paradigm Shift, critique of, 44; history, as critique, 60; homosexual, as species, reference to, 45; modern homosexual, as term, birth date of, 45; repressive hypothesis of, 54; and reverse discourse, 205n14
France, 66, 117, 120, 122, 128, 132, 177–78, 238–39n36, 244n91
Freccero, Carla, 52, 79, 85, 88, 129–20n76, 226n16
Freeman, Elizabeth, 9–10, 65, 266n15
Fry, Roger, 254n89
Fulbrook, Mary, 213n2

Gallagher, Catherine, 57
Gardiner, James, 33
gay liberation, 33, 51, 78, 83, 84
Gay Life and Culture: A World History (Aldrich), 54
gender, 84; and class, 139; as debased, 83; fluidity of, 20; performativity, 126; politi-

cal efficacy of, as diminished, 83; and sexuality, 20, 28, 82–83, 100–101, 133, 199; sexuality, in flux, 108; and transformation, 111

gender difference: and cultural change, 108

gendered body: as action-system, 144

gender history, 233n125

gender variance, 147; and identity, 140; and lesbianism, 100–101, 105; and same-sex desire, 77; and sexual deviance, 98; and sexual inversion, 105–6. *See also* female masculinity

genealogical project, 2, 15, 17–18, 23, 60–61, 65, 81, 86, 90, 101, 133, 138, 175, 186, 190, 197; and academic history, 62; and critical history, 89; proper history, as different from, 63; queer disavowal of, 80; and queer critical history, 87. *See also* identity history

genealogy, 2, 14, 162; conceptual underpinnings of, 93; definitions of, 15–16; and family tree, 58; and Foucauldian genealogy, 58; as problem, 92; as solution, 92

Germany, 66, 144, 185, 245n105

Gibbs, Philip, 145

Gilbert, Sandra M., 131

Gilbert, Sue, 66

Girl Guide movement, 100

GLQ: A Journal of Lesbian and Gay Studies (journal), 28

Glubb, Gwenda Mary, 166, 181–82, 188–89

Goldberg, Jonathan, 85, 266n15

Gould, Jenny, 98–101, 129–31

Gowing, Laura, 203n14

Gramsci, Antonio, 226n20

Graves, Robert, 9–10

Grayzel, Susan, 236n12, 241–42n61

Great Paradigm Shift, 67; critique of, 44–45

Great War. *See* First World War

Greenblatt, Stephen, 57

Gubar, Susan, 131

Hackett-Lowther Ambulance Unit, 238–39n36

Hacking, Ian, 169, 191

Halberstam, Judith, 67, 101, 191, 227–28n36, 237n23, 238n35, 247n135

Hall, Edward Marshall, 262n116

Hall, Radclyffe, vii–viii, 72, 77, 92, 99, 127–28, 195–96, 198–99, 219n73, 237n23, 264n2; and ambulance drivers, 21, 212n77, 265n5; daybooks of, 43; obscenity trial of, 40

Hallett, Nicky, 34

Halley, Janet, 215n21, 230n66

Halperin, David, xii, 45–46, 52, 58–59, 76, 84, 88, 97, 137, 162, 164, 211n68, 218n50; cultural historian, task of, 247n134; historicizing method of, 15; queer, definition of, *whatever* at odds with, 21, 44, 172, 191

Hamer, Emily, 34

Harker, Ethel, 244n95

Harley v. Carr, 173, 182, 186–87; class and war service, as determinants in, 180; and class codes, 185; moral perversion, charge of, in 175–76; press coverage of, 177, 185; sexual knowledge in, as crucial to, 187; verdict of, 185

Harley, Florence Eva, 1, 15, 21, 164–67, 173–89, 195, 253n85, 258n45, 258n47, 258–59n49, 259n52, 263n142; Hawes, friendship with, 173–74; as hero, 178; Mons medal, receiving of, 177–78. See also *Harley v. Carr*

Harmsworth, Cecil, 149, 152

Haverfield, Evelina, viii

Hawes, Decima, 164, 173–77, 179–88, 195, 258n45, 258–59n49, 259n52; Harley, friendship with, 173–74; and neurasthenia, 180

Hector Munro's Ambulance Unit, 144, 238–39n36. *See also* Flying Ambulance Column (FAC)

Her Husband Was a Woman! Women's Gender-Crossing in Modern British Popular Culture (Oram), 77

heritage, 195–96

Herring, Scott, 46–47, 79–80

Herrup, Cynthia, 208n40

heteronormativity, 19, 32, 69

Hidden from History: Reclaiming the Gay and Lesbian Past (Duberman, Vicinus, and Chauncey), 34

Hirschfeld, Magnus, 11

historical past: and history, 9; v. practical past, 10; and sexuality, 10

historical practice: as empiricist, myth of, 41; evidence, nature of, 40

historicism, 39

historicity, 29, 32, 39, 51; queer attentiveness to, 44, 56; and queer theory, 52

historiography, 33–34, 40, 42, 50, 53, 69, 229n51; and academic history, 6; and cultural turn, 72; dismissal of, 39; gay and lesbian, x; homosexuality, genealogical

245n105; appearance of, 144; background of, 144; hair cutting of, as transformative, 145–46; living arrangements of, 146–47; reputation of, 161; and sexual identity, 21

Krafft-Ebing, Richard von, 11, 263–64n149

Kunzel, Regina, 54–55

LaCapra, Dominick, 53

Ladies of Llangollen, 77

Ladies' Field (magazine), 106, 120, 237n18, 242n63, 243n79

Ladies' Field Supplement (magazine), 241n59

Leared, Mrs. R. I., 245n107

Lee, Janet, 99

Lee, Vernon, 77

lesbian: "lesbian-like," use of, 140; as word, 140, 142, 155–56. *See also* female masculinity; lesbianism

lesbian and gay history, 2. *See also* ancestral genealogy

lesbian, gay, or queer history, x–xi, 20, 22, 88; as collective project, and identity politics, as rooted in, 17–18; as genealogical project, 2; as term, 138

lesbian and gay social history: in academic history, 28; and cultural turn, 27; and "historical imagination," 31; marginalization of, 28; queer studies, tension between, 32; and queer cultural criticism, 50, 55–56; and queer history, 50; queer theory, at odds with, 27, 44; research methods, critiques of, 27–28; and slumming literature, 47; social identities, as historically shaped, 69; traumatic histories, alignment of with, 50; and unknowability, 47

lesbian historiography, 19

lesbian history, 66–67

Lesbian History Group, 34, 70, 72; and consciousness raising, 67; and history of origins, right of to, 67; political ambitions of, 74

The Lesbian History Sourcebook: Love and Sex between Women in Britain from 1780 to 1970 (Oram and Turnbull), 70, 160

lesbianism, 15, 20, 136; ambulance drivers, assumed link between, vii, 119; as danger, 4; feminism, association with, 98; historical fiction, important role in, 71; as knowable, 3; and origins myth, 21; outing of, 67; pathologizing of, 67; and patriar-

chy, 67; as threat, 236n13; and trials, 3–4. *See also* female masculinity; lesbian

Lesbian Lives Conference, 66

lesbian writing, 69; lesbian invisibility, countering of, 68; visibility in, 75

LGBT (lesbian, gay, bisexual, and trans) communities, 7; and history, 55–56, 229n51; as "history of the community," 72; and history project, 31; and studies, 34, 41

Liddington, Jill, 203n13

Light Car (journal), 129

Linton, Eliza Lynn, 77

Lister, Anne, 77, 203n13

literary criticism, 35–36; and contextualization, 224n171

literary studies, 12, 33, 35, 43

literary theory, 35

The Literature of Lesbianism: A Historical Anthology from Ariosto to Stonewall (Castle), 68

Lloyd George, David, 149, 152, 158, 258–59n49

Lochrie, Karma, 191

The Logic of Sense (Deleuze), 150

Love, Heather, 30, 46–47, 50–51, 72, 265n7

Lowther, Barbara "Toupie," viii, 101, 237n23

Macdonald, Nina, 106

Mack, Louise, 245n106

Macnaughtan, Sarah, 244n96

Making Sexual History (Weeks), 33

Manchester Evening News (newspaper), 237n18, 241–42n61, 242n63

Manchester Guardian (newspaper), 154, 160

Manners, Diana, 105–6

Marcus, Sharon, 89, 249n28, 256n10

Markham, Violet, 147–48, 251n54

Married Love (Stopes), 165, 184, 255–56n4

Medd, Jodie, 3

memory: psychoanalytic approaches to, 49

Menon, Madhavi, 85

Meyerowitz, Joanne, 233n125

militarism: female masculinity, public perceptions of, 99–100

Milk, Harvey, 39

misrecognition, 71, 84–85, 91, 119

"Miss Ogilvy Finds Herself" (Hall), 128, 212n77

Mitchell, David, 161, 251–52n58, 253n85

Moi, Toril, 115, 240n53

Montgomery County Times (newspaper), 151

morality, 169, 170, 172–73, 175, 189; homosexual acts, as moral weakness, 190; moral conduct, and medical examinations, 166; respectability, class-inflected notions of, 188; and sexual transgression, 137

Morning Post (newspaper), 151

Mort, Frank, 171

Mount, Ferdinand, 223n155

Munro, Hector, 144

name calling, 136, 139, 157, 162; and identity, 21; and self-naming, 142

Nameless Offences: Homosexual Desire in the 19th Century (Cocks), 54

naming, 162; habit of, 136–39; and identity, 21; and identity history, 163; and queer genealogy, 136–37; refusal to, 141; as unsaid way of knowing, 140

National Archives, 137

Nealon, Christopher, 51; archive, and pastness, 196

neurasthenia, 180

New English Weekly (newspaper), 252n63

Newman, Sally, 34, 170

New Woman, 19, 111; class-specific Englishness, as quintessence of, 113; womanliness, maintaining of, 241–42n61

Noakes, Lucy, 130–31

Nora, Pierre, 58, 71, 210n55

norm: categories of, emergence of, 168–69; queer history, "normal" and, elision of, 21–22; and social relations, 169; statistical norm, and group behavior, 169

normal, 188–89, 199; and deviant sexuality, 170; idea of, 171; norm, notion of, as linked with, 173; queer, at odds with, 172; queer history, "norm" and, elision of, 21–22; queer studies, historicity of, as sidestepping, 191; and sexuality, 198; sexuality, value of, assigning of to, 20; as statistical average, 169

normality, 191–92; idea of, 173; and normal/deviant binary, 172–73, 190

normativity, 20; and denormativizing, 173

North America, 11, 169

North Wales Chronicle (newspaper), 151

Norwood, Rev. Dr. F. W., 134, 154

Not a Passing Phase: Reclaiming Lesbians in History, 1840–1985 (Lesbian History Group), 67

nurses: ambulance drivers, contrast with, 120; as saintly, 245n105

Oakeshott, Michael, 9

Odd Girls and Twilight Lovers: A History of Lesbian Life in Twentieth Century America (Faderman), 66

O'Donnell, Katherine, 206n27

Oram, Alison, 34, 77, 99

Paine, Sir Godfrey, 147, 251n57

Palgrave Advances in the Modern History of Sexuality (Cocks and Houlbrook), 11, 209n46

Parker, Andrew, 215n21, 230n66

Passion and Power: Sexuality in History (Peiss and Simmons), 12

Peiss, Kathy, 12

Penn, Donna, 31

perverse presentism, 29, 227–28n36. *See also* presentism

Pervyse (Belgium), 126, 139, 143, 145–46, 161–62, 245n105

politics of recognition, 71

positivism: and empiricism, 220n81

postmodernism, 74; past, view of, 87; subaltern groups, defining of, 226n20

postqueer age, 234n144

poststructuralism, 56, 74

practical past: v. historical past, 10; and sexuality, 10

presentism, 46; and objectivity, 74; queer studies, as linked with, 29–30. *See also* perverse presentism

Pride events, 71

proper history, 53, 56; detachment, cultivation of, 9–10; genealogical project, as different from, 63. *See also* academic history; history

psychiatry, 141; and sexuality, 11

psychoanalysis, 67; as dangerous, 185; and memory, 49; and sexuality, 29, 205n14

Public Services Temporary Clerks' Association, 258n47, 259n52, 263n142

Punch (magazine), 132, 242n63; English upper-class woman in, as recognizable type, 113; upper-class women, social critiques of in, 113, 115–19; women, and men's work in, 241n59

Queen Alexandra Imperial Military Nursing Service Reserve, 177

queer, 210–11n63; as defined, 43–44, 171; fluidity of, 103; as historical and historicized category, 32; and history, 196; meaning

of, 103; normal, at odds with, 172; open-
endedness of, 7; and oppositionality,
168; as umbrella term, 7; as word, 7,
43–44, 168
queer activist politics, 18
queer archives: as collective memory, 48;
and genealogical project, 87; history, as
psychic need, 48; and "lost histories,"
47–48; past, constructing of, 49, 196
queer critical history, xii, 23, 43, 84, 175,
190; collective memory, and history,
198; and discontinuity, 91; and genealogical project, 87; and identity history,
163; and modern sexuality, multiple
configurations of, 198; norm, relational
values of, 171; normativity and deviance,
rethinking of, 91; oppositionality of,
18; past, severing of, 89; as practice, 62,
159, 168; present in, as historicized, 89;
and queer genealogy, 61, 88; and queer
methods, 198; and queerness-as-being,
187; queerness-as-method in, 90; refusal
to name, as historiographical method,
141; and sexuality, 4, 16; and structures of
knowing, 198. *See also* critical history
queer cultural criticism, 50, 57; alternative
"historical" practice, 56; "turn to affect"
in, 230n66
Queer/Early/Modern (Freccero), 79
*Queer Fictions of the Past: History, Culture,
and Difference* (Bravmann), 34
queer genealogy, 2–3, 15–16, 19, 23, 58, 70,
91, 138, 159, 168, 175, 187, 199; ancestral
genealogy, affinities between, 60, 63, 67;
ancestral genealogy, as evolving from,
84–85; ancestral genealogy, undoing of,
79, 86; and critical history, 84; critical
history and queer studies/queer theory,
exchange between, 92–93; denormativizing of, 59; as divided, against itself, 65;
and genealogical project, 88; historicizing, effects of, 196; identification, habit
of, 160; and identity, 76, 78–79; identity
and identification, 196–97; and identity
politics, 4, 65–66, 80; identity practices,
as indebted to, 17; as investigatory mode,
looking backward and forward, 77; and
methodologies, 85–86; and naming,
136–37; oppositional nature of, 80; and
queer critical history, 61, 88; sex and
identity, historical connections between,
as aim of, 78; sexual identity, deconstruc-

tion of, 59; traceability, logic of, 198; and
transhistorical continuities, 87. *See also*
queer history
queer historiography, x, 50
queer history, 2, 7–8, 31–32, 52, 199; binaries, and impulse to categorize, as based
on, 21–22; critical history, alliances
between, xii, 16; and cultural turn, 27;
history, and historicism, conflating of
with, 39; lesbian and gay social history,
50; "normal" and "norm," elision of,
21–22; and pastness, 40; queer deconstructionists, criticism of, 203–4n2; and
queer historicity, 56; and queer theory,
53, 56; as teleological, dismissal of, 16;
visibility, problem of in, 47. *See also*
queer genealogy
queering: primary cultural work of, as challenging norms, 190–91
*Queer London: Perils and Pleasures in the
Sexual Metropolis, 1918–1957* (Houlbrook), 226n17
queer methodology, 4–5; and cultural turn,
56, 70
"queer moment," 215n21
Queer Nation, 54
queerness: and identity, viii
queerness-as-being, viii, xii, 31, 61, 89–90,
137–38, 198; and nostalgia, 51; and queer
critical history, 187
queerness-as-method, viii–ix, xii, 31, 44,
89–90, 138, 168, 198
queer practical past: possibilities of resistance, creation of, 10
queer spectrality, 89
queer studies, 2, 7, 20–21, 37, 43, 55, 72, 88,
169, 170, 173, 186, 221n98, 265n17; and
academic history, 6, 8; 167; academic
history, estrangement with, 27, 44, 56,
62–63, 86; archive, appropriation of, 8;
contemporary cultures and representation, interest in, 29; and critical history
practice, 62; definition of, 171; high and
low theories in, 223n157; historicity,
interest in, 17; and historiography, 6, 8;
history, contrast with, 53; history, as discipline, 30; history, pastness of, 8; history,
depiction of, as positivist empiricism, 32;
history, queer misunderstanding of, 8;
history, raw material of, 42; lesbian and
gay history, tension between, 32; normal,
historicity of, as sidestepping, 191; and

187–90; sexual knowledge, as taint, 184; sexual transgression, and moral character, 137; and shame, 158; understanding of, through case histories, 11; and unknowing, 193; war work, effect on, 1; as word, 11

Sexuality (Weeks), 170

sexuality studies, 28, 37–38, 62; as burgeoning field, 11, 31; dismissal of, 12; gender, notion of, 82; as marginalized, 12, 84, 208n44; queer, as word, 7; secondary status of, 81

Sexuality in World History (Stearns), 12

sexual normality, 172

sexual perversion, 256n8

Shart, Dr. Alexander McGregor, 181

Sheffield Daily Telegraph (newspaper), 115

Simmons, Christina, 12

Sinclair, May, 124

Sinfield, Alan, 33

slander cases, 21, 176–77, 181, 186–87, 258–59n49. *See also* Harley v. Carr

social history, 48

sociology, 12

Souhami, Diana, 34, 219n73, 265n5

South Wales, 147

Spectator (magazine), 100

Stanhope, Lord, 151

Steedman, Carolyn, 49–50

Stein, Gertrude, viii, 119

Stonewall, 39

Stopes, Marie, 165–66, 168–69, 173, 184, 190; as radical, 255–56n4; as reactionary, 255–56n4

subaltern: as term, 226n20

subaltern studies, 64

Summers, Anne, 251n54

Sunday Chronicle (newspaper), 177

Surpassing the Love of Men: Romantic Friendship and Love between Women from the Renaissance to the Present (Faderman), 66

Syme, John, 154, 253–54n86

taxonomy. *See* categorization

Taylor, Charles, 71, 159

Telling the Truth about History (Appleby, Jacob, and Hunt), 226n20

temporality, 32, 56, 63

Terry, Jennifer, 97, 103–4, 257n28, 262n119

Thom, Deborah, 235–36n6

Thompson, E. P., 72

Thompson, H. N., 245n104

Thompson, Muriel, 122

Time Binds: Queer Temporalities, Queer Histories (Freeman), 9

The Times (newspaper), 129, 177, 241–42n61

Toklas, Alice B., viii

transhistoricism, 32, 45

Traub, Valerie, 52, 65, 70, 74, 78, 87–88, 91–93, 203n19, 218n50, 225n7, 225n12, 234n150; and anachronistic gaze, 76–77; on Renaissance lyric, 90

Trotter, David, 131

Troubridge, Una, 77, 195

truth claims, 40, 42

Ullman, Sharon R., 263n134

Umphrey, Martha M., 31

Under the Searchlight: A Record of a Great Scandal (Douglas-Pennant), 148–49, 153, 158, 253n85

undetermined history, 92, 141

uniformed women: as accepted, 237n18; as Amazons, 105; as ambulance drivers, 122; commentators on, 128; female workforce in war effort, as part of, 104; gender and class, 116; gendered boundaries, pushing of, 144; and gender stretching, 111–12; hostile criticism of toward, as rare, 242n63; as "ministering angels," 242n63; normalization, elasticity of, 107–8; press, fascination with, 144; press, overexposure of, 104; *Punch* cartoons, depiction of in, 113, 115–16; public attitudes toward, as shifting, 236n7; public culture, reaction to, 98, 104, 244n95, 244n96; public distrust of, 236n7; scandals and heterosexual behavior, 236n12. *See also* female war workers; women

United States, 71, 262n119. *See also* America

University of Glasgow Archives, ix

Unwin, Stanley, 253n85

Uranians, 105

Vernon, James, 89, 103

Vicinus, Martha, 28, 30, 34, 68, 77–78, 103, 105, 119, 140, 146, 217n40, 218n50; same-sex friendships, spiritualization of, 245n103

virginity: medical test of, 181–82, 186, 188–89, 261n96, 262n115

Voluntary Aid Detachment (VAD), 107, 113, 178

Walker, Jane, 181–82
Wallace, Robertson, 106
War Budget Illustrated (magazine), 111, 145, 239n39, 242n63, 245n105
Warner, Michael, 29, 31, 172, 213n3
Warner, Sylvia Townsend, 72
Waterhouse, Ronald, 251n57
Waters, Chris, 91
Waters, Sarah, 230n63
Watson, Janet, 101, 236n7, 244n97
Weeks, Jeffrey, 11, 33, 69, 170, 217–18n41; historical account of term "queer," 7; homosexual, idea of, 227n29
Weir, William Douglas (Lord Weir), ix–x, 134–35, 155, 202–3n10
The Well of Loneliness (Hall), viii, 40, 92, 130, 202n3, 212n77, 265n5; ambulance drivers, depiction of in, 195; protagonist in, 128
Western Front, 97, 102, 107, 139; ambulance drivers on, 119, 126, 238–39n36; male mothering on, 108. *See also* First World War
White, Hayden, 1, 8, 35, 37–38, 42, 45–46, 51, 53, 73, 206n24, 218n43
Wiegman, Robyn, 202n7
Wild, Ernest, 176–77, 179–81, 183, 184, 185–86, 262n116, 263–64n149
Wilde, Dolly, viii, 119
Wilde, Oscar, viii, 102
Wilson, Tyson, 148, 154, 157

The Woman's Motor Manual (de Havilland), 120
women: auto mechanics, knowledge of, rite of passage, 116; female labor, mobilization of, 107, 110; in labor force, during First World War, 107; in masculine public sphere, cultural anxieties over, 99; men, female subordination to, 19; in military uniforms, reaction to, 98; in military uniforms, as sexually deviant, 99; motor-car drivers, demand for, 243n80; national press, fascination with, 106–7; in "New Britain," 108; romantic friendship between, 249n28; as temporary man, concept of, 112; war, effects on, 1, 111, 142, 235n4, 241–42n61; and womanhood: reconfiguration of, 97. *See also* female war workers; First World War; uniformed women
Women and Soldiers (Alec-Tweedie), 97
Women's Army Auxiliary Corps (WAAC), 132, 237n18
women's history, 12, 64, 90, 233n125; lesbian history, reclaiming of in, 68; marginal position of, 83
Women's Land Army, 107
Women's Royal Air Force (WRAF), vii, ix–x, 134, 142–43, 147, 149, 151–52, 161
Women's Slander Act, 181
women's suffrage movement, 91, 99, 107
Woolf, Virginia, 75, 254n89
World War I. *See* First World War

Yale University, 47